D0944125

The Legacy of
KANO JIGORO

JAPAN LIBRARY

The Legacy of

KANO JIGORO

Judo and Education

The Committee for
the Commemoration of
the 150th Anniversary of
the Birth of Jigoro Kano

TRANSLATED BY Tom Kain

Japan Publishing Industry Foundation for Culture

Note to readers
This book follows the Hepburn system of romanization. Except for place names found on
international maps, as well as the Japanese names on the jacket, cover, and this page, long
vowels are indicated by macrons. The tradition of placing the family name first has been
followed for Japanese and Chinese names.

The Legacy of Kano Jigoro: Judo and Education
Edited by The Committee for the Commemoration of the 150th Anniversary of the Birth
of Jigoro Kano. Translated by Tom Kain.

Published by
Japan Publishing Industry Foundation for Culture (JPIC)
2-2-30 Kanda-Jinbocho, Chiyoda-ku, Tokyo 101-0051, Japan

First English edition: March 2020

This book is a translation of *Kigai to kodo no kyoikusha Kano Jigoro* which was originally
published by the University of Tsukuba Press.
English publishing rights arranged with the University of Tsukuba Press.

Jacket and cover design: Akiyama Masumi

Printed in Japan
ISBN 978-4-86658-136-1
https://japanlibrary.jpic.or.jp/

Contents

An introduction to the English edition

The year 2020 marks the 160th anniversary of Kanō Jigorō's birth. It also marks Tokyo's hosting of the thirty-second Olympic Games and sixteenth Paralympic Games. The two occasions share an important connection: in 1909, 111 years ago today, Kanō's induction to the International Olympic Committee (IOC)—as the IOC's first Asian member—initiated Japan into the Olympic Movement. Since then, Japan has played host to four Olympic Games, the third-most of any country. How did that come to be? Why is it that the Olympics, with their roots in Western tradition, have convened in Japan as many as four times in their history?

The answer lies in Kanō Jigorō, the man who ushered Japan into the Olympic fold and created a compelling fusion of sports and education.

This book, the English edition of *Kigai to kōdō no kyōikusha: Kanō Jigorō* (Tsukuba: University of Tsukuba Press, 2011), explores Kanō's enduring legacy from a variety of perspectives: Kanō the founder of Kodokan judo, Kanō the educator, and Kanō the champion of the Olympic Movement. Running through those dimensions, as readers will find, was a consistent focus on Kanō's philosophical tenets of *seiryoku zen'yō* (maximum efficient use of energy) and *jita kyōei* (mutual prosperity for oneself and others).

To all who helped make this edition possible, especially the Japan Publishing Industry Foundation for Culture, I extend my sincerest thanks.

March 1, 2020
Sanada Hisashi (on behalf of the authors)

Part I

Kanō Jigorō's early years and the origins of judo

Kanō Jigorō during the early Taishō era (courtesy of the Kodokan collection)

Chapter 1

Kanō Jigorō's family background and formal schooling

1. Early childhood and educational beginnings in Tokyo

Childhood studies

Kanō Jigorō was born on December 10, 1860, in Mikage, Ubara-gun, Settsu Province (now an area of Higashinada Ward in the city of Kobe). He was the third son in a well-established family in the brewing industry. His father, Jirosaku, was the son of the head priest at Hie Sannō Shrine (now the Hiyoshi-Taisha Shine) in Ōmi Province. Though sons of priests generally succeed their fathers at their home shrines, Jirosaku showed little interest in staying put; instead, he pursued his passions for Chinese philosophy and painting, moving from place to place. He eventually stayed for a time at the home of Kanō Jisaku, a brewer in the Nada area of Kobe, where he gave lectures on Confucian teachings. Jisaku, thoroughly impressed with the young man, suggested that Jirosaku marry his eldest daughter, Sadako, and become the family's adopted son-in-law. Jirosaku agreed. The Kanō patriarch even offered to leave the family estate to Jirosaku and make him the head of the household, but Jirosaku declined the succession offer. When his adoptive father-in-law died, Jirosaku left the brewery to Jisaku's biological son, Ryōtarō, and instead established his own separate Kanō household, agreeing to look after the brewing operation in a more custodial capacity. Jirosaku went on to forge a career doing business with the *bakufu* government (Japan's feudal shogunate regime), which entailed frequent trips to Edo (now Tokyo), Osaka, and other locations across Japan. One of his government contracts involved building battlements in Nishinomiya, a city in Hyogo Prefecture, under the supervision of famed naval engineer and public official Katsu Kaishū (1823–99). Those naval connections proved influential for Jirosaku, who later became a ship owner in his own right and oversaw shipping operations for government vessels. He dabbled in a variety of fields prior to the Meiji Restoration, but the navy eventually became his sole focus, and from that point on, he served exclusively as an administrator for the Japanese navy. With Jirosaku often away from home on official business, his son, Jigorō, spent most of his childhood with his mother, Sadako.

Kanō recalled his mother fondly, saying:

> I looked on my mother with both affection and fear. She raised me with all the care in the world, but she would take me to task whenever I made a mistake, refusing to yield until I either repented for my error or at least admitted fault. . . . One thing I do remember clearly about her is that she always put others before herself, even forgetting herself at times. She was always concerned about people, be it fretting about what she should do for someone or feeling sorry for what someone was going through.[1]

Sadako, whose penchant for strict discipline and consistent devotion to others would have an enormous impact on her son throughout his life, passed away when Jigorō was just eight.

Jirosaku, meanwhile, was determined to get Jigorō the best education possible. Mikage was home to more than twenty private elementary schools, but none had an instructor capable of teaching the Chinese classics at a level that met Jirosaku's exacting standards. He hired a private tutor, Confucian scholar Yamamoto Chikuun (1820–88), to teach Jigorō calligraphy and have him read through classical Confucian texts—full comprehension aside—from the age of five onward. Picking up a variety of Chinese characters from the Four Books and the Five Classics, as well as other works expounding Confucian principles, young Jigorō soon started compiling the things he learned into little home-made books that he would use for teaching his young relatives. "I named one book *Tenkishō*," he later wrote. "'*Ten*' was for the 'kingdom' [*tenka*] in the *Great Learning*, while '*ki*' and '*shō*' came from the middle two syllables of '*Shuki shōku*' [Passages (*shōku*) by Shuki (Zhu Xi, a renowned Confucian scholar)]."[2] Just six years old at the time, Jigorō was evidently already familiar with Confucius's *Great Learning* and Zhu Xi's school of Neo-Confucianism. After Sadako's death, Jirosaku took Jigorō (then nine) and his second-eldest son, Kensaku, to Tokyo in 1870. To place this move in historical context, it happened the year before the abolition of the *han* system requiring all of Japan's feudal lords to return their authority to the new Meiji government, as well as the Iwakura Tomomi-led diplomatic mission to Europe and the United States.

After making his way to Tokyo, Jigorō first studied at Seitatsu Shojuku, a private school in the Ryōgoku area. Jigorō's teacher at the institution was Ubukata Keidō, a prominent private-school affiliate whose intimate knowledge of Chinese literary classics and repute in the calligraphy world made him, in Jirosaku's eyes, the ideal instructor for his son. Jirosaku sought permission to have Jigorō study under Ubukata, who quickly recognized the boy's innate talents and poured his energies into educating him, convinced that Jigorō would one day serve the good of the nation.

Ubukata's biography, Onoda Sukemasa's *Ubukata Keidō-den* (A biography of Ubukata Keidō), details the type of education that Jigorō received at Seitatsu Shojuku. "[Kanō] had already learned to read the Four Books and Five Classics of Confucianism before coming to the school, so Ubukata-sensei had him read the *Kokushi ryaku* (A short history of Japan), *Nihon gaishi* (The unofficial history of Japan), *Jūhasshi ryaku* (Summary of the eighteen histories), and *Nihon seiki* (A record of Japanese government) in a sequential fashion," Ono writes. "He always wrote three *jō* [sixty sheets of Japanese paper] of calligraphy every day, as well, being as careful and attentive as possible. After his lessons, Kanō regularly joined two or three younger students to listen to Sensei impart his knowledge of history."[3] Having already established a basis in Chinese learning, then, Jigorō studied a curriculum that encompassed the three history books noted above and calligraphy, among other subjects. Ubukata was a Sinologist and calligrapher by trade, but he knew that times were changing; the

Kanō Jigorō (R), age nine (courtesy of the Kodokan collection)

Meiji Restoration (1868) had shifted the tides, ushering in a new era of cultural enlightenment that was bound to expand young boys' interests into Western learning. Aware that Chinese learning and calligraphy would give way to new developments in the coming generations, Ubukata wanted Jigorō to follow additional lines of study and even learn English as a gateway to Western learning. He sent his young student to begin studying at Sansha Gakusha in Kanda, Tokyo, where Jigorō gained a firm foundation in the English language. His teacher, Mitsukuri Shūhei (1826–86), was more than just the headmaster at the school in Kanda—he also helped form the "Meiji Six Society" with the likes of Mori Arinori (1847–89) and Fukuzawa Yukichi (1835–1901) in 1873, creating an intellectual coterie that introduced new ideas across the Japanese intelligentsia. Mitsukuri became supervisor of the Tokyo Normal School in 1875.

At the age of twelve, Jigorō entered another private school: Ikuei Gijuku, a boarding academy in the Karasumori-machi area of Shiba, Tokyo. It was his first time living away from his family, but that was far from the only daunting unfamiliarity that he encountered. The faculty at the school was mostly foreign, including Dutch and German instructors, and every class was in English. "I was equal to my classmates [academically]," Kanō wrote, remembering his time at Ikuei Gijuku. "Among my fellow pupils there were some who were physically weak, and as a result they were often under the domination of the bigger, stronger boys. The weaker ones were forced to serve the stronger. Since I was one of the weakest, I was made to run errands at the behest of the strong."[4] Jigorō, brainy and scrawny, found himself a target for bullying at the hands of older students, who had size and numbers on their side. It was around this time that Jigorō started developing an interest in jujutsu.

Looking at Jigorō's early education, his strongest academic foundations were apparently in Chinese learning and English. From that grounding, he enrolled in the English department at the Tokyo School of Foreign Languages at the age of thirteen and continued to absorb knowledge. The School of Foreign Languages, which opened its doors in 1873 as an arm of Tokyo Kaisei School (the forerunner of Tokyo University), was essentially a preparatory academy with a focus on training specialists. The curriculum was so immersive, in fact, that Kanō's letters to his friends were all in English. He went on to enroll at Tokyo Kaisei School in 1875. There, too, he had to confront the physical gap between him and his peers. Many of the boys were gifted scholarship students, boasting official recommendations from their clans and physiques hewn by years of martial-arts training; though the school emphasized academics, brawn still gave certain boys an outsize influence. Kanō had a competitive streak, however, and knew that he had to toughen up. "I still kept up with my classmates in scholastic attainments," he wrote, "but as for my physical abilities, I was nowhere near as strong or as robust as they were. Thus the urge in me to learn jujutsu finally became overwhelming."[5]

If those experiences formed Jigorō's impetus for taking up the study of jujutsu, living in the dormitories at Ikuei Gijuku and Tokyo Kaisei School was a life-changing juncture. At the time, though, his initial zeal to train was stymied; though he asked his father if he might be able to learn from a jujutsu practitioner who had been making frequent visits to the family household, Jirosaku rebuffed the request, claiming that jujutsu was quickly becoming a relic of a bygone age.

On to the Faculty of Letters at Tokyo University

In 1877, Kanō entered the Faculty of Letters at Tokyo University as a sixteen-year-old first-year student. He was in the first class in the history of Tokyo University, which formed that year through the consolidation and reorganization of Tokyo Kaisei School and the Tokyo Medical School. Starting as an organization comprising separate Faculties of Law, Science, Letters, and Medicine, the four departments integrated in 1881 under the leadership of Katō Hiroyuki (1836–1916). The Faculty of Letters originally had two divisions: the first consisted of studies in history, philosophy, and politics, while the second encompassed Japanese and Chinese literature. Kanō chose the first division, which quickly shifted to cover philosophy, politics, and political economy in 1879. The faculty included William Houghton (1852–1917), in charge of English literature; Toyama Masakazu (1848–1900), who taught psychology and English; Mishima Kowashi (Chūshū) (1831–1919), responsible for courses in Chinese classics; and Ernest Fenollosa (1853–1908), an American scholar who assumed the professorship in politics and political economy. Kanō, who specialized in politics and political economy during his time at Tokyo University, thus "studied primarily under Dr. Fenollosa"[6]—a figure who undoubtedly played a vital role in shaping Kanō's core system of thought.

Fenollosa ventured beyond his duties lecturing at Tokyo University as well. Taken with the beauty of traditional Japanese art, he eventually worked with Okakura Kakuzō (1862–1913, also known as Okakura Tenshin) on studies of

Japanese antiques and efforts to spark a revival in *nihonga* (Japanese painting), leaving behind a wealth of achievements. With those professors providing instruction, Kanō graduated from Tokyo University with a bachelor of arts degree in 1881, part of the second class of the Faculty of Letters. However, Kanō recalled, "As I had studied political economy, political philosophy, and economic philosophy in my fourth year, learning in all the Faculty's areas of studies except for philosophy, I had no experience in that discipline. Immediately following graduation, then, I enrolled as a special student on a further one-year course in philosophy."[7] Kanō's academic pursuits during that extra year of schooling included continued research on moral science and aesthetics, studies of Chinese classics under Nakamura Masanao (1832–91), and explorations of Western philosophy with Fenollosa and other members of the faculty. He completed his specialist course in 1882, after which he embarked on his journey toward becoming an educator and judo pioneer. He was still only twenty-one years of age.

2. Academic pursuits at Tokyo University

The impact of Ernest Fenollosa

During Kanō's time in the Faculty of Letters at Tokyo University, Ernest Fenollosa was a central figure in his academic growth. Studying primarily under Fenollosa, Kanō took it upon himself to read works of philosophy by William Hamilton and translate studies of ethics by Henry Sidgwick.[8] The exact workings and dynamics of the relationship between Kanō and his main academic mentor have remained largely unclear, however. The following section takes a closer look at their connection, using Kanō's course load at Tokyo University as a window into what Fenollosa was teaching in his lectures.

Of course, no exploration of the relationship between Kanō and Fenollosa would be complete without a basic overview of Fenollosa's background. Fenollosa's stint at Tokyo University lasted eight years, from August 1878 (the year after Tokyo Kaisei School officially became Tokyo University) to July 1886 (the year that Tokyo University renamed itself "Imperial University"). In other words, Fenollosa was on the faculty for nearly the entire span of the institution's existence as Tokyo University during the early years of the Meiji era, a time when Japan was modernizing dramatically. As a professor at a premier Japanese university, Fenollosa thus helped drive modernization forward through higher education. What led Fenollosa to Tokyo University was an invitation from American zoologist and Orientalist Edward Morse (1838–1925), then an instructor on the Tokyo University staff. At the time, Fenollosa was just twenty-five years old, only a few years out of the department of philosophy at Harvard College. Upon arriving at Tokyo University, he was assigned to teach politics, political economy (equivalent to modern-day economics), and philosophy in the Faculty of Letters. The university renewed his contract every two years and, after adopting new educational policies in 1881, tasked him with the disciplines of political economy, philosophy, and logic. While his teaching responsibilities may have gone through the occasional twist and turn, Fenollosa devoted himself to his work at Tokyo University for the full length of his stay there. He clearly made quite the impression on Kanō, who remembered his teacher with admiration:

> Of all the things that my experiences with Dr. F have shown me, one truth I have no hesitation in declaring, is that he possesses a clear, sharp intellect. Not only did that brilliant mind enable him to analyze whatever he intended to impart to his students, but he also had a unique ability to go beyond that initial analysis and synthesize the information for optimal clarity.[9]

To Kanō, Fenollosa not only had a brilliant mind but also possessed an extraordinary gift for analysis. When Kanō became principal at Tokyo Higher Normal School, he hired Fenollosa to teach at the institution from 1897 to 1900.

Fenollosa's lectures

Below is a list of Kanō's courses and instructors during his first year at Tokyo University, before Fenollosa made his way to Japan.

Kanō's first-year teachers and courses
William Houghton (English Literature), Frank Jewett (General Science), Edward Syle (History), Toyama Masakazu (English/Logic/Psychology), Yokoyama Yoshikiyo (Japanese Literature), Okamoto Kansuke (Chinese Classics)

In 1878, Kanō's second year of enrollment, Fenollosa joined the Tokyo University faculty. Kanō's courses and instructors for that year, along with Fenollosa's course description, were as follows:

Kanō's second-year teachers and courses

Toyama Masakazu (Psychology/Philosophy), Ernest Fenollosa (History of Western Philosophy), Edward Syle (History I), Charles Cooper (History II), Yokoyama Yoshikiyo (Japanese Literature), Kurokawa Mayori (Japanese Literature), Mishima Kowashi (Chinese Classics), William Houghton (English Literature), Koga Moritarō (French)

Fenollosa's course description for History of Western Philosophy (year two)

"This course provides a general outline of modern philosophy, from Descartes to Hegel and Spencer. . . Post-Cartesian philosophy has not only seen the rise of schools completely divergent from those of ancient philosophy but also formed the origins of contemporary thought. The objective of the course, then, is to study the progression of philosophy, particularly that of modern European thought, through the present day. Class sessions will cover Schwegler's *History of Philosophy*, mostly through lectures, and will examine the principles of the relevant philosophical schools. Through occasional memorization assessments and written examinations, the course will ensure that students develop the faculties necessary for thorough comprehension of works by various philosophers."[10]

The curriculum underwent several changes in 1879, Kanō's third year, with "political economy" replacing the history course and Fenollosa—responsible for courses in political economy—thus occupying a higher-profile role in the curriculum. Kanō's course load was as follows:

Kanō's third-year teachers and courses

Ernest Fenollosa (Political Economy/Politics), Charles Cooper (History/Moral Science), William Houghton (English Literature), Yokoyama Yoshikiyo (Japanese Literature I), Nakamura Masanao (Chinese Classics), Kimura Masakoto (Japanese Literature II and III), Konakamura Kiyonori (Japanese Literature I)

Fenollosa's course descriptions for Political Economy and Politics (year three)

"The Political Economy course will first engage students in the principles of political economy, using Mill's *Principles of Political Economy* as a foundational text. Thereafter, students will study Cairnes's *Character and Logical Method of Political Economy*, read works by Carey and other proponents of other political economics schools for comparative purposes with the political economics of

Mill and Cairnes, and sit for lectures thereon. References include works by Carey and related treatises by other authors discussed by Mill, which the instructor will lecture on in class sessions along with works by other authors. . . For the Politics course, meanwhile, the first and second terms will concentrate on ecology, or the study of the ways in which humanity has inhabited its environment and the mechanisms by which humanity has since evolved. In the third term, students will study the principles and functions of human life within the contexts of moral science and politics, after which the course will provide an overview of the methods of and interrelations between moral science and politics in practical application. The course will conclude with daily lectures providing a detailed analysis and criticism of practical moral science and politics under said methods. References include Spencer's *Principles of Sociology* and *Social Statics*, Morgan's *Ancient Society*, and Bagehot's *Physics and Politics*."[11]

Kanō entered his fourth year of studies in 1880, taking the following courses:

Kanō Jigorō (R) during his time at Tokyo Imperial University (courtesy of the Kodokan collection)

Kanō's fourth-year teachers and courses
Toyama Masakazu (Philosophy), Ernest Fenollosa (Political Economy/Politics), Charles Cooper (Western Philosophy), Hatoyama Kazuo (International Law/Politics), Shimada Chōrei (Chinese Classics)

Fenollosa's course description for Political Economy (year four)
"The fourth-year Political Economy course will comprise lectures during the first two terms, with students engaging in self-study on such topics as currency, banking, commerce, and foreign exchange. The third term will be devoted entirely to the composition of the students' graduation theses."[12]

Upon completing his fourth year in 1881, Kanō enrolled in the philosophy department for a year of further study in the following courses:

Courses in the philosophy department
Toyama Masakazu (Philosophy), Ernest Fenollosa (Western Philosophy), Nakamura Masanao (Chinese Classics/Chinese Philosophy), Nagamatsu Tōkai (Physiology), Hara Tanzan (Indian Philosophy), Yoshitani Kakuju (Indian Philosophy)

Fenollosa's course
Fenollosa grounded his lectures on the history of philosophy in the study of sociology. "That emphasis testified to Fenollosa's unique conviction that both politics and philosophy rested squarely on the foundation of sociology," Fenollosa scholar Yamaguchi Seiichi argues. "Considering that sociology represents a form of social evolutionism with roots in organicism, Fenollosa's 1881 curriculum bore strong signs of Herbert Spencer's influence."[13] In that sense, Spencerian social Darwinism likely formed the theoretical heart of Fenollosa's discourse.

The impact that Fenollosa had on Kanō at Tokyo University is hard to overstate, not only in terms of the actual coursework but also as an inspirational presence. When Kanō graduated from Tokyo University in March 1882, Fenollosa addressed the graduating class at the conferral ceremony, saying:

Today is the day, gentlemen, on which you proceed forth from this institution and begin to truly benefit society with what you have learned and achieved thus far. . . . I implore you never to cast aside your collegiate studies henceforth, never even for a day. I beseech you to carry your wisdom with you throughout your travails, your lifelong journey of training and discipline, and maintain the zeal with which you first embraced your academic pursuits with a spirit of true fairness, constantly and unfailingly. I sincerely hope that all of you commit yourselves to that spirit until your dying day, refusing to be confined or restrained in any way whatsoever, so that you may embody just ideals and benefit the nation as specialists in your fields.[14]

The fruits of academic study at the university level, Fenollosa emphasized to the graduates, were tools to employ in benefiting the country. Later, when Kanō went about explaining the essence of judo, he echoed a similar idea. "Judo is a way of using the powers of both mind and body most effectively," he wrote. "The purpose of judo training is to cultivate physical and mental discipline through the practice of attack and defense, fostering a comprehension of the essence of the Way. One thus attains completion of self and, in effect, contributes to the well-being of society at large."[15] Central to this description, which remains the definitive explanation of judo and its central objective, is Kanō's idea of "well-being"—a term essentially synonymous with Fenollosa's concept of "benefit" and inclusive of the same object: the "nation."

3. Education and the development of Kanō's personal philosophy

Kanō Juku and Kanō's educational vision

Kanō's early life was a chronicle of learning. At the age of five, in Hyogo, he read the Four Books and Five Classics of Confucianism under Confucian scholar Yamamoto Chikuun. At age ten, he enrolled at Ubukata Keidō's Seitatsu Shojuku and studied tomes ranging from the *Kokushi ryaku* (A short history of Japan) and *Nihon gaishi* (The unofficial history of Japan) to *Jūhasshi ryaku* (Summary of the eighteen histories). Upon commencing his academic career at Tokyo University, he continued to study Chinese learning with the likes of the geographer Okamoto Kansuke (1839–1904) and Mishima Kowashi. He stayed on at the university, taking the initiative to spend an extra year in the philosophy department as an undergraduate, delving deeper into Chinese classics and Chinese philosophy. A thread running through virtually the entirety of Kanō's education was Confucianism, which occupied a central position in his ideological background.

Having completed his university studies, Kanō started down his path as an educator in 1882. His relatives and friends began asking him to teach their children, so he decided to rent rooms at Eishōji temple in Kitainarichō, Shitaya, Tokyo, where the students could learn on a live-in basis. He also converted a portion of the temple premises into a dojo—the beginning of the Kodokan— and officially opened the "Kanō Juku" (1882–1919), a private academy. The *juku*, in Kanō's vision, would serve to help students "overcome the difficulties of life by developing the virtues of perseverance and self-denial that one often has to foster for worthwhile gains, especially so when seeking to help others."[16] Firm in his belief that experiencing hardship helped people develop into better-rounded individuals down the road, Kanō instituted a rather austere way of life at his academy, replete with strict rules and regulations. He divided the pupils into three age groups and assigned them to dwelling areas accordingly (the Children's Quarters, the Juveniles' Quarters, and the Adults' Quarters). Table 1-1 shows the daily schedule in the Children's Quarters.

In 1883, the "Fellow Residents' Agreement" took effect (see Table 1-2).

Table 1-1: Daily schedule for the Children's Quarters [17]

4:40 a.m.:	Wake up (5:40 a.m. on Sundays)
Immediately after waking up: Clean the washroom (inside and out) and then study until 6:00 a.m.	
6:00 a.m.:	Breakfast, followed by a break (roughly one hour) and study until leaving for school (roughly one hour)
12:00 p.m.:	Lunch, followed by a return from school and study (roughly one hour) until 4:00 p.m.
4:00 p.m.:	Evening meal
5:00–6:30 p.m.:	Judo training
6:30–8:00 p.m.:	Study
8:00 p.m.:	Bed

Table 1-2: Fellow Residents' Agreement [18]

I. Conduct with respect to instructors
   1. Students shall obey their instructors
   2. Students shall show respect to their instructors
   3. Students shall abide by the principle of loyalty
II. Conduct with respect to fellow students
   1. Students shall show faith and trust in their dealings with others
   2. Students shall show mutual love and respect for others, both young and old
   3. Students shall share both joys and sorrows with one another
   4. Students shall conduct themselves with modesty and humility
III. Daily duties
   1. Students shall welcome and bid farewell to their instructors
   2. Students shall bid courteous farewell to any guests leaving the establishment
   3. Students shall assemble at their instructor's station and make a courteous salute at the prescribed morning and evening hours
IV. Prohibitions
   1. Students shall not nap during the day
(rest omitted)

A Confucian influence is evident in the "Fellow Residents' Agreement": respect, loyalty, faith, modesty, and the idea of a courteous farewell all bear the marks of Confucian thought, for instance. The policies in the agreement share a common tenor with the principles of the Imperial Rescript on Education (the Meiji government's policy on education, promulgated in 1890), as well. Over a period of thirty-eight years, the Kanō Juku trained more than 300 students with a firm grounding in that core philosophy.

In 1889, Kanō addressed the Educational Society of Japan in hopes of convincing its members to incorporate judo into the standard curriculum of school exercises. His lecture, titled "Jūdō ippan narabi ni sono kyōiku-jō no kachi" (Judo and its educational value),[19] spelled out the benefits of the Way. Training in judo, he explained, would "engender a love for one's own country and what makes that country unique," "ennoble one's character and cultivate a valiant, active disposition," and "require a commitment to mutual devotion and kindness in one's actions." The process would help practitioners learn the "courtesy of human society" and how to "exercise self-restraint and moderation." In other words, the practice of judo was a path toward cultivating a well-rounded, moral character in multiple dimensions. While his discourse touched on the thoroughly Confucian virtues of patriotism, nobility, valiance, self-restraint, and courtesy, the speech avoided the feudalistic verbiage that characterized the principles of Edo-era jujutsu—phrases like service to one's country, loyalty to one's master, and filial piety. In forming a vision for judo, Kanō was apparently trying to rework the moral education that pervaded Japan's now-obsolete feudalism and bring it into alignment with the educational theory of the modern Meiji era.

The influence of Spencer's Education

During his studies of politics, political economy, and philosophy at Tokyo University, particularly in his pursuits of politics and philosophy, Kanō learned firsthand of Fenollosa's unique conviction that politics and philosophy depend heavily on the concepts of sociology. That focus on sociology, a form of social evolutionism with roots in organicism, meant that the theories of Herbert Spencer (1820–1903)—as communicated through Fenollosa's lectures—must have figured prominently in Kanō's studies. Spencer, who had a profound impact on Fenollosa, was a Scottish intellectual and a powerful presence in sociology and psychology. He essentially laid the synthetic philosophical foundation for British

Empiricism, and his *Education* (1861) stands as a touchstone for the idea that education rests on three pillars: intellectual, moral, and physical. The Japanese edition of the work appeared in 1880. From the Meiji era onward, Spencerian thought has had a substantial influence on Japanese education. Kanō founded judo to be a means of human education, a conceptualization that Spencer's *Education* surely helped shape. The work consisted of the following four chapters:

I. What Knowledge Is of Most Worth?
II. Intellectual Education
III. Moral Education
IV. Physical Education

The first chapter, "What Knowledge Is of Most Worth?" establishes the crux of Spencer's educational theory and delineates the optimal functions of education as a practice.

> In what way to treat the body; in what way to treat the mind; in what way to manage our affairs: in what way to bring up a family; in what way to behave as a citizen; in what way to utilize all those sources of happiness which nature supplies—how to use all our faculties to the greatest advantage of ourselves and others—how to live completely? And this being the great thing needful for us to learn, is, by consequence, the great thing which education has to teach. To prepare us for complete living is the function which education has to discharge.[20]

According to Spencer, education centered on preparing individuals for happy, fulfilling lives through the proper training of both mind and body. It also fulfilled a utilitarian purpose: to enable people to serve both themselves and others by making the most effective use of their individual abilities. In Kanō's vision, a conception that saw judo as a path toward both achieving self-realization and benefiting others on a balanced foundation of intellect, morality, and physical well-being, one can see clear traces of Spencerian educational philosophy.

In his third chapter, "Moral Education," Spencer situates education on three requisite pillars. "Whether as bearing upon the happiness of parents themselves, or whether as affecting the characters and lives of their children and remote descendants," he writes, "we must admit that a knowledge of the right methods of juvenile culture, physical, intellectual, and moral, is a knowledge second to none in importance."[21] In terms of intellectual education, however, Spencer underscored the need for language, imagination, and reasoning grounded in experimentation. Kanō's views flowed in a similar vein. In "Jūdō shūshin-hō" (The discipline of judo), for example, he argues that, in cultivating their intellect, people need the ability to verbalize the skills that they acquire through observation and the creative capacity to develop skills through their own power.

Kanō also argued that the idea of thinking deliberately and acting decisively was not only a key part of navigating a judo competition—it was, on a broader scale, a viable approach to conducting oneself in general. Spencer followed a similar line of thought in *Education*:

How to live?—that is the essential question for us. Not how to live in the mere material sense only, but in the widest sense. The general problem which comprehends every special problem is—the right ruling of conduct in all directions under all circumstances.[22]

To Spencer, then, the key was to conduct oneself properly in whatever one should encounter. That composite viewpoint was a clear link between the father of social Darwinism and the father of judo.

In "Physical Education," the fourth chapter of the work, Spencer outlines his ideas of what goes into success. "[T]he first requisite to success in life is 'to be a good animal'; and to be a nation of good animals is the first condition to national prosperity," he writes. "Not only is it that the event of a war often turns on the strength and hardiness of soldiers; but it is that the contests of commerce are in part determined by the bodily endurance of producers."[23] Essentially, the success of the individual and the prosperity of the nation itself both hinged on the ideal of the "perfect, complete human"—the physical fortitude to withstand labor and hardship. At the same time, Spencer also touched on the elements of nutrition, discussed the optimal clothing for physical activity, and argued that the exercise curriculum in school settings was no substitute for natural, spontaneous play in terms of physical movement. Spencer's philosophy on physical education likely formed a basis for Kanō's critiques of the general exercise and military drills that comprised the required physical-education curriculum then in place.

Another focus for Spencer was on the effective use of time and energy. ". . . And remembering how narrowly this time is limited, not only by the shortness of life, but also still more by the business of life," he explains, "we ought to be especially solicitous to employ what time we have to the greatest advantage. Before devoting years to some subject which fashion or fancy suggests, it is surely wise to weigh with great care the worth of the results, as compared with the worth of various alternative results which the same years might bring if otherwise applied."[24] Given the brevity of human life and the complexities of human activity, Spencer underlined the need to use time effectively—and also the need to mold that efficiency around the long-term benefits of a given pursuit. Spencer's take on the effective use of time informed Kanō's views as well: in 1915, he declared the fundamental principle of judo to be a way of using one's mental and physical energies as effectively as possible.

In 1918, *Jūdō* (vol. 4, no. 5) ran a piece titled "Muda no nai yō na seikatsu o seyo" (Live a life without wasting anything). In the article, Kanō called out Japanese people's habits of wasting time and money. There was no need to spend excessive amounts of time on things of no value, he wrote; people should instead devote their energies to whatever holds the most value. What kind of person embodied Kanō's ideal? It was not the samurai who swore allegiance to his domain in the Edo period, nor was it an individual who dedicated his or her entire life to the Japanese emperor. In a 1921 issue of *Yūkō no katsudō* (The principle of effective activity), Kanō stated that the lofty ideal of benefiting the greater good of the state was rooted in an individual's personal betterment. "By consciously adhering to the principle of effective activity in everything, one's normal conduct naturally and completely aligns with that ideal over time," Kanō wrote. "Individual self-reliance, success, and happiness all depend on whether one puts that principle into practice. The destiny of the nation, too, depends on whether each of its individual constituents lives by the principle of effective activity."[25] Kanō's belief that making the most effective use of one's mental and physical abilities would lead to individual self-perfection, which would then translate into benefits for the broader community, was a product of both judo as a discipline and the influence of Spencer and other British utilitarians.

Notes:

1   Kanō-sensei Denki Hensan-kai, ed., *Kanō Jigorō* (Tokyo: Kodokan, 1964), 21–22.
2   Ibid., 22.
3   Hasegawa Junzō, *Kanō Jigorō no kyōiku to shisō* [The education and thought of Kanō Jigorō] (Tokyo: Meiji Shoin, 1981), 6.
4   Kanō Jigorō, interview by Ochiai Torahei, "Jūdōka to shite no Kanō Jigorō (ichi)" [Kanō Jigorō, the judoka (I)], *Sakkō* [Promotion] 6, no. 1 (1927), trans. Brian Watson, *Judo Memoirs of Jigoro Kano* (Bloomington, IN: Trafford Publishing, 2008), 1.
5   Ibid.
6   Kanō-sensei Denki Hensan-kai, ed., *Kanō Jigorō*, 28.
7   Kanō Jigorō, interview by Ochiai Torahei, "Kyōikuka to shite no Kanō Jigorō (ichi)" [Kanō Jigorō, the educator (I)], *Sakkō* [Promotion] 8, no. 2 (1929), trans. Brian Watson, *Judo Memoirs of Jigoro Kano* (Bloomington, IN: Trafford Publishing, 2008), 12.
8   Hasegawa, *Kanō Jigorō no kyōiku to shisō*, 62.
9   Yamaguchi Seiichi, "Tōkyō Daigaku ni okeru Fenorosa (yon)" [Fenollosa at Tokyo University (IV)], *Journal of Saitama University (Foreign Languages & Literature)* 6 (1972).
10 Ibid.
11 Ibid.
12 Ibid.
13 Ibid.
14 Yamaguchi Seiichi, "Tōkyō Daigaku ni okeru Fenorosa (ni)" [Fenollosa at Tokyo University (II)], *Journal of Saitama University (Foreign Languages & Literature)* 6 (1972).
15 Kanō Jigorō, "Kōdōkan jūdō gaisetsu" [An overview of Kodokan judo], *Jūdō* [Judo] 1, no. 2 (1915).
16 Kanō Jigorō, interview by Ochiai Torahei, "Jūdōka to shite no Kanō Jigorō (go)" [Kanō Jigorō, the judoka (V)], *Sakkō* [Promotion] 6, no. 5 (1927), trans. Brian Watson, *Judo Memoirs of Jigoro Kano* (Bloomington, IN: Trafford Publishing, 2008), 35.
17 Kanō-sensei Denki Hensan-kai, ed., *Kanō Jigorō*, 128.
18 Kanō-sensei Denki Hensan-kai, ed., *Kanō Jigorō*, 124.
19 Kanō Jigorō, "Jūdō ippan narabi ni sono kyōiku-jō no kachi" [Judo and its educational value], *Dai Nihon Kyōiku-kai zasshi* [Journal of the Educational Society of Japan] 87 (1889).
20 Herbert Spencer, *Education* (New York: A. L. Burt, n.d.), 16.
21 Ibid., 170–71.
22 Ibid., 16.
23 Ibid., 239.
24 Ibid., 14.
25 Kanō Jigorō, *Yūkō no katsudō* [The principle of effective activity] 7, no. 6 (1922); Hasegawa, *Kanō Jigorō no kyōiku to shisō*, 269.

Chapter 2

The establishment of Kodokan judo and its principles

1. Kanō's jujutsu training

Motivations

Kanō's decision to train in the art of jujutsu likely stemmed from his initial experiences at Ikuei Gijuku in 1873, when he was twelve years of age. He recalls:

> . . . I was equal to my classmates [academically]. Among my fellow pupils were some who were physically weak, and as a result they were often under the command of the bigger, stronger boys. The weaker ones were forced to serve the stronger. Since I was one of the weakest, I was made to run errands at the behest of the strong. . . . In those days, although not sickly, I was, nevertheless, quite feeble . . . they often treated me with contempt and despised me. From an early age my curiosity had been aroused when I first heard mention of jujutsu, a Japanese method of fighting whereby one with little strength can overcome a physically more powerful adversary. I therefore seriously considered taking up training in this art.[1]

Having grown up small and frail, Kanō wanted to strengthen his body by learning jujutsu. His older sister, Yanagi Katsuko, noted the same motivations. "He [Jigorō] was so small and almost never won wrestling matches at school," she said. "Out of frustration, he decided to practice jujutsu in hopes that he might find a way to win against bigger foes despite his tiny frame."[2] Blessed with intellectual gifts but seemingly cursed by physical shortcomings, Kanō—who stood just 158 cm (roughly 5'2") tall and weighed 58 kg (around 128 lbs.) as an adult—took up jujutsu with the stubborn determination of a born competitor.

He sought out instruction in earnest. He asked Nakai Umenari, a family acquaintance and former shogunal vassal; he tried Katagiri Ryūji, the guard at his father's villa; he asked Imai Genshirō, another family acquaintance who had trained in the Kyūshin-ryū school; but he always came up empty. When Kanō matriculated at Tokyo Kaisei School in 1875 and saw all the well-built scholarship students there, he felt all the more inadequate and increasingly desperate for jujutsu tutelage. This time, he tried asking his father to set him up with a *jūjutsuka* (jujutsu practitioner) who often came by the family house, but it was to no avail; his father saw no need for his son to spend time learning the art. A path to jujutsu training would finally appear in 1877, right after Kanō began his studies at Tokyo University. Having heard that many bonesetters had trained in jujutsu, he began searching the city for one. By chance, he happened to spot a bonesetter's sign in Ningyō-chō, Nihonbashi, belonging to Yagi Teinosuke. Kanō told Yagi about the years he had been yearning for instruction in jujutsu, hoping that the bonesetter would agree to teach him. Yagi declined because he only had a single eight-mat room, which was much too small a space for proper instruction. Yagi did, however, tell Kanō about a teacher named Fukuda Hachinosuke (1826–80), a former *sewa kokoroe* (assistant professor) of jujutsu at the Shogunal Military Academy who was teaching Tenjin Shin'yō-ryū jujutsu in nearby Motodaiku-machi, Nihonbashi. Kanō soon paid Fukuda a visit, asked to become his pupil, and received permission. His dogged search for a jujutsu instructor had come to a serendipitous end.

Of all the trainees at the Fukuda dojo, only two—Kanō and a fellow student named Aoki—came every day. There were about four or five other students, most of whom were there less regularly. Kanō's daily training consisted of learning kata (forms) from Fukuda and then doing *randori* (free practice) with Aoki. There were times when Aoki missed a training session or Fukuda was out of commission after a moxibustion treatment, leaving Kanō without a practice partner. In those cases, Fukuda would swing a stick at Kanō so that he could practice falls on his own. The training was seldom, if ever, gentle. He described it as follows:

> One method that I recall in particular was the day when Fukuda threw me down repeatedly. I immediately picked myself up the first time and asked him to explain how he had executed the throw. He merely said, "Attack

again," which I did, and he threw me down once more. I faced him and repeated my question. Fukuda would only say, "Come on!" and yet again I was thrown. He then shouted, "Do you think you'll learn jujutsu by mere explanations each time? Attack again." Once more I was thrown to the mat.[3]

Instead of being given explanations of specific *waza* or methods for applying holds, Fukuda believed that students should learn by doing.

Kanō, however, began to question the prevailing jujutsu pedagogy. He decided to make his own jujutsu doll to learn more about the structure of the human body, and tinkered with ways of using that knowledge to break an opponent's balance. The training costume in use at the time was also far from ideal: unlike modern-day *jūdōgi* training uniform, the undershorts only came down to the wearer's thighs, while the top had wide sleeves, leaving practitioners' elbows and knees susceptible to scrapes. To manage the pain, Kanō was constantly applying an ointment called Mankin-kō, which had such a pronounced odor that his friends at Tokyo University would frequently tease him about the way his remedy made him smell. Realizing that modifications were necessary, he started wearing training apparel with longer legs and sleeves in order to avoid injury. This change also made it so that practitioners could attack and defend no matter what part of the uniform they grabbed.

In 1879, former US president Ulysses S. Grant (the eighteenth US president, in office from 1869 to 1877) was on his way to Japan as part of a lengthy world tour. Noted industrialist and philanthropist Shibusawa Eiichi (1840–1931) wanted to entertain Grant and the rest of the delegation, so he contacted members of prominent families—jujutsu masters Iso Masatomo (1819–81) and Fukuda Hachinosuke among them—to come to his villa in Asukayama, Tokyo, and show his distinguished guest what the art of jujutsu was like. On hand to assist Fukuda were Kanō and fellow student Godai Ryūsaku, who together gave a *randori* demonstration. Kanō, just twenty years old at the time, helped showcase jujutsu—an asset of traditional Japanese culture—for the former US president.

Tenjin Shin'yō-ryū kata

Kanō's training would soon take an unexpected turn. His sensei (master), Fukuda Hachinosuke, suddenly collapsed and died at the age of fifty-two in August 1879, shortly after the exhibition for Grant. Lacking a master to train with, Kanō decided to enroll at the dojo of Iso Masatomo. Iso, the prize pupil of

Tenjin Shin'yō-ryū founder Iso Mataemon and the third-generation master of the Iso school, had actually been Fukuda's sensei some years before. Iso was already over sixty years old by that time, however. While he was no longer fit to teach *randori*, he instructed his pupils in performing kata. In charge of *randori* at the Iso dojo were students by the names of Satō and Muramatsu, who would pair up with Kanō and Fukushima, another one of Fukuda's former pupils. The Iso dojo drew roughly thirty trainees a night. Remembering his time there, Kanō said, "Unlike today, the main practice session in those days was not considered to be *randori*, but kata. Customarily we did kata training first, followed by *randori*. . . . [I had] to do *randori* nightly with thirty or so partners. . . . I used to leave for the dojo after an early dinner and arrive back home late, sometimes well after 11:00 p.m."[4] Kanō's training regimen, then, began with a thorough run-through of the Tenjin Shin'yō-ryū kata and then proceeded on to *randori*.

Tenjin Shin'yō-ryū kata
· 12 *te-hodoki* (introductory techniques or hand releases)
· 10 *shodan idori* (basic seated techniques)
· 10 *shodan tachiai* (basic standing techniques)
· 14 *chūdan idori* (intermediate seated techniques)
· 14 *chūdan tachiai* (intermediate standing techniques)
· 20 *nagesute* (sacrifice throws)
· 24 *shiai-ura* (combat techniques)
· 10 *gokui jōdan tachiai* (highly advanced standing techniques)
· 10 *jōdan idori* (advanced seated techniques)
   Total: 124 kata

In June 1881, just two years after Fukuda's death, Iso Masatomo also passed away. In need of another master to study under, Kanō set out to find a sensei and eventually met Iikubo Tsunetoshi, a practitioner of the Kitō-ryū style. Iikubo was over fifty at the time, but he taught both kata and *randori*. The Tenjin Shin'yō-ryū style that Kanō had been learning consisted mostly of *waza* in the *heifuku kumiuchi* mold of grappling in regular clothing; most of the moves involved choking an opponent, reversing holds, and pushing opponents down. It also included throwing techniques like circular throws and foot sweeps. When Kanō began studying Kitō-ryū, however, he found differences in hold techniques and other unique traits specific to the school. Kitō-ryū also made

Table 1-3: Kitō-ryū kata

The 14 kata patterns	The 7 *ura* (back) kata
Tai (ready posture) *Yume no uchi* (inside a dream)	*Mikudaki* (body smashing)
Ryokuhi (strength dodging) *Mizu-guruma* (water-wheel)	*Kuruma-gaeshi* (turning wheel)
Mizu-nagare (water flowing) *Hiki-otoshi* (pulling drop)	*Mizu-iri* (water plunge)
Ko-daore (log fall) *Uchikudaki* (striking and smashing)	*Ryūsetsu* (willow snow)
Tani-otoshi (valley drop) *Kuruma-daore* (wheel throw)	*Saka-otoshi* (headlong fall)
Shikoro-dori (grabbing the neckplates) *Shikoro-gaeshi* (twisting the neckplates)	*Yuki-ore* (breaking under snow)
Yūdachi (shower) *Taki-otoshi* (waterfall drop)	*Iwanami* (wave on the rocks)

considerable use of body armor and had certain advantages over other disciplines, especially in terms of its hip and side-sacrifice techniques. With a new aspect of the jujutsu world open to explore, Kanō embraced his studies with fervor.

Around 1885, Kanō made an enlightening discovery while he was doing *randori* with Iikubo:

Normally, during our *randori* practice sessions, Iikubo, being superior in skill, threw me often. One day, however . . . I managed to throw him. . . . Although Iikubo tried quite desperately to throw me, he was unable to do so for the duration of our practice session, whereas my techniques on him were repeatedly successful. . . . He seemed a little surprised and looked somewhat puzzled, obviously wondering why such an unusual occurrence had happened on that particular day. I concluded that my success was undoubtedly the result of my study of *kuzushi*, or methods of breaking my opponent's balance.[5]

Kanō had reached an epiphany of sorts: the effectiveness of applying *waza* after first breaking his opponent's balance with *kuzushi*. When he told Iikubo of his discovery, the master *jūjutsuka* told Kanō that he had nothing left to teach him; there was no need to do any more *randori* together. Though it put an end to free practice with Iikubo, Kanō's realization laid the foundation for *roppō no kuzushi* and *happō no kuzushi* (the six and eight directions of breaking balance), key concepts that he would pass on to his students at the Kodokan. Iikubo granted Kanō his Kitō-ryū certification in 1883, along with a *densho* (a document that a master confers on a student who gains master-level proficiency) and everything else that he could bestow, and Kanō continued to train in Kitō-ryū techniques thereafter. He kept up his studies of Tenjin Shin'yō-ryū jujutsu all the while, too, having begun his training under Fukuda Hachinosuke in 1877, moving on to third-generation master Iso Masatomo, and then learning under Masatomo's successor Iso Masanobu and Inoue Keitarō, who had been Masatomo's top student and then gone on to become a jujutsu teacher at the Gakushūin (Peers' School). Not only was the Inoue dojo the place where Kanō would study the Tenjin Shin'yō-ryū on and off for a nine-year span, but it was also where he eventually found Saigō Shirō (1866–1922), a specialist in the *yama-arashi* (mountain storm) technique who went on to become a judo legend.

2. The establishment of Kodokan judo

From jujutsu to judo
Having trained in both Tenjin Shin'yō-ryū and Kitō-ryū jujutsu, Kanō had the feeling that he could reshape the martial art of jujutsu into something more transcendent—a practice that would have a meaningful impact on society through its potential for intellectual, moral, and physical education.

> In my younger days, I tended to be somewhat irritable and at times very hot-tempered. After a few years of training in jujutsu, however, I found that my health had improved. As a result, I had become calmer and possessed much greater self-control. I also concluded that the same spirit necessary to prevail in a life-or-death struggle against an enemy . . . could be similarly applied in overcoming difficulties that we often have to face in our daily lives. The training to acquire fighting skills that enable one to defeat an enemy in battle is, in a sense, also very valuable as intellectual training. . . . I concluded . . . that after modification, many of these same jujutsu techniques . . . could be of a practical nature for modern-day life and could be of value in the

exercising of one's intellect, body, and moral character.[6]

That mindset was the genesis of Kodokan judo, which Kanō officially established at Eishō-ji temple (Kitainari-chō, Shitaya, Tokyo) in May 1882. The first step in the formation process was changing the "jujutsu" name to "judo." In laying out the origins of the "judo" name, Kanō explained that judo had actually been a part of jujutsu terminology: "Allow me to explain the reasons for which I chose not to use the term 'jujutsu,' which describes what people normally practiced, and instead applied the name 'judo,' which had already been in use in one or two distinguished schools of jujutsu."[7] The schools with connections to the term were Chokushin-ryū "judo," a product of the Izumo region, and Kitō-ryū "judo," which Kanō had received a license to teach. From Kanō's standpoint, one of the reasons for the name change was that certain schools of jujutsu had already adopted the "judo" appellation. Another reason, as he explained, rested on a more philosophical premise.

> When we talk about jujutsu today, people often think of a technique in which one does only dangerous things, such as choking an opponent and bending his joints, or even, in extreme cases, killing him. Essentially, we think of something that is harmful to the body while offering no benefits . . . what I advocate is far from a violent or dangerous sport. . . . Because I did not wish the Kodokan techniques to be seen in the same light, I avoided the name "jujutsu."[8]

Jujutsu and judo share the same first character: *jū*, which means "soft." The difference between the two is in their second characters. *Jutsu* connotes special "techniques," "strategies," "tactics," and "schemes," which combined to give people an impression of danger—something that Kanō wanted to avoid. He decided to replace *jutsu* with something that had safer, less threatening implications, and he decided on *dō*: the "way."

Yet another motivation for the change lay in the developing connection between martial arts and the general population. Around 1873, Sakakibara Kenkichi (1830–1894), a former swordsmanship instructor at the Shogunal Military Academy, began organizing *gekiken kōgyō*, or public exhibitions of martial arts. Jujutsu was included in these shows. To Kanō, however, the performances made the art form into a cheap spectacle; he wanted to avoid the negative connotations of "jujutsu for show." He finally settled on *dō*, the way, but there were other options; he could have used suffixes like *rigaku* (science) or *riron* (theory), but Kanō felt that *jūrigaku* or *jūriron* would connote too much of a departure from jujutsu's existing legacy. "I merely wanted to ensure that the achievements of those who had gone before would not be lost," he wrote, "so I took a name that already existed and added the name of my dojo to it."[9] The achievements of his predecessors—some of whom had already adopted the *dō* in their own naming conventions—represented another factor in Kanō's decision to christen his discipline "judo."

The Kodokan Gokyō no Waza

After beginning the formal transition from "jujutsu" to "judo," Kanō started to establish the standard curriculum of judo *waza*. The syllabus of judo throwing techniques was the "Kodokan Gokyō no Waza" (the Kodokan's five sets of techniques) which came into being in 1895 and later underwent revisions in 1920 to establish the forty standard judo throws. The Gokyō no Waza presented trainees with a palette of techniques to choose from, proceeding in order from easiest to most difficult, with the first three sets comprising the skills for general learners. Each set consisted of eight *waza*; all in all, the syllabus contained instructions for six hand techniques, nine hip techniques, fourteen foot and leg techniques, three forward (supine) sacrifice techniques, and eight side sacrifice techniques. Much of the syllabus derived from Kanō's jujutsu training. Tables 1-4 and 1-5 show how the Gokyō no Waza line up with techniques from the Tenjin Shin'yō-ryū and Kitō-ryū, respectively.

Kanō's *waza* used names that were easier for contemporary learners to understand, first of all, and applied techniques that were less dangerous than their jujutsu counterparts were. The *katamuna-tori* and *shimoku* techniques from the Tenjin Shin'yō-ryū, for example, involved placing one's right hand near an opponent's throat and then reaping his leg from the outside rear. Given their potential for injury, Kanō designed his corresponding *waza* so that the person would grab the opponent's collar and sleeve and then sweep the leg. The name of the *waza*—*ōsoto-gari* (large outer reap)—was straightforward as well, simply expressing the basic principle of the technique. The Kitō-ryū's *yuki-ore* (breaking under snow) technique saw another transformation. In the original technique, when grabbed from behind, the *jūjutsuka* would flip the opponent forward over the shoulder. Kanō opted for a safer variation. Instead of being held from behind, the technique has the judoka face his opponent, grab his collar and sleeve, and then twist and throw him over his shoulder. In place of the abstract *yuki-ore*, Kanō gave his *waza* the more concrete name of *seoi-nage* (shoulder throw). That basic approach—a focus on popularizing *waza* by making them safer to do and easier to interpret—informed Kanō's alterations to jujutsu techniques like *mukō yamakage* (cross mountain shadow), which became *kata-guruma* (shoulder wheel), and *ushiro-kasugai* (rear clamp), which became *hadaka-jime* (naked choke).

By 1884, the Kodokan had established its basic setup. Entrants would take a five-point "oath of allegiance," sign an official register, and then seal their pledge in blood. The calendar featured regular events

The monument at Eishō-ji temple commemorating the birthplace of Kodokan judo (courtesy of the Kodokan collection)

like *kagami-biraki* (a ceremony to mark the opening of the dojo for the new year), monthly grading contests (tournaments), *kōhaku-jiai* (contests between a "red" [*kō*] team and "white" [*haku*] team), and *kangeiko* (midwinter train-

Table 1-4: Tenjin Shin'yō-ryū techniques and corresponding judo techniques

Tenjin Shin'yō-ryū jujutsu *waza*	Kodokan "Gokyō" *waza*
Mukō yamakage (cross mountain shadow)	*Kata-guruma* (shoulder wheel)
Shimoku (bell hammer)	*Ōsoto-gari* (large outer reap)
Katamuna-tori (single-lapel capture)	*Ōsoto-gari* (large outer reap)
Ryōte-tori (two-hand capture)	*Ippon-seoi* (one-armed shoulder throw)
Kataha-chijimi (single-wing constrictor)	*Kataha-jime* (single-wing choke)
Ushiro kasugai (rear clamp)	*Hadaka-jime* (naked choke)
Hidari muna-tori (left lapel capture)	*Waki-gatame* (armpit lock)

Table 1-5: Kitō-ryū techniques and corresponding judo techniques

Kitō-ryū jujutsu *waza*	Kodokan "Gokyō" *waza*
Yume no uchi (inside a dream)	*Yoko-wakare* (side drop)
Mizu-guruma (water wheel)	*Yoko-wakare* (side drop)
Hiki-otoshi (pulling drop)	*Uki-otoshi* (floating drop)
Yūdachi (shower)	*Uki-otoshi* (floating drop)
Tani-otoshi (valley drop)	*Tani-otoshi* (valley drop)
Yuki-ore (breaking under snow)	*Seoi-nage* (shoulder throw)

ing). The oath of allegiance, a prerequisite to entry into the Kodokan, professed that students would commit to learning the Kodokan techniques, persevere in their studies without discontinuing their training partway through, and abide by other stipulations. The register for 1882 contained nine signatures: Tomita Tsunejirō, Higuchi Naruyasu, Arima Sumiaki, Nakajima Tamakichi, Matsuoka Toraomaro, Arima Sumiomi, Saigō Shirō, Amano Genjirō, and Kawai Keijirō. The students then began training and taking part in the *kōhaku-jiai* and monthly grading contests, which Kanō conceived as a means of encouraging and motivating his pupils.

> For both events [the monthly grading contests and *kōhaku-jiai*], the contestant's name and that of his opponent are drawn and displayed in the dojo beforehand. The monthly grading contests are held once a month, on a Sunday. At the start of these contests, the lower grade bouts are held first [the lowest-ranking contestant facing off against the next lowest-ranking contestant]. If a contestant wins, he remains on the mat to face another opponent and should he defeat many of his opposers, he advances against higher and higher graded contestants from the opposing team until he is either defeated or the contest ends in a draw. Thus, the better contest men advance by defeating the less-skilled opposing team members. . . . These competitive events [between the red and white teams] were introduced . . . to encourage students to train more earnestly.[10]

Kangeiko began around 1884. Kanō specifically chose the coldest time of year for this mode of practice, which required students to do *randori* in frigid conditions every single morning, from 5 a.m. (sometimes as early as 4 a.m.) to 7 a.m., for thirty straight days. To Kanō, *kangeiko* benefited students in ways that extended beyond the mastery of techniques:

The Shimotomisaka dojo, completed in 1893 (courtesy of the Kodokan collection)

> Completing thirty days of training in these conditions is an undertaking that requires a sense of determination, a commitment to making good on a resolution. It also requires the will to fend off the drowsiness of the early morning and endure the cold of the midwinter months. Furthermore, it requires the type of meticulous care one needs to exercise in order to avoid falling ill or suffering an injury for a full month's time. Finally, it requires the understanding that, in whatever one does, there is no place for setting an aim and then arbitrarily deviating from that decision.[11]

The Kodokan also instituted midsummer practice routines under which students would train daily from 1 p.m. to 3 p.m.—the hottest time of day—for a full 30-day period. Wanting to encourage the same attributes he had designed the *kangeiko* to cultivate, Kanō saw summer practice as a means of developing a stronger spirit in his pupils. Students who successfully completed the set protocol for the month-long gauntlet received attendance certificates. These programs, along with the other activities at the dojo, came together to form the Kodokan judo training process.

Kangeiko (midwinter training) at the Shimotomisaka dojo (ca. 1930, courtesy of the Kodokan collection)

3. The development of Kodokan judo

The Kodokan begins to make a name for itself

The 1882 Kodokan operation was small: only nine students had taken the oath of allegiance, and they had a small space—just twelve tatami mats' worth—to practice in. Other students came in occasionally, of course, bringing the total number of trainees to around twenty. When the Kodokan was in its infancy, Kanō wanted to focus primarily on *randori*. "If students are left to their own discretion, the majority will no doubt practice *randori*, and kata will be neglected. In the early days of the Kodokan, I did not teach much kata," he said. "I decided, however, that when I did give the odd lesson, I would do so between bouts of *randori*."[12] The kata lessons between *randori* sessions simply presented forms from the Tenjin Shin'yō-ryū and Kitō-ryū jujutsu syllabi, with no modifications. As students kept filtering into the Kodokan dojo and *randori* became more and more of a logistical challenge, however, the increasing activity levels made it impossible for Kanō to give the pupils thorough, one-on-one instruction. Needing to give the trainees more to learn and practice, Kanō drew up *nage no kata* (throwing forms) and later added *katame no kata* (grappling forms)—a selection of techniques from the categories of *osaekomi-waza* (pins or hold-downs), *shime-waza* (chokes), and *kansetsu-waza* (joint locks)—in 1887. By that time, Kanō had stopped teaching Tenjin Shin'yō-ryū kata and replaced that form of jujutsu instruction with fifteen of his own *shinken shōbu no kata* (combat forms). Kanō retained the Kitō-ryū kata, meanwhile, as *koshiki no kata* (ancient forms) because of their importance in establishing the principles of throwing techniques and their sophisticated theoretical value. Kanō's pairing of *randori*, with its focus on attacking and defending safely via throwing *waza* and other techniques, and kata, including strikes and joint techniques, would be vital in shaping the subsequent development of judo.

It was a process, of course; judo did not make its way through society and establish a global presence overnight. One of the first steps forward in that long process came with the police martial-arts competition. In May 1885, Ōsako Sadakiyo (1825–1896), then the superintendent of the Tokyo Metropolitan Police, held the First Metropolitan Police Martial-Arts Competition in hopes of both promoting the art of swordsmanship, encouraging the practice of jujutsu, and giving the metropolitan police a way to attract high-level recruits. Ōsako's successor, Mishima Michitsune (1835–88), proceeded to make the competition an even bigger, higher-profile event from the second event onward. Around 1888, with Kodokan making itself a more familiar name in certain circles, tournament organizers began filling out the program with more and more matches between Kodokan practitioners and students in the Totsuka-mon Yōshin-ryū school—one of the foremost groups in the contemporary jujutsu world. At one of the competitions, Kanō recalled, "A contest showdown was called for between about fifteen representatives from the Kodokan and about the same number from the Totsuka Jujutsu School. Two teams of ten men competed, with the other four or five from each side pairing off with other partners . . . [and] apart from two or three draws, surprisingly, all the remaining matches were won by the Kodokan's representatives."[13] That resounding victory proved to be Kodokan's entry into broader recognition and growing acceptance. From that point forward, Kanō began working judo into the classes he was teaching at Gakushūin and later at the Fifth Higher Middle School in Kumamoto; judo began appearing in extracurricular activities at Keio Gijuku, Tokyo University, and other institutions of higher learning; and the Kodokan even began sending judo instructors to the Imperial Japanese Naval Academy.

In 1889, judo's expanding presence in the public eye prompted the Educational Society of Japan to invite Kanō to address national leaders on his creation. With Minister of Education Enomoto Takeaki (1836–1908) and other distinguished guests in attendance, Kanō delivered his "Jūdō ippan narabi ni sono kyōiku-jō no kachi" (Judo and its educational value) speech, touting judo's physical (bodily), competitive (martial), and spiritual (moral) benefits as grounds for immediately making the art a part of the middle-school curriculum nationwide. A year after becoming principal of the Tokyo Higher Normal School in 1893, Kanō created the school's judo training facility (the Yūshōkan) and formed a judo club at the school's affiliate middle school. The middle-school judo team apparently faced off in a competition with Gakushūin in 1898, but no records of the match exist. In 1899, the Kodokan hosted a competition pitting judoka from Tokyo pre-

Kanō Jigorō instructs young boys (courtesy of the Kodokan collection)

fectural schools and various dojos against each other. Some individual matches went on for as long as thirty minutes before a victor finally emerged; draws were few and far between, and there were no clear officiating guidelines. That same year, a team of five judo practitioners from the Tokyo Higher Normal School-affiliated middle school and five Kodokan students competed against a team of ten from Gakushūin. After several bouts with combined teams, the very first two-school showdown between Gakushūin and the Tokyo Higher Normal School-affiliated middle school came in 1903. While judo was clearly making solid inroads into school settings, though, the upswell in popularity was still not enough to convince the Ministry of Education to incorporate judo into the official school curriculum.

The path to the All-Japan Judo Championships
In 1898, Kanō founded the Zōshikai, an organization with a mission to guide young, motivated students, establish policies for individual success, and offer training for both mind and body. He also began making reference to judo teaching methods in the pages of the magazine *Kokushi*; the information therein would essentially form the first judo tutorial guide. As judo gradually gained a foothold through activities at the Kodokan and extracurricular Kodokan instruction, the need grew for an official set of rules and regulations. That came in 1900 with the creation of the "Kodokan jūdō randori shiai shinpan kitei" (Kodokan judo *randori* match and officiating regulations), which stipulated that judoka with ranks of first dan (*shodan* or first-degree black belt) or higher should devote two-thirds of their normal practice to throwing techniques and the other third to grappling techniques. The document also laid out the definition of an *ippon*, saying that a valid *ippon* must satisfy three conditions: "(a) excluding cases where one party deliberately drops to the mat or falls in error, a scored throw must be as a result of a deliberate attempt to throw or from the avoidance of that attempt; (b) the thrown party must fall faceup, even when it is difficult to determine the exact nature of the throw, and (c) the throw must have considerable *hazumi* [impetus] and *ikioi* [force]."[14]

Competition used the *nihon shōbu* (two *ippon*-decision) concept: in a match, the first judoka to score two *ippon* throws would be the winner. In addition to firming up the institutional roots of the sport with rules and standards, Kanō paid a visit to kendo (swordsmanship) practice at Kawagoe Middle School with Minegishi Yonezō (1870–1947, an instructor and kendo coach at the Tokyo

Higher Normal School) as part of a larger effort to make judo a required component of the school curriculum. Around the same time, martial-arts advocates Ozawa Unosuke (1865–1927) and Hoshino Senzō (1869–1917) were leading a movement to petition the national government to consider kendo for inclusion in the educational program. With support for the martial arts gaining momentum, the government

Kanō poses for a group picture with the Tokyo Higher Normal School judo club (courtesy of the Kodokan collection)

finally amended the Middle School Ministerial Administrative Ordinance in July 1911 to stipulate that "exercise shall consist of drills and exercises and shall include swordsmanship and jujutsu." While the legal provisions established these new requirements, the swordsmanship and jujutsu elements were electives in actual application—not required, but optional.

The advent of the Taishō period (1912–26) was an awakening for competitive sports in Japan. After the country's Olympic debut at the Games of the V Olympiad in Stockholm, Sweden, in 1912, it saw its first National Middle School Baseball Championships in 1915 and later its first National Middle School Judo Championships—featuring twenty schools—in 1919. Judo competition began surging in the first years of the twentieth century, but the progress came in fits and starts; there were more matches taking place—and also many cancellations.

One example was the Waseda University Judo (Combined) Tournament, which would later evolve into the famed Waseda-Keio Competition. The event took place for the first time in 1902—but then came to an abrupt end in 1905, just three years later. *Undōkai no rimen* (The other side of the sports world), a 1906 publication that covered student sports, gave the following account.

Keio suddenly asked tournament officials to increase the number of participants on each squad from thirty to thirty-five. Waseda, which had already struggled to amass a side of thirty, had no feasible means of adding five more tournament participants at such short notice. After deliberating on the

The Kodokan building in Suidōbashi, completed in 1933 (courtesy of the Kodokan collection)

matter, the organizers had no other choice but to assent to Keio's request. Upon that decision, Keio then demanded that the teams be expanded to forty members apiece. Waseda, no longer able to contain its frustrations, decided to cancel the event altogether.[15]

The issue of team size was a point of contention between the two institutions, it appears, and also prompted conflict at the Technical College Judo Championships, which began in 1914.

Table 1-6: All-Japan Judo Champions, 1930–41

		Amateur			
		Senior		Junior	
	Age	44	38–43	30–37	20–29
1930	First	4th dan Kōrogi Morifuji	6th dan Murakami Yoshiomi	5th dan Shimai Yasunosuke	5th dan Kasahara Iwao
1931	Second	5th dan Itō Tetsugorō	5th dan Kujirai Toramatsu	No champion	5th dan Nogami Chikao
1932	Third	4th dan Yoshimoto Kanji	5th dan Igarashi Kyūbē	3rd dan Lee Sun-kil	5th dan Iiyama Eisaku
1934	Fourth	5th dan Nakasuka Momomatsu	No champion	5th dan Koga Hiroshi	5th dan Nakajima Masayuki
1935	Fifth	4th dan Yamaguchi Ukichi	4th dan Matsumae Akiyoshi	5th dan Yokozeki Tatsuo	5th dan Nakajima Masayuki
1936	Sixth	5th dan Yamaguchi Ukichi	5th dan Tanaka Sōkichi	5th dan Yamauchi Jūjirō	3rd dan Murakami Kazuo
1937	Seventh	No champion	5th dan Lee Sun-kil	5th dan Kakizaki Shigeya	5th dan Murakami Kazuo
1938	Eighth	No champion	5th dan Lee Sun-kil	5th dan Makabe Ainosuke	5th dan Murakami Kazuo
1939	Ninth	Draw			
1941	Tenth	Matsumoto Yasuichi			

Controversy again arose at the 1920 match between the First Higher School and the Second Higher School, a regularly scheduled contest. The athletes on the Second Higher School team simply stayed on the mat, never engaging their opponents in anything but *ne-waza* (ground techniques). Irate at the nature of the matches, the First Higher School team pulled out of the competition on the spot. For Kanō, that brand of competition smacked of an overzealous, win-at-all costs mentality that he wanted to caution against. "When a competitor approaches a match showing no consideration whatsoever for his opponent, wanting only to win by even the most contemptible means," he said, "he leaves behind nothing but ill will, even if he should emerge victorious."[16] Every match has a winner and a loser, by nature, but Kanō underlined the importance of proper sportsmanship above simply winning or losing: "If one wins, one must win in accord with the Way, and if one loses, one must lose in accord with the

Professional			
Senior		**Junior**	
44	**38–43**	**30–37**	**20–29**
6th dan Amano Shinakichi	6th dan Ogata Genji	5th dan Sudō Kinsaku	5th dan Furusawa Kanbē
6th dan Yoshizawa Kazuki	5th dan Takahashi Shūzan	5th dan Kanda Kyūtarō	5th dan Ushijima Tatsukuma
6th dan Baba Jukichi	5th dan Matsunouchi Yasuichi	6th dan Furusawa Kanbē	6th dan Ushijima Tatsukuma
No champion	6th dan Aoki Takeshi	5th dan Tsushima Hyōichi	5th dan Tanaka Suekichi
6th dan Uto Torao	6th dan Nishi Fumio	5th dan Yamamoto Masanobu	5th dan Iiyama Eisaku
No champion	6th dan Kanda Kyūtarō	6th dan Yamamoto Masanobu	No champion
6th dan Takahashi Takamasa	6th dan Sudō Kinsaku	6th dan Tanaka Suekichi	5th dan Kimura Masahiko
6th dan Mitsuishi Shōhachi	5th dan Akagawa Tokujirō	5th dan Kusunoki Chikara	5th dan Kimura Masahiko
Kimura Masahiko			
Hirose Iwao			

Way. Losing in accord with the Way holds greater value than winning in defiance of the Way."[17]

In 1921, there were over 22,000 Kodokan members, more than 6,400 of whom held dan ranks.

The first All-Japan Judo Championships, Kanō's vision of a nationwide judo tournament, took place in 1930. Kanō created a set of tournament rules and regulations in the lead-up to the event, but ensuring an optimal competitive balance proved to be a challenging process. In the end, the tournament laid out several ground rules in view of proper parity. One had to do with geography: organizers decided to accept entrants from eight separate "zones" across Japan. The tournament also employed a two-class system to reflect the participants' skill and age levels. "Separating the participants into professionals and amateurs, as well as into four separate age groups, was a considerable struggle,"[18] Kanō wrote. Essentially, the tournament divided the entrants into two main groups—"professionals," who practiced judo full-time, and "amateurs," for whom judo was more of a hobby or a form of self-training—and then broke those two classes into smaller age groups. The motivations behind Kanō's arrangements lay largely in his goal of selecting the best judoka in individual groups of trainees, not simply crowning the best judoka of all. Another likely factor was his emphasis on physical education for the nation at large, a hope to make martial arts and physical education a part of the nationwide consciousness. The year after Kanō's death, however, the "All-Japan Judo Championships" became the "Japan Judo Championships" and did away with selecting winners by age group; there was just one "professional" champion and one "amateur" champion, with judoka of all ages competing against each other in the two classes (see Table 1-6).

The Kodokan's development was rapid over its first several decades. Starting out with an official membership of just nine in 1882 and a meager eight in 1883, the Kodokan had grown to a whopping 22,000 members in 1921 and ballooned to 48,000—23,000 with dan ranks—by 1930.

4. *Seiryoku zen'yō* and *jita kyōei*

The principle of seiryoku zen'yō *(maximum efficient use of energy)*

The year 1914 saw the effort to popularize judo take steps forward, with the Kodokan launching the Jūdōkai to help spread the sport through the journal *Jūdō* and judo-related lectures. The founding vision behind the Jūdōkai was, as

Kanō explained, in part a reaction to how the country was progressing at the time. "Our recent affluence has bred an inclination toward extravagance and indolence, an indulgent climate that seems to worsen by the day," he wrote. "Posing grave concerns for all of us upstanding citizens with love for our country, these tides of change demand that we do everything in our power to change the course thereof. It is my sincere hope that the discipline of judo . . . can contribute toward that cause."[19] In Kanō's eyes, then, judo had the potential to steer Japan away from the habits of careless opulence and wastefulness that he saw the country's citizens falling prey to. Japan had embarked on a rapid industrialization process in the wake of the Sino-Japanese (1894–95) and Russo-Japanese (1904–05) wars, cultivating a healthy, wealthy economy, but it also developed a haughty sense of pride as the victor in the two wars, while its commitment to proper labor practices showed signs of fading. The new Jūdōkai grew out of that context, testifying to Kanō's response to the state of society.

The Jūdōkai journal, *Jūdō*, was first published in 1915. The inaugural issue featured an article by Kanō himself: "Kōdōkan jūdō gaisetsu," a detailed explanation of using one's mental and physical energies as effectively as possible.

When you examine traditional jujutsu or my teachings in Kodokan judo, you find that both attack and defense go beyond *jū no ri* [the principle of gentleness, adaptability, and suppleness]; there are many more principles to explain. Say, for instance, that you are standing, and someone grabs you from behind. In that type of situation, a strict adherence to *jū no ri* would not be enough to free yourself from your predicament. There would be no way to react, adapt, and make use of the force that your assailant applies. . . .

It is becoming more and more difficult to explain methods of attack and defense solely through applications of the *jū no ri* principle. One truth that the techniques of judo uphold in any situation, however, is that one must choose the most effective method, be it physical or mental, for each specific setting. Thus, the most effective means of attack and defense must naturally equate to the most effective use of one's mental and physical faculties. While the exact reasons that jujutsu and judo make use of the character *jū* [for "soft" or "gentle"] may elude me, there is almost no room for doubt in my mind that the terminology has roots in the *jū* of *jū no ri*. What jujutsu and judo represent is an aggregate of multiple principles, acknowledging that applications of *jū no ri* are vital to methods of attack and defense but also incorporating principles from elsewhere. In hopes of further expanding the meaning of *jū*, I decided to use the word "judo" to refer to the most effective use of one's mental and physical energies, not just in attacking and defending alone, but also in whatever situation a person should find himself in.[20]

At the inception of the Kodokan, Kanō attributed the core principles of jujutsu and judo to *jū no ri*: the idea of adapting to an opponent's force and using that power to one's own advantage. As the above passage suggests, however, that foundation eventually gave way to the principle of making the most effective use of one's mental and physical energies. Kanō also expanded the scope of judo, explaining that it encompassed the way of "maximum effectiveness" (*seiryoku zen'yō*) in all its forms. In 1915, he defined the meaning of judo in explicit terms: it was the way of using one's mental and physical energies to their full effect; studying judo was a means of training the body, cultivating the mind, and learning the essence of the way through the practice of techniques for attack and defense; the ultimate purpose of the art was to converge all the dimensions of that self-improvement into self-perfection and thereby benefit the world outside the self. Kanō's description of judo marked a significant departure from the existing interpretations of jujutsu, which had never stretched beyond its role as a martial art for attack and defense, a method of doing combat. At the heart of Kodokan judo, however, was the process of self-realization and a commitment to the betterment of society at large—an ideal to *live* by.

The principle of jita kyōei *(mutual prosperity for oneself and others)*

The origins of *jita kyōei*, another Kanō tenet, go back as far as 1889. Kanō referenced the term in the "Jita no kankei o miru" (Examining the relationship between the self and the other) portion of his "Jūdō ippan narabi ni sono kyōiku-jō no kachi" (Judo and its educational value) speech to the Educational Society of Japan, underscoring the fact that judo training required mutual awareness between training partners. Herbert Spencer's influence was evident in Kanō's discourse, too, which at times included utilitarianist phrases like "co-existence and co-prosperity." Another essential contributing factor to the *jita kyōei* principle was Kanō's experience touring and promoting judo abroad. After visiting Europe for the first time in 1889, Kanō would travel overseas on four more occasions before making his thoughts on *seiryoku zen'yō* and *jita kyōei* public. Those initial encounters, which set the stage for a total of thirteen international voyages in Kanō's lifetime, must have been formative in terms of philosophical development. Table 1-7 provides a more detailed overview of Kanō's early trips overseas.

One of Kanō's most memorable experiences was his first trip to France and subsequent two-month stay in Paris in 1889, which he recounted in the pages of *Sakkō* (Promotion)(1929). "I had the opportunity to hear Gréard, the famous educator at the University of Paris. I listened to a lecture by Buisson, then the director of primary education, at the Ministry of Public Instruction. I was fortunate enough to meet numerous other principals, educators, and other professionals as well," he wrote, concluding, "The experience was a fruitful one."[21] "Gréard" was Octave Gréard (1828–1904), who went on to serve as the vice-president of the University of Paris for twenty-three years and fostered educational improvements under the French Third Republic. "Buisson," meanwhile, was Ferdinand Buisson (1841–1932), who organized the structure of French primary education in his meritorious service to the state. A renowned thinker, Buisson also discussed the relationship between religion and education, emphasizing the importance of respecting the basic essence of religion and human nature, rather than treating religion as a formal construct. Kanō, who would meet him again in 1920, held Buisson in high esteem, referring to him as one of the most powerful French voices in explaining morality as separate from

Table 1-7: Kanō's Foreign Travels

First trip abroad (Europe): Arrived in Marseille, France, in October 1889 to survey European educational approaches and introduce judo.

Second trip abroad (China): Spent approximately four months in China (July–October 1902) teaching about the origins of jujutsu and physical development.

Third trip abroad (China): Stayed in China from May to September 1905.

Fourth trip abroad (Europe/United States): Led the Japanese Olympic delegation at the Fifth Olympic Games in Stockholm, Sweden (June 1912); surveyed Western educational approaches; and worked to popularize judo. (Through this trip abroad, Kanō gained the confidence that his principle of *seiryoku zen'yō* would resonate with the global community.)

Fifth trip abroad (Europe): Led the Japanese Olympic delegation at the Antwerp Olympic Games (1920), toured educational institutions across Europe, and worked to popularize judo. Kanō's successful tours overseas convinced him to promote the ideas of *seiryoku zen'yō* and *jita kyōei*.

religion. In 1920, Kanō left his position as principal of the Tokyo Higher Normal School to attend the Summer Olympics in Antwerp, Belgium (the Seventh Olympic Games), and tour Europe. As Kanō visited schools, giving lectures and demonstrations on judo for audiences on the continent, the positive reactions must have convinced him that his messages spoke to people, that his views were worth proclaiming to a broader audience.

He also expressed the need for a core principle with a compelling, inclusive foundation. "Clerics often expound exemplary moral conduct, which is accepted and respected by the faithful. However, the principles and methods favored by varying religious groups differ somewhat. . . . If one religion is deemed to be favored . . . adherents of other faiths may well choose to ignore it," he argued.[22] Kanō's conclusion was that, in the absence of a fundamental principle capable of convincing anyone and everyone of its merit, there was no way to explain true morality. For Kanō, then, humanity needed a system of morality that rested on a stable cornerstone—a basis that Kanō envisioned as *jita kyōei . . . in order for one to live peaceably with one's fellows, a relationship fostering mutual help and cooperation is preferable. This means that we should be willing to give consideration to the opinions of others and to show an inclination to compromise."[23] The principle of *jita kyōei*, which Kanō forged as a means of unifying Japan's national morals, grew not out of a specific religious doctrine but rather from a grounding in virtue.

5. The creation of the Kodokan Culture Council

The core principles of the Kodokan Culture Council
After resigning from his post as principal of Tokyo Higher Normal School in 1920, Kanō reestablished the existing Jūdōkai (originally created in 1914) as the "Kodokan Culture Council" on January 1, 1922. In an interview, Kanō laid out the basic vision behind the new institution:

Recent world events have made international relations increasingly complicated. If nations fail to reconcile their differences, it will become difficult for them to maintain their independence. Since many in Japan are against such a trend spreading globally, Japan must strive to retain friendly relations with other nations. Reflecting on today's political affairs in Japan, many Japanese have little ambition, their ideology is confused, and the moneyed classes tend to be pleasure-seeking. There is continuing discord between landowners and tenant farmers. Further escalation of strife between capitalists and workers could possibly lead to the breakdown of society. There is clearly a growing struggle for equality between the underprivileged and the wealthy. All intellectuals recognize the fact that Japanese society needs to be rescued soon from this situation and brought into conformance with the trends of the world . . . Those with long experience of research in Kodokan judo have adopted the principle of *seiryoku saizen katsuyō*, the best practical use of one's energies, putting one's efforts to good use for the benefit of both oneself and society. By the establishment of the Kodokan Culture Council, this principle can be systematically promoted and make a further worthwhile contribution to the well-being of the public at large.[24]

The historical context of the time provides deeper insight into the origins of the Kodokan Culture Council. In the aftermath of World War I, European products had begun flooding into Asian markets; the influx had devastated Japan's trade economy, creating a significant unemployment problem. Political unrest was rampant as well; in 1918, for example, riots erupted when massive purchases of rice by large-scale merchants drove rice prices up to roughly four times their normal levels. The rebellion prompted a regime change, with Hara Takashi (1856–1921) assuming the office of prime minister—only to be assassinated three years later.

While conditions were far from stable at home, the global environment had its own set of circumstances: powerful imperialist ideologies remained as strong as ever in the postwar climate, and Japan had to maintain an active presence on the international stage as a permanent member of the League of Nations. Perceptive of the changing times, Kanō established the Kodokan Culture Council with a formal "Declaration" and a set of "General Principles."

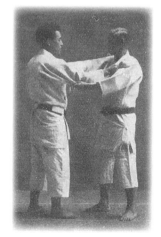

Shizentai (natural posture), 1931 (courtesy of the Kodokan collection)

Declaration

The purpose of the Kodokan Culture Council is to promote the idea of *seiryoku saizen katsuyō*, the best practical use of one's energies. This should be applied to all aspects of one's life. The doctrine of the Culture Council is focused on the following aims:

1. To seek the physical, intellectual, and moral perfection of each individual in order for him to be capable of benefiting society
2. To esteem the national polity of Japan and the history of Japan, and to work to improve whatever is deemed necessary for the good of the nation
3. To contribute to the harmonization of society by means of mutual help and mutual compromise between individuals as well as between organizations
4. To seek the peaceful elimination of racial prejudice worldwide through the promotion of cultural pursuits, and to pursue the mutual prosperity for mankind

General Principles

1. The perfection of oneself is ultimately the best use of one's energies
2. The achievement of self-perfection contributes to the self-perfection of others
3. The perfection of oneself and society is the basis for global prosperity

The "General Principles" took Kanō's 1915 definition of judo as a "way of using one's mental and physical energies as effectively as possible," reworded the phrase "one's mental and physical energies" into the more concise "one's energies," and championed the concept of *seiryoku saizen katsuyō* (the best use of one's energies)—human behavior serving the greater good as effectively as possible. In Kanō's eyes, *seiryoku saizen katsuyō* would enable self-perfection (the individual principle), which would immediately benefit others, which would then bring about social betterment (the social principle). It all centered on the connection between the individual self and the wider community. Kanō envisioned human happiness as *jita kyōei*, the process of joining the self (*ji*) and others (*ta*) in mutual prosperity (*kyōei*).

Kano's embodiment of seiryoku zen'yō *and* jita kyōei

The inaugural ceremony for the Culture Council took place on April 3, 1922, with members giving the following addresses.

1. Kanō Jigorō: Chairman's Opening Remarks
2. Tsurumi Yūsuke: Major Ideologies and the Sokol Movement in the Wake of World War I
3. Tsurumi Sakio: Japan's International Standing and National Consciousness
4. Hozumi Shigetō: What Makes a Man a Man?
5. Tokutomi Ichirō: Celebrating the Creation of the Council
6. Miyake Yūjirō: Introducing the Kodokan Culture Council

The Kodokan Culture Council spelled out the doctrine of applying *seiryoku saizen katsuyō* toward every objective in human life and represented a new attempt at building a framework for moral education in Japan. Although it originally issued two separate house journals, *Ōzei* and *Jūdōkai*, for financial reasons the organization eventually consolidated its publishing initiatives into a single publication under the name *Jūdō*. Kanō framed the *seiryoku zen'yō* in a far-reaching discourse, saying:

> There is no way for a person to do anything without employing the faculties of his mind and body, be it committing words to paper or wrapping a book in a *furoshiki* [traditional wrapping cloth]. If he aspires to write the most beautiful words or wrap a book in the most beautiful way possible, it follows that he must apply his mind and body as skillfully as he can toward fulfilling that purpose in the intended way. This, in a word, is the method or way of using one's mind and body as effectively as possible, the central, consistent path toward success in whatever endeavor one should pursue. This "way" is the Way of judo. In offering a means of attack and defense, the Way serves as a martial art. In fostering robust physical health and proving useful in everyday life, the Way serves as a form of physical education. In cultivating wisdom and nurturing virtue, the Way serves as a path toward deeper wisdom. In providing a guide for all things in social affairs, the Way serves as a foundation for life in the human community.[25]

Kanō thus defined judo as the "way of using one's mind and body as effectively as possible," a method that people could apply toward both martial arts and life in general. He would delve further into the scope of effective mental and physical application, saying, "Effective human activity and the use of one's energies for good also extend to issues currently commanding the public eye, including increases in efficiency, scientific management methods, and industrial rationalization."[26] The *seiryoku zen'yō* concept, as Kanō saw it, had a wide range of potential utilization—even in the fields of business and industry.

Kanō expounded on the "prosperity" element central to the *jita kyōei* concept as well. "In the commitment to thinking not only of oneself but also of others, devoting oneself to others but never forgetting to benefit one's own cause, and aiming to achieve both individual and communal prosperity," he wrote, "lies fertile ground for harmony, peace, and progress."[27] Efforts to better oneself and serve the community on an individual scale would pave the way for good on a much broader scope, leading to harmony and peace between nations.

Kanō worked constantly to delineate and elevate the judo spirit. From setting up the Zōshikai and using *Kokushi* in 1898 to lay out pathways to success for the youth demographic to creating the Jūdōkai and launching the *Jūdō* journal in 1914 to help popularize judo, he propelled organization and publicity initiatives. With the 1922 founding of the Kodokan Culture Council, a synthesis of the existing Zōshikai and Jūdōkai, Kanō's concepts reached full completion in the instructional philosophies of *seiryoku zen'yō* and *jita kyōei*.

These central concepts also featured prominently in Kanō's calligraphy. The work pictured on the left is attributed to "Shinkosai," one of Kanō's several pseudonyms. Until the age of sixty, he used the pen name "Kōnan" (featuring characters derived from the geography of his birthplace, Mikage, which was south—*minami*, or *nan* in the Sino-Japanese reading—of Mount Rokkō). He then proceeded to adopt the name "Shinkosai" (based on a phrase in the "Nourishing the Lord of Life" chapter in the *Zhuangzi*: "What your servant loves is the method of the Dao, something in advance of any art.") through his sixties. In his seventies, he wrote under the pseudonym "Kiitsusai."

Calligraphy of *seiryoku zen'yō* and *jita kyōei* brushed by Kanō Jigorō (courtesy of the Kodokan collection)

Notes:

1 Kanō Jigorō, interview by Ochiai Torahei, "Jūdō-ka to shite no Kanō Jigorō (ichi)" [Kanō Jigorō, the judoka (I)], *Sakkō* [Promotion] 6, no. 1 (1927), trans. Brian Watson, *Judo Memoirs of Jigoro Kano* (Bloomington, IN: Trafford Publishing, 2008), 1–2.

2 Yokoyama Kendō, *Kanō-sensei-den* [Biography of Professor Kanō] (Tokyo: Kodokan, 1941), 292.

3 Kanō Jigorō, "Jūdō-ka to shite no Kanō Jigorō (ichi)" [Kanō Jigorō, the judoka (I)], trans. Brian Watson, *Judo Memoirs of Jigoro Kano* (Bloomington, IN: Trafford Publishing, 2008), 4.

4 Kanō Jigorō, interview by Ochiai Torahei, "Jūdō-ka to shite no Kanō Jigorō (ni)" [Kanō Jigorō, the judoka (II)], *Sakkō* [Promotion] 6, no. 2 (1927), trans. Brian Watson, *Judo Memoirs of Jigoro Kano* (Bloomington, IN: Trafford Publishing, 2008), 10.

5 Kanō Jigorō, interview by Ochiai Torahei, "Jūdō-ka to shite no Kanō Jigorō (roku)" [Kanō Jigorō, the judoka (VI)], *Sakkō* [Promotion] 6, no. 6 (1927), trans. Brian Watson, *Judo Memoirs of Jigoro Kano* (Bloomington, IN: Trafford Publishing, 2008), 35.

6 Kanō Jigorō, interview by Ochiai Torahei, "Jūdō-ka to shite no Kanō Jigorō (san)" [Kanō Jigorō, the judoka (III)], *Sakkō* [Promotion] 6, no. 3 (1927); English translation based on Brian Watson, *Judo Memoirs of Jigoro Kano* (Bloomington, IN: Trafford Publishing, 2008), 15.

7 Kanō Jigorō, "Jūdō ippan narabi ni sono kyōiku-jō no kachi" [Judo and its educational value], *Dai Nihon Kyōiku-kai zasshi* [Journal of the Educational Society of Japan] 87 (1889).

8 Kanō Jigorō, trans. Nancy H. Ross, *Mind Over Muscle* (Tokyo: Kodansha International, 2005), 20–21.

9 Ibid., 21.

10 Kanō Jigorō, "Jūdō-ka to shite no Kanō Jigorō (roku)" [Kanō Jigorō, the judoka (VI)] trans. Brian Watson, *Judo Memoirs of Jigoro Kano* (Bloomington, IN: Trafford Publishing, 2008), 41.

11 Kanō Jigorō, "Kangeiko kyokō no shushi" [The purpose of midwinter training], *Jūdō* [Judo] 6, no. 2 (1935).

12 Kanō Jigorō, interview by Ochiai Torahei, "Jūdō-ka to shite no Kanō Jigorō (jūni)" [Kanō Jigorō, the judoka (XII)], *Sakkō* [Promotion] 6, no. 12 (1927), trans. Brian Watson, *Judo Memoirs of Jigoro Kano* (Bloomington, IN: Trafford Publishing, 2008), 78.

13 Kanō Jigorō, interview by Ochiai Torahei, "Jūdō-ka to shite no Kanō Jigorō (nana)" [Kanō Jigorō, the judoka (VII)], *Sakkō* [Promotion] 6, no. 8 (1927), trans. Brian Watson, *Judo Memoirs of Jigoro Kano* (Bloomington, IN: Trafford Publishing, 2008), 49.

14 Kanō Jigorō, "Kōdōkan jūdō kōgi" [A lecture on Kodokan judo], *Kokushi* [Patriot] 3, no. 24 (1898).

15 Undōjutsushi, *Undōkai no rimen* [The other side of the sports world] (Tokyo: Chūkōkan, 1906), 158–60.

16   Kanō Jigorō, "Taikō jiai no shin'igi" [The true meaning of inter-school competition], *Jūdō* [Judo] 4, no. 3 (1918).

17   Kanō Jigorō, "Kōdōkan jūdō no bunka-teki seishin no hakki" [Fulfilling the cultural spirit of Kodokan judo], *Yūkō no katsudō* [The principle of effective activity] 8, no. 2 (1922).

18   Kanō Jigorō, "Zen-Nippon jūdō senshiken taikai to seiryoku zen'yō kokumin taiiku" [The All-Japan Judo Championships and *seiryoku zen'yō* physical education for the nation], in *Kanō Jigorō chosaku-shū* [The collected writings of Kanō Jigorō] 2 (Tokyo: Gogatsu-Shobo, 1983), 390.

19   Kanō Jigorō, "Kōdōkan jūdō gaisetsu" [An overview of Kodokan judo], *Jūdō* [Judo] 1, no. 1 (1915).

20   Kanō Jigorō, "Kōdōkan jūdō gaisetsu (shōzen)" [An overview of Kodokan judo (cont.)], *Jūdō* [Judo] 1, no. 3 (1915).

21   Kanō Jigorō, interview by Ochiai Torahei, "Kyōiku-ka to shite no Kanō Jigorō (san)" [Kanō Jigorō, the educator (III)], *Sakkō* [Promotion] 8, no. 4 (1929).

22   Kanō Jigorō, interview by Ochiai Torahei, "Jūdō-ka to shite no Kanō Jigorō (jūroku)" [Kanō Jigorō, the judoka (XVI)], *Sakkō* [Promotion] 7, no. 4 (1928), based on a translation by Brian Watson, *Judo Memoirs of Jigoro Kano* (Bloomington, IN: Trafford Publishing, 2008), 107.

23   Ibid.

24   Ibid., 110.

25   Kanō Jigorō, *Jūdō kyōhon* [The fundamentals of judo] (Tokyo: Sanseido, 1931), 3.

26   Ibid., 29.

27   Ibid., 120.

Women's judo

1. The roots of women's judo: Accepting female students

The first female students

After founding Kodokan judo in 1882, Kanō began accepting female students in 1893. His first female pupil was Ashiya Sueko, who initially approached Tomita Tsunejirō (1865–1937)—the Kodokan's top student—and told him that she wanted to learn judo. Tomita relayed the request to Kanō, who consented, and Tomita began instructing Ashiya at Kanō's home dojo in the Kōjimachi goban-chō area. Several other women followed Ashiya's lead, training under Tomita until he left for the United States roughly ten years later. The Kodokan curriculum had laid down strong roots by then, first of all; with a strong foundation and smooth operations in place, it might have simply been an opportune time for judo to start expanding into instruction for women. Another contributing factor, however, was the role of Kanō's wife, Sumako, whom he wed in 1891. Even before the two married, Kanō had apparently been training Sumako in judo as a way of testing out approaches to teaching women. Kanō's daughter also said that her father would often get ideas for new *waza*—sometimes in the middle of the night—and enlist his students to practice them with. In some cases, Sumako would step in and be her husband's training partner. Kanō's first female judo student, then, was his wife. From what we know about the historical development of women's judo, Kanō had no particular qualms about the idea of women practicing judo. That stance was far from the norm at the time, however. The Meiji period may have been an age of "cultural enlightenment," but Japanese society still operated under the traditional gender consciousness; women were hesitant to ride bicycles or even let their legs show. Considering the cultural milieu he inhabited, Kanō had a progressive outlook—one that saw far beyond the immediate circumstances of his time.

Kanō's methods for training women

Initially, Kanō had no set training methods or policies in place for training women. The decision to accept female students put him in unfamiliar territory, leading to some hesitation. Miyagawa Hisako (1875–1930; née Ōba), who would later go on to become a leading figure in female education and serve as principal of Ōin High School, recalled Kanō's reaction when she applied to join the Kodokan:

> Shortly before I graduated from the Women's Higher Normal School, I began to consider what I would need in order to lead others as a professional educator if I did manage to graduate. I realized that academic expertise alone would not be enough; I also needed to train my body and especially my mind, to nurture the necessary physical and mental fortitude. For me, learning judo—a martial art that had developed out of Japan's longstanding warrior spirit—was the best path to developing that strength. I had hardly heard anything about women's judo at the time, but I got to talking with a few of my friends, and we decided to apply for entry to Professor Kanō's dojo in Kōjimachi. When we went, I remember how he struggled to give us an answer right away; the request must have caught him off guard. He told us that he would ask his wife, which he promptly did, and we received permission to train at the dojo.[1]

Miyagawa's account reveals another contour of Sumako's place in the judo story. Judging from Kanō's initial response to Miyagawa's application, it appears that he deferred to his wife when it came to women's judo—he respected her views. While her name rarely comes up in public discussions of judo, Sumako must have been an active, dynamic woman. Not only was she capable of serving as Kanō's training partner, but she was also athletic enough to convince her husband that he could effectively train women in the art of judo. Sumako's athleticism would prove to be a gateway for the development of women's judo.

As Kanō began teaching Miyagawa and a few other aspiring female judoka, both directly and indirectly, the process certainly brought instructional objectives and methods into clearer view—but not enough to convince him that he was going about the training in the right way. In 1904, Kanō received a visit from another young female judo hopeful: Yasuda Kinko, who would be a pioneering force in women's judo. What he told her at their first meeting betrayed his misgivings:

A judoka practicing judo with an American woman (courtesy of the Kodokan collection)

There are four or five girls training with me at the moment, but I have only been teaching girls for a short while—and I am still in the process of determining whether women's judo will have the intended effects. If you choose to come to the dojo, I want you to do so knowing that you are part of that process.[2]

Yasuda was the first female live-in student at the Kanō household and the first woman to pursue judo on a professional basis. Kanō took a cautious approach to teaching his female students. Yasuda had a weak constitution, so Kanō began by putting her on a strength-building diet and having her do basic, simple exercises on a continuing basis with dumbbells of various sizes. The next stage involved teaching Yasuda the *jū no kata* (forms of gentleness), having her practice *ukemi* (falling), and sending her for regular checkups at a university hospital. Once Yasuda was fit for more activity, Kanō implemented a program that included practicing *randori* and scaling Mt. Fuji. The training regimen, almost scientific in its meticulous progression, transformed Yasuda—she was tough, strong, and tenacious, worlds different from the frail young woman who had joined the Kodokan not long prior. While it may have been a trial-and-error process, piecing together the concrete elements of a viable, step-by-step instruction method convinced Kanō that instructing women in the ways of judo would work.

The birth of the Kodokan Women's Division
In the Taishō era (1912–25), women's judo proliferated in school settings, such as elementary schools, girls' schools, and women's teacher-training colleges. The Kodokan's Kaiunzaka dojo also implemented a formal full-scale training pro-

gram for women's judo in 1923, with Honda Ariya (6th dan) serving as the instructor. Meanwhile, the Kodokan also held a two-week judo course for female trainees in August 1926. The course had clear objectives in mind:

> This course, grounded in the conviction that "techniques such as judo kata represent not only an appropriate methodology for women's physical education, for which a viable method has yet to be proposed in Japan, but also a valuable means of self-defense," is designed to instruct participants, primarily "female physical education instructors at girls' middle schools and female instructors in other subjects with an interest in physical education," in "women's self-defense, comprising kata-based self-defense methods, to further the popularization of women's judo."[3]

The course drew just nine participants, but it was one of many initiatives that helped build momentum for the creation of the Kodokan Women's Division.

Female students practicing *randori* (courtesy of the Kodokan collection)

Kanō Jigorō teaches a kata to female students (courtesy of the Kodokan collection)

These efforts came to fruition with the formal establishment of the Kodokan Women's Division in November 1926. In 1931, the Women's Division got its own "oath ledger" (register), which new entrants would sign and seal. It was around this time, too, that female Kodokan members began full-fledged judo training. A powerful driving force behind the development of women's judo was Noritomi Masako (1913–82), who went on to become a renowned judo instructor. Her connection to the Kodokan came in Ōmuta, Fukuoka Prefecture, where she was training at a local dojo. Kodokan coach Samura Kaichirō happened to make a visit to the establishment one day, and he was so impressed with Noritomi that he encouraged her to come to Tokyo and train at the Kodokan. She initially declined, saying that it hardly mattered where she did her training; whatever she could do in Tokyo, she argued, she could do in Fukuoka. When her dojo instructor and parents joined in with their support for a move, however, Noritomi made the decision to relocate to Tokyo; she moved into the Kanō residence, and began her studies at the Kodokan. What she encountered there was a far cry from her freewheeling training in Fukuoka, where she had regularly practiced with boys and even fought in match competition:

> At the Kodokan, practice required us to be "ladylike." The instructors drummed proper etiquette and language into us relentlessly; if I ever accidentally hit someone's leg, for example, I would have to apologize with a deferential "Forgive me."[4]

Given its recent appearance and extremely short history, women's judo was still a curiosity in the public eye. Curiosity, though, can breed rumors and stereotypes, something that Kanō surely recognized; the last thing he wanted was for people to see female judoka as violent, rough, or wild. The "etiquette" curriculum at the Kodokan, then, must have come out of that awareness.

Women wore the same attire as men did. The only difference was that women donned caps. At that time, women often used hair oil, which would get on the *tatami* mats and make for slippery conditions—hence the headwear.

In January 1930, the Kodokan held matches for public viewing at Hibiya Public Hall as an extension of its *kagami-biraki* ceremony. It was there that the Kodokan Women's Division performed judo in public for the first time. The showcase featured a demonstration of *jū no kata* by three pairs of women who, interestingly, all wore different types of clothing: one pair wore *hakama* (a skirt-like Japanese garment worn over a kimono), another bloomers, and the other Western clothing. Kanō probably wanted to highlight the fact that anyone, even a woman, could do *jū no kata* in comfort, regardless of attire.

The Kodokan also announced an official set of "Kodokan Women's Division Regulations" at the 1934 *kagami-biraki* ceremony, spelling out nine articles under the heading, "The Kodokan Women's Division shall be under the direct supervision of Kanō, head of the Kodokan." The regulations officially permitted females to train at the Kodokan dojo in the same fashion as their male counterparts. Also announced were the following personnel appointments, by which three women became holders of dan ranks.[5]

Kodokan Women's Division leaders
· Division director: Watanuki Noriko (Kanō's eldest daughter, then 41)
· Manager: Uzawa Takashi
· Head instructor: Handa Yoshimaro
· Assistant instructor: Noritomi Masako

The Kodokan also instituted the following Women's Division Regulations. The decision to establish specific rules for the Women's Division likely stemmed from Kanō's aims to help popularize judo among women, a goal that he believed would be easier to accomplish by operating the Division as a separate, distinct entity from the training programs for men.

Kodokan Women's Division Regulations
1. The Kodokan Women's Division shall be under the direct supervision of Kanō, head of the Kodokan.
2. Kanō shall appoint the following leaders of the Kodokan Women's Division.
   Division director (one)
   Manager (one)
   Head instructor (one)
   Assistant instructors
   (a) The division director shall, in accordance with Kanō's instructions, administer the operations of the Division. In the absence or disability of the division director, Kanō shall serve in place thereof.
   (b) The manager shall, under the supervision of the division director, execute the responsibilities assigned thereto.
   (c) The head instructor shall, under Kanō's supervision, instruct students in *randori* and kata and serve as referee. Kanō shall, as the circumstances may require, appoint qualified individuals to train students.
   (d) Assistant instructors shall assist the head instructor.
3. The Kodokan Women's Division shall have several delegates who shall be appointed by Kanō and serve terms of three years in length.
4. The delegate committee shall convene at Kanō's request and provide Kanō with advisory support.
5. The Kodokan Women's Division Admission Regulations and Ranking Regu-

lations shall be as stipulated separately. All other matters shall be as stipulated in the relevant Kodokan regulations and guidelines.

The Women's Division Admission Regulations read as follows:

Kodokan Women's Division Admission Regulations

1. Those seeking admission to the Kodokan Women's Division shall submit an admission application and accompanying resumé to the Kodokan, in person, on any day (except holidays) between the hours of 9 a.m. and 3 p.m.
2. Those admitted to the Kodokan Women's Division shall sign the following five-point "oath of allegiance":
   Article 1. From this day forth, I promise to persevere in judo and shall not quit training for any frivolous reason.
   Article 2. I shall not bring dishonor on the Kodokan.
   Article 3. I shall not divulge to others any of the secret arts of judo to any person or persons whatsoever without authorization from the Kodokan.
   Article 4. I shall not instruct others in the art of judo without authorization from the Kodokan.
   Article 5. I shall abide by the rules of the Kodokan dojo both before and after receiving a Kodokan judo teacher's license.
3. Those admitted to the Kodokan Women's Division shall pay an admission fee (three yen) and the dojo fee (one yen and fifty *sen*) for the corresponding month.
4. On the day of admission, each new member shall bring her personal seal and wear either a *hakama* or formal Western attire.
5. Practice times shall be as follows:
   Weekdays: 3:00–6:00 p.m.
   Saturdays: 2:00–5:00 p.m.
   Sundays: Closed on *taisaijitsu* (major national holidays)
6. Those from foreign countries or faraway locations seeking admission to the Kodokan Women's Division shall send their admission application, resumé, certificate of sponsorship, and a signed and sealed copy of the five-point "oath of allegiance," along with their admission fee and an endorsement from a holder of a Kodokan dan rank, to the Kodokan. Upon receiving said documents, the Kodokan shall deliberate on the content thereof and, where appropriate, admit the applicant to the Kodokan Women's Division.

7. Dojos in foreign countries or faraway locations must first gain written permission to operate and then choose which of these Regulations to apply.
[The following year, the two items below were added.]
8. The Kodokan Women's Division shall, for the foreseeable future, limit admission to a small number of students.
9. Those admitted to the Kodokan Women's Division shall submit a certificate of sponsorship.

Women applying for admission to the Kodokan had to undergo family background checks, submit health certificates, and present copies of their official family registers, not to mention sit for personal interviews. At a glance, the hurdles that applicants had to clear appear to have been daunting; the arrangements, in some ways, made gaining admission to the Kodokan seem akin to young women apprenticing in reputable households to learn proper manners. There was, indeed, an emphasis on etiquette. While not part of the actual rules and regulations, there were practice supervisors who kept a close eye on any male instructors leaving or entering the dojo or male judoka leading practice. These supervisors would make sure that the proper manners were being minded and the proper morals upheld. The main aim of the arrangement was all to put the minds of the girls' parents at ease. At a deeper level, too, the Kodokan put an emphasis on etiquette and morality because women's judo stood out in the contemporary social climate—popular perceptions of girls practicing a martial art were probably not altogether accepting. By focusing on propriety, Kanō had his eyes on finding and developing a select group of first-grade female judoka with the potential to blaze trails for women's judo.

From time to time, Kanō would ask Noritomi about her thoughts on dan ranks for women, the connections between women's physical limitations and judo, and the rigorous selection of female entrants to prevent rumors from developing. His ideas occasionally puzzled Noritomi, and she sometimes voiced her own opposing opinions. When it came to dan ranks for women, for instance, Kanō's associates suggested naming the dan after flowers to give the names a more feminine ring. Noritomi begged to differ. "It would make little sense to award different qualifications to men and women practicing the exact same judo," she said. "I suggest that you handle dan ranks for women just as you handle them for men." Kanō had a progressive vision, to be sure, but he obviously harbored reservations about treating female students the same as male trainees; he might have struggled with the idea of women wanting to undergo the same training that the men were doing. Noritomi, looking back on her experiences, remembered her disappointment and frustration at making it into the Kodokan only to embark immediately on a rigidly formal, propriety-oriented training regimen. The decision to prohibit women from competing in matches must have embittered Noritomi, too.

Kanō's ban on match competition for women

In discussing his instruction of female trainees, Kanō noted the following.

> Above all, there are, to a greater or lesser extent, some differences between men and women in terms of physical constitution and also mental nature. Most young women, generally speaking, will eventually become mothers. Given these conditions, no woman may commence *randori* training unless she has enhanced her physical constitution through the abovementioned methods of physical education for the nation and developed sufficient physical strength to withstand and be fit for both *ukemi* and *randori*. More than anything, I want female judo trainees to engage in their studies in as sensible and reasonable a manner as possible, never overexerting themselves.
>
> Overexertion causes injury and illness. The reason I have chosen to prohibit women from competing in judo matches lies therein; contests and matches naturally foster a single-minded desire to win and avoid losing at all costs, leading competitors to push themselves past their limits. My decision to ban women from match competition comes from my hope never to see that overexertion lead to an unnecessary injury, illness, or, at worst, a misfortune with life-altering consequences.[7]

Women's judo in 1926 (courtesy of the Kodokan collection)

The quote sheds valuable light on how Kanō approached training female students. He instructed men and women differently, citing physical and mental differences between the two—a policy that arose from nothing else but his vision for the future of women's judo. He situated the Women's Division dojo near his office at the Kodokan, close enough for the sounds of students training to be audible. When he heard practice in session, he would often walk over and give a lesson or train with the women. He hand-picked instructors to teach the female students, selecting teachers adept in *waza* and practice techniques. He refused to allow anyone—even high-ranking judoka—into the Women's Division dojo for practice without his permission. It was under his close, watchful eye that women's judo gradually laid down firm roots: the number of women learning judo began to rise, not just in the Kodokan Women's Division but at rural dojos, as well.

Women's judo as the ideal embodiment of the judo spirit

Another quote reveals Kanō's deeper feelings about women's judo. "To me," he said, "women's judo is the heir to the true spirit of Kodokan judo." Kanō believed that men's judo was "judo of strength"; with their superior physical power, men often competed on sheer force. Women's judo, on the other hand, captured "true judo"—the "gentle way"—because women's relative lack of pure physical strength made supple flexibility vital. Kanō's view of women as the successors of true judo points to a knowing insight. Men's judo often comes under fire these days for its lack of a fluid rhythm; to critics, who liken it to "jacket wrestling," men's judo is turning into a crude form of combat where competitors forsake concepts like *kuzushi* (breaking an opponent's balance) and *tsukuri* (setting up maneuvers) for leg-grabbing and brute force. Women's judo, however, raises less concern along those lines. While women's competition might be showing signs of the same trends, the essential movements and techniques are still there, with the female judoka less prone to men's wrestling-like tendencies. Kanō consistently strove to highlight judo's benefits to the world, but he worried that people would lose sight of judo's core *waza* and movements as the sport moved across borders. He saw women as the ideal heirs for preserving *real* judo into future generations—and opening the doors to women's match competition, in his eyes, might have put that inheritance in peril.

A good number of the pioneering women who joined the Kodokan Women's Division and went on to pour their energies into judo instruction, such as Noritomi Masako, ended up foregoing marriage altogether and devoting their whole lives to judo. Kanō would try to set them up with eligible bachelors from time to time, but it was often to no avail. The social norms at the time made it virtually impossible for a woman to get married, start a household, and still head to the Kodokan to teach. For all intents and purposes, the women had to make a tough choice: judo or marriage. Many chose judo, opting to continue down the path that they had committed themselves so strongly to. To Kanō, the women's dedication to judo was obvious—they were just as passionate as his male instructors were. They were leaders he could trust with ushering judo into the future.

2. Fukuda Keiko and judo's expanding presence in the United States

Fukuda's relationship with Kanō Jigorō

Fukuda Keiko (1913–2013) was the first female judoka to hold the rank of 9th dan from the Kodokan. In September 2010, when the author interviewed her, she was 97 years old, living in San Francisco, and was one of the few judoka still living who knew Kanō personally. Her story is captivating, bringing Kanō's teachings and the spirit of women's judo into illuminating focus.

Fukuda Keiko was the granddaughter of Fukuda Hachinosuke, the man who taught Kanō Tenjin Shin'yō-ryū jujutsu. When Hachinosuke died, however, the Fukuda family fell out of touch with Kanō until he invited them to the Kodokan's fiftieth anniversary celebration in 1934. After the event, Kanō personally visited the Fukuda family house, commemorative gifts in hand, and met Keiko there for the first time. She remembered the encounter fondly:

> I'd heard he was famous, but there wasn't much of an aura about him when we met. He was small and slight. My grandmother just called him "Kanō"—never adding the polite -san suffix—and he didn't strike a very imposing figure. He wasn't intimidating, by any means. I remember seeing a handful of candy and chocolates in his overcoat pocket, even. He seemed charming, a bit of a character.[7]

During his visit, Kanō asked Fukuda if she wanted to train in the Kodokan Women's Division—and that was essentially how Fukuda's judo career began. The idea of young women practicing judo raised some eyebrows at the time, considering the contemporary social mores, but Fukuda's was a unique case. Her family agreed to her starting judo; they may have wanted her to keep Hachinosuke's legacy alive into the next generation. Her older brother, the head of the family and thus another obvious potential heir to the Fukuda martial-arts heritage, had been small and weak since boyhood. The chances that he would choose the judo path were slim.

Whatever her motivations, Fukuda agreed to begin learning judo. Seeing judo for herself was an eye-opening experience, she said. When she took a tour of the Women's Division dojo, she marveled at "women spreading their legs to do maneuvers on each other," a sight she found a bit alarming. Her surprise was natural, of course; she had grown up in a household where simply breaking *seiza* (sitting on one's knees) was grounds for a reprimand. Adding to the shock were the girls doing the training, who came from elite backgrounds—family history and bloodline figured prominently into Kanō's admission criteria, so Keiko was watching the likes of Kanō's granddaughter and the daughter of the Tokyo Higher Normal School principal grapple and throw each other around. Considering the high-ranking pedigrees of the trainees at the dojo, the girls often used extremely polite, refined language with each other: "Forgive me" was a frequent apology, while a reverent "Did I hurt you?" followed a potentially painful maneuver. The contemporary context was powerful in shaping women's judo as a suitable pursuit for "proper young ladies" from good families to develop self-defense skills.

The Kodokan Women's Division

Fukuda joined the Kodokan Women's Division at age twenty-two and trained under the Division's head instructors: Handa Yoshimaro, Uzawa Takashi, and Noritomi Masako. She had little memory of ever learning *waza*, which suggests that the training process centered primarily on learning kata and watching *waza* being performed.

What hooked Fukuda on judo was the elegance of its style. When your opponent executes a technique, you respond by gracefully breaking your fall; if an opponent lunges at you, you respond by using her own force against her to execute a throw. Besides studying under her three main instructors, she also had the chance to learn from famed "airplane throw" master Mifune Kyūzō (1883–1965). Fukuda remembered Mifune going about *randori* like a "light, nimble dance" and imparting nuggets of wisdom—"Judo is round," for example.

By the time Fukuda made her way into the Kodokan, Kanō was already advanced in years. He no longer did any training himself, but he did give frequent lectures. "Kanō talked about '*seiryoku zen'yō*' and '*jita kyōei*' so much," Fukuda recalled, "that some students would roll their eyes every time he started into those all-too-familiar refrains; you could almost hear them thinking, 'There he goes again.'" Still, the magnitude of his influence remained immense. When Kanō exhorted the members of the Women's Division to "go abroad and spread judo around the world," several young women immediately signed up for English lessons. Fukuda was no exception; she started learning English at a church. At the time, of course, Fukuda never thought she would one day travel to the United States and spend the rest of her life there as an ambassador for judo.

Fukuda's first trip to the United States

The Kodokan had already opened its doors to foreign students, who came from a variety of different countries to visit the dojo. Fukuda remembers a student from Hawaii coming to the Kodokan, for example, after studying with Women's Division instructor Uzawa Takashi in Hawaii. Fukuda eventually went stateside, too, at the age of forty. A woman who was married to the director of a dojo in Oakland, California, brought a group of students to the Kodokan for official dan promotions. Upon their arrival, Nangō Jirō (the second director of the Kodokan) assigned Noritomi, Niboshi Haruko, and Fukuda to teach their American guests. Fukuda was the only one of the three with any command of English. When the program was over and the woman was getting ready for her return voyage, she told Fukuda that she wanted her to come to the United States—and that she would pay Fukuda's way there. It was a moment that would shape the course of Fukuda's life. She teetered on the fence initially; on top of all the unknowns of moving to a new home, the woman could only pay her a paltry instruction fee. Her brother, though, urged her to go. "Going abroad is a valuable experience," he told her. "If you ever need any extra spending money, just let me know. You'll be fine." It was the push she needed.

The voyage was by cargo vessel, not a normal passenger ship, and took a full two weeks. When she finally arrived, the quality of the judo she saw was nothing to write home about. The students were enthusiastic, though, attentively watching and studying every last move their instructor from Japan made. The response was phenomenal. Fukuda had originally planned to be in the United States for a few months at most, but the students were so enraptured by their training that she ended up staying a year and three months. When she finally had to head back to Japan, her charges were obviously disappointed—and she remembered how one trainee's offhand parting words kindled a new spark in her. "I told her I doubted I'd come back to the United States again. I wasn't getting any younger, of course," she said. "But the woman said, 'Don't say that! You know so much about judo!' I'd never really thought about it, but she made me realize that, yes, I *did* know a lot about judo."

The Kodokan had a profusion of instructors. There were certainly times when people saw the impressive roster of teachers and assumed Fukuda, a woman, to be a second-rate instructor relative to her male counterparts. Fukuda's stay in the United States showed her something different. If a woman knew how to teach, Fukuda learned, she could earn students' respect—and that awareness made Fukuda much more confident in her abilities. The experience must have also given her an inkling that the international stage could hold more promise for her, as a woman, to thrive.

Laying permanent roots in the United States

At one point, late in Kanō's life, Fukuda's mother petitioned him to help find a husband for her daughter. He apparently gave the issue some thought before his sudden death on his way back from an International Olympic Committee meeting, as his eldest daughter approached Fukuda with an idea for a potential spouse. Fukuda declined. Kanō's daughter asked if she wanted to devote her life to judo, not a man. "Yes," Fukuda replied.

For a woman in 1930s Japan, getting married meant settling down in the home. For Fukuda, getting married thus would have meant leaving judo behind. Fukuda's conversation with Kanō's daughter made it clear that she had to choose between judo or married life—it was one or the other. It was an agonizing decision, Fukuda recalled. Her eventual decision to head back to the United States when she was past the age of fifty was the product of many factors—and the marriage issue was certainly one of them. Knowing how hard it would be for her to make her way as a single woman in Japan, with judo her only source of income, left her with little choice but to pursue her passions where she would have a better chance of success.

When judo became an official sport at the Tokyo Olympics in 1964, Fukuda and Noritomi made an appearance to demonstrate *jū no kata*. The Northern California Judo Association invited Fukuda to do a six-month residency two years later, and she made another trip to the States. She was fifty-three at the time. Providing instruction at Mills College, San Francisco State University, and other institutions in the area, she again made an impression on her students. They, like the students she had coached during her first stay in the United States, wanted to keep learning from Fukuda and asked her to stay on. Fukuda agreed, rented a room at a student's house, and set up a ten-mat dojo—the Sōkō (San Francisco) Joshi Judo Club—in the basement. Additional space opened up when Suzuki Shunryū (1904–1971), the chief priest at Sōkō-ji temple in San Francisco's Japantown district, let Fukuda use a corner of his temple as a dojo. The parallels to Kanō renting part of Eishō-ji temple and establishing the Kodokan were striking; it was almost as if she was following in her former teacher's footsteps, albeit on a different continent.

Teaching and popularizing judo abroad

Teaching in the United States proved an extraordinary challenge for Fukuda. Since the students were still learning judo at its most rudimentary level, teaching a single *waza* was an arduous, time-consuming task. "It was impossible to get through anything in a single bound. It takes time to learn the maneuvers, after all," she recalled. "But that's what instruction is all about. Everyone there really *wanted* to learn; their drive was obvious. That made me more invested in teaching them." Fukuda also taught at nursing schools and flew to Australia, the Philippines, France, Canada, Norway, and spots all across the map working to popularize judo. While she said that some audiences were dismissive at first, not expecting much of a little lady, they always ended up marveling at her technique in the end and lavishing her with gratitude for her guidance. She was confident in her instruction, on point in her techniques, and passionate about what she did, but there was another element that won people over: her personality. Mild-mannered and never overbearing, Fukuda never lost her temper—even when people were hostile to her or a frustrating situation developed. It was the principles of judo personified, in a way: instead of confronting an opponent with force, she adhered to the *jū no ri* (the principle of gentleness). She understood Kanō's judo spirit at the deepest level, put it into practice, and made it a guide for whatever she did. Whenever someone would ask her to do some calligraphy, one of her favorite pastimes, Fukuda would always write, "Be strong, be gentle, be beautiful." The words summed up what she had learned from Kanō, what she rooted her judo philosophy in, what shaped her entire outlook on life itself.

Part of the reason that Kanō prohibited women from taking part in match competition was his conviction that women could seek out a deeper understanding of *true* judo, an art where embodying elegance holds more value than winning by force. Fukuda captured that same sentiment when she spoke about her favorite kata. "The kata I worked hardest to master and really fought to understand deep, deep down was *jū no kata*, which has roots in jujutsu. You can see that foundation when you realize how much it depends on *jū no riai* [using correct, sufficient motion for maximum efficiency]. Noritomi-san was always talking about that concept, telling me never to let force dictate my movements. That's as far as she would go, though—she never got to where the whole concept of *jū no riai* came from," she explained. "From that point on, I was on my own. I think I worked harder than anyone else to understand it, and that's something I'm proud of. Honestly, I doubt my judo would've been worth anything if I hadn't figured it out. When I finally did, I was in my nineties. It was such a moving moment that I broke down in tears on the spot, right there in the kitchen."

Winning in competition is a moment of self-satisfaction, a gratifying experience with an immediate payoff: a visceral *understanding* of what judo is. Countless judoka have emerged from a match with that sense, to be sure. Judoka who have never been in a match, however, never get a taste of judo mastery on those binary terms; the only way to find it is through practice. The journey there is a long, solitary one, as Fukuda's experience suggests. Perhaps that path of inquiry is what Kanō was hoping women would illuminate.

Fukuda's lifelong devotion to judo is both astonishing and humbling. While no one will ever know exactly what Kanō expected of her, he would surely have been proud of how she worked and trained just as hard as any of her male counterparts did. Kanō might have known that women had more dedication, a fiercer persistence in seeking understanding, than men could ever have.

Kanō's teachings

Every life needs some kind of core. For Fukuda, it was judo. Describing what judo had done for her and how she had pursued her studies, Fukuda said, "Kanō-sensei's ideas of *seiryoku zen'yō* and *jita kyōei* are always in my heart, reminding me that I have to do good. That's the philosophy that I always need to embrace—and holding true to that concept is why I've made it in judo. I want everyone in the judo world to take Kanō-sensei's words to heart, straight and true, and do what they can to put them in practice." While Fukuda was still as bright and positive as ever in her later years, old age took its toll on her legs, making it hard for her to walk. Despite that physical wear and tear, she still made it a point to go to the dojo twice a week—and her students handled all her transportation. Not only did they help her get to and from practice, but they were the ones taking care of her meals, shopping, and everything else she needed to get by day to day. The fact that so many American students went the extra mile for their aging Japanese instructor is more than just a heartwarming thought. It also speaks to the depth of the relationships that Fukuda forged throughout her life's work.

When Fukuda was studying at the Kodokan, there was a high-ranking sensei who said that he came there "to see Kanō-sensei, above all." Through the end of her life, Fukuda inspired the same admiration. She no longer had the ability to perform *waza*, but students flocked to her anyway. To those women, Fukuda was a master—and to Fukuda, her gift for instruction traced back to her growth under Kanō.

The future of women's judo

If Kanō were alive today, what would he think of women's judo in its current state? Just as he had envisioned, women's judo expanded its reach throughout Japan and into the international community. With that spread came the gradual development of organized competition. In 1980, the first Women's World Judo Championships convened in New York; at the Seoul Olympics in 1988, women's judo debuted as a demonstration sport; and in 1992, women's judo became an official Olympic sport at the games in Barcelona. Since the first All-Japan Women's Judo Championships in 1978, judo competitions for people ranging from elementary school students to working adults have added women's components. Female Japanese judoka may have gotten a late start in the competitive arena, but they have leveraged Japan's judo legacy, historical background, and host of first-rate coaches to level the global playing field—and dominate it. Japanese women are as competitive as ever, exhibiting both technical prowess and a tenacious approach. Although most of the female judoka today likely have no idea that women were banned from match judo competition for years, their performance in competition is a clear reflection of the vision that Kanō had for women's judo, an ideal that has passed from generation to generation. Numerous female judoka have gone on to become coaches and referees after retiring from competition, as well. The realities of female roles—marrying, bearing children, and raising families—have largely remained the same over time. What *has* changed, however, is that women no longer need to choose between judo and a family. Judo is about more than just match competition. While the lifting of the longstanding ban on female judo competition has enabled so many gifted judoka flourish and shine like they never could before, Kanō's hope for women's judo—to serve as a conduit for *true* judo, a pursuit of the "perfection of the self" and the "well-being of society at large"—holds true today. The fulfillment of that vision depends largely on women who embody those principles both on and off the competitive stage.

The timeline below highlights the major events in the history of women's judo.

1882: Kanō Jigorō founds the Kodokan.

1893: Ashiya Sueko and other aspiring female judoka begin training at the Kodokan.

1923: The Kodokan begins full-scale training for women.

1926: The Kodokan holds a judo course for women and creates the Kodokan Women's Division.

1933: Kosaki Katsuko becomes the first female to achieve the rank of first dan (*shodan*).

1934: The Kodokan establishes the "Kodokan Women's Division Regulations," and three more women earn dan ranks.

1972: Italy proposes holding a women's event at the 1972 general meeting of the International Judo Federation.

1974: The Kodokan Women's Division hosts a test run of women's match competition; the Oceania Women's Championships are held.

1975: The first Women's European Judo Championships are held.

1977: The first Pan-American Union Women's Judo Championships are held.

1978: The first All-Japan Women's Judo Championships (with four weight classes) are held.

1979: The first Pacific Rim Judo Championships are held; the event features four Japanese women, all of whom place.

1980: The first Women's World Judo Championships are held in November (New York City); Japanese women compete in seven of the eight weight classes (with Yamaguchi Kaori winning the silver medal in the 52 kg and under division).

1988: Five Japanese women compete at the Summer Olympics in Seoul, South

Korea, where women's judo was a demonstration sport; Sasaki Hikari wins the gold medal in the 66 kg and under division, while the Japanese contingent also take home one silver and three bronze medals.

1992: Women's judo makes its debut as an official Olympic sport at the Barcelona Olympics; Tani (née Tamura) Ryōko earns the silver medal in the 48 kg and under division; Japanese women win two silver and two bronze medals in other weight classes.

Notes:

1   Kanō-sensei Denki Hensan-kai, ed., Kanō Jigorō [Kanō Jigorō] (Tokyo: Kodokan, 1964), 456.

2   Ibid., 457–.

3   Ibid., 453.

4   Noritomi Masako, Joshi jūdō kyōhon [The fundamentals of women's judo] (Tokyo: Junsensō, 1972), 10.

5   Ibid.; the Women's Division Regulations and Women's Division Admission Regulations are from the same source.

6   Kanō-sensei Denki Hensan-kai, ed., Kanō Jigorō, 464–65.

7   Fukuda Keiko, interview with the author, February 9–11, 2009, at Fukuda's residence in San Francisco; all subsequent quotes attributed to Fukuda are from this interview.

Part II

Kanō Jigorō
in the educational sphere

Kanō Jigorō, principal of the Higher Normal School

Kanō's educational reforms

1. Kanō the educator

Kanō's career as school principal

Kanō Jigorō's combined tenure at the Higher Normal School and Tokyo Higher Normal School spanned twenty-three years across three separate periods.

Period 1: September 1893–August 1897 (four years)
Period 2: November 1897–June 1898 (seven months)
Period 3: May 1901–January 1920 (eighteen years, eight months)

Kanō landed an instructor position at Gakushūin in January 1882, marking his entry into the educational sphere. While that was his first step, his educational career gained more momentum when the institution made Kanō both a professor and the assistant principal, which meant that he took part in all Gakushūin management. Recalling that it was from that point onward that he began to study education in a larger sense,[1] Kanō gradually began to commit himself to education and school management.

Kanō got along well with the first two Gakushūin presidents that he worked under, Tani Tateki (1837–1911) and Ōtori Keisuke (1833–1911), but eventually butted heads with Ōtori's successor, Miura Gorō (1847–1926). After heading abroad in 1889 and returning home in 1891, Kanō promptly left his position at Gakushūin. That was the beginning of a whirlwind academic streak in Kanō's career, one that would see him assume leadership of the Higher Normal School on three separate occasions in just over two decades.

In April 1891, the Japanese government appointed Kanō a councillor to the

Ministry of Education. That August, he complicated his duties as councillor by moving alone to Kumamoto and assuming the post of principal at the Fifth High School in Kumamoto. Not even two years later, however, the Ministry of Education brought him back to Tokyo to work on textbook inspections and other tasks. New roles and responsibilities kept coming, with Kanō taking up an additional post as principal of the First High School in June 1893 and then receiving an order to serve concurrently as the principal of the Higher Normal School that September. Shortly thereafter, he was relieved of his duties at the First High School and left in charge of one institution: the Higher Normal School, where he began his first term as principal.

Initially, Kanō showed little interest in the training of secondary-school teachers. As he began to recognize the importance of the functions and roles played by the Higher Normal School in developing educators, however, he pushed through a handful of reforms at the school—expanding the scale of the institution, extending the academic track (from three years to four years), and establishing special courses. Kanō foresaw that the number of secondary schools would grow after the Sino-Japanese War, prompting a need for more teachers, but the prospects for action were unclear because the personnel situation at the Ministry of Education—the head decision-making body—was in flux. In the spring of 1897, Minster of Education Hachisuka Mochiaki (1846–1918) was planning to name Tsuzuki Keiroku (1861–1923) deputy minister—a move that Kanō opposed. Buttressed by Hamao Arata (1849–1925) and other allies within the ministry, Kanō voiced his opinion that Tsuzuki was unfit for the position. In the end, Kanō's outspoken criticism ruffled feathers, and he was dismissed. A shakeup at the top, however, brought Kanō full circle: when Hamao replaced Hachisuka atop the ministry at the end of September 1897, Kanō reclaimed his post and began his second official term as principal of the Higher Normal School in November.

A further shift in ministry leadership brought about yet another change

Kanō Jigorō during his time as assistant principal at Gakushūin (courtesy of the Kodokan collection)

The main gate of the Higher Normal School (Ochanomizu, ca. 1900)

in Kanō's duties. Hamao resigned as minister of education due to an illness in January 1898. Succeeding Hamao was Saionji Kinmochi (1849–1940), who promptly tapped Kanō to head up the Bureau of Common Educational Affairs. Although he was initially able to manage both positions (principal of the Higher Normal School and director of the Bureau of Common Educational Affairs), Kanō took the advice of former Education Minister Toyama Masakazu (1848–1900) and eventually stepped down as principal in June 1898 to concentrate on his duties at the bureau. Kanō's second stint as principal thus lasted just seven months. Even though he had resigned from the school to focus exclusively on his position at the Bureau of Common Educational Affairs, his time there would be short-lived as well: a clash with then-Deputy Minister of Education Kashiwada Morifumi (1851–1910) led to Kanō's dismissal that November.

After two and a half years out of the educational field, Kanō began his third term at the helm of the Higher Normal School in May 1901. True to form, he held additional offices over the course of his time there—including important leadership roles at the Educational Society of the Empire of Japan. Kanō was driven by a constant passion for education.

Secondary education during Kanō's third tenure as principal

Countries on the path to modernization generally focus their educational efforts on bolstering their systems for primary (compulsory) education, which serves to raise the floor for national academic performance, and higher education, which forms an elite class of well-educated citizens. Japan was no exception. In 1872, the Japanese government instituted a school system with three levels—elementary, secondary, and higher education—in a single-track framework, a rarity at the time. The process of developing the three levels was uneven, however. Considering that the national government was absorbed in establishing universities and regional communities were preoccupied with opening elementary schools, secondary schools sat on the back burner while the other two segments of the framework took priority.

The slow-starting initiative to firm up a secondary-education structure picked up steam in the late 1890s and early 1900s. First came a reorganization effort on the legal side. February 1899 saw a flurry of action, with lawmakers revising the Middle School Order, promulgating the Vocational School Order, and developing the Girls' High School Order in quick succession. That spurt of activity stemmed partly from the 1897 Normal Education Order, which reworked the normal-school system. With that structure in place, the next step entailed making the legal arrangements for a variety of secondary institutions to follow the six-year course of elementary education. At the same time, the framework of secondary education continued to fill out and grow. As figure 2-1 shows, the numbers of secondary schools and secondary-school students climbed steadily around the turn of the twentieth century. Children who went on to further education after their compulsory schooling were few and far between in prewar Japan, but their numbers jumped as options for secondary education increased: a look at the percentages of students choosing to continue their education at the secondary level shows a nearly threefold increase, going from 4.3 percent in 1895 to 12.3 percent in 1910.

Along with the larger scale of secondary education came the need for larger numbers of secondary-school teachers. The responsibility for meeting that growing demand fell on the Higher Normal School, which primarily served to

Figure 2-1

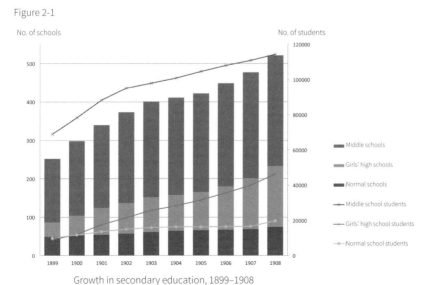

Growth in secondary education, 1899–1908

train teachers, but there was no way for the separate men's and women's normal schools to produce enough instructors by themselves. The country needed new teacher-training institutions and more opportunities for aspiring educators. A new higher normal school opened in Hiroshima in 1902 (which resulted in the renaming of the existing "Higher Normal School" as the "Tokyo Higher Normal School" to differentiate the institutions). In 1908, the second higher normal school for women launched operations in Nara.

In addition to new normal schools, there were other sources of secondary-school teachers. A sizable number came from Tokyo Imperial University, which had already been awarding secondary-school teaching certificates to graduates. A new imperial university opened its doors in Kyoto in 1897, boosting the supply. People interested in becoming secondary-school teachers had several other routes to certification, as well. These included the examination certification system, which gave licenses to people who passed the official Ministry of Education test, and the non-examination certification system, under which students from authorized and designated schools could receive teaching licenses upon graduation. Like higher normal schools and imperial universities, both certification frameworks played important roles in training secondary-school teachers. Despite all the different paths to licensure, however, Japan still faced a shortage of secondary-school teachers. The government responded with a new approach: in 1902, provisional teacher-training centers began operating as annexes to higher-learning institutions across the country.

These were the circumstances that Kanō stepped into when he began his third stint as principal of the Higher Normal School. Secondary education in Japan was spreading rapidly, sparking the creation of new teacher-training institutions and certification methods. While those additions helped, the sheer scale of the country's teacher shortage transcended what the diversification of training options could do. As secondary education gradually became more accessible and familiar to the average citizen, the need for higher-quality, better-skilled teachers also began to emerge.

2. The showdown over secondary-school teacher training

Frequent curriculum changes

Kanō spearheaded an array of educational reforms at the Tokyo Higher Normal School in 1903, including changes in academic faculties, courses, and weekly class hours. Even before that juncture, however, the curriculum at the Higher Normal School had undergone numerous adjustments. In 1894, during Kanō's first stint as principal, the school consolidated its three existing faculties (literature, science, and natural history) into two faculties (arts and sciences). When the Normal Education Order came into effect in 1898, during Kanō's second term as principal, the school split its faculties into six smaller departments: pedagogy, Japanese language and classical Chinese literature, English, geography and history, physical mathematics, and natural history. The following year, Izawa Shūji (1851–1917) took over as principal. Under Izawa, the Higher Normal School overhauled its curriculum in 1900. One key part of the sweeping changes was the course of study, which the new framework divided into two parts: a one-year preparatory course followed by a three-year regular course. Like the preceding initiatives, the 1900 reforms also reorganized the academic clusters. The new departments had numbers corresponding to a primary subject of study: Department I focused on Japanese language and classical Chinese literature, Department II on geography and history, Department III on mathematics and physical chemistry, and Department IV on biology and natural history.

The frequent reshuffling of the Tokyo Higher School curriculum—three departmental overhauls in less than ten years' time—is evidence of the changing needs of the times. With the need for secondary-school teachers quickly mounting at the turn of the twentieth century, the school had to align its academic approach with the shifting demand. The approach varied from principal to principal, however, and the reforms that Izawa initiated after Kanō's second term were a stark departure from what his predecessor envisioned. Kanō was frustrated with the direction the school was taking.

Izawa and Kanō: Opposing viewpoints

Izawa and Kanō were noticeably different in their approaches. Table 2-1 shows Izawa's 1900 curriculum for Department I, which focused on Japanese language and classical Chinese literature. Table 2-2, meanwhile, shows Kanō's curriculum for the Japanese language and classical Chinese literature department in 1903, the year he began his third term as principal. According to education historian Funaki Toshio, Kanō's 1903 reforms aimed to "segmentalize the curriculum in hopes of helping students deepen their expertise in a specific field of learning" and "make drastic cuts to the number of hours students spent learning pedagogical elements."[2] In other words, Kanō wanted to replace much of the specialized

Table 2-1: Curriculum reforms under Izawa (Japanese language and classical literature, Department I, regular course)

Term \ Course		Ethics	Pedagogy	Psychology	Japanese language	Classical Chinese literature	
Year 1	Weekly class hours	2		3	(6) [2]	(6)	
	First trimester	Practical morality History of Eastern ethics		General psychology	Reading Reading	Reading Composition	
	Weekly class hours	2		3	(6) [2]	(6)	
	Second trimester	Same as above		Same as above	Same as above Same as above	Same as above	
	Weekly class hours	2		3	(6) [2]	(6)	
	Third trimester	Same as above		Same as above	(Same as above) [Same as above]	(Same as above)	
Year 2	Weekly class hours	2	4	2	(6) [2]	(6)	
	First trimester	Practical morality History of Western ethics	Educational theory and application	Applied psychology	(Reading) [Comparative grammar Literary history]	(Reading Literary history Composition)	
	Weekly class hours	2	4	2	(6) [2]	(6)	
	Second trimester	Same as above	Same as above	Same as above	(Same as above) [Same as above]	(Same as above)	
	Weekly class hours	2	4	2	(6) [2]	(6)	
	Third trimester	Same as above	History of education	Same as above	(Same as above) [Same as above]	(Same as above)	
Year 3	Weekly class hours	2	6		(6)	(6)	
	First trimester	Practical morality Ethics	History of education Department-specific instructional methods		(Reading Grammar Literary history)	(Reading Composition)	
	Weekly class hours	2	6		(6)	(6)	
	Second trimester	Same as above	Department-specific instructional methods Teaching practice		(Same as above)	(Same as above)	
	Weekly class hours	2	14		(2)	(2)	
	Third trimester	Same as above	School hygiene Educational laws Teaching practice		(Literary history)	(Reading)	

English	German/French	History	Philosophy	Linguistics	Biology	Physiology	Physical education	Total
(2) [12]		3			2		3	27
(Reading) [Reading, Grammar, and Composition]		Japanese history			Introduction to biology		Gymnastics and games Military drills	
(2) [12]		3			2		3	27
(Same as above) [Same as above]		Same as above			Biological evolution		Same as above	
(2) [12]		3			2		3	27
(Same as above) [Same as above]		Same as above			Same as above		Same as above	
(2) [8]	[4]					2	3	27
(Reading) [Reading, Composition, and Literary history]	[Reading, Grammar, and Composition]					Human physiology	Gymnastics and games Military drills	
(2) [8]	[4]					2	3	27
(Same as above) [Same as above]	[Same as above]					Same as above	Same as above	
(2) [8]	[4]					2	3	27
(Same as above) [Same as above]	[Same as above]					Same as above	Same as above	
[8]	[4]		2	3			2	27
[Reading, Composition, and English literature]	[Same as above] [German/French literature]		Introduction to philosophy	General phonetics			Gymnastics and games Military drills	
[8]	[4]		2	3			2	27
[Same as above]	[Same as above]		Same as above	Same as above			Same as above	
[2]	[2]		2	3			2	27
[Same as above]	[Same as above]		Same as above	General philology			Same as above	

Items in parentheses correspond to courses for students focusing on Japanese language and classical Chinese literature; items in brackets are for students focusing on foreign languages.

Table 2-2: Curriculum reforms under Kanō (Japanese language and classical Chinese literature department, regular course)

Term \ Course		Ethics	Psychology and Pedagogy	Japanese language	Classical Chinese literature
Year 1	Weekly class hours	2	2	6	6
	First trimester	Ethics	Psychology	Reading, Grammar, and Composition	Reading
	Weekly class hours	2	2	6	6
	Second trimester	Same as above	Psychology	Same as above	Same as above
	Weekly class hours	2	2	6	6
	Third trimester	Same as above	Psychology	Same as above	Same as above
Year 2	Weekly class hours	2	3	7	7
	First trimester	Ethics	Pedagogy	Reading, Grammar, and Composition	Reading Literary history
	Weekly class hours	2	3	7	7
	Second trimester	Same as above	Pedagogy	Same as above	Same as above
	Weekly class hours	2	3	7	7
	Third trimester	Same as above	History of education	Reading, Grammar, Composition, and Literary history	Same as above
Year 3	Weekly class hours	2	5	6	7
	First trimester	Ethics	History of education Instructional methods	Reading Literary history	Reading
	Weekly class hours	2	5	6	7
	Second trimester	Same as above	History of education, Instructional methods, School hygiene, and Educational laws	Same as above	Same as above
	Weekly class hours				
	Third trimester				

English	History	Philosophy	Linguistics	Physical education	Total
5	3			3	27
Reading	Japanese history			General gymnastics and games Military drills	
5	3			3	27
Same as above	Same as above			Same as above	
5	3			3	27
Same as above	Same as above			Same as above	
3	3			3	28
Reading	Eastern history			General gymnastics and games Military drills	
3	3			3	28
Reading	Eastern history			Same as above	
3	3			3	28
Reading	Eastern history			Same as above	
		2	3	2	27
		Introduction to philosophy	Linguistics Phonetics	General gymnastics and games Military drills	
		2	3	2	27
		Same as above	Same as above	Same as above	

Students will undergo on-site training in the third trimester of their third year.

content on the teaching profession itself (an emphasis of Izawa's reforms) with specialized content on the actual subjects the future teachers would be teaching. The overhaul was an important project for Kanō, who apparently made a conscious effort to guide the reforms to his liking. An article in the *Yomiuri Shimbun* reported that Kanō had headed into negotiations with the Ministry of Education with "a proposal to reform the policy at the Higher Normal School away from the conventional approach of 'training instructors over deepening scholarship,' in place since the time of former principal Mr. Izawa Shūji, and revising the curriculum to address the lack of scholarship among students, which represents the school's primary shortcoming."[3]

Why did Kanō place such an emphasis on specialized subjects in academic fields? The title of his proposal points to the root cause: a perceived lack of academic ability among Higher Normal School students, especially relative to graduates of imperial universities. For Kanō, shedding that reputation would mean adopting a new academic focus. At imperial universities, students would spend long hours on their specific fields of study, and each student had just one specialization. The Higher Normal School, on the other hand, trained students to teach multiple subjects at secondary schools; the nature of the program forced students to divide their time between several subjects, inevitably preventing them from developing the levels of scholarship that their peers at imperial universities could. Observers had been aware of that dilemma for some time. If the Higher Normal School wanted to produce secondary-school teachers with scholarly expertise approaching the pedigrees of the graduates coming out of imperial universities, it would need to implement a narrower, stronger emphasis in specialized areas. And as long as there was a limit on the total number of class hours students could complete, there was no way for the Higher Normal School to simply add specialized content to the curriculum—it would first need to remove content focused on the practice teaching and then fill the holes with specialized content.

However, there were also worries that replacing teaching-oriented subjects with academic subjects would make the curriculum at the Higher Normal School the same as the curriculum at imperial universities. "Should the Higher Normal School continue its current endeavors to refine its academic offerings and rival universities on the basis of scholastic excellence," a 1904 article in *Kyōiku jiron* (The educational review) read, "would it not be neglecting the very features that define its character?"[4] Competing with imperial universities could very well make the Higher Normal School curriculum indistinguishable from the imperial university curricula. If that were to happen, some asserted, there would be no practical need for a Higher Normal School in the first place. Arguments claiming that the Higher Normal School was redundant had surfaced on numerous occasions in the Meiji period, but Kanō's reforms actually ended up providing opponents with even more ammunition in their campaign to eliminate the institution. To understand why Kanō would be so adamant about a shift toward academics—even if it meant putting the Higher Normal School at risk—it is necessary to take a closer look at the contemporary practices of training secondary-school teachers.

Higher Normal School badge

The Higher Normal School and provisional teacher-training centers

Japan needed enormous numbers of secondary teachers in the late 1890s and early 1900s. The Ministry of Education, recognizing the demand, opened five provisional teacher-training centers (PTTCs) in 1902. The PTTC system created five two-year teacher-training facilities, each attached to an existing institution of higher education and designed to serve a different specialization (albeit not entirely exclusively): Japanese language and classical Chinese literature, and natural history (PTTC I); physical chemistry (PTTC II); mathematics (PTTC III and IV); and English (PTTC V). True to their name, the institutions were provisional. Besides PTTC III, which remained active for around ten years, most of the PTTCs closed their doors after only around four to six years in operation. It was an unorthodox approach to teacher training, a stopgap measure to meet an urgent need.

However, the PTTCs posed several discomfiting threats to the Higher Normal School almost as soon as they opened. First of all, the PTTCs were annexes to imperial universities, high schools around the country, and the Tokyo School of Foreign Languages—a selection of higher-learning institutions that did not include the Higher Normal School. In certain circles at the Higher Normal School, being excluded from this assignment raised suspicions that the Ministry of Education's PTTC assignment was an intentional slight. Being a core institution for training secondary-school teachers, the Higher Normal School was an obvious choice for a PTTC site, considering the circumstances. It certainly seemed to some, then, that the ministry had passed over the Higher Normal School on purpose and gone out of its way to open the PTTCs at imperial universities. There were even rumors among Higher Normal School officials that the Ministry of Education had deliberately turned a deaf ear to Kanō's arguments for a PTTC at their institution. The Ministry of Education denied any antagonism on its part, saying, "This rumor has no grounds whatsoever. The Higher Normal School has its own curriculum, so Dr. Kanō would never have suggested such a thing in the first place."[5] However, skepticism ran strong among Higher Normal School officials.

Another threat emerged as the PTTCs garnered a sterling reputation as training institutions, defying critics who considered their two-year program prohibitively short. An article in a 1902 issue of *Kyōiku jiron*, for example, drew favorable comparisons between the PTTCs and the Higher Normal School: "The provisional teacher training centers have performed surprisingly well. The mathematics institution in Sendai is a case in point; of the center's thirty graduates, a full eighteen earned honors. After completing their two-year curriculum, the graduates have shown themselves to be no less capable than Higher Normal School alumni."[6] Table 2-3 shows the curriculum for Japanese language and classical Chinese literature at the PTTCs. Students spent fifty-five hours studying Japanese and sixty-one on classical Chinese literature—a course load that surpassed the requirements Kanō implemented in his rigorous academics-focused reforms to the Higher Normal School regular course. A serious cause for concern lay in the implications of the qualifications of the PTTC graduates, whom the author of the *Kyōiku jiron* piece deemed "no less capable than Higher Normal School alumni." If the products of a two-year program could measure up to the graduates of the Higher Normal School, how would the public react? *Kyōiku jiron* laid out one possibility:

> If these rumors prove true, logic would clearly dictate that the Higher Normal School would be an uneconomical facility; that the institution, thereby redundant, should be done away with; and that the provisional teacher training centers should be expanded in its stead.[7]

Kanō's efforts to put the Higher Normal School on a scholastic par with imperial universities came at the risk of diluting the institution's characterizing

Table 2-3: The academic program at the provisional teacher training center for Japanese language and classical Chinese literature (hours)

Term	Course	Ethics	Education	Japanese language	Classical Chinese literature	English	History	Total
Year 1	First trimester	2		9	10	3	4	28
	Second trimester	2		9	10	3	4	28
	Third trimester	2		9	10	3	4	28
Year 2	First trimester		3	9	10	3	3	28
	Second trimester		3	9	10	3	3	28
	Third trimester		6	10	11	3		30

traits, a turn of events that had the potential to make the Higher Normal School seem superfluous. The possibility of redundancy took on a deeper dimension when PTTCs—designed specifically for training secondary-school teachers, one of the Higher Normal School's core practices—opened at imperial universities. To keep pace with the elite academic performance of the imperial universities at the front of the pack and keep the PTTCs at a safe distance, the Higher Normal School had to focus on academics.

Kanō's deadlock with the Ministry of Education

Kanō was likely eager to get started on his reforms, but the Ministry of Education was slow to react. The article that mentioned Kanō's intentions to undo Izawa's policy of "training instructors over deepening scholarship" also noted that Kanō "had already brought his proposal to the Ministry of Education long prior." Considering that the ministry had yet to take any action on the proposal by that point, the author concluded that there must have been a breakdown in communications between the two sides.

Some media outlets attributed the delay to a personal rift between Kanō and then-minister of education Kikuchi Dairoku (1855–1917). A writer for

The main gate of the Tokyo Higher Normal School (Ōtsuka, 1931)

the *Yomiuri Shimbun* floated that very theory in no uncertain terms, writing that "the friction between Minister of Education Kikuchi and Higher Normal School Principal Kanō has long stirred rumors in the educational community, and the two have reached non-negotiable terms."[8] According to another paper, "Minister of Education Kikuchi and Principal Kanō have been on less-than-friendly terms from the outset." Despite the fact that Kanō had sought meetings with the Minister of Education time and time again to discuss reform proposals for the Higher Normal School, the minister had turned up his nose at every request and continued to brush Kanō off.[9]

The feud between Kanō and Kikuchi would remain at a bitter standstill until the "Matter Concerning the Faculties, Subjects, and Weekly Study Hours at the Higher Normal School" finally came up for discussion as a draft for deliberation at the seventh meeting of the Higher Conference on Education near the end of 1902. At long last, the Ministry of Education got around to addressing Kanō's proposal.

Table 2-4: Higher Conference on Education draft for deliberation (preparatory course/Japanese language and classical Chinese literature department, regular course hours)

Year \ Course		Ethics	Pedagogy	Japanese language	Classical Chinese literature	
Preparatory course		1		4	3	
Regular course	Year 1	2	2	5	7	
	Year 2	2	3	6	7	
	Year 3	First trimester	2	5	6	7
		Second trimester	2	5	6	7
		Third trimester	2	5	4	4

3. The goals of the secondary-school teacher-training reforms

Discussions at the Higher Conference on Education

The Higher Conference on Education, established via the promulgation of the "Higher Conference on Education Organization Order" in 1896, was a panel of experts charged with advising the minister of education on various matters. Comprising the president of the Imperial University, the heads of the various colleges of the Imperial University, the heads of bureaus in the Ministry of Education, the principal of the Higher Normal School, the principals of other higher-level commercial schools, and other representatives from academic circles, the assembly was akin to Japan's present-day Central Council for Education. It was at the Higher Conference's seventh meeting at the end of 1902 that Kanō's long-pending proposal for curriculum modifications at the Higher Normal School finally made it onto the agenda as a draft for deliberation. Considering the context, the Ministry of Education's draft for deliberation was likely a faithful reflection of Kanō's original proposal. Kanō, himself a member of the Higher Conference, headed in to the debates on the matter ready to field questions and comments on his ideas.

For all the back-and-forth wrangling that must have taken place between Kanō and the Ministry of Education over the curriculum reforms, however, the matter hardly sparked any substantive discussion at the Higher Conference on Education. As table 2-4 indicates, the members addressed the curriculum proposal for the preparatory course and regular course for the Higher Normal School's department of Japanese language and classical Chinese literature—but

English	History	Mathematics	Philosophy	Linguistics	Physical education	Total
12		4			3	27
5	3				3	27
4	2				3	27
			3	2	2	27
			3	2	2	27
				2		12

Library I, Tokyo Higher Normal School (1914)

the matter apparently failed to strike the panel of experts as anything meriting much special attention. The proposal still managed to make its way through the Coordinating Committee and reached a second reading, which fell to a committee of five members (which included Kanō). Although there are no available records of the Coordinating Committee's talks on the proposal, unfortunately, reports from the second reading indicate that the Coordinating Committee had made several revisions.

According to Kanō, the Coordinating Committee's amendments centered on two main points. The first was the curriculum for the preparatory course, which the members modified by making slight reductions to the class hours for Japanese and English and adding logic, drawing, and music. Second, the Coordinating Committee switched the name of the "pedagogy" component to "psychology and pedagogy" to show that psychology was part of the curriculum's educational scope. After a brief discussion, the assembly approved the revisions unanimously. The decision to rename "pedagogy" to "psychology and pedagogy" was for the sake of clarity: while psychology was part of the pedagogy component in the original, the committee added "psychology" to "make that fact even more obvious."[10] Under Izawa's foregoing curriculum, the Higher Normal School taught pedagogy and psychology in separate classes. Kanō, on the other hand, wanted to integrate the two—ideally into a "pedagogy" package. The committee's revisions to the preparatory-course curriculum entailed other interesting changes, most notably the inclusion of drawing classes. The members most likely made the addition with middle school graduates in mind,

Table 2-5: Final draft for deliberation by the Higher Conference on Education (preparatory course hours)

Year \ Course	Ethics	Japanese language	Classical Chinese literature	English	
Preparatory course	1	3	3	10	

probably aiming to train the students in art of some kind, but exactly what they were hoping to teach is unknown.

The premise of the draft for deliberation was to ensure consistency between the curricula at the Tokyo Higher Normal School and the Hiroshima Higher Normal School, which had opened that year. Once the distribution of class hours was in place, the two schools were to iron out the specifics of their respective class plans. The next section takes a closer look at the 1903 Tokyo Higher Normal School curriculum, which Kanō formulated based on the Ministry of Education notice resulting from the Higher Conference on Education deliberations.

The blackboard and practice teaching

Table 2-5 lays out the preparatory-course curriculum that came out of the Higher Conference on Education. The additions include logic, music, and drawing, the last of which was to receive two class hours a week. In Table 2-6 is the more concrete version of the curriculum, which the Tokyo Higher Normal School administration formulated according to the Ministry of Education notice. The institution, then using a trimester schedule, planned to teach drawing—covering an overview of projection methods, an overview of mirror-drawing methods, and blackboard drawing—in the second trimester. With that plan, the school was aiming to instruct future teachers in an essential skill as early as the preparatory-course stage.

Kanō's plan for the regular-course curriculum, meanwhile, left the third trimester of the final year completely open across all the academic departments. In the margin of the curriculum table, Kanō wrote, "Students are to undergo on-site training in the third term of their third year"—implying that he envisioned students finishing off their academic careers with a trimester of practice teaching.

Compared to Izawa's curriculum, Kanō's approach certainly shifted the class-hour distribution away from pedagogy and toward specialized academic subjects—but classroom skills still received their due attention. Kanō's revised

Logic	Mathematics	Drawing	Music	Gymnastics	Total
2	4	2	2	3	30

Table 2-6: Curriculum reforms under Kanō (distribution of class hours in the preparatory course)

Term \ Course		Ethics	Japanese language	Classical Chinese literature	English	
Preparatory course	Weekly class hours	1	3	3	10	
	First trimester	Overview of ethics and morality	Reading, Composition, and Grammar	Reading	Reading, Grammar, Composition/ Conversation, and Transcription	
	Weekly class hours	1	3	3	10	
	Second trimester	Same as above	Same as above	Same as above	Same as above	
	Weekly class hours	1	3	3	10	
	Third trimester	Same as above	Same as above	Same as above	Same as above	

curriculum made blackboard writing a part of the preparatory course, thereby helping students develop a practical skill that they would need as teachers, and set aside an entire block of the three-year program for intensive, on-site educational training. The reform was thus more nuanced than a simple teardown. If bolstering the academic rigor at the Higher Normal School had been his only goal, he could have simply increased the number of academic class hours, such as those for Japanese language and classical Chinese literature. However, Kanō's decision to clear the class schedule for the third trimester of every student's third year slashed the total class time down by more than twenty hours compared to Izawa's curriculum—and that reduction automatically bumped the relative proportion of academic (non-pedagogy) course hours up. It was addition by subtraction, in a sense, but nothing drastic. In the end, students' class times in

Mathematics	Logic	Drawing	Music	Gymnastics	Total
4	2	2	2	3	30
Arithmetic and Geometry	Deduction	Writing Sketching	Singing and theory	General gymnastics and games Military drills	
4	2	2	2	3	30
Algebra, Geometry, and Trigonometry	Induction	Overview of projection methods Overview of mirror-drawing methods Blackboard drawing	Same as above	Same as above	
4	2	2	2	3	30
Same as above	Methodology	Watercolor	Same as above	Same as above	

Japanese language and classical Chinese literature rose by just one or two hours. Kanō's reforms, therefore, aimed to find a better balance between academics and pedagogy. The effort was about more than simply trying to compete with imperial universities in terms of scholastic rigor. After all, the trends of the times dictated versatility: with secondary education undergoing a rapid expansion at the turn of the twentieth century, secondary-school teachers needed skillsets that stretched more broadly than refined expertise in a specific discipline.

A closer examination of the contemporary state of secondary education and Kanō's actual statements on secondary-school teachers brings the contours of Kanō's curriculum into sharper focus.

4. How Kanō approached changing notions of the ideal secondary-school teacher

School disturbances and expectations of secondary-school teachers

In the late 1890s and early 1900s, Japanese middle schools saw a rash of sporadic school disturbances, ranging from student strikes and class boycotts to student-on-student violence. The outbreaks made frequent headlines in the papers, spotlighting what many saw to be a growing social concern. Secondary education was beginning to transition from a form of privileged education for an exclusive elite to something more accessible, a resource that children from relatively well-to-do families in outlying areas could access. With more and more students reaping the benefits of secondary education, the public blamed the school disturbances on the teachers—the people with whom the "true fault" lay, according to some. Terada Yūkichi (1853–1921), a former Ministry of Education councillor, was of this view: "When school instructors are consummate in their deportment, proficient in their disciplines, versed in the true purport of education, and adept in the proper teaching methods, they earn the respect and admiration of their students, not their opposition and rebellion."[11]

Terada's appraisal of the situation also points to the contemporary expectations of secondary-school teachers. They needed virtue, academic expertise, and a command of teaching methods, the last of which took on an even weightier significance in the early 1900s:

In today's educational sphere, secondary-school teachers with degrees from provisional teacher training centers and other institutions are assigned to schools and paid handsomely for their services. Be that as it may, their general lack of knowledge in teaching methods, that quality so inherently necessary to what an instructor does, is beginning to pose difficulties for every school across the country. Graduates rest comfortably on their lofty laurels, their scholastic pedigrees, and the prestige of their schools, ignorant

Tōka Dormitory, Tokyo Higher Normal School (ca. 1914)

of their own instructional incompetence, simply parroting their university lectures with virtually no regard for their pupils' abilities. The current state of affairs indeed represents a concern for the public at large.[12]

The notion that anyone with high-level expertise in a given specialization could be a secondary-school teacher was, evidently, already a thing of the past. As secondary education spread, covering broader swaths of the population, the public expected aspiring instructors to develop their skills in youth pedagogy, hone their educational methods, and accumulate practical experience in the classroom.

Kanō's perspective

How, then, did Kanō envision the ideal secondary teacher? According to *Kyōiku jiron*, Kanō defined nine essential traits at the Tokyo Higher Normal School graduation ceremony in March 1908: (1) refined ideals and the ability to realize them; (2) an awareness of how important the effects of education are; (3) a deep interest in education; (4) an assured, rich base of academic knowledge; (5) a mastery of educational methods; (6) a compassion for one's students; (7) a strong will; (8) a strong, able body; and (9) a sensible understanding of society.[13]

Items (4), (5), and (6), which emphasized the need for specialized academic expertise, a practical proficiency in secondary-school teaching methods, and an upstanding character, respectively, coincided almost perfectly with the core elements of Terada's arguments. The Higher Normal School had been a frequent target for comparisons with imperial universities, which observers had long deemed superior in terms of scholastic excellence. As the critiques of the PTTCs suggest, however, the turn of the twentieth century saw a rise not in the need for higher-level expertise but rather in the demand for teachers adept in instructional methods. Considering its function in the educational sphere, the Higher Normal School was where that demand converged. Not only was it an institution where instilling both solid academic knowledge and practical pedagogical techniques was imperative, but it was also a school capable of meeting those needs. In his address at the Higher Normal School graduation ceremony, Kanō's words evinced an awareness of the institution's role in that context.

On a different occasion, Kanō touched on the differences between the pedagogy taught at imperial universities and the pedagogy studied at the Higher Normal School:

I do not expect normal educators to engage in abstract, sophisticated inquiries into the underlying principles of pedagogy; these are topics of study better suited to university settings. . . . What we do at the Higher Normal School is to transform the principles that emerge from university research into practical, tangible skills that students may apply; to deduce the proper educational policies, instructional doctrines, and pedagogical methods; and to present our findings as a model for normal schools across the nation.[14]

Instead of directing his institution toward research into the basic fundamental principles of education, Kanō envisioned the Higher Normal School as a place for pedagogical studies with a practical focus—a platform for helping students apply abstract principles in concrete ways. His insistence on combining pedagogy and psychology into a single, integrated subject might have had something to do with that underlying vision.

Kanō's curriculum reforms at the Higher Normal School were not simply an attempt to close the scholastic gap with imperial universities, it would appear. He did assign considerable value to enhancing academic capabilities, of course, but he also attached importance to helping students learn instructional methods and educational techniques—the elements that gave the Higher Normal School its identity. Kanō wanted students to master basic educational techniques in the institution's preparatory course; he designed the course of study to culminate with an intensive practice-teaching program. Considering how purposefully he wove pedagogical components and teaching methods into his curriculum, Kanō was clearly on a mission to find a compatible fusion of academic subjects and teaching-oriented subjects. The Ministry of Education was trying to meet the demand for larger numbers of secondary-school teachers by diversifying the teacher-training field. Kanō was trying to satisfy that quantitative demand through a qualitative transformation.

Kanō's reforms hinged on a complicated balancing act. If teachers were to find themselves responsible for higher-level content, training institutions would need to focus on the academic side; if problems in actual school operations were to arise, training institutions would need to devote more attention to the professional, practical side. Finding an optimal balance between the two was never an easy task, since a teacher-training course always has a definite endpoint. The institution needs to apportion the different components within that framework—and that problem is just as challenging for secondary-school teacher—training facilities now as it was in Kanō's day. It was during the late 1890s and early 1900s that this issue first emerged in all its vexing intricacy, and Kanō was one of the first educators to set out in search of an effective solution.

5. The Higher Normal School as a model for secondary-teacher education

Clues to solving the dilemma at the heart of secondary-teacher training—whether to develop teachers with high-caliber academic expertise or teachers with a thorough command of instructional practices—lie in the evolution of research on teaching methods, which integrates both into one question: how to teach a given subject. Since Izawa's time as principal, the Higher Normal School had offered classes on teaching methods. Research in the field was disjointed, however; even in the late Meiji period, there were gaps in progress. "In the field of primary-school education, research on teaching methods is profoundly detailed and thorough; the capabilities of primary-school educators merit praise, likewise. At middle schools, however, progress in teaching methods is far from sufficient."[15] Against that backdrop came the Chūtō Kyōiku Kenkyūkai (Secondary Education Research Society), which formed in 1908. The group's charter laid out the reasons behind its founding: "While the state of primary and professional education in Japan appears to be making slight progress as the nation continues to advance, progress in secondary education remains sluggish." Conscious of how studies on secondary education were lagging behind work in other fields, the Secondary Education Research Society set its sights on making up ground.

The Society operated out of the Tokyo Higher Normal School, with Kanō presiding as chair. One of the group's activities was the publication of *Chūtō kyōiku* (Secondary Education), a journal featuring research papers on the subject of pedagogy along with other writings—including occasional pieces by Kanō, who played an active role in the group. He even assisted with the various

Tokyo Higher Normal School tennis club (1904)

subject-specific subgroups that eventually took shape within the larger organization. Through numerous initiatives by Kanō and other leaders, the Higher Normal School had become a hub of practice-oriented research in the realm of secondary education.

The Higher Normal School curriculum continued to serve as a model for secondary-school teacher training in prewar Japan. The training schools that gained authorization via non-examination certification represent one clear example of that influence. Under the system, which came into effect in 1899, public or private schools that passed the screening process and obtained authorization from the minister of education could award secondary-school teaching licenses to their graduates. In making authorization decisions, the Ministry of Education required schools to have curricula comparable to those of the Higher Normal School or Women's Higher Normal School. The screening process thus hinged on the benchmark of the Higher Normal School, a recognized standard for accreditation.

Several prewar-era reports detailing on-site screening surveys at authorized schools still survive. One dates to 1927, when an inspector surveyed the curricula for Japanese language and classical Chinese literature and geography and history at a professional school in Tokyo that was seeking authorization. "The weekly class hours in both Japanese language and classical Chinese literature and geography and history compare with the same quantities in Departments I and IV at the Tokyo Higher Normal School," read the report, which also included a table comparing the class hours at both schools and noted that "the school's weekly class hours in morals were fewer than those at the Higher Normal School." To secure official recognition as an authorized school, an institution thus needed to align its curriculum with the model of the Higher Normal School.[16]

From a broader viewpoint, the Higher Normal School's position as the criterion for teacher-training accreditation meant that Kanō's curriculum reforms ended up shaping the curricula at the authorized schools aiming to train secondary teachers. Essentially, the Higher Normal School curriculum became the national curriculum for secondary-teacher training in prewar Japan.

The Higher Normal School was obviously influential in steering the contemporary approach to implementing secondary education and training secondary-school teachers. Over the course of that development, Kanō Jigorō maintained his leadership role as principal—and his constant presence across the years deserves recognition.

In exploring notions of the "ideal" secondary-school teacher and weighing different strategies for teacher training, the Higher Normal School's various initiatives under Kanō and the impact of the institution's systems in the educational sphere still offer valuable insights today. As scholars continue to look at secondary-school teacher training in the post-Meiji era, Kanō is well-deserving of close attention and a reputation as one of the key figures in shaping Japan's pedagogical milieu.

Notes:

1   Ōtaki Tadao, *Kanō Jigorō: Watashi no shōgai to jūdō* [Kanō Jigorō: My life and judo] (Tokyo: Shinjinbutsu Oraisha, 1972), 65–66.

2   Funaki Toshio, *Kindai Nihon chūtō kyōin yōseironsō-shiron* [Tracing the history of the controversy surrounding secondary teacher training in modern Japan] (Tokyo: Gakubunsha, 1998), 106.

3   "Monbushō tai Kōtō Shihan (zoku)" [The Ministry of Education versus the Higher Normal School (cont.)], *Yomiuri Shimbun*, October 29, 1902.

4   "Gakusei kaikaku no yōkō" [The principles of educational reform], *Kyōiku jiron* [The educational review] 677 (February 1904).

5   "Monbu tōkyokusha no danwa" [A discussion with Ministry of Education officials], *Yomiuri Shimbun*, October 30, 1902.

6   "Kōtō Shihan o hai shite wa ikan" [Should Japan do away with the Higher Normal School?], *Kyōiku jiron* [The educational review] 625 (August 1902).

7   Ibid.

8   "Monbushō tai Kōtō Shihan" [The Ministry of Education versus the Higher Normal School], *Yomiuri Shimbun*, October 28, 1902.

9   "Kanō kōchō haiseki no koe (tsuzuki)" [Voices call for the ousting of Principal Kanō (cont.)], *Nihon* [Japan], September 3, 1902.

10   "Dai nana kai kōtō kyōiku kaigi giji sokkiroku" [Proceedings of the 7th Higher Conference on Education], vol. 8, December 2.

11   Terada Yūkichi, *Gakkō kairyō-ron* [School improvement] (Tokyo: Nankōdo, 1898), 40–41.

12   "Gakkō sotsugyō chūtō kyōin" [Secondary teachers with school diplomas], *Kyōiku jiron* [The educational review] 770 (September 1906).

13   "Kōtō Shihan sotsugyō-shiki" [The Higher Normal School graduation ceremony], *Kyōiku jiron* [The educational review] 828 (April 1908).

14   Kanō Jigorō, "Konnichi no kyōikuka wa nani o nasu beki ka" [What are today's educators called to do?], *Kyōiku jiron* [The educational review] 749 (February 1905).

15   "Chūgaku kyōiku no kaizen" [Improving secondary education], *Kyōiku jiron* [The educational review] 795 (May 1907).

16   "Kōritsu shiritsu gakkō sotsugyōsha ni tai shi mushiken kentei no toriatsukai o kyoka shitaru gakkō" [Public and private schools authorized to provide non-examination certifications to graduates], National Archives of Japan.

Kanō Jigorō and the development of athletics in Japan

1. The School Council at the Tokyo Higher Normal School

How Kanō viewed sports

At the Tokyo Higher Normal School, Principal Kanō led the creation of new organizations to oversee student athletics; namely, the Athletic Association and the School Council. Through the School Council, in particular, the Tokyo Higher Normal School would propel the spread and development of physical education and sports in Japan.

For Kanō, "sports" encompassed everything from judo to Western sports and games, racewalking, swimming, and other activities with long histories in Japan. He saw significant value in sports, which featured prominently in his 1910 book *Seinen shūyō-kun* (Teachings for the cultivation of the young).[1]

First, given the fact that sports develop muscular strength and harden the physique, one shall strive to spend one's spare time, however brief it may be, engaging in exercise through sports and methods of one's choice.

Second, one shall engage in sport not only for the betterment of one's own body but also to cultivate stronger morality and integrity in relation to both oneself and others.

Third, one shall not discontinue the habit of said exercise upon the completion of one's studies; rather, one shall continue to engage in exercise thereafter to help maintain a youthful vigor, in both mind and body, over time.

Sports thus held enormous value in Kanō's eyes. In addition to recognizing their capacity for enhancing physical function, Kanō also saw sports as pathways to stronger morals, a means of building integrity, and a pursuit that would offer consistent benefits throughout the course of one's life.

The moral aspect of sports was key to Kanō's perspective. Consider-

Boating (ca. 1914)

ing that he followed his studies at Tokyo Imperial University with additional research on moral education as a special student in a one-year philosophy course, morality had long been an area of interest for him.

In requiring students to practice judo and engage in physical education (distance running, swimming practice, and more), Kanō was hoping to do more than just help them develop healthier bodies—he also believed that sports could shape young people mentally and morally, cultivating a sense of justice, fairness, and modesty with an impact on both the self and the other. He also held that people could retain a youthful zest and live happier lives by making physical education a lifelong practice.

Kanō's conception of "morals" likely coincides with the "mental training" component that he outlined in his 1889 "Jūdō ippan narabi ni sono kyōiku-jō no kachi" (Judo and its educational value), along with the "physical education" and "combat" elements.[2] For Kanō, the mental education that came along with the practice of judo was inseparable from the process of physical education. He pointed to numerous benefits for the mind, including judo's capacity to cultivate moral faculties like justice, fairness, and modesty; its power to sharpen the intellect; and the way practitioners can apply the theories of combat in everyday life. In his claim that judo could "sharpen the intellect," Kanō was alluding to being receptive to progressive ideas, abandoning preconceptions, and taking an objective, scientific stance on what one observes. Applying the theories of combat, meanwhile, meant drawing on one's subjective experiences in judo training in the public realm of social life.

Kanō's take on the value of sports—a recognition of their physical benefits, mental benefits, and life-spanning merits—holds true today. His piercing foresight into what represents the basis for modern-day sports education appears to have been an outgrowth of his own firsthand experience in implementing judo.

How Kanō utilized the athletic element

Firm in his belief that sports were vital to human development and a beneficial component of education, Kanō actively incorporated athletics into student life at the Tokyo Higher Normal School during his time as principal.

Judo, a reconception of a traditional martial art for modern application, was one sport that Kanō encouraged as a means of physical and mental growth. There was much more than just judo, however. Kanō brought numerous Western sports into the picture, giving the Tokyo Higher Normal School educational system a diverse athletic mix. A look at Kanō's initiatives as principal of the Higher Normal School and the Tokyo Higher Normal School reveals the breadth of that variety.

The beginning of Kanō's tenure as principal of the Higher Normal School coincided with a sharp increase in participation in physical education and sports-related activities among the student body, with the principal's directives providing the impetus. The following timeline traces the major developments:[3]

1894 Athletic meet held, with all students and faculty participating

1896 Athletic Association established to manage the school's athletic clubs; students encouraged to join one or more clubs and exercise for at least thirty minutes a day

1898 "Healthy-leg race" (marathon) from Ochanomizu to Ikegami Honmon-ji temple held

1901 Athletic Association reorganized into the School Council, created to supervise extracurricular activities, with Kanō serving as council chairman; track-and-field meet held in Ōtsuka in the fall; races held for students from middle schools and normal schools nationwide

1905 All new preparatory-course students required to take part in summer swimming practice (roughly two weeks in duration)

1908 All new students required to practice judo or kendo; first footrace competitions (marathons) held on a biannual (spring/fall) basis

If you were a student at the Tokyo Higher Normal School under Principal Kanō, whether you studied on the arts track or in the sciences, you would have learned either judo or kendo, run long-distance races in both the spring and fall, spent two weeks practicing swimming in the summer, competed in a track-and-field meet in the fall, and also taken part in a variety of school-council activities. During Kanō's time at the helm, few higher-education institutions in Japan were more heav-

Tokyo Higher Normal School judo club (ca. 1914)

ily invested in physical education and sports than the Tokyo Higher Normal School was.

Athletics at the Tokyo Higher Normal School blossomed over Kanō's tenure. New clubs included those for judo, kendo, archery, apparatus gymnastics, sumo, lawn tennis, football (soccer), baseball, cycling, boating, footrace, swimming, table tennis, and rugby.

From judo, kendo, and other martial arts to Western sports like tennis, soccer, and rugby, the sports that Kanō encouraged as ways of getting exercise seem virtually limitless.

The principles behind the School Council athletic clubs

To celebrate the fortieth anniversary of the Tokyo Higher Normal School's founding, the School Council released a special commemorative issue containing a short piece by Kanō (who also served as the chairman of the council). Titled "Kōyūkai-in ni tsugu" (A message to the members of the School Council), the missive verbalized Kanō's vision for the organization:

In my view, it would be difficult to consider a school education complete if it were to consist solely of providing instruction in the classroom and supervision in the dormitory. A school must encourage students to make known their intentions and act thereupon. All students must learn how to observe the fruits of education in the classroom and dormitory settings, and must then draw on those observations to develop effective methods of instruction for the future, of their own volition, seizing every opportunity to apply their findings in determining the teachings that merit conveyance. In order to do so, it is imperative for students to assume roles within the various arms of the School Council and fulfill their corresponding duties. I have thus created within the School Council nearly a dozen separate divisions whose respective student members bear the responsibilities for performing their roles and thereby accustom themselves to performing the necessary tasks. The School Council also holds occasional long-distance races and track-and-field meets, participation in which is mandatory for all students. By uniting students who spend the bulk of their time in separate departments and separate dormitories, these school-wide athletic events enable students to develop the beneficial practices of cooperation and fellowship.

The School Council thus represents the most essential component of school education outside the general learning that takes place in the classroom and dormitory settings. This school has therefore bestowed upon its School Council a prominent emphasis, subjected it to close scrutiny, and carefully advised the organization in bringing it to where it now stands. While it still retains certain flaws and requires numerous improvements, I believe the School Council compares favorably with its many counterparts, occupying a commendable standing that owes itself to the efforts of its leaders, professors, and student officers. I would like to extend my gratitude to all those who have contributed to the organization and, on behalf of the entire school, offer my sincerest congratulations to the School Council on achieving many of its founding aims.

Thus conclude my remarks for the present year. In the days and years to come, I hope to see the School Council sustain its progress toward complete development and bring the entirety of its founding goals to fruition.[4]

Tokyo Higher Normal School footrace club (ca. 1914)

The special issue came out in 1911, ten years after the School Council's formation. In recalling the council's first decade of activities, Kanō explained that he had created the organization for the express purpose of encouraging physical education.

Kanō also noted his determination to "encourage students to make known their intentions and act thereupon" and ensure that students would "assume roles in their respective divisions of the School Council and fulfill their corresponding duties." He valued proactivity, hoping that students would embody the type of initiative that he considered crucial to learning the instructional methods of the future.

He also underlined his aim to develop a feeling of camaraderie in

Certificate from the Tokyo Higher Normal School School Council (1904; courtesy of the Nakamura Tōtarō collection)

shared customs by having the entire student body take part in long-distance races and track-and-field meets.

According to student counselor Minegishi Yonezō, the School Council also helped bridge the teacher-student gap. Instructors and pupils were supposed to be open with each other and communicate freely, but that was easier said than done; it was often difficult for the two sides to connect. The School Council served to forge a stronger, friendlier rapport between teachers and students, Minegishi wrote, through activities that brought them together.

In addition to driving the development of sports through a variety of student-led athletic clubs, the School Council at the Tokyo Higher Normal School also worked to help students cultivate the qualities that they would need as future instructors and strove to nurture a cooperative spirit through races and track-and-field meets. The School Council's far-reaching activities made the organization a trailblazing force in solidifying the position of sports within the realm of school education.

The School Council became an incorporated association in 1907 and drew up its official articles, which stipulated that council membership would also be open to alumni and school personnel (as "special members"). With students and alumni joining forces, the School Council athletic clubs had an extensive, organized support system to grow on.

How the School Council athletic clubs helped popularize sports

The School Council athletic clubs at the Tokyo Higher Normal School proved to be a major force in expanding the reach of sports in Japan. Taking every opportunity to establish tournaments at vocational schools, set up competitions at middle schools, and send instructors on teaching assignments nationwide, the organizations laid a sturdy foundation for growth across a broad athletic landscape.

Track and field

The Higher Normal School's first athletic meet took place in the fall of 1894. Gathering in a roped-off area in front of the Yūshōkan (the school's facility for judo training), students competed in more than twenty events—from races and soccer to a three-round sumo elimination tournament, swordplay, tug of war, and sword dancing.

After the establishment of the School Council, the "Athletic Meet" became the "Track-and-Field Meet" and grew in scale. On October 2, 1901, the School Council held its first Track-and-Field Meet at the school's new building in Ōtsuka. A look at the event expenses suggest that the meet was expanding: the costs quadrupled in the span of a year, going from 74 yen in 1900 to 297 yen in 1901. That gave way to even more expansion in the second Track-and-Field Meet (October 1902), which included over thirty events, including a special race for guest middle schools and normal schools. It also featured participants from other middle schools and normal schools in Tokyo, along with the Chiba, Kasukabe, and Saitama normal schools. That geographical diversity was a product of the alumni factor. When Higher Normal School graduates who had taken teaching positions at provincial normal schools learned of the new Track-and-Field Meet at their alma mater, they signed their schools up to join the competition. As it continued to introduce events, the meet also extended its reach to a growing number of normal schools via the School Council's graduate network.

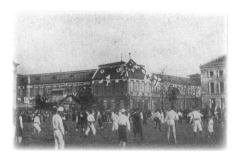

Tokyo Higher Normal School Fall Track-and-Field Meet (1904)

The Higher Normal School was an institution for training teachers, so there were alumni on teaching faculties at normal schools throughout Japan. With all those connections paving the way for the School Council's athletic efforts, the Track-and-Field

Meet was just one of the events that brought in swelling numbers of participants from other institutions—the organization's long-distance races and swimming-practice programs also developed a sizable footprint.

The third Track-and-Field Meet, convened on the Tokyo Higher Normal School ground in November 1903, marked the debut of the Normal-Middle School Championship Race. The winner of the inaugural race was a runner from the Tokyo Prefectural Normal School, who bested contestants from other participating institutions. In the run-up to the fourth meet in 1904, the School Council decided to formalize the operational structure for the event. The new framework outlined specific roles for venue managers, decorators, athletic officials, prize officials, receptionists, meal staff, shop managers, record keepers, and administrative assistants, creating a clear-cut division of duties for optimal efficiency.

At the 1904 meet, which boasted a total of twenty-seven different events, the Normal-Middle School Championship Race had forty entrants from twenty schools. The Tokyo Prefectural Normal School topped the podium again. The meet drew a staggering 10,000 spectators; among them was Minister of Education Kubota Yuzuru.

In the 1905 meet, a total of twenty-two schools—ranging from Yokote Middle School (Ugo, Akita) in the east to Miyazaki Prefectural Normal School in the west—took part in the Normal-Middle School Championship Race.

While the field of competitors continued to diversify, audiences continued to grow in both size and prominence—including even members of the imperial family. At the seventh meet (1907), three imperial grandchildren were on hand; during the eighth meet (1908), members of royalty watched sumo, club swinging, *kibasen* (a mock cavalry battle with students riding the shoulders of their teammates), and children's games (for students from affiliated elementary schools); and the ninth meet (1909) drew seven members of the imperial family.

Student-led initiatives continued to appear as well. In 1906, for example, several student volunteers formed a study group

Tennis (ca. 1914)

devoted to "running form" and began training competitors on an organized basis.

Judo club

Upon the completion of the new judo facility in Ōtsuka in 1902, the School Council's judo club held its first judo tournament with students from the Tokyo Higher Normal School and vocational schools from around Tokyo. Most Normal School graduates went on to take teaching positions at secondary schools across the country, which meant that many served as judo "messengers"—they brought the fundamental judo knowledge that they had gained at the Normal School with them into their professional careers and began passing the practice on to the next generation. The development of the National Secondary-School Judo Championships, for example, stemmed from the Normal School's alumni presence in the country's school system. Tournaments were just one facet of the judo club's lasting impact, however; from 1921 on, the organization sponsored summer training sessions for secondary students throughout Japan. Establishing a broader base for judo was a major focus for the club.

Soccer club

In 1903, the soccer club published *Assoshiēshon futtobōru* (Association football)—Japan's first-ever soccer guidebook. That same year, club members began visiting schools around the country to provide soccer instruction. The ensuing decade (through 1912) proved a bustling period for the club, which made stops at a bevy of normal schools and middle schools on its mission to popularize soccer:

- Saitama Prefectural Normal School
- Tochigi Prefectural Normal School
- Gunma Prefectural Normal School
- Tokyo Prefectural Aoyama Normal School
- Physical Exercise School of Nippon Taiikukai
- Fukushima Prefectural Normal School
- Ibaraki Prefectural Normal School
- Ibaraki Prefectural Shimotsuma Middle School
- Hyogo Prefectural Himeji Normal School
- Yamagata Prefectural Normal School
- Nara Prefectural Normal School

· Shiga Prefectural Normal School
· Aichi Prefectural Third Middle School
· Niigata Prefectural Takada Normal School

The club was also part of Japan's first-ever international soccer match, a 1904 contest against a team from a Yokohama-based sports club for foreigners. (The Japanese side lost). At the end

The Tokyo Higher Normal School soccer club that played against the Yokohama-based sports club for foreigners (1904)

of November 1909, the Tokyo Higher Normal School's athletic facilities shut down to facilitate the construction of the institution's attached middle school. In stepped Principal Kanō, who filled the need for a practice venue by giving the club access to his Toshimagaoka property. Kanō obviously felt that the school's athletic clubs warranted special investment.

2. The growing popularity of distance running

What Kanō saw in running

Of all the athletic pursuits in existence, Kanō Jigorō thought walking, distance running, and swimming were the ideal activities for Japanese people. He wrote specifically about walking and distance running, highlighting their strengths:

One must exercise at least every other day, if not on a daily basis, ideally. . . . Given the need for frequency and regularity, I gradually began to realize that one of the preconditions for encouraging the Japanese people to exercise was that it should be an activity that anyone and everyone could do. It would be inappropriate to recommend an activity that is possible for the dexterous and coordinated among us but impossible for the less-skilled. First and foremost, the activity would need to be one that people of both sexes and all ages could perform to a reasonable degree. Second, it would need to be an activity that required nary an expense nor any type of special equipment. Third, it would ideally be an activity that would have a general appeal among boys, girls, men, and women, regardless of age, but not fuel impassioned competition. The activity that satisfies these three criteria best, I came to understand, is walking . . .

While walking is the ideal method of exercise and should therefore be the most prevalent form, the next-best exercise technique is running. As running also meets the above conditions, involving no equipment or monetary burden whatsoever, I believe it to be a good form of exercise as far as one's age and physical constitution allow.[5]

The Higher Normal School (Tokyo Higher Normal School) was among the leaders of the process of popularizing distance running across Japan.

The Higher Normal School held its first and second marathons ("healthy-leg races") in 1898 and 1901, respectively, both at Ōmiya Hikawa Park. In 1904, the school made its fall "run" a "footrace"; in 1908 it did the same for its spring event. From that point on, the Tokyo Higher Normal School's biannual long-distance footraces became fixtures on the calendar. Participation was essentially mandatory for all students, who would set off from the starting line and dash off to destinations like Tamagawa and Ōmiya. As was the case with judo, Higher Normal School graduates often took their distance-running experience with them and passed on their knowledge at the institutions where they taught. Soon enough, marathons started popping up at a number of Japanese middle schools and normal schools.

Kanakuri Shisō's role in expanding distance running

Another key player in the popularization of distance running was three-time Olympic marathon runner Kanakuri Shisō (1891–1983), who also happened to be a graduate of the Tokyo Higher Normal School. After winning Japan's 1911 Olympic marathon qualifier, Kanakuri joined Tokyo Imperial University student Mishima Yahiko (1886–1954) to form Japan's first Olympic delegation at the 1912 Games of the V Olympiad in Stockholm. Although blistering heat ultimately forced him to drop out of the marathon event mid-run, Kanakuri—the "marathon king," as many came to call him—would go on to set a world record and lead the Japanese delegation at both the 1920 and 1924 Olympics. His legacy remains enormous. As a competitor, he developed the altitude-training approach; as an ambassador of long-distance running, he brought the marathon to new heights of visibility in Japan.

Kanakuri's track record as a runner is equally impressive, as the time-line below shows. With every step, he raised the profile of distance running significantly.

April 1917: Organized Japan's first *ekiden* (a long-distance relay race), the "Tento Kinen Tōkaidō Gojūsantsugi Ekiden Kyōsō" (New Capital Memorial Tōkaidō Fifty-Three-Stage Ekiden Race), and also served as the anchor for the winning team

July 1917: Competed in the Fuji Mountain Race (a race up Mt. Fuji)

July–August 1919: Ran from Shimonoseki to Tokyo (1,300 km) in twenty days

November 1919: Ran from Nikkō to Tokyo (120 km) in ten hours

February 1920: Organized and ran in the Tokyo-Hakone Round-Trip Ekiden Race

August 1922: Ran from Sakhalin to Tokyo in twenty days

1931: Ran the Kyūshū Isshū Marathon (a marathon around the island of Kyushu)

In 1920, Kanakuri made his second Olympic appearance in the marathon at the Games of the VII Olympiad (Antwerp Olympics). Observers pegged him as one of the favorites for the race, but Kanakuri ended up finishing sixteenth, with a time of 2:48:45, hobbled by a leg injury and frustrated by other factors. One was the weather—a steady downpour made the high-temperature training he had done all for naught. He decided to follow his Olympic journey with a trip to Germany, where he saw that country's exemplary program for women's physical education firsthand. The experience was an inspiring one for Kanakuri; after returning to Japan, he decided to make physical education for women a priority and lay the groundwork for a better system at home.

At the age of thirty-three, Kanakuri won the marathon qualifier for the Games of the

Japanese Olympian Kanakuri Shisō (1911)

VIII Olympiad (Paris Olympics) in 1924. That success, however, belied the inevitable effects of aging. Having already passed his physical peak, Kanakuri overpaced himself during the first half of the marathon in Paris and became so fatigued that he pulled out of the race at the 32-kilometer point. The 1924 Olympics marked the end of Kanakuri's career as a front-line runner, but putting a halt to his competitive career gave him more time to devote to popularizing track and field and advancing the sporting community.

One of Kanakuri's biggest contributions was the Hakone Ekiden, which he both developed the idea for and turned into an actual event. The first race—officially the "Four-University Ekiden Race"—took place in 1920; the Tokyo Higher Normal School squad bested teams from Meiji University, Waseda University, and Keio University. As the Ekiden proved increasingly popular, gaining a following among a broader collection of universities and vocational schools, event organizers renamed the race the "Hakone Ekiden." That competition would prove instrumental in giving distance running a pervasive presence throughout Japan.

Kanakuri's treks across Japan, meanwhile, were about more than simply getting from point A to point B. Along the way, he made numerous stops at schools to give lectures on the joys of running, and occasionally found himself joined by groups of student runners; wherever he went, he was rarely alone. He was a promoter through and through.

According to the journals he kept on his twenty-day, 1,400-km run from Sakhalin to Tokyo in 1922, for example, Kanakuri stopped at major towns and cities along the route to give talks and teach sports to children.[6] His lectures would delve deep into his personal history, including his experience running the marathon at the Stockholm Olympics as one of the first Japanese Olympic athletes, his other travels, his stories, and, from time to time, his views on education.

Almost everywhere Kanakuri went, communities received him with open arms. Welcoming committees would greet him as he trotted in, make accommodation arrangements, and even take care of his meals. Local newspapers would devote considerable space to Kanakuri's visits, as well. Considering the warm, celebratory reception that Kanakuri encountered along his journeys, it would be safe to assume that the general public took a considerable interest in his ambitious endeavors. The element of national pride was another wind at Kanakuri's back: donning the Japanese flag connoted much more honor and esteem in Kanakuri's time than it does now. As they looked up at a man who had represented Japan in competition and continued to run with the symbol of the "rising sun," the people who listened to Kanakuri speak must have been in awe of what they were experiencing.

Kanakuri's journals also note that young men and students—in groups of as many as twenty—would occasionally join him for portions of his journey, sometimes lengthy spans. Many had a keen interest in distance running and sports in general, and their experiences of being with Kanakuri on the trail helped further the development of distance running as a popular pursuit. While Kanakuri never even placed in Olympic competition, he won the admiration of legions across the country; people in communities from coast to coast went out of their way to honor a runner who had represented Japan on the international stage for more than a decade.

Distance running in Japanese school settings traces its beginnings to the Tokyo Higher Normal School in more ways than one: not only did Tokyo Higher Normal School alumni add their running experience to the scope of student activities where they went on to work, but Kanakuri, a Tokyo Higher Normal School alumnus with an Olympic pedigree, also served as a compelling advocate.

3. The popularization of swimming (long-distance swimming and the Tokyo Higher Normal School swimming style)

The inception of swimming practice at the Tokyo Higher Normal School
According to "Yūeibu-shi" (The history of the swimming club), an article by Tanaka Keiji, appearing in a 1911 issue of the *Kōyūkai hatten-shi* (History of the School Council) and the journal of the School Council at the Tokyo Higher Normal School, the first years of the school's swimming-practice program transpired as follows.

In July 1902, a group of sixty students headed to Kagamigaura for a two-week swimming program, leaving on a steamship at eight at night and arriving in Hōjō at four the following morning. The students practiced diving and floating, with Kobori Heisaku, a master of the Kobori-ryū style of swimming, providing instruction. The program was extended from two weeks to two months in 1903. During that stint, students took part in six 3-*ri* (roughly 11.8-km) endurance swims; a total of eighteen students successfully swam the full distance. The instructor was Ueda Seiji, a master of the Shinden-ryū swimming style, and the students bunked at Hamada-ya and Nakamura-ya, inns near the Hachiman Shrine. The 1904 trip had sixty participants, forty-three of whom finished the 3-*ri* endurance swim. The group lodged at the Iwaya villa.

These initial years saw the development of the Tokyo Higher Normal School swimming style. In the *Kōyūkai hatten-shi*, one finds the following description of how the method was formed.

Master Nakano Jirō (Tokyo University), a formidable expert in Shinden-ryū swimming, made the bold, unprecedented decision to combine techniques from a variety of schools, such as the Suifu-ryū *noshi-oyogi*, Kobori-ryū *tō-suijutsu*, and Kankai-ryū *hira-oyogi*, and to use a scientific naming system to unify the different methods (*aori yoko-oyogi ichidan* [level-one scissor-leg sidestroke], for example) into an educational curriculum: the "Tokyo Higher Normal School swimming style," a monumental achievement that will forever remain a proud legacy.[7]

The "Tokyo Higher Normal School swimming style" was born. The fifth volume of the School Council journal, which came out in 1904 (just after the development of the *aori yoko-oyogi ichidan*), contains a "Swimming Practice Policy" section that specifically identifies the Suifu-ryū *noshi-oyogi* (scissor-leg sidestroke), Kobori-ryū *tōsuijutsu* (circular movement of the legs), and Kankai-ryū *hira-oyogi* (breaststroke with frog kick) as particularly useful techniques for inclusion in a swimming curriculum. The book also discussed how the Tokyo Higher Normal School swimming style took shape through a reorganization of elements from other schools:

With the progress of society today must come commensurate progress in swimming techniques. It is for that very reason that the Tokyo Higher Normal School swimming

Participants at the inaugural Tokyo Higher Normal School "swimming practice" (1902)

club has undertaken the endeavor to assemble techniques from various schools, never disproportionately partial to a specific tradition, into an elegant form ideal for practical use, conducive to well-balanced physical development, of value to the cultivation of the spirit, and effective in enabling learners to apply said spirit in practice settings, thereby establishing an educational art of the utmost merit.[8]

The Tokyo Higher Normal School swimming style, as the book explained, took traditional techniques and consolidated them into a practical, educational package.

Developing the Tokyo Higher Normal School swimming style

In 1905, the year after its new swimming style was created, the Tokyo Higher Normal School began requiring all preparatory-course students (first-year students) to take part in swimming practice. The first year's program sent the entire preparatory-course student body—students in the arts and the sciences alike—to Hōjō Beach for a full two weeks of swimming, day in and day out. The order for the trip came straight from the top, suggesting that Principal Kanō was determined to establish and disseminate the new swimming style in an educational context. The program's instructor was Nakano Jirō, assisted by students from the First Higher School.

An article in the School Council journal shows just how serious Kanō was about the swimming program. Getting to the Hōjō area, nearly 100 kilometers away on the Bōsō Peninsula, was no easy task in the first years of the twentieth century. Despite the transportation difficulties, the article states, Kanō made annual trips to Hōjō to observe the training sessions and give the students pep talks. As the practice camp began taking more and more participants, the group gradually outgrew its rented accommodations. The developments prompted a proposal to build a dedicated lodging facility for the swimming-practice participants in one of two possible locations: Hōjō (on the Bōsō Peninsula) or Matsuwa (on the Miura Peninsula). Kanō went so far as to survey both sites himself, eventually deciding on the Hōjō location, and the swimming club's very own dormitory, the Hōshokusha, wrapped up construction in 1906. Even the name of the facility, which translates roughly to "venerable remains," was Kanō's creation. The 1906 program brought in an additional instructor, Suifu-ryū Ōta-ha master Honda Ariya (1870–1949), who joined Mukai-ryū specialist Hishikura

Tokyo Higher Normal School swimming club dormitory (ca. 1914)

Yoshikichi and Shinden-ryū master Nakano Jirō on the teaching staff. Judging by the individual backgrounds of the instructors on the roster, the Tokyo Higher Normal School swimming style continued to draw on the techniques of different schools.

On August 6, 1906, the Tokyo Higher Normal School and First Higher School held the first Kantō Federated Swimming Tournament at Hōjō Beach. The competition would thereafter be a yearly event. In addition to the two founding schools, the tournament would feature participating teams from the School of Foreign Languages, Waseda University, Awa Middle School, Kaisei Middle School, Kawagoe Middle School, the Tokyo Higher Normal School's attached middle school, the Imperial Fisheries Institute, Saitama Prefectural Normal School, the Higher Commercial School, and more.

That competitive element fit well with Kanō's basic stance. Competition, Kanō believed, was a vital component in making physical education exciting enough to draw young people in. In the end, the Kantō Federated Swimming Tournament would provide a blueprint for the Japan Amateur Athletic Association's first National Swimming Championships in 1914.

As early as 1902, the swimming program already had a grading system in place. Students would work on their techniques in smaller groups that met for instruction sessions and training activities, and they would also take part in long-distance swims and graded tests. Based on the students' progress, officials would announce grade promotions several times over the course of the program. Swimmers could also earn promotions based on their day-to-day performance in practice. Issues of the School Council journal between 1902 and 1905 provide additional details on the system's inner workings and grading standards. Initially, the only criterion for grade assessment was the distance of the swim. In 1903, its second year in operation, the program made technical skills another factor in the grading. Looking at the journal's swimming-related entries, one can see that the distance benchmarks for the various grade ranks grew longer over the four-year span from 1902 to 1905; evidently, the students' swimming skills were improving to levels that necessitated a more challenging grading rubric and more ambitious curriculum. The program eventually incorporated dan ranks and began holding dan ceremonies, where Principal Kanō would present certain high-performing students with special certificates.

When the 1904 winter swimming event wrapped up, students gathered in the Tokyo Higher Normal School lecture hall for an official ceremony. Principal Kanō was on hand to award medals to twenty-seven swimmers for completing long-distance (3-ri, roughly 11.8-km, or 1.5-ri, approximately 5.9-km) events and *shodan* (first dan) certificates to three deserving students. The corresponding journal article notes that Kanō then gave an hour-long lecture to the group.

Tokyo Higher Normal School swimming club *shodan* certificate (1903; courtesy of the Nakamura Tōtarō collection)

In 1906 the Tokyo Higher Normal School began sending students to middle schools to teach swimming. With the swimming club solidly established after four years in operation, the school was eager to start proselytizing the Tokyo Higher Normal School swimming style nationally on a broader scale. Kanō's approach to establishing a swimming style bore a remarkable resemblance to his efforts to establish judo: the swimming curriculum borrowed liberally from a variety of traditional schools; the formative process involved a healthy dose of competition; grades and dan ranks gradually entered the picture; and the drive to popularize the style relied on groups of trained, experienced students heading into middle schools and inculcating the younger generation with the techniques. In the first ten years of the Tokyo Higher Normal School swimming program (1903–13), 1,321 preparatory-course students, 733 specialized-course students, and 986 regular-course students—over 3,000 in total—participated. The practice programs at Hōjō Beach would continue through the summer of 1942.

Swimming practice in detail: Techniques and schools

While the Tokyo Higher Normal School's swimming-practice program obviously focused its instruction on the Tokyo Higher Normal School swimming style, the process was a fluid mix of tradition, innovation, and concurrent development. At the same time that students were learning techniques from a variety of existing schools to form a base of routine exercises, the pieces comprising what would eventually become the "Tokyo Higher Normal School swimming style" were still falling into place—and the traditional techniques had a palpable influence on that developmental process. The program initially covered the Kobori-ryū and Shinden-ryū schools of swimming. In 1904, the curriculum incorporated the first elements of the Tokyo Higher Normal School style, which gradually became the main focus of the program and finally arrived at completion in 1909.

The 1909 arrangement, which constituted the program's core curriculum through the onset of World War II, included components from the Tokyo Higher Normal School swimming style as well as from Kobori-ryū, Mukai-ryū, Shinden-ryū, and Suifu-ryū Ōta-ha. Kanō explained his thoughts on the Tokyo Higher Normal School swimming style in *Yūei kyōju yōroku* (Swimming instruction record), which came out in 1913:

First, in order to provide a unique, effective form of training, the style uses practical techniques from a variety of existing schools as a required subject and continues to incorporate additional required techniques as appropriate.

Second, as various games and distance-swimming events not only generate interest in swimming but also cultivate courage, the style also implements such activities as a means of augmenting the benefits of swimming practice.

Third, given that rowing is a valuable skill to acquire in tandem with swimming proficiency, the style requires students to practice both swimming and rowing.

Fourth, club members holding the rank of grade one or higher are appointed as "research students" who study techniques and instructional methods of all kinds, assist in the creation of a complete swimming curriculum via the standardization of techniques from existing schools, and establish a complete instructional method therefor.[9]

Participants at the 10-*ri* endurance swim (ca. 1914)

For Kanō, the focus was thus always on creating a practical swimming curriculum and an effective accompanying instructional method—an amalgam of the best techniques from all the existing schools. The style gained traction across the country as Tokyo Higher Normal School students honed their craft and then passed it on to others. When a student achieved a grade-two ranking and obtained approval from Master Honda, Principal Kanō would officially authorize the student to teach swimming at the middle-school level. With these licensees thus taking instructional positions at middle schools and Tokyo Higher Normal School graduates of all types bringing their shared swimming experience with them into their pedagogical careers, the Tokyo Higher Normal School swimming style began to become more widespread. The evolutionary trajectory of the new style led to certain complications, however. As many of the graduates had developed their swimming skills under Suifu-ryū Ōta-ha master Honda, the public sometimes conflated the Tokyo Higher Normal School swimming style with the Suifu-ryū Ōta-ha, one of the several schools it borrowed from.

Just as he had done in founding judo, Kanō endeavored to create a new swimming curriculum by restructuring traditional elements into a modern mold. He set out to construct a new framework without any special allegiance to a single existing school, not even the well-established Suifu-ryū Ōta-ha. What emerged, in the end, was the new Tokyo Higher Normal School swimming style: a systematic approach that would go on to gain a dominant presence in Japan's pre-war context. Instrumental in giving the new style such an extensive reach were Tokyo Higher Normal School students, many of whom became swimming instructors at normal schools and middle schools across the country.

4. The gymnastics special course becomes the faculty of physical education

The creation of the special course for physical education

One of Kanō's most significant achievements in his tenure as principal of the Tokyo Higher Normal School was the conversion of the school's existing gymnastics course into the faculty of physical education. The move redefined the academic landscape at the institution, elevating physical education to a level that the two big divisions—arts and sciences—had long occupied by themselves.

In April 1899, the Tokyo Higher Normal School offered five special courses:

manual arts, physics and chemistry, zoology and botany, agriculture and earth sciences, and gymnastics. The gymnastics course had an enrollment cap of thirty and an initial span of two years and one academic term, which would drop to two years after curricular revisions in January 1900. Coursework in the gymnastics division included classes in ethics, pedagogy, Japanese, physiology and hygiene, regular gymnastics, and military gymnastics.

The next incarnation of the gymnastics course, the government-endowed "moral gymnastics special course," ran from September 1902 to March 1905—a period of two years and two academic terms; that is, two terms longer than the previous gymnastics course. Accompanying that extension was an expansion in the course's academic curriculum, which added classes in Chinese classics, English, and music.

The course continued to evolve. On four separate occasions (in April 1906, April 1907, April 1909, and April 1911), the Tokyo Higher Normal School offered a special course with a dual emphasis on arts and gymnastics. The first was a three-year government-funded program, but the rest were privately funded arrangements with four-year tracks. The number of enrollment slots hovered around thirty-five in 1906, 1907, and 1909 before dropping to about thirty in 1911. In the "arts-gymnastics special course," ethics, pedagogy, gymnastics, and physiology and hygiene represented the bulk of the students' studies. Students also had to choose one of three arts minors to complement their focus on gymnastics: Japanese language and classical Chinese literature, English, or geography and history (all equivalent to the departments in the regular course).

According to Kanō, he established the two-pronged special course because he saw the potential for synergy between academics and athletics in developing better teachers. "If Higher Normal School alumni were to teach both their academic subjects and judo," he explained, "I believed that they would be able to further their performance to even greater effect."[10] However, the balancing act between the two disciplines proved challenging; providing enough instruction for students to earn qualifications to teach in the arts—a requisite component of the course—made it difficult to develop human resources capable of devoting their full attention to the development of the gymnastics course. In the end, Kanō decided to scrap the arts-gymnastics special course and revert to a single focus on gymnastics.

The Tokyo Higher Normal School offered the "gymnastics special course" in April 1913 and April 1914. In both years, the course was a three-year, privately funded program with an enrollment limit of around sixty. Two distinctions set this special course apart: it had no dual focus, first of all; and it marked the debut of a "gymnastics" major with both judo and kendo in its curriculum. The inclusion of martial arts was a reflection of the government's

The Ōtsuka area (ca. 1930)

July 1911 amendments to the Middle School Ministerial Administrative Ordinance, which stipulated that gymnastics "shall consist of drills and exercises and shall include swordsmanship and jujutsu." Now that the government had made martial arts a required subject, schools across Japan confronted a pressing need for teachers with the proper qualifications—hence the creation of a corresponding training course (and majors) at the Tokyo Higher Normal School. The institution's decision to separate the course into the three separate major tracks of gymnastics, judo, and kendo would later play into the formation of the faculty of physical education as a separate, special organization.

In 1918, the gymnastics special course graduated its last group of students. Over its five-year run, the course generated a total of exactly 200 graduates, the overwhelming majority of whom went on to take teaching positions. A full four-fifths of the graduates wound up joining the faculties at normal schools or middle schools; figuring in the graduates who secured jobs at higher women's schools and vocational schools, the proportion grew to an impressive 86 percent. Records also list several students whose post-graduation careers fell into the "Other" category. This included twelve graduates who decided to pursue additional studies at the Tokyo Higher Normal School. Presumably, a good number of those dozen graduate students went on to teach at secondary schools after completing their advanced work. Nearly all of the 200 graduates of the gymnastics special course apparently embarked on careers in schools, drawing lines from the Tokyo Higher Normal School to the next generation of students.

Kanō framed the creation of the gymnastics special course as follows:

Though schools do have instructors of technical gymnastics, what they offer remains incomplete. It is my hope that, through the creation of this special course, students will be able not only to develop their technical proficiency but also to gain a thorough understanding of the underlying theories and master today's advanced methods.[11]

In Kanō's eyes, the goal was to train instructors who would be more than mere technicians—he was aiming for teachers who could combine that practical expertise the ability to apply sound theoretical knowledge. The gymnastics special course was one manifestation of that intent, which culminated in the establishment of the faculty of physical education.

Establishing the faculty of physical education

In February 1915, the Japanese government revised the Higher Normal School Regulations under an order from the Ministry of Education and amended the Tokyo Higher Normal School Regulations accordingly. The second article of the revised regulations stipulated, "The school shall divide its faculties into the faculty of arts and the faculty of sciences, each of which shall comprise three departments, and, in addition to the faculties specified in the preceding paragraph, institute a special faculty of physical education." Into the school's academic landscape thus came the faculty of physical education, a unique entity outside the scope of the school's other faculties, in the spirit of the first article of the regulations: "The school shall endeavor to cultivate in its students the qualities befitting the principals and faculty of normal schools, middle schools, and higher women's schools and pursue studies of the methods of regular education."

The new faculty was of a decidedly different nature than the previous gymnastics special course, which the Tokyo Higher Normal School had created under the Special Course Regulations as an ad hoc measure designed to offset a shortage in physical-education instructors. In Article 5, the regulations stated that the faculties of the arts, sciences, and physical education were each to have a "course term of four years in length" with the "first year being a preparatory course." Whereas the gymnastics special course had been a three-year program, the new faculty of physical education was to follow the same four-year protocol as the faculties of arts and sciences. From an institutional standpoint, this meant that physical education was now on par with the other faculties. In a historical context, meanwhile, the creation of the faculty of education at the Tokyo Higher Normal School and the development of a richer curriculum represented the rebirth of full-scale teacher training for gymnastics programs and dedicated institutional research into physical education—two initiatives that had been dormant since the closure of the National Institute of Gymnastics in 1886.

The third article of the regulations stipulated that the faculty of education would provide education in "morals; pedagogy; gymnastics, drills, and games; judo; kendo; theory of physical education; anatomy, physiology, hygiene, and first aid; psychology and logic; Japanese and Chinese classics; English; and history." Gymnastics drills and games, judo, and kendo were to form the primary curricular components, while English was to be an elective. The faculty's diverse mix of courses included two disciplines that were absent from the gymnastics special course curriculum: "psychology and logic" and "history." Article 10 provided additional details on what each field of study would cover:

· Morals: Practical ethics, ethics, national morality, history of Western ethics, history of morality, and history of Eastern ethics
· Pedagogy: Pedagogy, history of education, teaching methods, school hygiene, and educational laws
· Gymnastics, drills, and games: Gymnastics, drills, and games
· Judo: Basic judo, advanced judo, kata, *randori*, catechism, and teaching methods
· Kendo: Basic kendo, advanced kendo, kata, match competition, catechism, and teaching methods
· Theory of physical education: Theory of physical education
· Anatomy, physiology, hygiene, and first aid: Anatomy, physiology, hygiene, and first aid
· Psychology and logic: Logic and psychology
· Japanese and Chinese classics: Reading, grammar, and composition
· English: Reading and grammar
· History: Japanese history, Eastern history, and Western history
· Elective: English

The gymnastics special course had been a stopgap measure, a means of compensating for a practical lack of instructors, with an official term of three years. The faculty of physical education, on the other hand, featured a full four-year track. In 1921, the new faculty became a regular course, effectively eliminating any institutional differences between it and the faculties of arts and sciences. From that perspective, the creation of the faculty of physical education consummated Kanō's vision of the ideal approach to the development of physical-education instructors: training students so that they could "not only . . . develop their technical proficiency but also . . . gain a thorough understanding of the underlying theories and master today's advanced methods." Kanō also saw the new faculty as a platform for cultivating physical-education instructors with a comprehensive command of martial-arts techniques and theory, as the dedicated programs for judo and kendo within the faculty of physical education suggest. The faculty's design served to actualize what Kanō conceived of as the epitome of physical education: a judo instructor with deep, probing insight, all grounded in an understanding of pedagogy, physiology, and other scientific foundations. Once the Tokyo Higher Normal School opened its faculty of physical education in 1915, there was no dislodging physical education from the academic arena.

The faculty's founding also gave the School Council's athletic clubs a significant boost, enhanced the institution's curriculum, and led to an increase in the number of students specializing in judo and kendo. It was a major accomplishment for Kanō. It also proved to be his swan song at the Tokyo Higher Normal School. Having seen the first graduating class of the faculty of physical education off, Kanō resigned from his position as principal in 1920 after a quarter of a century on the job.

Notes:

1   Kanō Jigorō, *Seinen shūyō-kun* [Teachings for the cultivation of the young] (Tokyo: Dōbunkan Shuppan, 1910), 100–101.

2   Kanō Jigorō, "Jūdō ippan narabi ni sono kyōiku-jō no kachi" [Judo and its educational value], *Dai Nihon Kyōiku-kai zasshi* [Journal of the Educational Society of Japan] 87 (1889).

3   Naganuma Akira, "Kōyūkai ippan-shi" [A general history of the School Council], *Kōyūkai-shi* [The School Council journal] 29 (1911).

4   Kanō Jigorō, "Kōyūkai-in ni tsugu" [A message to the members of the School Council], *Kōyūkai-shi* [The School Council journal] 29 (1911).

5   Kanō Jigorō, "Kokumin no taiiku ni tsuite" [On national physical education], *Aichi kyōiku zasshi* [The Aichi journal of education] 356 (1917).

6   Kanakuri Shisō, *Karafuto–Tōkyō-kan tōha-shi* [From Sakhalin to Tokyo on foot] (1932; in the collection of the Tamana City Kokoropia Historical Museum).

7   Tanaka Keiji, "Yūeibu-shi" [The history of the swimming club], *Kōyūkai hatten-shi* [History of the School Council] 29 (1911).

8   Tokyo Higher Normal School, School Council Swimming Club, "Yūei renshū no hōshin" [Policies for swimming practice], *Kōyūkai-shi* [The School Council Journal] 5 (1904).

9   Tokyo Higher Normal School, School Council Swimming Club, *Yūei kyōju yōroku*

[Swimming guidance record] (Tokyo: Tokyo Higher Normal School School Council Swimming Club, 1913).

10 Ōtaki Tadao, *Kanō Jigorō: Watashi no shōgai to jūdō* [Kanō Jigorō: My life and judo] (Tokyo: Shinjinbutsu Ōraisha, 1972), 108.

11 "Kanō-sensei ikuei sanjū-ncn-shi" [Professor Kanō's three decades in education], *Kōyūkai-shi* [The School Council Journal] 67 (1920).

The university-promotion movement

1. The Special Council for Education and Kanō: The development of the "normal university" proposal

Special Council for Education

Kanō Jigorō was appointed a member of the Special Council for Education, an advisory panel established by the Terauchi Masatake cabinet, in October 1917. From its inception to its dissolution in May 1919, the Special Council submitted recommendations on topics ranging from elementary education and higher general education for men to university education and professional education, normal-school education, the school-inspector system, women's education, vocational education, popular education, and the degree system. In addition to providing the government with expert opinions on those nine main themes, the group also wrote proposals on implementing military calisthenic drills in school settings and raising the concept of "national polity" (*kokutai*). As such, the Special Council for Education was instrumental in forming an array of post-World War I educational policies from the second half of the Taishō period (1912–26) to the early Shōwa period (1926–89).[1]

Kanō was a force on the Special Council, chairing the deliberations on elementary education, university education and professional education, normal education, and the promotion of military calisthenic drills. Whatever the report, whatever the proposal deliberation, no member was more vocal than Kanō—and he tended to be particularly outspoken on the issues of elementary, normal, university, and professional education, four areas with significant connections to the Tokyo Higher Normal School.

Elementary education was a key focus for Kanō, and he made his stance clear on a number of points. The first was the best approach to securing capable elementary teachers. Echoing an opinion he had maintained since his days as the director of primary education at the Ministry of Education, Kanō argued that forming a solid base of elementary teachers was contingent on ensuring reasonable conditions for educators—in terms of both pay and support. He also touched on moral education, noting that Japanese teachers were adept at teaching book knowledge but inept at imparting moral values. To right the situation, Kanō declared, the government would need to reinterpret the Imperial Rescript on Education and move away from what he considered an overemphasis on knowledge-oriented education. Physical education was another facet of his take on improving the elementary-school approach. For Kanō, what Japan's physical-education curriculum needed was an emphasis on nurturing respect for the body, encouraging the general public to value physical activity, and making gymnastics more enjoyable. He also criticized the uniformity of elementary-education methodology, saying, "I do not think it necessary to teach the same subjects with the same textbooks and the same methods";[2] he saw rigid standardization as an ineffective approach, one that upheld fixed ideals that would inevitably fall out of touch with people's day-to-day lives.

After deliberating on the issues, the Special Council for Education drafted a report recommending several elementary-education policies: combining national funding and municipal coffers to pay for elementary teachers' salaries, eventually halving the national government's share of teacher-pay expenses, steering the curriculum away from its focus on memorization, enhancing national moral education, and prioritizing the improvement of physical education.

The discussions on elementary education also included an assessment of teachers' overall performance, another area where Kanō offered a variety of input. While praising elementary teachers for their performance in their duties, particularly in light of their professional status and working conditions, he also highlighted three weaknesses: a tenuous grasp of their roles as educators, substandard

The Tokyo Higher Normal School's affiliated elementary school (1932)

scholarly aptitude and expertise in educational methods, and an overly pedantic approach to moral education, one that placed acquiring knowledge over cultivating a just, healthy conscience through an understanding of emotion and behavior. In Kanō's eyes, any initiative to improve elementary education would necessarily entail measures to elevate teachers' principles and academic abilities. In time, that basic position would inform efforts to enhance the normal-school system, promote higher normal schools to normal universities, and bolster the teacher-training framework.

Improving the normal-school system

With talks on improving the training of elementary teachers naturally came discussions on remodeling the normal-school structure, another area where Kanō had an obvious interest and emphasized the need for change. Normal schools were rife with issues at the time, and admission procedures represented one of the biggest frustrations. Graduates of higher elementary schools hoping to enroll at normal schools had no choice but to take an entire year off and bide their time until the admissions period opened. With working conditions for elementary teachers already on the decline, the prospect of idling away for a full year before embarking on the teacher-training process was another factor deterring graduates from the teaching profession. The number of aspiring teachers was shrinking.

To address the issues contributing to that dwindling interest, Kanō recommended two countermeasures: enabling graduates of higher elementary schools to enroll at normal schools without a year-long gap, and establishing a system that would use state funding to help raise normal-school teacher salaries. He also stressed the importance of cultivating higher-caliber teachers through an even stronger focus on morals, Japanese, geography, mathematics, singing, and gymnastics. Although funding constraints made Kanō's reform ideas impossible to implement straight away, they did come to fruition after an advisory consultation by the Educational and Cultural Policy Council (formed in 1924) with the resulting revisions to the Normal School Regulations made in April 1925.

When it came to hiring female teachers, however, Kanō had qualms. "When girls become teachers, the home crumbles into disorder," he said. "Every girl has a unique vocation: raising the citizens of the future," Kanō asserted, referring to women's roles as mothers. "The thought of depriving girls of that immense responsibility and instead making them teachers seems to me a quizzical notion."

Kanō's beliefs were not unique at the time; save for Japan Women's University founder Naruse Jinzō (1858–1919) and a handful of others, the entire Council membership subscribed to the idea that a woman's place was in the home, not at the head of the classroom. The Special Council for Education's report to the government recommended "training normal-school students under a policy that will ensure a proper difference in the proportions of male and female teachers at elementary schools" on the grounds that "placing national education primarily in the hands of women is not the way toward nurturing simple, sturdy citizens."[3]

Opposition to employing female teachers did not mean opposition to educating women, of course. Recognizing that everything from politics and the military to finances and economics had roots in home education and social education, the Council saw women's education as a fundamental piece of the national framework. Kanō, whose vision of women's education centered more on spiritual education than on practical knowledge in the narrower scope of domestic economy, stressed the need for "high schools befitting girls" and "higher girls' schools with a central focus on nurturing a sound Japanese national spirit" so they could eventually raise children befitting the country.

The effort to transform higher normal schools into normal universities

Kanō wanted higher normal schools to occupy a more elevated position in the educational sphere. "I want to see the Tokyo Higher Normal School contribute even more fully to improvements in education," he explained, "and, in order to do so, I believe we should promote the institution to university status. In addition to training more educators of stronger character and greater ability, normal universities would also include research institutions with the ability to facilitate valuable research not only on moral education but also education of all kinds." For him, that meant adding a year to higher normal schools' academic programs, establishing more courses for advanced study, and effectively transforming the institutions into full-fledged "normal universities."

At the time, secondary-teacher training took place via programs at Japan's four higher normal schools (the Tokyo and Hiroshima institutions for men and the Tokyo and Nara establishments for women), national and private universities, and was verified through licensing examinations. The structure was in place, but a slew of problems—the challenge of training high-caliber teachers, among others—hindered the framework in practice. In Kanō's view, higher normal schools needed to satisfy three main conditions. First, the academic departments at normal schools needed to match the academic departments at the schools where graduates would be teaching, without any superfluous departments or curricular holes leading to incongruencies. Second, normal schools needed to have dormitory arrangements so that students could focus on their academics. Third, departments needed to educate learners not just in purely academic knowledge but also the finer points of tailoring lessons for optimal application in middle-school settings. What defined the educational practices at higher normal schools was the process of "cultivating an educator spirit," Kanō argued with conviction, hammering home the point that higher normal schools played a unique role in secondary-teacher training—the philosophy that laid the foundation for Kanō's "normal university" proposal.

The response to Kanō's proposal was hostile at worst and chilly at best. House of Peers member Egi Kazuyuki (1853–1932), Tokyo Imperial University president and fellow House of Peers member Yamakawa Kenjirō (1854–1931), and Sanjūshi Bank president Koyama Kenzō (1858–1923), flanked by others, stood in fierce opposition, contending that imperial universities should have their own colleges of education to stand alongside their colleges of literature and science. Special Council for Education Vice-President Kubota Yuzuru (1847–1936), meanwhile, suggested that higher normal schools be promoted to normal universities, situating the normal universities within imperial universities, and splintering the teacher-training facilities at higher normal schools off into auxiliary bodies within normal-school operations.

Discussions within the Special Council for Education developed into a struggle between two camps: Kanō's side, which aimed to give normal schools chief responsibility for secondary-teacher training, and Egi's coterie, which wanted imperial universities to occupy the central role. The split likely stemmed from divergent opinions on university education and professional education. Whereas Kanō's stance on university education favored single-faculty colleges or multi-college universities with a priority on professional education, Egi and Yamakawa threw their weight behind the development of large, multi-faculty universities that would steer their energies toward deep, comprehensive research across the academic landscape.

A bird in the hand is worth two in the bush
As the Special Council for Education was full of detractors who opposed the idea

of promoting higher normal schools to normal universities, Kanō shifted gears. Instead of aiming for the glory of an against-all-odds campaign for university promotion, an enterprise whose prospects appeared dim, he opted for objectives with better chances of success. His new approach involved expanding the two-year courses of specialized study (which had been in place since April 1911) into their own faculties. Revisions to the Higher Normal School Regulations in February 1915 had consolidated the faculties at higher normal schools into two organizations—the faculties of arts and sciences, each with three constituent departments—and established a third, separate faculty of physical education (except for the framework at the Hiroshima Higher Normal School, where the third faculty was the faculty of education). Due to budget cuts, however, the only specialized courses that ever took shape were the moral-education Chinese-literature and English courses, each of which only appeared in the curriculum once. The Special Council for Education thus convened with the curricula at higher normal schools in an underdeveloped state.

In July 1918, the Special Council for Education issued recommendations detailing a host of improvements to the nation's higher normal schools. One pertained to the programs of study at the schools, which would "continue to exist as special institutions with the purpose of training teachers," strive to better working conditions for staff members, work to improve their educational offerings, and feature "permanent" graduate-study programs and specialized courses. Considering the growing demand for secondary teachers, the Council also advised the government to expand the capacity of the country's higher normal schools. Another point dealt with student funding, with the Council recommending that policymakers reinstitute the government's scholarship program. In line with the report, Kanō began the process of putting higher normal schools in position to make an easier transition to university status via a broader selection of specialized courses, better support systems for staff members, and similar measures. The palette of specialized courses, for example, featured a moral-education course every year through 1928.

The Special Council for Education report touched on the mechanisms for teacher training as well. To prepare for surging numbers of teachers in higher education, the group called on the government to establish faculties of education at arts-oriented universities and ensure that universities would "funnel large numbers of human resources into the educational community and elevate the standing of teachers." The report also underscored the need for "continued reciprocity between imperial universities and higher normal schools" and "enhanced expediency in research," which would entail imperial universities sending students to higher normal school-affiliated institutions for teaching practice, on the one hand, and students in specialized courses and graduate programs at higher normal schools making use of lectures and facilities at imperial universities to further their studies.

Kanō opted for a bird in the hand rather than two in the bush. He took surefire reforms, which would essentially make the Higher Normal School a "university" in substance, over the recognition that might come with a "university" designation. Kanō made the Tokyo Higher Normal School—a long-standing bastion of Japanese education—an even more vital force.

2. The Higher Normal School: Kanō's to serve or Kanō's to lead?

The promulgation of the University Order

On the recommendations of the Special Council for Education, the Japanese government promulgated the University Order in December 1918 and thereby promoted the existing vocational schools (under the Vocational School Order) into bona fide universities. Joining the university ranks, which had long consisted solely of the imperial universities—Tokyo, Kyoto, Tohoku, Kyushu, and Hokkaido—were a host of new additions. Osaka Medical University, a public institution, received accreditation in 1919. The following year saw the official approval of Tokyo University of Commerce (formerly Tokyo Higher Commercial School) and Aichi Medical University, both public, and eight private (foundation-funded) universities: Keio, Waseda, Meiji, Hosei, Chuo, Nihon, Kokugakuin, and Doshisha.

Vocational schools of all stripes—whether government-run, public, or private—were transitioning into single-faculty colleges left and right, but the momentum pushing Tokyo Higher Normal School's entry into the university ranks was petering out. One of the factors holding the Higher Normal School back was the impasse that had soured deliberations on the Special Council for Education. The government was divided on whether to elevate the Higher Normal School to university status, and the opponents to the idea held a firm line. Including the likes of former minister of education Okada Ryōhei (1864–1934), Egi Kazuyuki, Kubota Yuzuru, and other parliamentary heavyweights, the old educational guard bristled at the idea of making higher normal schools into universities. They adhered to the views of Mori Arinori, the first minister of education, who saw the country's higher normal schools in a class separate from universities—to Mori, higher normal schools were special institutions devoted exclusively to training aspiring educators. For that camp, higher normal schools should remain higher normal schools, outside the university realm, upholding their unique raison d'être as a collective centerpiece of education. The conventional wisdom still held strong. As far as the existing higher normal schools went, Okada and his allies were staunch, formidable protectors of a proud legacy. They also represented a staunch, formidable barrier to the university-promotion campaign.

The resistance was not necessarily a crisis for Kanō, however, whose views still occupied a common ground with Okada's general stance. While the Tokyo Higher Normal School may not have "attained university status in name" in the Special Council for Education's report, it had all but "gained the university designation in substance." Kano knew that as long as the government promptly implemented the Council's recommendations as intended, there would be "no impediments of note," and the school would be free to teach its students as it liked.

The university-promotion movement

After Osaka Higher Technical School and Tokyo Higher Technical School started movements to gain university status, a similar university-promotion initiative started to gain traction at the Tokyo Higher Normal School in December 1919. Students, staff, and members of the Meikeikai (the Tokyo Higher Normal School's alumni association) banded together behind the promotion effort, spurred on by a series of external factors. As the university-promotion movement gained steam at Tokyo Higher Technical School, for example, Minister of Education Nakahashi Tokugorō (1861–1934) declared his hope to "select a number of worthy technical schools for conversion into single-faculty colleges in 1921." Reports of Akita Mining College's intentions to seek university promotion were also beginning to surface. People at the Tokyo Higher Normal School, taking note of the developments, felt that their institution deserved a place in the discussion. They prided themselves on the institution's primacy among the country's government-controlled schools and its high-ranking status, just a rung below the elite imperial universities. For the advocates of university promotion, that sense of honor and self-worth was central to their undertaking.

The university-promotion movement got its start on December 3, when a declaration reading "Promote us, or close us! Rise up, fellow students! Gather tonight and join the cause!" went up on a Tokyo Higher Normal School bulletin board. At five o'clock that evening, six hundred students made their way to the lecture hall for their first student meeting. "Throw no bombs that fail to ignite," the meeting's basic statement urged. The participants came to an official resolution, stating that "We call for the Tokyo Higher Normal School to be promoted to university status," and also produced a sealed covenant. "We hereby pledge to take concerted, decisive action in hopes of fulfilling the resolution dated December 3, 1919," read the pact, which all the students signed. After hours of discussions, the student meeting finally broke up at two the following morning.

Just hours later, student council officers began making door-to-door visits to faculty members to rally support for the initiative. The faculty council met and gave the university-promotion movement its unanimous approval, while Chairman Miyake Yonekichi assembled a fourteen-member Central Committee to drive the effort. The second student meeting convened at 7:30 p.m. that same day and arrived at a series of next-step resolutions, agreeing to bring students in specialized courses on board, circulate written appeals to Meikeikai members nationwide, and "continue to attend classes as usual, always remaining dutiful to our roles as students in the name of proper order." Hanging in the lecture hall were banners proclaiming the two main slogans of the university-promotion movement: "Respect for Education" and "Enhancement of Spiritual Culture."

The next day, December 5, school personnel, students, and Meikeikai members forged a three-party alliance. The meeting of staff members also heard reports on a series of new developments, including the formation of the "Hakunetsu-dan" (the "Barn Burners")—a support group of specialized-course students—and the writing of the "Sen'yōka," or "enhancement song." The lyrics of the song, written by a second-year regular-course student named Jō Yasuo, were as follows:

Verse 1:
Like the leaves of the paulownia
wither not on the branch but fall in grace
We must cast off the ashes of our name
and awake, fellow brothers, arise!

Verse 2:
In the wisdom of the shining sun
our school most hallowed shall prevail
For the waters of the Meikei
are better dry than defiled

Set to the melody of the Keio University fight song, the Tokyo Higher Normal School's "Sen'yōka" became a popular anthem for the university-promotion movement.[4]

The Higher Normal School: To serve or to lead?

The university-promotion movement proved to be a dilemma for Kanō, who found himself torn between acting on his personal vision for the Tokyo Higher Normal School and honoring his responsibilities as principal. In a 1923 piece for *Kyōiku* (Education), Kanō opened up about his inner conflict:

On the Special Council for Education, I decided to abandon my dogged pursuit of the university name and instead opt for substance over name. I explained my reasoning to the assembly and assured my fellow council members of my intention to secure the Ministry of Education's commitment to implement our resolutions the following year. Having ceased my appeals for the promotion of the Tokyo Higher Normal School, I thus tried to convince the proponents of the promotion movement to forswear their cause. However, it was already too late; my dear students, staff, and graduates would hear nothing of my pleas, so committed they were to effecting the institution's promotion. They are unbending in their determination to see their mission through even now; the progress of their initiative is their sole focus. However, it is an undeniable fact that the government has long been indifferent toward normal education. Moreover, the movement also represents an attempt to achieve exactly what I had first proposed at the Special Council for Education. Their passion to serve the cause of normal education, too, is exactly the spirit that I have endeavored to instill in them. I am no more able to stifle the movement than I am to give it my blessing.[5]

As the above passage suggests, suppressing his sympathies for the university-promotion movement was no easy task for Kanō—and he ultimately decided to go with his heart. On December 5, the third day of the university-promotion movement, Kanō made a clandestine visit to Egi Kazuyuki's residence and told him that he would do everything in his power to "pacify the unrest in Ōtsuka" [where the Tokyo Higher Normal School was located] but noted that "circumstances may force him to join with the protesters."[6] In the wake of that meeting came the formation of the three-party alliance among students, staff, and Meikeikai members. Kanō then made an appearance at a meeting of the Meikeikai committee, which had already resolved to "go hand in hand with its allies" to elevate the Tokyo Higher Normal School to university status, and pledged to take "concerted, decisive action" with the alliance:

> In light of my statements last year at the Special Council for Education, I was prepared to forego the glory of university promotion in favor of practical progress (by expanding and enhancing the school's specialized courses, establishing research institutions, and annexing attached high schools). However, you fine gentlemen have taken a step forward in pursuing the very aims and ideals I had long championed. Here, I find myself surrounded by professors and graduates with whom I have forged lasting ties; here, I stand before young students now devoting themselves to their studies; and here, you resound in unison, unwavering in your convictions. How could I ever abandon you for the sake of nothing more than my own interests, my personal reputation in the public eye? I hereby vow to join you, gentlemen, in taking concerted, decisive action.[7]

On December 6, a formal report was issued to the students. "Of greatest concern to us was where Principal Kanō would stand, considering the course of events that has transpired since the Special Council for Education," the report read. "Fortunately, however, he has overcome countless challenges and hardships to pledge his support for our actions, seeing as our beliefs coincide with his long-held views." The alliance, now "sharing a solid bond," became "all the more impassioned." At the third student meeting at 6:30 that evening, attendees belted out a rousing rendition of the "Sen'yōka."

Over 700 students lent their voices to another "Sen'yōka" chorus at the following day's Meikeikai assembly, where Kanō delivered an address to the crowd:

> First, not once since taking my position at this institution in 1894 have I

witnessed all of its professors, all of its graduates, and all of its students join as one for the sake of the school. This truly is a joyous moment for me.

Second, the roots of the nation lie in education. Over my tenure at the Ministry of Education and ever since, I have devoted myself to and championed the causes of both general education and the development of this institution.

But for reasons I cannot comprehend, the ministry authorities have furtively curtailed the budget time and time again. Whenever I submit a proposal that they deem unsatisfactory, they remain silent, refusing to inform me of the necessary revisions.

Third, I seriously considered leaving the school on countless occasions, so frustrated was I that my arguments never once found a receptive ear. However, I was never able to bring myself to act on that impulse. While some may exceed my academic knowledge and expertise, I doubt there is anyone whose passion for general education surpasses mine.

Fourth, our best faculty members have routinely been poached away by universities. On occasion, I would recruit promising educators toiling in obscurity to teach at this institution; I would send them abroad to further their studies on my personal recommendations; they would return, ready to apply their newfound skills in the classrooms here; I would take heart in the prospects of welcoming them to the faculty as full professors; and then, just as I was ready to breathe a contented sigh of relief, universities would swoop immediately in and make off with the teachers I had so carefully groomed. Imagine how that made me feel. Still, I was never able to stand in their way. They would come to me to discuss their prospects, their futures weighing heavily on their minds. Had I forced the teachers to stay, they surely would have remained. But I let them go. In my heart, I wanted nothing more than to see them find happy fulfillment. If only we had had the types of research institutions that universities possess, I doubt I ever would have had to confront such a bitter fate.

Fifth, despite the fact that I was seeking university status in substance alone, if not name, I still met with reduced budgets and unexecuted plans. Was the momentum behind the effort not enough? Were the authorities not able to understand the circumstances? Or was I simply a fool?

Sixth, the fact that I am agreeing to stand with you, considering my circumstances, may very well put my reputation in peril. However, my personal honor is but a selfish motive. I cannot bear to remain a distant spectator on these crucial events before us, nor can I stand in their way. I have no time to be busying myself with the worldly concerns of praise and censure; I must instead commit myself to your cause.

This you must understand, gentlemen. Should we fall short of our aims, I fully intend to fall with you.[8]

A summary of Kanō's speech also appears in the records of the Meikeikai Executive Committee:

Today, for the first time, I vow to stand with you in solidarity in the effort to secure promotion for the Higher Normal School. I had been in such dire straits and long contemplated this. I decided that the institution did not need to be a university in name; as long as I continued my dogged pursuits of better education and made the institution the leading authority in general education, I told myself, that would suffice. I convinced myself that there was no need to obsess so desperately over a nominal designation. Now, however, I realize that I was mistaken. Whatever may come, whatever the cost may be, we must devote ourselves to promoting the institution to university status in both substance *and* name. Though mine may be a sudden change of heart, it is an unavoidable consequence of the spirit of the times we now inhabit, a force against which we can no longer resist. We must thus fight with all our might and in all sincerity, invoking the spirit of Yoshida Shōin, for the respect of education.[9]

To Kanō, then, "the institution did not need to be a university in name"; as long as he continued his "dogged pursuits of better education and made the institution the leading authority in general education . . . that would suffice." That line of reasoning points to one of his inspirations for Tokyo Higher Normal School: Kanō originally envisioned the institution as a spiritual cousin to the École normale supérieure (ENS), France's higher normal school.

The ENS was founded by the National Convention in October 1794, during the French Revolution, to train a body of teachers for the country. Although it closed for a time shortly thereafter, Napoleon eventually reopened the institution in March 1808. Now located at the rue d'Ulm in Paris, the ENS is currently one of France's "grandes écoles"—selective, prestigious institutions of higher education—specializing in the training of university instructors and researchers. France is currently home to four higher normal schools, two in Paris and two in Lyon, but singular references to the French "higher normal school" generally correspond to the institution at the rue d'Ulm. Seeing elements of the ENS in the Tokyo Higher Normal School, Kanō referred to his institution as a "normal graduate school" in his addresses and asserted that "the Higher Normal School now measures up to a university."[10]

Kanō's speech on December 7 resonated with the audience, engendering sympathy for his position. He laid out his personal vision of the Higher Normal School, spoke from the heart about his inner conflict, and vowed his support for the university-promotion effort as principal, rallying the assembly to "fight with all our might and in all sincerity, invoking the spirit of Yoshida Shōin." The Tokyo Higher Normal School's School Council even offered the following interpretation of Kanō's mindset:

> The principal is an official of the national government in control of a school. Serving as a member of the Special Council for Education, he also passed recent resolutions concerning the Japanese school system. Given his standing, it would obviously be a virtual impossibility for him to take part in a student-led university-promotion movement—the very type of matter one would expect a man in his position to suppress. However, the movement's commitment to promoting the Higher Normal School to university status coincides with the principal's long-standing vision for the institution. Unable to turn his back on the four-thousand graduates and seven-hundred students who have undertaken their mission in the name of respect for education and the enhancement of spiritual culture, the principal has instead chosen to sacrifice his stature and spearhead the movement himself.
>
> Seeing the principal take up the leadership of the movement, emanating the heroic valiance of Saigō Takamori, we could not help but choke back tears of inspiration.[11]

Kanō's decision to join the movement stirred controversy in the press. One newspaper called the promotion initiative "Professor Kanō's vengeful insurrection" against the Ministry of Education for effectively pushing him out of office; another writer saw it as a "misguided boycott at the hands of Professor Kanō." A particularly harsh critic of the university-promotion movement, however, was

Minister of Education Nakahashi. In the December 10 issue of the *Osaka Asahi Shimbun*, a piece titled "Principal Kanō's outrageous, meaningless mission to promote the Higher Normal School to university status" included a selection of Nakahashi's vitriolic barbs on the topic.

> For the Tokyo Higher Normal School to launch a university-promotion movement is an exercise in meaningless futility—and even more disgraceful is the fact that Principal Kanō himself has linked arms with professors and students in all the ruckus rather than fulfill his role as a model for principals nationwide. Why in the world would the Higher Normal School, with its specific duty of training schoolteachers, need to be a university, anyway? A university is the highest institution of learning, a place where students explore the mysteries of academic knowledge. The distinction between a university and the Higher Normal School, inherently a teacher-training institution, is self-evident. I have no idea what grounds the institution is basing its calls for promotion on, what logical arguments corroborate its contentions that it will never be able to attract human resources unless it carries the university designation, but my question is this: what point does it serve for the Higher Normal School to attract university-type human resources in the first place? The Meikeikai is all caught up in the commotion, too. That may be their way of doing things, but forming old-boys' clubs like the Meikeikai and raising commotion is nonsense. Government-controlled schools must be one with the Ministry of Education, but here we have one fancying itself some kind of independent body and making a scene with its baseless demands. The last thing students should be doing is involving themselves in political movements or government affairs. Only in places like China and Russia do students concern themselves with political movements. Japan, as a result of the Paris Peace Conference, now stands shoulder to shoulder with the powers of the day—and yet here we find ourselves in a sad state, a first-rate country acting like China, like Russia, like a second-class nation. This is absolute nonsense. This is why we have things like the Ministry of Education and principals. And again, here we have a principal joining the fracas. . . . A school operating under that brand of principal deserves to be closed.

Despite the opposition, the university-promotion movement eventually achieved its aims, for all practical purposes, thanks in large part to a concerted effort uniting Kanō, Central Committee chairman Miyake, and Tokyo Higher Normal School graduate and House of Representatives member Mitsuchi Chūzō (1871–1948). With that faction of advocates making a united push, Minister of Educa-

Attendees at a party celebrating the school's promotion (1929)

tion Nakahashi announced on December 15 that he would "work to improve normal education" and "give due consideration to calls for the special establishment of universities." The minister thus gave his blessing to the promotion of five schools—Kobe Higher Commercial School, Osaka Higher Technical School, Tokyo Higher Technical School, and the higher normal schools in Tokyo and Hiroshima—to university status.

Nakahashi's announcement effectively brought a sense of completion to the Higher Normal School's university-promotion movement, whose members then gathered around the Meikeikai and shifted toward the focus of "serving as the alumni association's voice in society." The successes of the five schools sparked university-promotion movements at other specialized schools, meanwhile. Having seen how going after the Ministry of Education with strong, consistent demands was a viable way of securing the university designation, groups of graduates at various schools—or school principals, bowing to pressure from their graduates—began to descend on the Ministry with fervent pleas for promotion.

Kanō's resignation

With the university-promotion movement having quieted, Kanō gave the following address on December 28, 1919, at a special meeting of the Meikeikai, which had resolved to "ensure the promotion of our alma mater and establish the institution as an educational authority."

I joined this movement to stand with my students and the Meikeikai in the fight for the promotion of this institution, and fortunately, our efforts came to fruition. We successfully convinced the authorities to answer our calls. That the movement has come to this successful juncture fills me with overwhelming pride and gratification. Over the roughly twenty-four years that have passed since I first began my career at this school, I have put my position on the line numerous times in addressing a host of different challenges. When it came to the progress of general education, however, I knew that I could not make the decision a matter of my personal interest. But I now see the earnest passion of the Meikeikai. I now see the solidarity that binds you all together. I now know that the school is in good hands—and I now understand that I can leave my position at any time. I may stay on for another twenty or thirty years; I may bid farewell tomorrow.[12]

True to his word, Kanō stepped down as principal on January 9, 1920. Some time after tendering his resignation, he explained his decision to an audience of Tokyo Higher Normal School students:

First, I no longer needed to go on as principal because the promotion issue had come to a favorable conclusion. There were also people whom I was willing to recommend to serve as my successor.

Second, I felt I was no longer able to meet the demands of the position due to my diabetes, whose treatment requires my full attention.

Third, I wanted to travel to the West, see the postwar reconstruction efforts for myself, return home with a bounty of new knowledge, and apply those insights toward the betterment of general education. I also simply wanted to support the school from the outside, however small my contributions may be.[13]

The government accepted Kanō's resignation on January 16, and Kanō said goodbye to the Tokyo Higher Normal School—the institution where he had worked over three separate periods and a total of twenty-three years. In a letter that went out to relevant recipients upon his withdrawal, Kanō explained that his resignation had nothing whatsoever to do with the recent promotion issue and instead attributed his departure to a yearning to see the world, develop the Kodokan, and undergo treatment for his diabetes.[14]

The press was abuzz yet again after Kanō's announcement, voicing a mixture of praise and speculation. "It was an elegant exit," one article read, "like a bird taking flight from its familiar nest." Others, meanwhile, thought Kanō's resignation was either his way of taking responsibility for the promotion movement or a result of the Ministry of Education "recommending retirement." What Kanō's address and written statement make clear, however, was that he resigned on his own accord, chiefly out of concern for his health. He accepted the course of events, putting his mindset in metaphorical terms. "Developing the Higher Normal School was like pulling a heavy cart up a steep slope," he wrote, "and every last millimeter of progress took an arduous, backbreaking tug by an enormous team of pullers. One slip of the hand would send the cart tumbling down. If the story of the Higher Normal School were an ascent of Mount Fuji, all our years of toil would have only put us at the eighth or ninth station" [out of ten].[15] Kanō was ready to entrust the rest of the climb—the final trek to the summit of "normal university" recognition—to Miyake Yonekichi (1860–1929), his successor.

A special farewell ceremony for Principal Kanō took place on January 23. A young student representing the Tokyo Higher Normal School's affiliated elementary school gave a thank-you message. "I was always proud to tell people that 'my principal was Professor Kanō,'" he said. "We admire you, Professor Kanō, and we will never forget you."[16]

In July 1921, half a year after Kanō's resignation, the Tokyo Higher Normal School and the Meikeikai held a "Professor Kanō Appreciation Ceremony" that drew three hundred attendees. There, Miyake—the new principal—remembered his predecessor:

Looking back over your more than two decades at the Tokyo Higher Normal School, Professor Kanō, you recalled that the process of developing the institution was akin to "pulling a heavy cart up a steep slope." It was an apt metaphor, I must say. Yet I feel such a sense of regret in the fact that, all owing to your years of dedicated service, we are now on the cusp of becoming a university—but you are not here to witness that moment firsthand. The cart is at the eighth station, nearing the apex, but we have left our guide behind. . . . While you may have resigned your position, Professor Kanō, that departure was nothing more than a formal gesture. Your spirit breathes life into this school; your soul inhabits its walls.[17]

Evolving into the Tokyo University of Literature and Science

In July 1921, the Ministry of Education gave the newly formed Education Council its proposal for promoting five schools to university status. The Education Council, examining the bills for deliberation, began discussing the proposal to "establish single-faculty colleges with an educational focus on literature and science in Tokyo and Hiroshima." Deciding that the terms of the proposal might fail to do justice to what the higher normal schools could represent as full-fledged universities, the Council approved the bill with three conditions: that the specialized courses at the higher normal schools would be converted into universities of literature and science with attached higher normal schools; that the universities of literature and science would offer special education requisite to educator training; and that the protocols at the universities of literature and science would apply the same admission requirements to both graduates of the higher normal schools and graduates of high schools. The Council weighed the issue of university promotion in a series of discussions, trying to determine whether the new universities should be single-faculty colleges pursuant to the University Order, normal universities with the specific aim of training teachers, or universities of education. In the end, the Council decided to operate under the provisions of the University Order: creating universities of literature and science with attached higher normal schools.

An arch celebrating the school's promotion to university status (1929)

In April 1929, under a government-run system of universities for literature and science, new universities of literature and science (both with a single school of literature and science) opened in Tokyo and Hiroshima. The aftereffects of the Great Kanto Earthquake in 1923 stalled the process somewhat, but the end result was the culmination of the Tokyo Higher Normal School's promotion efforts: the Tokyo University of Literature and Science, an institution comprising faculties of education, philosophy, history, literature, mathematics, physics, chemistry, biology, geography, research, elective courses, and more.

University promotion had been the dream of countless students at the Tokyo Higher Normal School and the members of the Meikeikai. That dream finally became a reality—ten years after the movement gained its first momentum.

Notes:

1 Kaigo Tokiomi, ed., *Rinji Kyōiku Kaigi no kenkyū* [Examinations of the Special Council for Education] (Tokyo: University of Tokyo Press, 1960).

2 "Rinji Kyōiku Kaigi (sōkai) sokkiroku" [A shorthand record of the Special Council for Education (general meeting)] 3 (October 4, 1917), in *Shiryō: Rinji Kyōiku Kaigi* [Documentary materials on the Special Council for Education], vol. 2 (Tokyo: Ministry of Education, 1979).

3 "Rinji Kyōiku Kaigi (sōkai) sokkiroku" [A shorthand record of the Special Council for Education (general meeting)] 23 (September 17, 1918), in *Shiryō: Rinji Kyōiku Kaigi* [Documentary materials on the Special Council for Education], vol. 5 (Tokyo: Ministry of Education, 1979).

4 Executive Committee and Periodical Committee, "Shōkaku mondai no keika" [The development of the promotion issue], *Kōyūkai-shi* [School Council journal] 66 (1920; published by the Tokyo Higher Normal School School Council).

5 Kanō Jigorō, "Tōkyō Kōtō Shihan Gakkō shōkaku no yurai to sono shōrai ni tsuite" [On the origins and future prospects of the promotion of the Tokyo Higher Normal School], *Kyōiku* [Education] 480 (April 1923; published by the Meikeikai).

6 Aizawa Hiroshi, *Nihon kyōiku hyakunen-shi-dan* [A century of Japanese education] (Tokyo: Gakukei Tosho, 1952), 343.

7 Executive Committee Director, "Bokō shōkaku undō nichiroku" [A daily record of the promotion movement at my alma mater], *Kyōiku* [Education] 443 (March 1920; published by the Meikeikai).

8 Executive Committee and Periodical Committee, "Shōkaku mondai no keika."

9 Executive Committee Director, "Bokō shōkaku undō nichiroku."

10 "Sōritsu no keii o kataru (zadankai)" [The story behind our founding (roundtable)], in *Tōkyō Bunrika Daigaku heigaku kinen-shi* [A commemorative farewell to the Tokyo University of Literature and Science] (Tokyo: Tokyo University of Literature and Science, 1955), 83.

11 "Jōhoku Ōtsuka no jukkanen (kōki)" [Ten years in Jōhoku-Ōtsuka (later years), *Kōyūkai-shi* [School Council journal] 67 (Tokyo: Tokyo Higher Normal School School Council, 1920).

12 Executive Committee Director, "Bokō shōkaku undō nichiroku."

13 "Jōhoku Ōtsuka no jukkanen (kōki)."

14 Kanō Jigorō, "Tōkyō Kōtō Shihan Gakkō shōkaku mondai no shinsō to sessha jishoku no riyū to ni tsuite" [On the issue of the promotion of the Tokyo Higher Normal School and the reasons for my resignation], *Yūkō no katsudō* [The principle of effective activity] 6, no. 2 (February 1920).

15 Kanō Jigorō, "Kaiko rokujūnen" [Reflecting on the last sixty years], *Kyōiku* [Education] 457 (May 1921; published by the Meikeikai).

16 "Shaji" [Messages of gratitude], *Kōyūkai-shi* [School Council journal] 67 (Tokyo:

Tokyo Higher Normal School School Council, 1920).

17 "Kanō-sensei shaon-shiki" [The ceremony honoring Professor Kanō], *Kyōiku* [Education] 460 (August 1921).

.

Chapter 4

Educating international students

1. Educating international students at Kōbun Gakuin

Kanō's decision to admit Chinese students

Kanō Jigorō was the first educator in Japan to admit government-funded international students into an educational program after the start of the Meiji era. The students came from Qing China, which was looking to implement sweeping reforms in the wake of its defeat in the Sino-Japanese War. Aiming to effect change amid the flux of the times, the Chinese government recognized the pressing need for human resources capable of executing effective policies—and its eyes turned to Japan, which had emerged from the Meiji Restoration and achieved successful modernization. The government thus began sending numerous students across the East China Sea to gain valuable insight. At the request of the Chinese government, then-minister of foreign affairs and minister of education Saionji Kinmochi approached Kanō Jigorō about enrolling international students at the Tokyo Higher Normal School (where Kanō was principal), and Kanō agreed. That opened the door for the first cohort of international students at the school: a group of thirteen government-funded Chinese students in 1896. To accommodate the students, Kanō established a special academy in Kanda-Misaki-chō, Tokyo, put Honda Masujirō (a professor at the Tokyo Higher Normal School) in charge of the new establishment, and recruited several instructors to teach classes in Japanese and general subjects.

When seven of the students graduated in 1899 and the next cohort made its way to Japan, Kanō expanded the academy and christened it "Ekiraku Shoin." The curriculum for the international students centered on Japanese instruction, with linguistics scholar Mitsuya Shigematsu (1871–1923) responsible for the bulk of the teaching.

The steady stream of Chinese students coming to Japan to study under Kanō would continue to swell, prompting another expansion. In 1902, Kanō decided to move Ekiraku Shoin to Ushigome ward and rename it "Kōbun Gakuin," creating an institution that would provide international students with Japanese-language education and general-education classes at a secondary-school level. The academic framework included a three-year "general education course," which covered Japanese and general-education classes for Chinese students, a six-month "intensive normal course," which functioned as a teacher-training program, and a three-year "police course," which concentrated on knowledge and skills for aspiring police officers, among other offerings.

Kanō explained his reasoning for accepting Chinese students:

Over the last several decades, Japan has imported the civilization of the West in hopes of applying the merits thereof to compensate for its own shortcomings, drawing on that enlightenment to pursue reforms on myriad fronts, and taking great strides forward as a nation. Those efforts have met with a mix of success in certain areas and failure in others. For China, then, Japan's experiences of modernization hold invaluable lessons as the country undertakes its own transformations. . . . Thus, we must welcome Chinese students hoping to study in Japan; we must befriend them, guide them, show them kindness, and afford them every facility. . . . The learned individuals among us and those in the employ of China must not think merely of their own benefits but go forth with China's interests in mind. Only through a commitment to truly amiable neighborly relations may we reap benefits to call our own. It is for that very purpose that I have resolved to found Kōbun Gakuin, thereby affording facilities to those students who elect to depart China and pursue their studies in Japan.[1]

Kōbun Gakuin (courtesy of the Kodokan collection)

Kanō adopted a remarkably

objective, distanced perspective on Japan's modernization, whose entire narrative—from its triumphs to its shortcomings—he saw as a meaningful precedent for China to learn from. In exhorting Japan to think past its own interests, embody a commitment to China's advantage, and adopt the role of a "good neighbor," those components he deemed vital to Japan's benefit, Kanō laid out the basic elements of what he would later distill into the *jita kyōei* concept.

At the graduation ceremony for the first cohort of seven international students in 1900, Kanō addressed the group as follows:

> Some of you gentlemen will further your academic studies in this country, and some of you will go on to serve as interpreting officials in official capacities, be it at legations or consulates, or return to your native land and commence employment at an institution of learning. Whatever the path you may choose, you will undoubtedly transfer your knowledge of the Japanese language into practical application. The prospects of your future endeavors fill me with an immense sense of gratification and pride. Yet I urge all of you gentlemen never to be satisfied with your station. With the proficiency that you have heretofore gained in the Japanese language, you must strive for even deeper academic expertise and absorb the new knowledge that comes to light in the present day. Now, amid the eventful state of Oriental affairs, I hope to see you gentlemen devote yourselves both to your beloved homeland and to the peace and prosperity of the Eastern world.[2]

While Kanō intimated his joy in knowing that the graduating international students would apply their Japanese toward careers in academics and interpretation, he also urged them to sustain their studies and direct their energies toward the well-being of China and the regional international community.

Following Kanō's address, the graduates gave the following response.

Kōbun Gakuin (courtesy of the Kodokan collection)

The wisdom you have been so kind to impart unto us over the last three years, Sensei, has permeated our minds, thoroughly transforming us. How could we ever contain our excitement, our joy, at learning from such a fine teacher?[3]

As their words suggest, the international students had apparently grasped and embraced Kanō's teachings over the course of their three-year program.

At the time of its founding, the school had a set regimen of thirty-three hours per week for forty-three weeks per academic year. Covering a full three years of study, the curriculum for the general education course included a broad range of subjects:

Year 1: Morals (*shūshin*), Japanese, geography and history, *sangaku* (a form of geometry), science, and gymnastics
Year 2: The subjects from year 1 plus geometry, algebra, physics and chemistry, drawing, and English
Year 3 (Part 1): Morals, Japanese, trigonometry, geography and history, zoology, botany, English, and gymnastics
Year 3 (Part 2): Morals, Japanese, geometry, algebra, trigonometry, physics and chemistry, zoology, botany, drawing, English, and gymnastics

Besides its comprehensive curriculum, Kōbun Gakuin's athletic clubs represented another distinctive feature. "The school will establish athletic clubs to encourage instructors, staff, and students to engage in physical activity on a regular basis," read the school's announcement on its efforts. "The requisite funding for the creation of the clubs will be subsidized in part by the institution, and the maintenance expenses will be borne by the members of the corresponding clubs. . . . An Athletic Club Committee, comprising three members appointed by the president, shall not only aid in fostering the progress of the athletic clubs but also tend to matters of institution-wide hygiene and contribute to the development of athletic meets." With that organizational framework in place, Kōbun Gakuin formed archery, tennis, and distance-running clubs and began holding annual athletic meets. The school's various athletic activities naturally followed the model of the Tokyo Higher Normal School's School Council. For the international students at Kōbun Gakuin, education meant more than just book learning: physical education and sports were substantial pieces of the curriculum as well.

Those two key components of Kōbun Gakuin's activities took a variety of forms. Gymnastics classes, for example, consumed five hours a week—second only to Japanese in terms of actual in-class time—and often took place on the Tokyo Higher Normal School grounds or gymnasium. Judo also played a sizable role. As early as 1903, Kanō renovated the Kōbun Gakuin house into the Kodokan Ushigome Branch Dojo, giving international students an environment where they could learn judo. Thirty-three international students at Kōbun Gakuin—including Lu Xun (born Zhou Shuren, 1881–1936), who would go on to become a renowned Chinese writer—even joined the Kodokan. Kōbun Gakuin also began holding its own track-and-field meets in 1904. At his institution for international students, Kanō worked to create as many opportunities as possible for both the study of judo and a diverse mix of other physical activities.

Forging connections with the Chinese educational community
Kanō spent three months (July–October) in China in 1902 by official invitation. In addition to touring locations ranging from Beijing, Tianjin, and Shanghai to Anhui, Jiangsu, and Zhejiang, he met with Zhang Zhidong (1837–1909) as well as other political leaders, and a variety of educators to discuss efforts and methods to promote education. At the meetings, Kanō underscored the need for a moral dimension in general education and emphasized the importance of elementary-school teachers, along with explaining the art of judo and the process of mental training.

An issue of *Kokushi* (Patriot) ran an article detailing Kanō's thoughts and impressions on his visit to China. In the piece, Kanō noted that only a small minority in China felt that sweeping reforms were necessary; if proponents of change were to voice their position with any amount of urgency, they would inevitably encounter opposition from the authorities. What China needed, Kanō argued, was a means of putting the country on a natural, reliable course toward progress without sowing resistance among the people. In his eyes, the ideal approach for China was to interact more frequently with foreign countries and enhance the country's presence in the global community.[4] He also assigned the blame for China's decadence and corruption to the country's politics and education, criticized the old-fashioned system of imperial examinations as an "impractical exercise in useless learning," and warned of the grave consequences that improper educational methods could have. In his analyses of contemporary China, which were often biting in their appraisal, Kanō acknowledged that reforms could foment confusion and leave the country vulnerable to Western powers—and thus stressed the need for peaceful, gradualist reforms through educational measures and similar means. Some of the international students at Kōbun Gakuin called for a more violent revolution, but they always received the same message from their school president: Kanō consistently advocated for social change through education.

The Kōbun Gakuin teaching faculty
In 1906, Kōbun Gakuin had the following teaching faculty.[5]

- · 1 director
- · 85 professors and instructors
- · 33 administrative clerks
- · 18 assistants
- · 37 temporary assistants

The educational approach at Kōbun Gakuin was obviously influenced by the Higher Normal School. Kanō asked for help writing texts that would guide Kōbun Gakuin's educational reforms, and Tokyo Higher Normal School faculty members wrote a significant share of the documents.

The transcripts illustrate just how closely Tokyo Higher Normal School officials were involved in educating international students at Kōbun Gakuin. As part of its efforts, Kōbun Gakuin set to compiling a Japanese textbook. Led by Matsumoto Kamejirō (1866–1945) and Mitsuya Shigematsu, both instructors of Japanese at the institution, the team poured their energies into researching the usage of honorifics (keigo) and pedagogical techniques for grammar acquisition. Their efforts produced Nihongo kyōkasho (Japanese textbook) in three volumes, published in 1906. Not only was Kōbun Gakuin providing international students with in-class instruction, it was also a pioneering force in the methodology of Japanese-language education.

Kanō complemented the faculty members from the Higher Normal School with a hand-picked array of renowned educators. In 1904, for example, he hired Makiguchi Tsunesaburō (1871–1944)—a notable educator who had published Jinsei chirigaku (The geography of human life) in 1903, drawn attention to the field of human geography, and also served as a clerk for the Meikeikai (the

Tokyo Higher Normal School alumni association). *Jinsei chirigaku* would go on to be published in a Chinese edition, whose translation, incidentally, was the work of international students at Kōbun Gakuin.

To make its curriculum as relevant and actionable as possible, Kōbun Gakuin went to great lengths to align the content of its classes with conditions in contemporary China. When covering mineralogy in science classes, for example, instructors restricted their lectures to discussions of common minerals in China and tailored their teaching styles to international students learning science for the first time. Botany units began with a comparison of common plants in Japan and China. The institution's lessons in geography, a field that includes subdivisions like astronomical, natural, human, and continental geography, put the primary focus on Chinese geography. Detailing everything from China's topography, climate, and natural resources to its people, transportation, shipping, and trade, Kōbun Gakuin's geography coursework revolved around giving Chinese students an objective grasp of their home country. In world history classes, meanwhile, teachers provided a basic overview of colonization efforts in Asia and Africa—all part of an effort to open students' eyes to world affairs with particular implications for China and Japan.

Thanks to the pertinent, thorough education they received as a result of the institution's various reforms and pedagogical adjustments, many Kōbun Gakuin graduates enrolled at institutions of higher learning. Of the 140 students who enrolled at Kōbun Gakuin in 1906 (32 government-funded students and 105 privately funded students), at least 118 went on to continue their studies. The known destinations are as follows:[6]

· Former high schools and imperial universities: 19 (6 percent)
· Technical colleges: 42 (36 percent)
· Tokyo Higher Normal School: 7 (6 percent)
· Vocational schools (private universities): 44 (37 percent)
· Other schools: 6 (5 percent)

After Kōbun Gakuin made its reforms, Japanese institutions were the destinations of choice for many Kōbun Gakuin graduates. Law, law and politics, economics, and commerce were the most popular fields of advanced study, followed by education and medicine. In terms of sheer academic breadth, Kōbun Gakuin graduates were a diverse mix.

The effects of the reforms at the institution would prove to be short-lived, however. The number of students from China coming to Japan plummeted, due mostly to the discontinuation of short-term (intensive) study-abroad programs and also partially to national policies in different countries: China was trying to cut down on education expenses, while Western countries were embarking on projects to attract Chinese students. For Kōbun Gakuin, the ramifications of the changes were debilitating; the school soon found itself with no other option but to close its doors, which it did in July 1909. Over its brief time in operation, Kōbun Gakuin had admitted 7,192 enrollees and graduated 3,810 students. That small legion of graduates, so active in so many fields, undoubtedly had a significant impact on China's push toward modernization.

The closure of Kōbun Gakuin did not mark the end of Kanō's involvement in educating international students, however. The focus simply shifted to the Tokyo Higher Normal School, where Kanō continued to admit students from abroad.

2. International students at the Tokyo Higher Normal School

Admission

The Higher Normal School admitted its first group of eight international students in 1899. To make it easier for international students to continue their studies at Japanese universities and vocational schools, Kanō negotiated with the Ministry of Education, which eventually issued a notice in 1901 that enabled graduates of the Kōbun Gakuin's three-year general education course to enroll at Ministry-controlled schools like Kyoto Imperial University, Sapporo Agricultural College, Sendai Medical College, Okayama Medical Specialty School, the Higher Normal School, and the Women's Higher Normal School. The notice did stipulate some restrictions, however. If the number of applicants for admission ever exceeded the available international-student slots, the Ministry would implement a selection test to determine who would secure enrollment—entering a higher normal school without sitting for an examination was not always a possibility. Despite the system's hurdles, the selection-test process was how Lu Xun, for one, gained admission to Sendai Medical College.

The system's quotas created complications for China, which was hoping to send more students to Japan. Through discussions between the Chinese government and the Japanese Ministry of Education, a new, more lenient framework took form in 1907 with the signing of the "Special Treaty of Five Schools." Under the agreement, the "five schools"—namely, the First Higher School, Tokyo Higher Normal School, Tokyo Higher Technical School, Yamaguchi Higher School of Commerce, and Chiba Medical College—would admit a combined total of up to 165 international students per year for the ensuing fifteen years. At the Tokyo Higher Normal School, the enrollment cap was twenty-five international students per year from 1908 to 1922. That number occasionally climbed to around thirty in some years. While the number may not have amounted to a staggering total, the Tokyo Higher Normal School's relatively small student body—around 700 at the time—meant that its ratio of international students to Japanese students was by no means negligible.

The student population of the Tokyo Higher Normal School just before Kanō's resignation as principal in 1920 broke down as follows:[7]

1919
· Japanese students: 616
· Special students (from Korea): 7
· Foreign students (from the Republic of China): 113
· Total: 736

1920
· Japanese students: 665
· Special students (from Korea): 7
· Foreign students (from the Republic of China): 125
· Total: 797

The total number of Korean and Chinese students in 1919 came to 120, representing over 16 percent of the student body (736 students). That proportion held steady in 1920, with 132 of 797 students (over 16 percent) hailing from outside Japan.

When the Xinhai Revolution (Chinese Revolution) erupted in 1911, the tumult threw the existing Chinese government into disarray. Chinese students in Japan suddenly confronted the possibility that the instability would bring an end to their state-sponsored funding. Recognizing their concerns, Kanō called a meeting of the Chinese students at the Higher Normal School. The group gathered in a lecture hall, where Kanō assured them that he would take care of the situation—that they should stay in Japan and continue their studies, even if it meant him paying their tuition out of his own pocket. It was a moving gesture, a clear sign of Kanō's generosity and commitment to his students.

Graduation and career development

According to the Tokyo Higher Normal School's alumni association roster, the *Meikeikai kyakuin meibo*,[8] many Chinese students became university professors or took positions at the Chinese Ministry of Education after graduating and returning to China. Given the positions of influence they often occupied, the Chinese graduates of the Tokyo Higher Normal School likely had a hand in shaping education in the Republic of China. A look at the third department of the general-education arm of the Republic's Ministry of Education makes that influence apparent: all four officials in the department had graduated from Kōbun Gakuin, and three had completed their studies at the Tokyo Higher Normal School. The four graduates held significant sway, too, as their department oversaw the operations of normal schools across the Republic. The Tokyo Higher Normal School's connection to the educational system in China was clear, with numerous graduates leaving an obvious imprint on the pedagogical landscape. Below are several examples.

Fan Yuanlian (1876–1927) served three separate terms as minister of education of the Republic of China, occupying the office for over three years in total. After making his way to Japan in 1899, Fan eventually enrolled at the Tokyo Higher Normal School. When Kōbun Gakuin opened in 1902, he helped interpret lectures into Chinese, suggesting that Kanō trusted him with conveying knowledge. Fan then headed back to China in 1905 and forged a career in education. Serving in successive leadership roles, he worked to pave the way for Japanese-style normal education in China. Fan's obvious prowess in the educational realm earned him another top-level appointment after the country's transition into the Republic of China: as minister of education, he continued to construct the institutional infrastructure for normal education and a variety of other educational frameworks. Fan even wrote the lyrics to the school song for Beijing Advanced Normal School, which later became Beijing Normal University—the institution where he would serve as president during the later years of his life.

Tian Han (1898–1968), born in Changsha, Hunan Province, enrolled in the English department at the Tokyo Higher Normal School in 1917 and went on to become a prominent literary figure after returning home. An enduring hallmark of his career was the text of the song "March of the Volunteers," the theme of the 1935 film *Children of Troubled Times*. The song's legacy has transcended mere cinema: it has also been the national anthem of the People's Republic of China since 1982. Whenever a Chinese athlete takes the podium at the Olympics, a song with words by a former Tokyo Higher Normal School student fills the air.

On Kanō's advice, Yang Changji (1871–1920) followed his studies at Kōbun Gakuin by enrolling at the Tokyo Higher Normal School. Upon graduating, he then studied philosophy, ethics, and education in Scotland before returning home and devoting himself to bettering the country through education. Yang taught at Hunan First Normal University, where he met a young Mao Zedong (1893–1976) in 1913. According to Mao, Yang had a considerable influence on him—the future founding father of the People's Republic of China would go on to call Yang a mentor during his formative years.

Both Yang Changji and Chen Duxiu (1879–1942), another former student at the Tokyo Higher Normal School, helped mold Mao Zedong's perspective on physical education. That influence manifests itself in "Study of Physical Education," a piece by Mao that appeared in *Xin qingnian* (New Youth). Not only did the text mention Kanō Jigorō by name, but it also referenced some of the same tropes that Kanō often employed in discussing the subject:

In today's civilized nations, Germany is the most advanced [in terms of physical education]. The popularity of fencing spreads in the entire country. Japan has its samurai and recently, influenced by China, judo. They are most impressive. . . .

Physical education supplements ethical and academic education. Yet, virtue and wisdom both rely on the body. Without the body, there can be neither virtue nor wisdom. . . .

Virtue is truly valuable. It is order and equity among men. Yet what is the lodge of virtue? The body is the vessel of knowledge and the lodge of virtue. . . .

Physical education should be of primary importance. Once the body is strong, one can advance vigorously and effectively in the academic and the ethical aspects. . . .

Famous athletes in the West, such as America's Roosevelt, Germany's Sandow, and Japan's Kano, all attained the greatest of strength from the weakest of bodies. [9]

Certain themes of Kanō Jigorō's philosophy run through Mao's arguments, especially in his assertions that social order hinges on virtue and that studying morals is the path to interpersonal equity. The article also makes mention of long-distance running, which Mao considered the best method of developing physical stamina—another belief that he shared with Kanō.

The Tokyo Higher Normal School also graduated a number of Korean students, one of whom even went on to become the president of South Korea: Choi Kyu-hah (1919–2006). After completing his studies in the English department at the Tokyo Higher Normal School in 1941, Choi became a professor at the Seoul University College of Education in 1945, took a government job the following year, served as the country's minister of foreign affairs from 1967 to 1971, and later occupied the position of prime minister from 1976 to 1979. His ascendancy up the leadership ladder culminated in 1979, when he became acting president in the wake of then-president Pak Chong-hui's death. Although a coup d'état by Chun Doo-hwan and his allies brought Choi's administration to an end less than a year after its formation, Choi's many accomplishments as foreign minister made his legacy a lasting one. Choi remained a popular figure in South Korea for reasons outside his public influence, too; after his political career was over, Choi focused on his private life and stayed home with his wife, who was suffering from Alzheimer's.

Sports

Sports, of course, were a central focus at the Tokyo Higher Normal School under Kanō. A look at issues of the *Kōyūkai-shi* (the Higher Normal School's School Council journal) between 1909 and 1915 reveals that international students participated in club athletics along with their Japanese counterparts.

The journal's recap of the 1909 track-and-field meet, for example, noted that Japanese students were cheering on their fellow international students by name during the "international student 200-yard dash" event.

Once that was through, a balloon with a banner hanging under it announced the next event: the 32nd international student 200-yard dash. The venue buzzed with excitement, with a throng of spectators on hand to watch the race. When the starting pistol fired and the runners began streaking down the track, the crowd erupted in volleys of cheers: "Go, Sun!" "Faster, Dong!" "Off you go, Kwon!" Chiang emerged victorious in the end, besting the field by ten meters.[10]

Eighteen Chinese students also participated in the aquatic (boating) athletic meet on May 11, 1909, the second sports event they had competed in that year.

In 1910, twenty-nine Chinese students joined the School Council. The Chinese members were able to take part in all student-association activities, including its athletic clubs; records indicate that the student soccer team indeed had Chinese players.

At the Tokyo Higher Normal School soccer tournament on January 31, 1909, a group of twenty-two Chinese students also faced off, eleven to a side, and played to a 0–0 draw. A match between Chinese students also took place at another soccer tournament in November 1909. January 1911 saw yet another "international friendly," so to speak, pitting the international students from the arts faculty against the international students from the sciences faculty. The same pattern held in 1912 and 1913, as well, with the soccer tournaments in both years featuring contests between Chinese students. The soccer club, it certainly appears, had a healthy complement of international players.

While Kōbun Gakuin closed in 1909, international students continued to enroll at the Tokyo Higher Normal School. There, they took active part in a variety of sports, including soccer, and eventually went from competing on an intramural basis to taking on teams from other schools. The first inter-school matches took place in June and November 1910, when the Tokyo Higher Normal School hosted a team from the Tokyo Prefectural Toshima Normal School. The June game went to the international students by a score of 1–0. The Tokyo Higher Normal School squad appeared to be on the verge of a repeat victory in November, but the Toshima Normal School rallied and salvaged a split of the two contests. According to the accounts of the matches, the Tokyo Higher Normal School team had a boisterous cheering section of around eighty other international students—including students from other schools.

The School Council Journal included a brief story on the match between the international students and the Toshima Normal School in the fall of 1910:

On the thirteenth of the same month, a team from the Toshima Normal School and a squad of Chinese students from the Tokyo Higher Normal School met on the athletic ground at two o'clock in the afternoon for their second soccer match of the year. After the Chinese squad won the spring tilt at a score of one-nil, the Toshima team practiced enthusiastically, aiming to avenge their loss, while the Chinese students continued to polish their play, refusing to relent. Both sides headed into the contest determined to win, and the competitive fire filling the air was palpable.

By the time Referee Kojima signaled for kickoff at two o'clock, a mass of supporters, seventy to eighty strong, had gathered to cheer the Tokyo Higher Normal School side on. The Chinese students dominated the match at the outset, but a spurt of pressure from the Toshima strikers created enough confusion in the home side's backfield for the visitors to capitalize and put the ball in the net for a 1–0 lead. The second half saw the Chinese squad make a sustained offensive push, but nary a shot managed to make it past the goalkeeper. Toshima held the line, emerging victorious by the score of 1–0.[11]

In June 1913, the Tokyo Higher Normal School's international students also took on the Taihei Club—a team of Korean students in Japan—and came out of the match with a 2–0 victory. Beyond the score, however, was the captivating nature of the game: Chinese students versus Korean students on a Japanese field.

The last mention of an international-student match in the School Council Journal was a January 1915 contest against the Saitama Prefectural Normal School, another 2–0 win for the Tokyo Higher Normal School squad. Given their solid record in inter-school play, the Chinese students appear to have been a relatively skilled, formidable team by the mid-1910s.

A 1909 article in the School Council Journal highlighted another dimension of the international students' athletic activities—the support they received from their fellow Japanese students:

The weather was clear and mild, with hardly a breeze to speak of. At seven-thirty in the morning, our fine band of international students made its way onto the pitch. It was a marvel to bear witness to the transformations they had made. While they had been stiff and sluggish upon their first arrival in Japan, occasionally drawing dismissive sneers from Japanese onlookers, they had evinced such an indominable spirit and tackled their training with such fervor that they now rivaled those of their adopted home in skill and physical prowess.

It is our sincerest hope that, upon culminating their studies and making their triumphant returns home, our international students make themselves of benefit both through their knowledge and on the athletic front.[12]

Starting off with little more than an average command of soccer skills, the international students at the Tokyo Higher Normal School gradually trained and developed their techniques until they were proficient enough to hold their own with higher-level Japanese players. Besides praising the athletic development among the international students, the author also expressed hopes to see the students apply their training toward nurturing a physical-education culture at home. The cross-cultural bonds linking the Japanese students and their Chinese counterparts may have never formed if not for the activities of the Tokyo Higher Normal School School Council, which Principal Kanō was very much invested in.

The *Meikeikai kyakuin kaiin meibo* also noted the career paths of the first international members of the Tokyo Higher Normal School soccer club, many of whom went into education.

Zhu Wenxiong (1883–1961; a graduate of the chemistry department in 1910) and Chen Yinghuang (natural history, 1912) took personnel positions in the Ministry of Education's National Institute for Compilation and Translation. Sun Bing (natural history, 1912) also worked for the Ministry of Education, serving as a secretary. University-level education was another popular route, with Huang Jiyu (mathematics, 1910) teaching at Shandong University, Shu Zhiliu (English, 1912) transitioning from journalism to university teaching, and Tang Tingzhi (natural history, 1912) teaching at the College of Agriculture. It would be safe to assume that these and other graduates brought their athletic pursuits back home with them, from soccer to the other sports that they had learned and practiced in Japan.

In many cases, Chinese graduates of the Tokyo Higher Normal School embarked on important educational careers in their home country—and they played pivotal roles in enhancing their nation's framework for normal education. Their time under Kanō's tutelage also exposed them to a diverse mix of athletics, which helped unite students across national boundaries. More than a century ago, then, the Tokyo Higher Normal School was home to an active, international brand of educational exchange. It all harmonized with Kanō's notion of progress: knowledge, physical education, and athletics helped foster deeper insights and stronger virtues in individuals, who together formed stronger communities, which together had the ability to reshape society as a whole.

Notes:

1   Kanō Jigorō, "Shinkoku" [Qing China], *Kokushi* [Patriot] 44 (1902).

2   Kanō-sensei Denki Hensan-kai, ed., *Kanō Jigorō* (Tokyo: Kodokan, 1964), 168.

3   "Shinkoku ryūgakusei sotsugyō-shiki" [The graduation ceremony for students from Qing China], *Kokushi* [Patriot] (21) 1899.

4   Kanō Jigorō "Shinkoku jun'yū shokan (ichi)" [Thoughts on a tour of Qing China (I)], *Kokushi* [Patriot] 50 (1902).

5   Kōbun Gakuin catalog (1906).

6   Kageyama Masahiro, "Kōbun Gakuin ni okeru Chūgoku-jin ryūgakusei no tenkai" [Chinese students at Kōbun Gakuin], in *Kyōiku no naka no minzoku: Nihon to Chūgoku* [Peoples in the context of education: Japan and China], ed. Saitō Akio, Doi Masaoki, and Honda Kōei, 154–156.

7   Tokyo Higher Normal School catalogs (1919, 1920).

8   Meikeikai, *Meikeikai kyakuin kaiin meibo* [The official roster of Meikeikai members and guest members] (1930).

9   Mao Zedong, "Study of Physical Education," *Xin qingnian* [New youth] 3, no. 2 (1917).

10 "Rikujō daiundōkai" [The track-and-field meet], *Kōyūkai-shi* [The School Council Journal] 20 (1909).

11 "Kōyūkai hōkoku: Shūkyū-bu" [School Council report: Soccer club], *Kōyūkai-shi* [The School Council Journal] 21 (1910).

12 "Kōyūkai hōkoku: Shūkyū-bu" [School Council report: Soccer club], *Kōyūkai-shi* [The School Council Journal] 18 (1909).

Part III

Kanō Jigorō
on the international stage

Kanō Jigorō doing an interview for NBC (1936) (courtesy of the Kodokan collection)

Chapter 1

Kanō Jigorō and the West

1. Lafcadio Hearn and the spread of judo

Kanō meets Hearn

In September 1891, Kanō Jigorō moved to Kumamoto to take up his position as principal of the Fifth High School. It was there that he would meet prolific writer Koizumi Yakumo (known in the West by his birth name, Lafcadio Hearn), whom he hired to teach English. Not only did Hearn become close friends with Kanō, but he also observed judo and penned treatises about judo techniques and principles of thought. Framing an Oriental martial art through the lens of an incisive Occidental intellect, Hearn's writings were instrumental in introducing judo to the West.

Lafcadio Hearn (1850–1904), born in Greece and raised in Ireland, took the name Koizumi Yakumo upon becoming a naturalized citizen of Japan. After first arriving in Japan in 1890 at the age of forty, Hearn married Koizumi Setsu, the daughter of a samurai from the former Matsue *han* (domain). During his career in Japan, he taught English and English literature at Matsue Middle School, the Fifth High School in Kumamoto, Tokyo Imperial University, and Waseda University, among other institutions. He also wrote numerous works on Japan in English ranging from personal impressions and essays to discussions of folklore, including *Kwaidan: Stories and Studies of Strange Things*; *Kokoro: Hints and Echoes of Japanese Inner Life*; and *In Ghostly Japan*. The meeting between Hearn and Kanō in Kumamoto opened the doors for a deep exploration of jujutsu (judo) in the English language.

Hearn spent three years in Kumamoto, arriving in November 1891 and leaving in November 1894. Even before setting foot in Japan, he had developed an interest in the country. He not only saw compelling dimensions in modes of Japanese life, but he also had a clear fondness for the Japanese people, and was awed by the country's breathtaking natural beauty. At the same time, however, Hearn's delicate sensitivities made him susceptible to disillusionment. While he found the innocent, unvarnished simplicity of Japanese society endearing, he could see that the rising tides of efficiency-first thinking would wipe away the purity that so enchanted him about the place. The thought of Japan's warmhearted kindness disappearing in the face of rationalization saddened and disgusted Hearn—sentiments that he made clear in letters to friends but never in his published works. Whatever his private feelings were, Hearn poured his extraordinary literary talents into providing the world with a revealing glimpse of Japanese customs, traditions, and folk heritage.[1]

Kanō recruits Hearn to teach at the Fifth High School

In April 1890, Hearn settled in Matsue, a city in the former province of Izumo (now the eastern part of Shimane Prefecture). His early experiences there were formative, bringing him into contact with the natural landscapes of Japan, the warmth and sensitivity of the people, and his soon-to-be wife, Setsu. Hearn spent just more than a year in Matsue teaching English at Matsue Middle School, but he quickly uprooted himself and moved to Kumamoto. Kanō Jigorō had handpicked him to teach at the Fifth High School in Kumamoto, and Hearn took up the offer. Kanō later recalled:

Aside from the many unremarkable things I did during my time as principal, there were a small handful of episodes that merit special note. One was convincing Lafcadio Hearn to leave his position at a middle school in Shimane Prefecture and come to instruct pupils at the Fifth High School.[2]

Hearn eagerly accepted Kanō's invitation. Despite having just settled in Matsue a year prior and apparently finding his adopted surroundings full of charm, Hearn jumped at the chance to relocate. One might wonder why he would leave his first home—and his wife's hometown—behind so quickly. As it turned out, Matsue's chilly climate offset its allure. Hearn often corresponded with Basil Hall Chamberlain (1850–1935), an esteemed British linguist and Japanologist who taught at Tokyo Imperial University. Chamberlain helped lay the roots of modern linguistics and developed the field of Oriental comparative linguistics; he was a valuable source of support for Hearn. When Hearn was in search of a position in Japan, for example, Chamberlain's goodwill helped him secure employment at Matsue Middle School. The two exchanged numerous letters, which shed valuable light on Hearn's inclinations. During his stay in Matsue, Hearn wrote Chamberlain saying that he was hoping to find a position somewhere else—and what should arrive but Kanō's offer to join the teaching staff in Kumamoto. For Hearn, the timing was impeccable. In November 1891, he set off to teach English under Principal Kanō at the Fifth High School. The encounter came three months after Kanō had begun his stint in Kumamoto. Hearn was forty-one, Kanō eleven years his junior. After that, their paths would remain in relatively close alignment. Kanō left to assume the principalship of the Tokyo Higher Normal School in 1893; Hearn resigned his position at the Fifth High School in 1894 and eventually made his way to Tokyo in 1896, with a stay in Kobe in between. He proceeded to teach English literature at Tokyo Imperial University and Waseda University in Tokyo, where he would spend the rest of his life.

In an interview twenty-five years after Hearn's death, Kanō remembered his time in Kumamoto and his impressions of Hearn:

Hearn was, as many know, a highly unusual man, blessed with a literary mind with few rivals in the Anglosphere, a thoroughly singular individual in all respects. I was acquainted with him, so I also knew his wife, who had grown up in a samurai family in Shimane Prefecture, and her familiarity with traditional propriety may have had an effect on him. Be it wearing traditional Japanese clothes on a daily basis or smoking a traditional Japanese pipe, he embodied Japanese taste. He was extraordinarily talented in the pedagogy of the English language and had an immense knowledge of English literature, of course, but he also conducted himself in a remarkably idiosyncratic, eccentric fashion. I remember the time we attended some sort of celebratory function at the [Imperial Japanese Army's] 6th Division headquarters in Kumamoto, and the governor, school principals, judges, and numerous other elites were there, as well. Every military officer was in uniform; every civil servant was in a frock coat; seemingly every single guest was clad in formal Western attire. Only one man was dressed in Japanese kimono, complete with a family crest: Lafcadio Hearn.[3]

Out of the East

Hearn's *Out of the East* (Boston: Houghton Mifflin, 1895) contains the author's ruminations on jujutsu. An abridged translation of Hearn's jujutsu discourse eventually appeared in the fifth issue of *Kokushi* (Patriot) in 1899, making the author's unique viewpoint more accessible to Japanese readership. The translation was by Kanō Kotarō, who was the firstborn son of Kanō Jigorō's eldest brother and himself a standout student at the Kanō Juku. Titled "Seigan ni eizeru jūdō" (Judo in the Western eye), the Japanese version of Hearn's writings begins with a translator's foreword explaining that Hearn was the first non-Japanese person to take significant interest in—and write insightfully about—Kanō's judo practices:

Since the Meiji Restoration, I would surmise that as many as one thousand foreign guests have traversed this land, either for the purposes of trade, in the calling of missionary work, or by means of a round-the-world voyage. Some have esteemed the art of Japan; some have extolled the beauties of our scenery. None, however, has discussed the ancient Japanese martial arts or understood the way of *bushidō*, nay even speculated vaguely thereon, much less expounded on jujutsu and the infinite applications thereof. Judo, meanwhile, represents an evolved form of jujutsu, an elegant sublimation of the ancient art. Only to one versed in jujutsu would the lofty concepts of judo be discernible. In all of the tomes that those travelers in the Orient have penned, I have yet to come across even one mention of the word "judo." Hence my sheer amazement when I perused *Out of the East* to find a thorough, meticulous discussion of judo, with its writer, Lafcadio Hearn, devoting a full sixty pages to the art with impassioned sympathy and piercing insight. It was as if by fate, it seemed, that I came across the passage, which filled me with a delight I had theretofore never encountered, and I later met Hearn at Yōrō Falls by some felicitous circumstance in the sweltering heat of high summer. As Hearn refers to his subject as "jujutsu" ["jiujitsu" in the actual text of *Out of the East*] throughout, however, some might harbor doubts that his treatise does, in fact, concern judo. What follows is my reasoning for interpreting the passage, so unlike any of its predecessors, to be an exposition of which judo is the primary theme.

When the former president of this association [Kanō Jigorō] was principal at the Fifth High School in Kumamoto, Hearn assumed a position

With students from the Fifth High School (Kanō at center; Hearn facing left), 1893 (courtesy of the Kodokan collection)

lecturing in the subjects of English and English literature at the school. To Hearn thus came frequent opportunities to observe judo at the school's dojo, the Zuihō-kan, and pose any questions he might have to the master himself. In doing so, Hearn gained a refined understanding of the art, perceiving the depths of the practice with remarkable clarity. In his piece on "jujutsu," Hearn forms his introduction around the Zuihō-kan before commencing his exposition of the topic at hand. One could very well presume, then, that the "jujutsu" to which Hearn refers is, in fact, none other than Kodokan judo.[4]

Kanō Kotarō continued, noting Hearn's prolific interests. "Hearn's pen spilled torrents of words across the page, touching on themes far and wide, even discussing the modes of Japanese life, the products of her institutions and civilization, and a litany of other topics lying on the fringes of his primary subjects." He went on to write, "So, in this abridged version, I will only translate the vital, exceptional portions of the work. I hope that readers understand my reasoning in doing so." Besides offering a discourse on jujutsu, Hearn also touched on Japanese customs and practices. To situate Hearn in the context of Kanō, however, the key question is how Hearn saw jujutsu.

Hearn's perceptions of jujutsu
Hearn wrote about jujutsu at length in *Out of the East*.

Jiujutsu is not an art of display at all: it is not a training for that sort of skill exhibited to public audiences; it is an art of self-defence in the most exact sense of the term; it is an art of war. The master of that art is able, in one moment, to put an untrained antagonist completely *hors de combat*. By some terrible legerdemain he suddenly dislocates a shoulder, unhinges a joint, bursts a tendon, or snaps a bone,—without any apparent effort. He is much more than an athlete: he is an anatomist. And he knows also touches that kill—as by lightning. But this fatal knowledge he is under oath never to communicate except under such conditions as would render its abuse almost impossible. Tradition exacts that it be given only to men of perfect self-command and of unimpeachable moral character.

The fact, however, to which I want to call attention is that the master of jiujutsu never relies upon his own strength. He scarcely uses his own strength in the greatest emergency. Then what does he use? Simply the strength of his antagonist. The force of the enemy is the only means by which that enemy is overcome. The art of jiujutsu teaches you to rely for victory solely upon the strength of your opponent; and the greater his strength, the worse for him and the better for you. I remember that I was not a little astonished when one of the greatest teachers of jiujutsu (Kanō Jigorō, as Hearn indicates in an accompanying note) told me that he found it extremely difficult to teach a certain very strong pupil, whom I had innocently imagined to be the best in the class. On asking why, I was answered: "Because he relies upon his enormous muscular strength, and uses it." The very name "jiujutsu" means to conquer by yielding.[5]

Hearn ostensibly had a clear understanding of jujutsu's fundamental core: the principle of gentleness, adaptability, and suppleness; or, in his words, conquering by yielding. What *Out of the East* also reveals, however, is that Hearn saw more than just a martial art in jujutsu (and judo). In his eyes, jujutsu was a window on the soul of the new, modernized Japan in the aftermath of the Meiji Restoration.

The modernization of Japan and the spirit of jujutsu
Hearn argues that the spirit at the heart of jujutsu is what enabled Japan to bring itself into the world of modernity:

Much more than a science of defence is this jiujutsu [upon closer examination]: it is a philosophical system; it is an economical system; it is an ethical system . . . and it is, above all, the expression of a racial genius as yet but faintly perceived by those Powers who dream of further aggrandisement in the East. . . . That Japan might only be practising jiujutsu, nobody supposed for a moment . . . such beliefs were due to an unavoidable but absolute ignorance of the character of the race.

Twenty-five years ago,—and even more recently,—foreigners might have predicted, with every appearance of reason, that Japan would adopt not only the dress, but the manners of the Occident; not only our means of rapid transit and communication, but also our principles of architecture; not only our industries and our applied science, but likewise our metaphysics and our dogmas. Some really believed that the country would soon be thrown open to foreign settlement; that Western capital would be tempted by extraordinary privileges to aid in the development of various resources; and even that the nation would eventually proclaim, through Imperial Edict, its sudden conversion to what we call Christianity. But such beliefs were due to an unavoidable but absolute ignorance of the character of the race,—of its deeper capacities, of its foresight, of its immemorial spirit of independence. That Japan might only be practising jiujitsu, nobody supposed for a moment: indeed at that time nobody in the West had ever heard of jiujutsu.

And, nevertheless, jiujitsu it all was. Japan adopted a military system founded upon the best experience of France and Germany, with the result that she can call into the field a disciplined force of 250,000 men, supported by a formidable artillery. She created a strong navy, comprising some of the finest cruisers in the world;—modelling her naval system upon the best English and French teaching. She made herself dockyards under French direction, and built or bought steamers. . . . She modelled her public-school system upon a thorough study of the best results obtained [abroad] . . . but regulated it so as to harmonise perfectly with her own institutions. She founded a police system upon a French model, but shaped it to absolute conformity with her own particular social requirements. . . .

Despite her railroad and steamship lines, her telegraphs and telephones, her postal service and her express companies, her steel artillery and magazine-rifles, her universities and technical schools, she remains just as Oriental to-day as she was a thousand years ago. She has been able to remain herself, and to profit to the utmost possible limit by the strength of the enemy. She has been, and still is, defending herself by the most admirable system of intellectual self-defence ever heard of,—by a marvellous national jiujutsu.[6]

To Hearn, then, Japan's post-Restoration push into modernization was a crystallization of jujutsu's core principles of adaptability and suppleness. The Japanese had held fast to their traditional Oriental spirit, never straying from that fundamental mentality, but still willingly absorbed the merits of Occidental ways and practices to their advantage. That modernization process was an outgrowth of the jujutsu spirit, Hearn posited: using an opponent's force to one's own benefit. That was the very mindset that enabled Japan to uphold and protect its own traditions while at the same time allowing it to elevate its standing as a civilization.

In *Out of the East*, Hearn presented jujutsu as a vital engine of Japanese modernization, a tradition with an influence on events unfolding at the time. Kanō's emerging practice of judo now had a Western audience, laying international roots that would later flourish.

2. Kanō's first European voyage

Touring the educational arena in Europe

When he was thirty years of age, serving as a professor at Gakushūin, Kanō ventured abroad for the first time on a voyage to Europe. On September 15, 1889, he set off for Europe aboard the *Caledonian*, a French steamer operated by Messageries Maritimes, from the port of Yokohama. He was traveling with a delegation of the Imperial Household Ministry to tour Europe and learn more about the educational practices in use there.

At the time, Kanō was embroiled in a heated philosophical standoff with Gakushūin chancellor Miura Gorō. It was a deadlock, with neither Kanō nor Miura willing to back down from their respective educational stances. Kanō loathed working under someone he never saw eye to eye with—and Miura, too, wanted nothing to do with his adversary. Before the *Caledonian* shipped out, Miura gave Kanō a leave of absence, effectively dismissing him from his position as assistant principal.

Essentially in exile from Gakushūin, Kanō departed for Europe at something of a loss—he needed to take serious inventory and think hard about how he would chart out the rest of his life. He was free of the weighty onus of his duties at the school, which ranged from his research in political science and economics to his status as assistant principal, and was now at liberty to steer his career any way he chose. What would he make his life's work? How would he channel his youthful, energetic spirit into that pursuit? As Kanō's internal

Kanō Jigorō around the age of twenty-three (courtesy of the Kodokan collection)

dialogue deepened, the tour of the educational scene in Europe gave him the answers he was seeking so fervently.

Anchors aweigh, the *Caledonian* hit the seas, and Kanō was off on his first voyage to Europe. On the opposite shore lay Western society, a new milieu that Kanō and his fellow travelers were about to take in. According to extant records, Kanō departed the Port of Yokohama on September 15, 1889, and returned on January 16, 1891. The trip therefore spanned a total of one year and four months. On that lengthy sojourn, Kanō chronicled his first overseas experiences in a diary—and the entries were in English. Kanō was an able writer in the language, wielding a command that had already made an impression on his classmates years before; he even frequently wrote to his Japanese friends in English. His compositional skills were just one facet of his English aptitude. His penmanship, too, was so exceptional that a foreign acquaintance suggested he use his own writing as a model for others to emulate. Kanō kept English diaries throughout his life; the one he wrote on his first voyage was just the beginning.

Having mastered Tenjin Shin'yō-ryū jujutsu, attained proficiency in Kitō-ryū jujutsu, and established Kodokan judo, Kanō had a youthful verve, his own school of martial arts, and a ticket to Europe. The diaries provide a window on how judo figured into his survey mission.

Kanō's English diaries

The Kodokan eventually assumed possession of Kanō's English diaries from the Kanō estate and made the documents part of the Kodokan Library collection. The pages seem to be from small, unlined notebooks or pocketbooks, measuring roughly 7 by 10 inches in size. The first entry is dated September 14, 1889, and the last December 31, 1931.

The English diaries were a collection of small notebooks marked I and II, but parts of volume II are nowhere to be found. The first contains the entries from September 14, 1889, to March 23, 1890, the last of which Kanō composed in Berlin.

The *Caledonian* left port on September 15, 1889, which means that Kanō jotted his first entry on the eve of his departure. Why he started the diary on the day before his voyage is an unknown, but the early timing certainly suggests that Kanō was itching to start logging his trip as soon as possible.

The Kodokan was kind enough to provide access to the journals (within a limited scope, given the privacy concerns inherent to diaries). The entries pertaining to Kanō's European expedition—which have never appeared in publication since their writing more than 120 years ago—represent an illuminating firsthand account, a primary source of incredible value.

The diaries are old, the pages not always in optimal condition, the words not always easily legible or properly spelled. That said, they merit inclusion here due to three distinct, important factors: their value as previously untapped primary documents on the history of judo; their academic significance in offering a new, first-person historical perspective; and the unique, distinguishing dimension they offer in commemorating Kanō's 150th birthday. While the authors understand that the journals may be excessively long at times, the entries' value as new sources for historical study—and firsthand accounts, no less—far outweighs any potential drawbacks. The diaries, in a sense, provide a direct interface with a young Kanō, a resource unlike any other.

What follows is a selection of entries from Kanō's diaries, which shed valuable light on his meticulous attention to detail and forward-looking insight.

[Note: Illegible words, unidentifiable names, and explanatory notes are given in brackets.]

September 14, 1889
Rose up about 3 in the morning after one or two hours' sleep in the upstairs. Returned to order all the bits of papers and [diverse?] furnitures which were scattered about in different rooms. Gave directions as to the places where

those things should be kept. Then put into a trunk and a portion [illegible] all the luggage I had to carry with me. Then I met with several friends who came to see me away whom was Mr. Miyauchi of the Police Department who entrusted to me a number of Japanese swords to be sent to [Zushiza-ki?]. Then as the time came for my going the Palace for Haiyetsu [likely a variation of *haietsu*, Japanese for "audience with the Emperor"] I went out, going to the Kunaidaijin [*kunai-daijin*, or Imperial Household Minister], Nagasaki, Nanma [Nomura?] and Mishima in my way. Haiyetsu and Sanpai [*sanpai*, or worship] in the Kashikodokoro [*kashikodokoro*, or palace sanctuary] about 11 o'clock in the morning then after half a hour's talk in the office of the Kunaishō [Imperial Household Ministry] with Nagasaki, Sugi, Tsutsumi etc. I went to bid adieu to Harunomiya. He being absent I came back leaving a word to the [illegible]. . . .

Then I came back and saw at my house besides Okura [Saigo?] and others Mr. [Kensaku?], Kondō and Iwanami the last of who were in my house since the day before. Then came Hayashi, Iijima and in a moment Hijikata, the Kunai Daijin [Imperial Household Minister] came to bid farewell and returned after a few minutes talk with me. I dined with the rest. Shidachi [likely Shidachi Tetsujirō, a prominent banker] also came to see me at half past two.

I left my house committing the care of the house and others matters to those who were remaining. I first went to see Mr. and Mrs. Nango the latter of whom was already absent having gone to see me at Shimbashi. After more than half an hours' talk with my sister I went to see Mr. and Mrs. Yanagi both of whom were still at home. After a few minutes talk went [left him?] and went to Shimbashi. It was about 20 [30?] minutes to the time the train leaves the station (4.45) pm. From a distance I could see crowds of people waiting to see me[.] For most of all were [ranged?] hundreds of people, people all clad in white. This was the Gakushūin students assembled in a body. When I came near to them two from the body, Mr. Minami Iwakura and [Ikutsuji?] stepped out of the body to the front and addressed to me in the following words: We came to bid farewell to you and we wish your good health in your journey. Then I made a short reply. Behind these Gakushuin students and to the left were all full of Kōdōkwan [Kodokan] students and those from my house. I made a salute to them and stepped in into the Station House. The large house was full of [illegible] faces [illegible] familiar to me. To the left I could recognize my mother, my aunt, my brother and sister, Mr. Yoshimura, Mr. Yoshita [Yoshida?], Mrs. Tomita, Mrs. Matsumoto, etc. Making a general salutation to them all, I stepped into the First and Second Class Waiting Room, where I saw again a large assembly of familiar faces occupying the large room allmost full. Among these faces were. . . .

[Note: The original versions of the remaining pages of the entries for September 14–17 have unfortunately been lost. What follows is a paraphrased version of the text, translated into English based on existing Japanese translations.]

. . . Mr. Yanagi, accompanied by Yoshizawa, Mr. Nangō, accompanied by my sister, Fujii, Hayashi, Gojō, [Hanksnet?], Yamagata, Mōri [Genpin?], [Katō Chōmatsu?] and his son, Ōshima and his son, Hattori, Kuwahara, Takasaki, Yatabe, Iwamura, Ōkubo, and others.

It was nearly time for the train to leave Shimbashi, so I left the waiting room. On my way to the train, I saw two groups of people on the path open to me. There I found [Hanabusa?], [Tatsumi?], and a number of other close acquaintances. Everywhere on the way to the train was filled with people.

I departed for Yokohama with Mr. and Mrs. Nangō, Iwanami, Fukushita, Ōkura, Saigō, Tokujirō, Tamura, Higuchi, Sekiba, Ōshima, Arima, Miwa, Hirayama, Chōmatsu, Satō, Saneyoshi, Kondō, Shidachi, Kitō, [Hokawa?], Kanō [Goichi?], Sumitomo, Maruo, Mine, and others. [Kaketa?], Kubota, and several others were already in Yokohama. All of us stayed in Nishimura. After that, some went home, and several lodged elsewhere.

The first part of the evening tonight I spent talking about a variety of topics and other matters of business. After that, I called Ōkura, Saigō, Iwanami, Arima, and Higuchi to a small room, where we discussed what to do about the Kodokan, the academy, and expenses in my absence. I gave Ōkura the money that would be required for all the expenses through the end of February. I also asked Mr. Kensaku to handle the affairs in Masago-chō.

At 7:30 the next morning [September 15], a number of people arrived from Tokyo. Among them were Ōkubo, [Sagane?], and several academy students (Ōta, Katō, [Mine?], [Konami?], Nojima, Kotarō, Jirō, Saburō, and younger students). Around 8:00, we all went to the Yokohama dock, where half of the group boarded a launch. At 8:30, we made our way to the *Caledo-*

nian. The vessel would take us to Shanghai, where we would board a waiting ship bound for Marseilles. At around 8:50, I bid farewell to my family and stepped aboard the *Caledonian*. The only Japanese person accompanying me to Berlin was Mr. Yumoto.

The ship departed at 9:00 and then arrived in Kobe at 10:00 the next morning [September 16]. The sea was calm, making for a pleasant voyage. In Kobe, I saw Kōda, [Jiheida?], and Munakata, who had come to meet me. We then went to the Nishimura Hotel. Next, I went to see Arai and Fuku-saburō. With Arai, Fukusaburō, and Munakata, I then set off for Mikage, where we first went to visit Jirōemon and then my family's gravesite. After that, we went to Mikage's new Sankairō, where we had a nice salt bath. I saw a number of acquaintances at Jirōemon's home and Sankairō. Besides those who were already there, I saw Hachisuke, Oyone, [Haruichi?] and his wife, Jirōemon's wife and mother, an elderly retiree from [Jōnen?], Mr. Hisano, Mr. Takai, and Den'emon. I then took a train to Kobe around 8:30 and went to Kōda's home, where I saw the entire family except for Keiichi, who was in Hokkaido. Ryōzō also came to see me there, where I spent the night.

The next day [September 17], Kōda, [Jiheida?], and [Sasuzō?] accom-panied me to Nishimura, where Munakata, Ryōzō, Jirōemon, Jirōsuke, and Fukutarō were waiting for me. They, Yumoto, and I went back to the *Cale-donian* around 8:30. The vessel left Kobe for Shanghai at 9:00. When we left, I said goodbye to Fukutarō, who was at the dock. Others left before our departure. The ship sailed through the Awajishima Strait and then into the Seto Inland Sea. The scenery was more beautiful than any I had ever seen; the sky was clear and the waters calm. It was the most pleasant trip I had ever taken. We are now, at 12:00, sailing in the Seto Inland Sea.

The above entries, dated September 14 to September 17, include names and places that would require additional research to identify and explanations to place in context. Considering the scope of this biography, however, there is simply not enough space to cover everything. The primary focus of this chapter is Kanō's experience of his European voyage, which took him and the other pas-sengers through the Shimonoseki Straits, the Oki Islands to the left and Tsushi-ma Island to the right, before arriving at Shanghai on September 20. There, the passengers disembarked from the *Caledonian* and got on the *Irrawaddy*, another vessel in the Messageries Maritimes fleet. After a two-day layover in Shanghai, the long leg of the voyage began. The *Irrawaddy* shipped out of the Port of Shanghai on September 22, sailed straight for Europe, and arrived in Marseille at 9:00 p.m. on October 25. Kanō had finally set foot on the European continent, the culmination of more than a month at sea. He wrote exclusively about his travels during his time aboard the *Irrawaddy*, never once mentioning judo. His subsequent entries are almost completely devoid of the word "judo" as well. It was only mentioned in passing descriptions of doing judo with Japanese acquaintances who lived in Europe.

[The following is a transcription of Kanō's original English diary entry.]

After returning home read books till very late almost to the morning therefore slept till past 11 the 22nd morning when Tsuzuki [Keiroku, Kanō's fellow classmate at Tokyo University] came in and said Kawakita has come [and] as he told me his one of my students of jūdō I got up soon and dressed and ate a piece of bread with tea and saw him. Spoke with him for an hour lend him my lecture on Judo delivered before the Educational Society in Japan. He went off [and] we [Kanō and Tsuzuki] took [our?] dinner. After that went to see Musée royale de [peinture?] near the Palace Royale. There stayed till 4 then walked about the streets, saw Cathedral of St. [Gudula?], Place du Congrés and its column, [Place de le Societes Circle?] etc. Came back about half past 5. Finished dinner and [went?] looking and marked over the [plan?] of Brussels in Baedeker when Tsuzuki came in and said "Matsukata has come and wants to see me." So I descended the staircase, saw him in the parlor. We entered into a long conversation on jūdō after awhile we came up stairs to the room of Tsuzuki and there talked till 12, promised to go to him tomorrow evening to have some exercise on jūdō. After twelve began to read books till about 2.

[The following is a paraphrased version of Kanō's diary entry, rendered here in English based on existing Japanese translations.]

23rd Monday [1889; Brussels, Belgium]
Matsukata, Kawakita, Tanaka, and Tsuzuki came. Went with Kawakita, Tanaka, and Matsukata to the house of Matsukata. I laid out some futon and demonstrated five or six jūdō *waza*. Went home accompanied by Kawakita

around 11. Wrote in my diary and read books before going to bed at 2 a.m.

Judo makes another appearance in a brief entry dated March 5, 1890.

[The following is another paraphrase, created based on existing Japanese translations.]

Tanaka, Hidaka, Dr. [Aline?], Mr. [Liebig?], and two other Swiss men were there. What was interesting was that I got up quickly after being brought down by [Aline?] but he was unable to.

The March 5 entry suggests that Kanō gave a judo demonstration to a small group, possibly as a form of post-dinner entertainment. Among the party was a person identified only by the name of Dr. [Aline?] on whom Kanō appears to have executed a *nage waza* or *osaekomi waza*. By the time he made his way to Europe, Kanō had already established the Kodokan and honed his skills to master-level proficiency; regardless of how big his European counterparts may have been, the small-statured Kanō could effectively immobilize anyone and render them unable to recover quickly. On the way back from Europe, incidentally, Kanō applied a hold to a Russian officer—and the outcome was more of the same. The officer was literally floored.

From Marseille, Kanō headed to Paris, where he would spend the bulk of November. Staying roughly a month in France, Kanō was surely busy—and one might expect judo to have made an appearance. His diaries from his time in France, however, make no reference to judo. University of Bordeaux Professor Michel Brousse, who recently completed his degree with a dissertation on the history of French judo, suspects that Kanō's diaries were most likely an accurate portrayal—that judo played virtually no part in the European mission. Not only are there no historical resources pointing to any judo activity, but Brousse doubts Kanō would have ever seriously considered the idea in the first place. It was Kanō's first time ever setting foot in a foreign land, first of all; the chances that he would have been in the frame of mind to start demonstrating judo right away in that new environment are slim. Even if he had been, Kanō was apprehensive about pitting Kodokan judo against other martial-arts traditions in any sort of competitive setting. He was also there as part of an official delegation. Judo certainly lay outside the scope of the mission; a demonstration would have undoubtedly raised eyebrows, not to mention what might have transpired if someone were to have suffered an injury doing judo. Kanō had plenty of grounds not to do any judo in Europe, and it appears that he heeded reason. He only showed a handful of maneuvers on occasion, limiting his audience to Japanese students he knew.

Kanō's observations
While Kanō's English diaries might not contain much in the way of judo, the pages do hold a smattering of interesting travel anecdotes. The entry for December 20, 1889, lists Kanō's main observations from the first three months or so of his journey.

[The following is another paraphrase, created based on existing Japanese translations.]

(1) After seeing the odd houses of the Chinese in Shanghai, I wanted to show my Japanese friends that, indeed, different countries do have different customs.

(2) The Chinese society was so impressive to me that I genuinely wanted to study it in detail.

(3) In Hong Kong, I was amazed at how the British had built such a powerfully fortified port.

(4) From a sociological standpoint, I wanted to learn more about why the frugal, productive Chinese had lost to the British.

(5) I learned that the port and large rivers I saw in Canton were means of trade, and that waterways were useful in the distribution of goods.

(6) In Saigon, I wondered why the French had only been able to seize the port. I also saw a priest wearing a silver hair ornament, which I found interesting.

(7) In Singapore, I sensed the might of the British.

(8) In Colombo, I saw the lack of material development that the Indian people had achieved, and in Aden, I marveled at how the British had carefully selected numerous ports with ample facilities for both war and trade.

(9) Marseilles was just as I had imagined, the streets and houses very European in style.

(10) The houses in Lyon, like those in Marseilles, were beautiful, good, and clean.

(11) Paris, unlike Shanghai and Canton, was full of energy, beautiful, and massive in scale. My first impression of the Place de la Concorde in particular confirmed this. As I had expected, the exhibition was too magnificent for words. My interest in European culture and civilization grew by the day. In the end, I was amazed at how large and splendid the buildings and everything else in Paris were.

For Kanō, an Oriental elite with delicate sensibilities, insatiable curiosity, and a piercing intellect, encountering the lands and peoples of Europe must have been like the soil of the earth soaking up nurturing rains.

3. Kanō becomes an IOC member

On June 23, 1894, the International Athletic Congress (at the University of Paris) unanimously approved two motions by Pierre de Coubertin: a revival of the modern Olympics and the creation of the International Olympic Committee (IOC). Two years later, in 1896, that adoption bore fruit: the first modern Olympic Games convened at the Panathenaic Stadium in Athens, Greece, where the ancient Olympic tradition first began.

In the spring of 1909, Kanō, then principal of the Tokyo Higher Normal School, received an unexpected request from Auguste Gérard (1852–1922), the French ambassador to Japan. Gérard wanted to arrange a meeting—one that would add another international dimension to Kanō's life.

Gérard had received a letter from his former classmate Baron Pierre de Coubertin, seeking his help. The missive explained that Coubertin and a cohort of like-minded leaders had created an "International Olympic Committee," which had organized the first international Olympic Games in 1896. The event had taken place every four years since, featuring competitions in track and field, swimming, and a variety of other sports. Now, the organization was hoping to extend the scale of its efforts with an eye to the future. One issue to address was the makeup of the organizing body itself: although the IOC comprised members from nations around the world, there were no members from Asia. Coubertin was looking for someone who could represent Asia on the IOC and bring the Olympic ideals to new shores. Coubertin charged Gérard with finding a good candidate, and Gérard chose Kanō.

Kanō was a promising prospect for a number of reasons. He had cachet, first of all, as the founder of Kodokan judo. He also fit the bill in terms of the Olympic spirit. For years, he had shown commitment to youth athletics and sports; as principal of the Tokyo Higher Normal School, he began encouraging students to run long-distance courses and swim in Tateyama in 1898. That made him a leading figure in the Japanese athletic world. With the addition of his exceptional language skills, he had a bevy of favorable traits.

Kanō weighed the offer and ultimately decided to accept. In his reasoning, becoming a member of the IOC would open doors to a number of worthy aims: promoting friendly relations with other countries, fueling interest in athletics on a domestic level, and drawing on the growing prevalence of sport to foster a stronger, more able-bodied populace and cultivate a healthier mindset.

After getting word of Kanō's decision via Ambassador Gérard, Coubertin passed the news on to a meeting of the IOC members in Berlin in May 1909 and gave Kanō his official recommendation to become the first IOC member from Asia. The following year, Japan received an invitation to participate in the Stockholm Olympics from both the IOC and the government of Sweden, the host country. Coubertin's letter contained a concrete suggestion for facilitating Japan's entry into the Olympic brotherhood, as well. He informed Kanō that countries taking part in the Olympics had a "National Olympic Committee" (NOC), an umbrella organization responsible for overseeing sports at a national level, and he encouraged Japan to institute a similar organization as quickly as possible.

Kanō was conflicted. Though he had already decided to accept the invitation from Coubertin and Sweden and envisioned Japan taking part in the 1912 Olympics, the issue of an organization for selecting athletes posed a headache. No such body existed in Japan, not to mention the fact that the very ideas of "national athletics" or "national sports" had yet to take root there.

Recognizing the need for an organized group that would amount to an NOC, Kanō thus founded the Japan Amateur Athletic Association on July 10, 1911—Japan's first-ever athletic association—and named himself president.

4. The 1912 Summer Olympics in Stockholm: Japan's first Olympic Games

The first Olympic qualifiers

With the games of the fifth Olympiad fast approaching, not more than a year away, Japan had to hold qualifiers to select its athletes. The Japan Amateur Athletic Association held trials, the first of their kind in Japanese history, at the Haneda Athletic Grounds (eventually the site of Haneda Airport) on November 18 and 19, 1911. In the run-up to the competition, the Japan Amateur Athletic Association drew up an "International Olympic Qualifiers" pamphlet comprising an event prospectus, athlete application guidelines, competition regulations, and other information, and distributed the document nationwide. The prospectus underlined the need for physical education—reflecting the contemporary state of Japanese athletics—along with providing an overview of the Olympic Games and verbalizing the Japan Amateur Athletic Association's raison d'être.

The qualifiers drew ninety-one entrants. Kanō was on hand as head judge, although he was battling an illness at the time. Responsible for the day's logistic operations were several school representatives, under the leadership of Director Ōmori Hyōzō (1876–1913), Director Nagai Michiaki (1869–1950; head instructor of physical education at the Tokyo Higher Normal School), and Director Abe Isoo (1865–1949; director of the athletics department at Waseda University), who ran frantically around the venue tending to various matters.

After the qualifiers were complete, the Japan Amateur Athletic Association turned its attention to forming the roster for Japan's Olympic team. The discussion took longer than expected, delaying the announcement of the Olympic athletes until February 15, 1912, but eventually resulted in the following lineup:

Executive: Kanō Jigorō (president of the Japan Amateur Athletic Association and member of the IOC)
Manager: Ōmori Hyōzō (director of the Japan Amateur Athletic Association)
Athletes: Mishima Yahiko (1886–1954; sprint; Tokyo Imperial University) and Kanakuri Shisō (marathon; Tokyo Higher Normal School)

Kanō imparted a message to Kanakuri, a former student at the Tokyo Higher Normal School:

Japan sits below its advanced Western counterparts in several respects, one of the most prominent gaps being in the realm of physical education and sport. Western nations spearheaded the Olympic Movement, having held four Games over the previous two decades. In my role as principal of the Higher Normal School, I have required every student to spend one hour exercising after school each day. You have done your part in that regard, running day in and day out with the track team. However, virtually no other Japanese university makes physical exercise part of its daily schedule. Should you find yourself unable to emerge victorious from your race in Stockholm, know that the responsibility for that defeat is not yours to bear alone. The work of a true pioneer, regardless of whatever transpires, is a struggle. So it always has been, and so it always will be. In that struggle, however, lie the seeds for the future, seeds that will one day bloom. You are sowing those seeds, Kanakuri. Your appearance in the Olympic Games will allow Japanese sport to take root.[7]

With the Olympic delegation now final, the Swedish chargé d'affaires in Japan invited Mishima and Kanakuri to a celebratory luncheon at the Tsukiji Seiyōken, a hotel in Tokyo. The gathering served as an Olympic primer of sorts for the two runners. Attendees gave the Japanese athletes a rundown of international competition, covering rules and other points to keep in mind, while two American embassy officials offered some tips on training methods and promised to provide additional help in the coming weeks. Soliciting advice from embassy personnel might seem an odd choice, but these were far from ordinary employees: both were Olympic veterans themselves.

Kanakuri Shisō's recollections
Kanakuri Shisō remembered the experience in detail:

Right before we set off for the Olympics, Sensei [Kanō] gave us some words of encouragement. "Go and set the course for the future of Japanese sport," he said, adding that he would be there with us in his role as an IOC member. He asked us if we were ready to go. He looked each one of us up and down, checking to see if our cuffs were buttoned and our collars crisp. After we arrived in Sweden, he would make frequent stops by the practice facilities to see how we were doing. "It doesn't matter how many of you there are," he told us. "Just give it your all. . . ."[8]

Ōmori (with his American wife, Annie), Mishima, and Kanakuri departed for Stockholm together; Kanō left on June 6 and made his way to Sweden via the United States. Once in Sweden, Japan's duo of runners set to the task at hand: preparing for Olympic competition.

After making our arrival in Stockholm, we took a few days off before starting our training regimens for the marathon and sprint events. Training was vital to success, of course, and we worked day in and day out to prepare ourselves for our respective races. In the afternoons, we would walk from our lodgings to the practice ground, where Mishima would head to the track to work on his starts and run 100-meter dashes. I coached him. We had no other choice, really, as there were no coaches with us. We were utterly alone, and the solitude made the need for teammates and coaches painfully clear. After helping Mishima with his training, I ran the marathon route by myself. I remember feeling comfortable at first, with the heat still relatively mild and only a small number of foreign runners training with me. When the temperatures began climbing in late June and the route filling up with more and more runners, however, I started to feel more uncomfortable. Just sharing the course with so many unfamiliar fellow runners was a source of stress, making the fatigue harder and harder to bear. I wished I had someone there to encourage me. The marathon route itself was ideal for running, following tree-lined, quiet roads through the countryside, but the pavement was extremely hard. The soles of my *tabi* [traditional Japanese cloth shoes] fell apart, so I had to send away for emergency reinforcements via telegram. My knees could hardly

withstand the pain of all the impact, either. It all interfered with my training regimen, leaving me woefully unprepared for the marathon. . . . The race was on July 14, the last day of the track and field competition, and the sun was beating down on the fifty or so runners in the field. I was in the middle of the pack at the starting line. Looking around, I saw that some of the runners from other countries were smaller than me. At least in terms of

The Japanese delegation marches in the Parade of Nations at the Stockholm Olympics (courtesy of the Kodokan collection)

size, I felt little in the way of intimidation or physical inadequacy. But when the race actually started, the other runners set off in a sprint, and I eventually fell to the back of the pack. I was thrown for a loop, completely bewildered. Whatever "rhythm" I might have had was off from the start. About half of all the runners succumbed to sunstroke in the scorching heat, and I was one of them. Everyone—athletes and coaches alike—paid his own way to and from Stockholm. The government had no interest in the competition, nor was the fledgling Greater Japan Amateur Athletic Association in any financial position to provide monetary support. The entire delegation wore tailcoats and silk hats to the official Olympic functions as well.[9]

On July 6, the day of the opening ceremony, Mishima Yahiko ran in the sixteenth heat of the 100-meter qualifiers. He missed the cut, placing fifth, and also failed to make it out of the 200-meter qualifiers on July 10. He did qualify for the 400-meter race, despite unusual circumstances. Running in the fourth group, he placed last—but there were only two runners. That made him "runner-up," which technically earned him a place in the semifinals. He pulled out of the race, however, due to an injury. Kanakuri Shisō, meanwhile, appeared in the marathon but succumbed to piercing abdominal pains mid-race. "I started to drop back [and withdrew from the race] at around mile 18 of the 25-mile marathon," he recalled. Kanakuri also remembered how Kanō consoled him after pulling out:

"You two might have come up short in both events, but that does not mean that Japanese people lack the physical strength to compete. It doesn't prove a thing. You have your whole lives ahead of you—just stick with it," Sensei said with a smile. It was a heartening moment. His words inspired us to take another shot.[10]

Kanō, too, recalled the events in an article years later:

Kanakuri was in the spotlight in Stockholm. His world record-breaking run had put his name in the American papers and given him a reputation in Europe. Even so, he practiced alone, silently running along the route. The same went for Mishima. It was nothing like the attention the runners from the United States and other countries got, with throngs of fans and coaches crowding around for support and instruction. Looking on, I felt so sorry for

Kanakuri and Mishima.

The environment must have had quite an effect, too. The skies in Stockholm stayed light deep into the night, which made it hard to get comfortable, and the sounds of automobiles driving around the vicinity of the accommodations made it all the more impossible to sleep. The food was different. Hardly anyone spoke to anyone else. On top of all that, the two had the pressure of the competition to contend with, the burden of a responsibility that must have felt immense. They were far from their normal selves, to say the least. We came up short in every event, save for Mishima's first qualifying run in the 400-meter race. Honestly, I thought we might have a chance—but not even Mishima could measure up to the athletes from other countries, and that was a sobering realization to come to.[11]

The experience made Kanō acutely aware of Japan's status as a latecomer to the sports world. The shock hit particularly hard given the high hopes Kanō had placed in Kanakuri.

I was partial to Kanakuri; I was sure that he would win. When it finally came time for the marathon, the fifty or so marathon runners gathered at the starting line and set off en masse. The runners started to arrive back at the finish line some time later, on schedule, but Kanakuri was nowhere to be seen. Minister Uchida [Japan's minister to Sweden] turned to me and asked if I knew what might have happened to Kanakuri, but I had no answer to give him.

I began to suspect that Kanakuri might simply have returned to his lodgings, so I went to the hotel. He was there, in his room. "What happened?" I asked. "I'm sorry," Kanakuri replied. "I felt like my heart was going to burst. I collapsed. I couldn't go on." All I could do was console him. Never in the slightest did the thought of rebuking him for losing the race ever cross my mind.

We must train our athletes harder to ensure that they have the requisite physical fortitude. We must send athletes to the Olympics in greater numbers. It all has to do with enhancing Japan's national power. My experience in Stockholm made it clear that we had a broader aim for which we needed to strive.

The Stockholm Olympics also presented me the opportunity to visit several times with Chairman Coubertin, who explained that the Olympics represented the paragon of education. With an earnest conviction, he repeatedly spoke of his desire to see Japan lead the way for the Oriental world in contributing to the future of the Olympic Movement. Even without Baron Coubertin's fervent pleas, I came to a powerful, overwhelming realization of the virtues inherent to the Olympic spirit when I first saw the competition with my own eyes: that every athlete was well-built and conditioned, well-disciplined, courteous, and teeming with an ardent sense of patriotic pride.[12]

Evident in Kanō's words are his clear understanding of the Olympic spirit—that the Olympics served an educational ideal, as Coubertin had intended them—and his archetype of the human ideal, a strong, orderly, courteous, and patriotic person. The discourse hints at an undercurrent of universality, suggesting that people on both sides of the East-West "divide" see humanity and existence through a common lens. What Kanō Jigorō saw in Olympism resonated with the concepts of *seiryoku saizen katsuyō* and *jita yūwa kyōei*, the precepts that he would continue to advocate throughout his life.

Notes:

1 Higashi Ken'ichi, "Kumamoto ni okeru Kanō Jigorō to Rafukadio Hān" [Kanō Jigorō and Lafcadio Hearn in Kumamoto], *Tōkyō Gaikokugo Daigaku ronshū* [Area and Culture Studies (Tokyo University of Foreign Studies)] 51 (1995), 187–202.

2 Kanō Jigorō, interview by Ochiai Torahei, "Kyōiku-ka to shite no Kanō Jigorō (roku)" [Kanō Jigorō, the educator (VI)], *Sakkō* [Promotion] 8, no. 8 (1929).

3 Interview by Ochiai Torahei, 25–26.

4 Kanō Kotarō, abridged translation, *Kokushi* [Patriot] 5 (1899), 25–26.

5 Kanō Kotarō, 27–28.

6 Kanō Kotarō, 28–29.

7 Kanō-sensei Denki Hensan-kai, ed., *Kanō Jigorō* [Kanō Jigorō] (Tokyo: Kodokan, 1964), 600–601.

8 Kanō-sensei Denki Hensan-kai, 658–659.

9 Japan Amateur Athletic Association, *Nihon Taiiku Kyōkai nanajūgo-nen-shi* [The 75-year history of the Japan Amateur Athletic Association] (Tokyo: Japan Amateur Athletic Association, 1986), 248.

10 Kanō-sensei Denki Hensan-kai, ed., 659.

11 Kanō Jigorō, "Waga Orinpikku hiroku" [My secret Olympic notes], *Kaizō* [Modification] 20, no. 7, 1938.

12 Kanō Jigorō, "Waga Orinpikku hiroku."

Chapter 2

Judo in Europe and the roots
of the "World Judo Federation" vision

1. Shaping the "Budokwai" in the United Kingdom

The creation of the Budokwai

If we have learned a great deal from other countries but have nothing to teach them, not only must we feel ashamed, but it will also be difficult to avoid being looked down upon. So, what shall we teach them? We have judo.[1]

Kanō Jigorō made his first trip to Europe in 1889, departing Japan in September and returning home roughly eighteen months later. Over the course of the journey, he turned twenty-nine, most likely laid eyes on the brand-new Eiffel Tower—the architectural symbol to mark the 1889 world's fair in Paris, France—and undoubtedly was awed by a world with a civilized, cultured polish, the likes of which he had never seen. Taking in that milieu firsthand must have kindled his desire to put judo shoulder to shoulder with the sports of the West. He never conceived of that process as a competition, however: it was not judo *versus* Western sport as much as it was judo *with* Western sport, a mutual development by which the Orient and the Occident would take advantage of the other's cultural traditions. What grew out of that conceptualization was a vision for the "World Judo Federation," that shaped Kanō's efforts to popularize judo in the United Kingdom.

In January 1918, the "Budokwai" (originally the "London Budōkan") was established in London. The organization, founded by a group with Koizumi Gunji and Tani Yukio at the center, started out as a far-reaching "culture school," hosting jujutsu and swordsmanship practice along with classes on Japanese tea ceremony, Japanese flower arrangement, Buddhism, and more for Japanese citizens on business in the United Kingdom and British citizens with an interest in Japanese culture. Kanō made his first visit to the Budokwai on July 15, 1920, on his way to the 1920 Antwerp Olympics, which he was attending as a member of the International Olympic Committee (IOC). His visit was more than just a cursory peek, however—he was there to sow the seeds of judo. That had been the plan from the outset. He even brought Aida Hikoichi, a young Kodokan stalwart, along. The sheer scope of the visit suggests that the Budokwai held significant promise in Kanō's eyes, representing a potential base for popularizing judo in the United Kingdom and, by extension, across Europe. The Japanese presence at the Budokwai must have added to the site's appeal. The main cogs of the Budokwai operations—Koizumi and Tani, among others—were fellow countrymen, making it easier for Kanō to forge a solid link with organizational leadership. Koizumi would eventually be instrumental in gaining judo a following in Europe, essentially serving as Kanō's ambassador, and would hold the elite rank of seventh dan.

Considering their roles in shaping European judo, Tani and Koizumi are vital players in the judo story.

Tani Yukio (1881–1950), a Tokyo native, learned Tenjin Shin'yō-ryū ju-jutsu[2] from his father. He moved to the United Kingdom at the age of nineteen, in 1899, on the invitation of E.W. Barton Wright (1860–1951), an Englishman who had studied jujutsu in Japan. In the United Kingdom, Tani made a living as a professional mixed martial artist of sorts: he fought area wrestlers and boxers at local music halls and other venues. The draw was the sheer gap in size between Tani—"Little Tani," as spectators dubbed him—and his larger foes. As he continued to force opponent after opponent into submission, Tani helped bring "jujutsu" into the contemporary British vernacular. In a similar vein is the story of Maeda Mitsuyo (1878–1941), the Kodokan-trained practitioner who helped spread jujutsu to the South American continent. Tani and Mae-

A demonstration in Vienna (courtesy of the Kodokan collection)

Kanō Jigorō demonstrates judo to police officers in Berlin (courtesy of the Kodokan collection)

da were just two of the many *jūjut-suka* (and judoka) who brought the "jujutsu" name across borders, proving that Japanese jujutsu was a legitimate martial art with systemic roots in the Edo period (1603–1868). A look around the Budokwai premises is enough to appreciate Tani's legacy: in 1933, the organization voted to place his picture on the wall for posterity, never to be removed.

Another driving force for the Budokwai was Koizumi Gunji (1885–1965). The "Father of British judo," as he came to be called, Koizumi studied jujutsu (Tenjin Shin'yō-ryū, among other styles) in his early years and moved to the United Kingdom in 1905. After a brief stint in the United States, he headed back to the United Kingdom in 1910 and settled in London, where he would live for another fifty-five years until his death in 1965. While Koizumi and Tani both occupy central places in the history of British judo, their paths to that position were quite different. Tani initially paid the bills with martial-arts sideshows; Koizumi got his footing in the United Kingdom dealing in antiques and pursuing other business ventures. As soon as the Budokwai got off the ground, however, Koizumi devoted himself to the organization's operations.

Kanō's judo vision extends its reach

Tani and Koizumi both left Japan at a young age, never having studied Kodokan judo. Why, then, did they wholeheartedly take up the cause of spreading Kanō judo internationally? It may have had something to do with Kanō's magnetic personality, but it most likely went beyond that.

In terms of technique, both Tani and Koizumi shared a common foundation with Kanō: Tenjin Shin'yō-ryū jujutsu, which formed the building blocks of judo. Kanō, of course, had studied Tenjin Shin'yō-ryū and Kitō-ryū jujutsu after matriculating at Tokyo University. Fellow Kodokan founding members Saigō Shirō (1866–1922; the inspiration for the novel *Sugata Sanshirō* by Tomita Tsuneo, 1942) and Yokoyama Sakujirō (1864–1912) traced their martial-arts roots to the Tenjin Shin'yō school as well. Kanō explicitly associated judo with the school's teachings, saying, "The Kodokan judo that I now teach partially applies the secrets of the [Tenjin Shin'yō-ryū] teachings."[3] Many of the Kodokan judo *waza* do, in fact, appear to be adaptations of Tenjin Shin'yō-ryū maneuvers. Kanō even awarded Tani and Koizumi the rank of second dan in Kodokan judo on his first visit to the Budokwai in London. If one meeting was enough for Kanō to recognize and commend the skills that Tani and Koizumi had, the fact that all three came from the same jujutsu school must have been at least something of a factor. Kanō saw their performance as conducive to judo and took the initiative to accelerate their development with dan grades. From that point on, all he had to do was guide them along the way in his own school.

Also contributing to the evolution of the Budokwai was Aida Hikoichi (1893–1973), whom Kanō dispatched to London. Aida was undoubtedly well-versed in judo teachings and capable of instruction, having trained in the judo club at the Tokyo Higher Normal School and at the Kodokan. Armed with a solid skillset, Aida became the Budokwai's first official judo instructor—and his prowess made an indelible impression. Then-Budokwai member and eventual Budokwai president E.J. Harrison called Aida "one of the most successful pioneer judo instructors to spread knowledge of the art beyond the boundaries of their native land."[4] Had Aida been any less technically adept, it would have been hard for him to win the acceptance of the Budokwai. After all, Tani and the rest of the London-based Japanese contingent had fought a multitude of foreign martial artists in their adopted home—they were not about to be fooled.

Aida taught judo at Oxford and Cambridge universities, as well, but his stay in the United Kingdom was relatively brief. After around two and a half years in the country, he relocated to Germany and later France.

Kanō's philosophical bent surely played a role in drawing Tani and Koizumi to judo. At its heart, Kanō's brand of judo boiled down to the two concepts of *seiryoku zen'yō* and *jita kyōei*. In just eight Chinese characters, the two phrases encapsulated the tenet of using one's physical and mental energy as effectively as possible (*seiryoku zen'yō*)—in every aspect of life—to bring mutual prosperity to both the self and the other (*jita kyōei*). The philosophy made such an impression on Koizumi that he championed the concepts in his own writing, praising the educational framework that Kanō and Kodokan judo established through the "principle of deriving the maximum effect from the minimum effort" and the "method of discipline for body, mind, and logic."[5]

The internal features of judo, from its techniques to its core ideology, represented a type of value that opened Tani's and Koizumi's eyes to the fledgling practice, to be sure—but that value alone was likely not able to win them over completely. There were probably other external motivators at work.

The reason that the Budokwai sought direct contact with Kanō in the first place was to gain access to judo instructors from the Kodokan. According to the organization's official records, the liaison for the instructor request was a British judoka by the name of W. E. Steers, who himself had previously studied at the Kodokan facilities in Japan.[6] The Budokwai probably saw recruiting top-level instructors from Japan as a way of stabilizing its financial standing while simultaneously maintaining its influence. Why the organization wanted judo instructors—as opposed to conventional jujutsu teachers—is hard to pin down precisely, but Budokwai leaders probably knew that judo had carved out a prominent place in the Japanese jujutsu realm. Kanō's work for the Dai Nippon Butoku Kai (Greater Japan Martial Virtue Society), a group with a far-reaching sway in the world of martial arts, had helped judo establish credibility. Even more important, however, was Kanō's prominence as an IOC member. If its leader was both Japanese and a man of the world, judo certainly must have seemed a particularly appealing martial art to focus on at the Budokwai.

The influence of Nitobe Inazō's Bushido

The Budokwai had invited another Japanese cosmopolitan besides Kanō: Nitobe Inazō (1862–1933). Nitobe had made a name for himself as the author of *Bushido: The Soul of Japan*, written during his studies in the United States and translated into numerous languages. A look at the Budokwai's records reveals that Nitobe gave a lecture on Japanese loyalty on October 11, 1919, roughly nine months before Kanō appeared at the Budokwai. Nitobe apparently drew quite a crowd, with people packing the lecture hall. Nitobe and Kanō knew each other, too, and shared a common viewpoint on finding an optimal, two-way balance between nationalism and internationalism.[7] Given the relationship and similarities between the two, the chances are good that Nitobe passed at least some kernels of information on the Budokwai along to Kanō. Whether that exchange happened directly or indirectly, Nitobe's input on the Budokwai must have motivated Kanō to forge ties with the organization.

Instrumental in strengthening that bond between Nitobe and Kanō, mean-while, was Sugimura Yōtarō (1884–1939). Sugimura had been a student at the Kanō Juku before entering and graduating from Tokyo Imperial University, after which he thrived as an elite-track diplomat. His ties to both Nitobe and Kanō had an official, international dimension. When the League of Nations formed in 1920, Nitobe served as an under-secretary general; Sugimura inherited the post from him in 1927. Nitobe saw Sugimura as a top-of-the-line successor, calling him "a Japanese man with a true grasp of the pathos of things."[8] For Kanō, too, Sugimura represented a promising candidate to take up the mantle of leadership. In 1933, Kanō recommended that Sugimura become the third Japanese IOC member, a post that Sugimura would hold until 1936. Sugimura was also an adept judoka (eventually earning the rank of seventh dan) and gave several judo demonstrations during his time at the Japanese embassy in France. He had even more ties to the Kodokan: he made the acquaintance of Aida Hikoichi after Aida left the UK for France.[9]

From Tani and Koizumi to Aida and Sugimura, Kanō's impressive personal network helped judo broaden its reach in Europe. Past research, however, has largely attributed the spread of the art to the proficiency of the practitioners active in the area. The skill factor was, of course, an ingredient in the mix—without high-level technical aptitude capable of impressing the local commu-nity, it would have been next to impossible for judo to land an audience. That said, judo also owed part of its growing European presence to Kanō's circle of acquaintances. The connections linking Kanō—and thereby judo—with the likes of intellectuals, politicians, and financiers were another important part of the picture.

Going back to Tani and Koizumi, Kanō entrusted the pair with fostering a fertile environment for British judo. Kanō, seeing how well the two had tak-en up the judo cause, reflected on his second visit in 1928 as follows: ". . . I journeyed to England to meet again with Koizumi and Tani, both third dan grade holders. They were living in London and were engaged as judo instruc-tors at the Budokwai judo club to which I paid several visits during my stay. I was pleased to see a larger number of trainees practicing there than during my previous visit some eight years earlier. Moreover, the general level of skill of the members had improved markedly during the interim."[10] According to Kotani Sumiyuki (1903–91; member of the Tokyo Higher Normal School judo club and eventually tenth dan holder), who accompanied Kanō on his third visit to the Budokwai in 1933, Tani and Koizumi had done their jobs remarkably well. "Thanks to Koizumi and Tani, who had settled down in the UK, taken British wives, and spent years teaching judo to British audiences," Kotani wrote, "the judo in London was proper and true to the correct principles."[11]

Living up to Kanō's hopes and expectations, Tani and Koizumi helped fuel the rise of judo in Europe. Kanō also proposed making the Budokwai a branch (*yūdanshakai*) of the Kodokan at a meeting with Budokwai officials and members on August 26, 1933. According to the meeting minutes, the gathering "closed with an outpouring of gratitude to Kanō." Incidentally, the audience was mostly British; the contingent had embraced Kanō, who obviously made a sizable impact on the Budokwai. A year after the meeting, the link between the Kodokan and Budokwai solidified: the Budokwai agreed to become an official *yūdanshakai* of the Kodokan, in line with Kanō's proposal.

2. The "World Judo Federation" vision

Cultivating German judo

Germany was another nation where the local community had embraced judo. Along with the United Kingdom, Germany lent considerable weight to the growth of European judo. Looking at European judo before the onset of World War II, Kanō himself noted, "Germany was superior in terms of quantity; the United Kingdom had the edge in quality."[12] The United Kingdom and Germany even teamed up on a judo exchange program beginning around 1929, manifesting a cross-Europe judo trend that inspired Kanō to conceive of the "World Judo Federation"—an international community of judo. As nations began hurtling toward World War II, however, crippling breakdowns in international relations prevented Kanō's vision from being realized.

Judo summer camp in Frankfurt (*KRAFT SPORT*, August 1932)

Kanō gave a lecture on the topic of judo in Berlin, Germany, in 1928, eight years after making his first visit to the British Budokwai. In the years leading up to this lecture, a style of juju-tsu with dubious, unidentifiable origins had become popular and lodged itself in the German consciousness. Aida Hikoichi had left the United Kingdom in 1923 to spend a year or so teaching judo to police officers and other groups in Germany, and fellow former Tokyo Higher Normal School judo member Kudō Kazuzō (1898–1970; younger than Aida and later ninth dan) also studied in Germany from 1926 to the end of 1928, spending much of his time working to popularize judo. While their efforts may have helped give judo a foot in the door, the smattering of various jujutsu styles around the country had made it hard for judo to establish firm local roots. A shift in popularity came when Kanō was in Berlin in 1928, however. He met Werner Glasenapp (1904–86), the face of German jujutsu, who told Kanō that he wanted to make "judo Germany's na-tional sport," entreated Kanō for help with judo instruction, and even expressed his hopes of forging a European judo federation.[13]

The "judo" name began carving out a niche in the German athletic scene in 1929, when the British Budokwai and judo teams in Frankfurt, Berlin, and else-where around the country started holding matches together. The driving force behind the effort on the British side was Koizumi Gunji. Kanō may have pushed Koizumi to forge ties with Germany, considering the relationship between the two and Kanō's vision of a cross-border judo community. The photo on the pre-vious page depicts Japanese instructors at an international judo summer camp in Frankfurt during the month of August 1932: Koizumi at the far right, Tani second from the right, Ishiguro Keishichi (member of the Waseda University judo club, later eighth dan; taught judo in Paris, France, and around Europe for the Kodokan) second from the left, and Kitabatake Kyōshin (then studying in Germany; fourth dan) at the far left. When a team of German judoka headed to the UK at the end of November 1932, meanwhile, the Germans bested the teams from the University of Oxford, the University of Cambridge, and the Budokwai. The Budokwai members were impressed: "German judo is making improvements by leaps and bounds," the organization's records note.

In July 1933, after an IOC meeting in Vienna, Kanō made a stopover in Berlin. It was there that he met German chancellor Adolf Hitler, an encounter that came shortly after the Hitler Cabinet formed in January that same year. "I had no particular intention to meet Hitler," Kanō wrote later, "but he was insistent that we do so."[14] The meeting, obviously, did not place high on Kanō's agenda; his stance was passive, at best. The fact that Hitler had a reputation as an enthusiast of boxing, jujutsu, and judo, however, makes it ever the more compelling to speculate on what he discussed with Kanō. With Kanō on his appointment to meet Hitler were Kotani Sumiyuki and Takasaki Masami (later ninth dan). According to Takasaki, Kanō "met with Chancellor Hitler and fielded questions on a variety of topics, including Japanese education, national education (a state-directed system for nurturing the qualities and skills essential to the betterment of the nation) and differences between Japan and China."[15] Specifics on the conversation between Kanō and Hitler are absent from Kotani's writings, but he did note that the meeting took place at a "banquet" (with many other attendees present) and that several high-ranking German officials "came over to pay their respects to Sensei [Kanō]."[16]

On the heels of the meeting between Kanō and Hitler, the National Socialist League of the Reich for Physical Exercise (the government organization in charge of sports and physical education) listed "judo" in its "heavy athletics" (*Schwerathletik*) category. That official recognition essentially created a framework for bolstering judo on a national level—a step that Germany may have taken in hopes of making judo an Olympic sport for inclusion at the 1936 Berlin Olympics (the Games of the XI Olympiad), which were three years away at the time. The archives of the British Budokwai, too, suggest that may have been the case: according to an entry from 1934, "Germany appears to have launched an initiative to add judo to the list of sports at the upcoming Olympics."[17]

Concerns on the British side

As Kanō met with central players in the German government and German judo continued to make significant headway, the British side began to put up its guard—their change in attitude was cause for concern. Official Budokwai records show that Koizumi resigned his position as an organization official in December 1933. In his prolonged efforts to bolster relations with the German judo community, Koizumi had rankled several Jewish Budokwai members. His departure, it seems, stemmed from their objections to the organization's affiliations with the Nazi regime. Hitler, of course, touted the superiority of the Germanic race and harbored a vehement opposition to Jews, a thoroughly anti Semitic stance that informed a host of suppressive policies against the Jewish population. One can imagine how Koizumi's efforts to extend a conciliatory hand and take up with the German side must have looked to the Jewish members of the Budokwai. For a period after his resignation, Koizumi found his involvement in Budokwai operations shrinking as the organization began distancing itself from him and, consequently, Kanō. In December 1934, Budokwai leaders pressed Kanō for answers about the meaning of recent occurrences: why Germany had already announced the creation of the "World Unions of Judo," with Kanō at the helm, and why Glasenapp was professing himself the chairman of the European Unions of Judo. Kanō was slow to respond to the organization's questions, however, further deepening the impasse. The relationship reached its nadir in June 1935, when the Budokwai resolved to "render invalid any and all promises and arrangements made with Kanō during his visits in 1933 and 1934." In effect, the resolution made the Budokwai's agreement to become a branch of the Kodokan null and void.

The reasons behind Kanō's seemingly sluggish response represent crucial points that delineate the course of that falling-out. For one, he may have simply been too busy to address the concerns of the British judo community. The onset of the 1930s saw Kanō attempting to balance the challenges of forming a global judo community with his significant responsibilities as an IOC member. One of the more critical projects on his plate was the 1940 Olympics. Since 1931, talks about holding the Games of the XII Olympiad in Tokyo—which would make Tokyo the first-ever host city in Asia—had been on the table. As a Japanese IOC member, Kanō obviously had to make that effort a priority. Kanō was getting on in years, too, and he often found himself in less-than-ideal health from around 1934 onward. With all those factors in play, not to mention the tumultuous international situation of the time and his position as a representative of Japan, the notion of playing the middleman and mending relations between the British and German judo communities must have seemed an arduous, cumbersome task to Kanō—even if the conflict did center on judo, the art he had developed. In 1933, Japan and Germany withdrew from the League of Nations; in November 1936, they went on to sign the Anti-Comintern Pact. The bond between the two nations was growing increasingly tight. It was a swirling maelstrom of global proportions, and it swallowed Kanō up.

The vision of a "World Judo Federation," rooted in Kanō's pacifist philosophy

The Budokwai's historical resources also include a document containing "conversations" between Kanō and Koizumi in 1936, the year of the Berlin Olympics. Titled "Judo and The Olympic Games," the document contains the following piece of illuminating insight.

> I [Kanō] have been asked by people . . . as to . . . the possibility of judo being introduced at the Olympic Games. My view on the matter, at present, is rather passive. . . . For one thing, judo in reality is not a mere sport or game. I regard it as a principle of life, art, and science. In fact, it is a means for personal cultural attainment. . . . In addition, the Olympic Games are so strongly flavored with nationalism that it is possible to be influenced by it and to develop Contest Judo as a retrograde form. . . . Judo, as an art and a science, should be free from external influences—political, national, racial, and financial. . . . And all things connected with it should be directed to its ultimate object, the benefit of humanity.[18]

Taking a detached, objective stance on the contemporary scene surrounding the Olympics and athletics in general, Kanō sought to preserve the ideals at the heart of judo—an art that bore his personal stamp. He was wary of the possibility that political nationalism might continue to dominate the Olympics, much as it had in making the Berlin Games the "Nazi Olympics," and render the competition a means of asserting national prestige. If that trend were to take firmer hold, he wanted to keep judo out of its grasp. In Kanō's eyes, judo had to exist outside the political sphere of influence; it needed to be an independent, neutral form of Japanese culture, not a political tool.

> Judo is nothing but the teaching of *seiryoku zen'yō*; it would be irrational to conceive of the art as a teaching of militarism or statism. Only a warmonger or some jingoistic sophist would ever associate the essence of *seiryoku zen'yō* with any military connotation. Judo is a peaceful art, and the use thereof for any other false pretense is both a manifestation of malicious intent and a threat to world peace.[19]
>
> The judo spirit dovetails harmoniously with an international spirit aspiring toward world peace. A World Judo Federation, therefore, would represent a true League of Nations with Japan in a leadership role.[20]

As the above quotes suggest, Kanō's vision for a World Judo Federation rested squarely on the foundation of his pacifist standpoint. That ideal of peace, however, would fade amid worsening hostilities. As the clouds of war continued to enshroud the international community, Kanō's world federation did not come to fruition in his lifetime.

Today's International Judo Federation (IJF) took form in 1951, thirteen years after Kanō's death, establishing its roots in a European community that was still recovering from the ravages of World War II. Japan joined the organization in 1952. Kanō's vision of a World Judo Federation finally took shape, having endured a catastrophic war before coming to life. Now, the IJF includes as many as 200 member nations and regions—the body is, as Kanō envisioned it, an umbrella organization for the entire judo world.

Kanō's pacifist stance, which formed the basis of the World Judo Federation concept, also bore fruit in postwar Japan. In the aftermath of World War II, Japan came under the control of the Supreme Commander for the Allied Powers (GHQ), which banned all the martial arts in the school curriculum—including judo—for being "military arts." The Dai Nippon Butoku Kai (DNBK; Greater Japan Martial Virtue Society), which had overseen martial arts of all kinds under Japan's military regime, also had to disband in 1946 due to concerns about its complicity in the war effort. The Kodokan, however, lived on; despite being a larger organization that subsumed the DNBK, the Kodokan avoided suppression and survived the postwar years. Judo itself made a rapid comeback, reentering the school curriculum in 1950 thanks in part to the help of the Ministry of Education. Of the various factors that helped spare judo from a more ruinous fate, the larger philosophy Kanō embedded in his practice—a thoroughly pacifist stance—was surely a significant one. The Ministry of Education and the broader judo community based much of their arguments around Kanō's "judo pacificism," which the GHQ must have acknowledged as a redeeming quality that it recognized in Kanō's concept of a World Judo Federation.

In the end, Kanō embodied a vital truth: that the creation, sustenance, and development of culture hinge on committing to ideals and beliefs, not simply pandering to the circumstances of the times.

Notes:

1   Kanō Jigorō, "Kōdōkan no hōfu to sono jitsugen no hōhō [An approach to bringing the vision of Kodokan judo to fruition], *Sakkō* [Promotion] 8, no. 1 (1929), trans. Nancy H. Ross, *Mind Over Muscle* (Tokyo: Kodansha International, 2005), 149.

2   Much of the past literature has subscribed to the theory that Tani originally studied Fusen-ryū jujutsu, but there is no extant proof substantiating that hypothesis. Here, the author posits that Tani's background actually lay in Tenjin Shin'yō-ryū jujutsu

based on the contentions of Koizumi, who spent considerable time with Tani and was also a master of Tenjin Shin'yō-ryū. See Koizumi Gunji, "Eikoku jūdō-kai no jittai" [The state of the British judo community], *Jūdō shinbun* [The judo newspaper], March 1, 1955.

3 From Kanō's introduction to *Tenjin Shin'yō-ryū jūjutsu gokui kyōju zukai* [The illustrated secret teachings of Tenjin Shin'yō-ryū jujutsu] by Yoshida Chiharu and Iso Mataemon V, originally published in 1893; see Watanabe Ichirō, ed., *Shiryō meiji budō-shi* [The documented history of martial arts in the Meiji period] (Tokyo: Shinjinbutsu Ōraisha: 1971), 127.

4 Aida Hikoichi, *Kodokan Judo*, trans. and ed. E. J. Harrison (London: W. Foulsham and Co., Ltd., 1956), 5.

5 Koizumi Gunji, *My Study of Judo* (London: W. Foulsham and Co., Ltd., 1960), 18.

6 W. E. Steers began studying judo at the Kodokan in 1911 and was thus acquainted with Kanō. See Richard Bowen (vice-president of the Budokwai, 1999), Budokwai website (http://www.budokwai.org/history.htm; accessed: March 16, 2011). On Kanō's first trip to the Budokwai, he was welcomed by Steers and Koizumi at Waterloo Station.

7 Nagaki Kōsuke, *Kanō jūdō shisō no keishō to hen'yō* [Kanō's judo philosophy: Legacy and transformation] (Tokyo: Kazamashobō, 2008), 128–129.

8 Sugimura Yōichi, ed., *Sugimura Yōtarō no tsuioku* [Memoirs of Sugimura Yōtarō] (no commercial release; 1940), 57.

9 For example, Aida, while in France, served as the coach and manager for Naitō Katsutoshi, who took home Japan's first-ever bronze medal in Olympic wrestling at the 1924 Paris Olympics (the Games of the VIII Olympiad) and originally held a second dan rank in judo. Sugimura was also involved, providing additional support. See Japan Amateur Athletic Association, ed., *Dai hachi-kai kokusai Orinpikku kyōgi taikai hōkokusho: Pari/1924* [The official report on the Games of the VIII Olympiad: Paris, 1924] (Tokyo: Taiikukenkyūsha, 1925), 91.

10 Kanō Jigorō, interview by Ochiai Torahei, "Jūdō-ka to shite no Kanō Jigorō (nijū)" [Kanō Jigorō, the judoka (XX)] *Sakkō* [Promotion] 7, no. 12 (1928), trans. Brian Watson, *Judo Memoirs of Jigoro Kano* (Bloomington, IN: Trafford Publishing, 2008), 129–130.

11 Kotani Sumiyuki, *Jūdō ichiro: Kaigai fukyū ni tsukushita gojū-nen* [A life of judo: Fifty years promoting the art abroad] (Tokyo: Baseball Magazine Sha, 1984), 39.

12 Kanō Jigorō and A.F. Thomas, trans. T.U., "Kanō shihan ni jūdō o kiku (ni)" [Talking to Master Kanō about judo], *Jūdō* [Judo] 5, no. 8 (1934).

13 Kanō Jigorō, "Tenran budō taikai ni tsuite" [On martial-arts performance in the imperial presence], *Sakkō* [Promotion] 8, no. 6 (1929).

14 Kanō Jigorō, "Sekai no yūshū kokumin-kan no kyōsō ni oite Nihon-jin ga kachieru yuiitsu no hōhō" [The only way for Japanese athletes to defeat counterparts from the world's leading countries], address at a welcoming party at the Meikei Kaikan, 1933, in *Kanō Jigorō taikei 9-kan* [An introductory overview to Kanō Jigorō, vol. 9], comp. and ed. Kodokan (Tokyo: Hon no Tomo-sha, 1988), 326.

15 Takasaki Masami, "Kanō Kaichō zuihan-roku" [Notes from my travels with President

Kanō], *Jūdō* [Judo] 4, no. 9 (1933).

16 Kotani Sumiyuki, *Jūdō ichiro*, 38.

17 Letter from Budokwai secretary H. A. Tricker to Kanō, dated December 16, 1934, C-65, Bowen Collection.

18 Quoted here are documents published by Koizumi in the Budokwai journal in April 1947, which can be found in the Bowen Collection (C-563). See also Brian Watson, *Judo Memoirs of Jigoro Kano* (Bloomington, IN: Trafford Publishing, 2008), xviii–xvix. There are several pieces of evidence indicating that Kanō was relatively reluctant to make judo an Olympic sport; see, for example, Nagaki Kōsuke, *Kanō jūdō shisō no keishō to hen'yō*, 138–39.

19 Kanō Jigorō and A. F. Thomas, trans. T.U., "Kanō shihan ni jūdō o kiku (ni)," 4.

20 "Jūdō Sekai Renmei sosei e no kiun shinten: Hachigatsu jūyokka-zuke Tōkyō Nichi Nichi Shinbun: Rondon shikyoku tokuden" [Momentum for the World Judo Federation builds: *Tokyo Nichi Nichi Shinbun*, August 14, London Office special telegram], *Jūdō* [Judo] 4, no. 9 (1933).

Chapter 3

Bringing the Olympics to Tokyo

1. Why Kanō embraced the Olympic Movement

Promoting youth education through physical education

Japan joined the Olympic Movement after Kanō Jigorō became Japan's first IOC member in 1909. Kanō was the impetus—but what compelled him to embrace Olympism? It came down to three main causes: the desire to promote youth education through physical education, an understanding of the element of goodwill intrinsic to sport, and the commitment to promote physical education on a national scale.

The first motivating factor, then, centered on applying physical education toward the development of Japan's youth population.

In Kanō's view, practicing judo and engaging in various forms of physical education—distance running, swimming, and the like—had multiple layers of benefit for young people. He believed not only in the physical benefits that athletics deliver, but also in the mental and moral foundations they cultivate in everything ranging from justice to fairness and humility, all of which extend beyond the individual self and affect others. He also contended that consistent pursuit of physical education would enable young people to maintain their youth both physically and mentally, and thereby live happier, more fulfilling lives. As the chief purveyor of judo and the principal of the Higher Normal School, Kanō made physical education a vital component of his educational framework, requiring young students to run long distance, practice swimming, and take part in athletic meets. Simply mandating physical activity would not be enough, of course; he knew that students might very well lose interest without a competitive element in the mix. For Kanō, then, competition-centric Western sports held enormous potential for igniting the spark of physical education in young people. At the Higher Normal School, club teams practicing sports that ran the gamut of Western athletics—lawn tennis, soccer, baseball, cycling, boating, table tennis, and rugby, to name a few—sprouted up as Kanō made extracurricular athletics a priority. That outlook harmonized with the Olympic Movement, which Kanō saw as another means of fueling interest in physical education among the younger population.

Understanding the element of goodwill intrinsic to sport

Kanō also touched on the concept of goodwill and peace in explaining his reasons for embracing the Olympics. "Just as the ancient Olympics forged the Greek spirit," he wrote, "the modern Olympics can bring together the thoughts and feelings of countries across the globe and help clear paths toward civilization and peace worldwide." He saw Olympic competition as a means of uniting the nations of the world in a way that would "transcend victory and defeat to deepen bonds and cultivate mutual amity,"[1] in addition to other benefits. Kanō already knew firsthand how sports made it possible for young people to enhance their physical health and build their character, creating a fertile environment for establishing strong relationships. His efforts to accept Chinese students and put them through a curriculum of physical education and sports, including judo, exemplified this belief. Between 1896 and 1920, when he left his position as principal of the Tokyo Higher Normal School, Kanō admitted roughly eight thousand international students to his private school, and later to the Kōbun Gakuin, the school he set up for the education of international students. Their studies at these institutions included Japanese and standard secondary-education subjects—and, of course, athletics.

Sports occupied a sizable portion of the activities for international students under Kanō's supervision. Not only did students participate in two sports days each year (one in the spring and the other in the fall), but they also had opportunities to play club sports (tennis, archery, and distance running). Judo was another focus. In 1903, the Kōbun Gakuin received

Volleyball at the Tokyo Higher Normal School (ca. 1931)

official recognition as the Kodokan's Ushigome branch dojo. Renowned Chinese writer Lu Xun even studied at the institution. Upon finishing the Kōbun Gakuin program, many of the school's international students went on to enroll at Tokyo Higher Normal School. There, too, they joined club-sport teams, including the soccer squad, and competed against teams of Japanese students from other schools. The Japanese students, in turn, cheered on their international counterparts. Sports were a platform that brought young people from divergent backgrounds together for mutual betterment; Kanō had already seen that process at work. His practical knowledge dovetailed perfectly with the Olympic philosophy.

Promoting national physical education
The final motivator for Kanō lay in his hopes for the advancement of national physical education: a Japan where every single citizen would learn and engage in physical activity. He envisioned a framework that would provide physical education for the long haul, a foundational wellness that would enable the entire Japanese population to maintain hardy physiques, stay in good health, and work productively. For Kanō, the ideal approach would maximize accessibility: there would be no need for special skills, monetary expenditures, or equipment, first of all, and there would be no limitations on gender or age. Judo, walking, running, and swimming were ideal pursuits, meeting all of Kanō's criteria. This helps explain why, in response to the IOC's suggestion to set up a national Olympic committee, Kanō established the Japan Amateur Athletic Association instead of a formal Japanese Olympic Committee—more than the Olympics specifically, what took paramount importance in Kanō's eyes was physical education on a national scale. The Japan Amateur Athletic Association was an organization with the dual function of sending teams of athletes abroad and energizing the national physical-education initiative.

Kanō's embrace of the Olympic Movement was generated by a dogged determination to further physical education and sports at the national level. He also knew, however, that Japan needed to produce high-caliber athletes. Citing the examples of Germany and other countries, Kanō argued that developing a competitive base of Japanese athletes would be essential to establishing a foundation of physical education for the whole of Japan.

2. How Kanō envisioned and campaigned for Tokyo's bid to host the 1940 Olympics

Kanō's efforts to make Tokyo the host of the 1940 Olympics

As an IOC member, Kanō poured his energies into making Tokyo's bid to host the 12th Olympic Games in 1940 a success. Efforts to bring the Olympics to Japan began in 1931 after the Tokyo Municipal Diet passed a resolution to pursue staging the event. As the following timeline indicates, Kanō played a significant role in the process.

· July 1932: Kanō attends the IOC Session in Los Angeles, where he presents IOC president de Baillet-Latour with an official letter of invitation and explains Tokyo's bid for the Olympics
· June 1933: Kanō attends the IOC Session in Vienna, where Sugimura Yōtarō (former under-secretary of the League of Nations) is appointed the third Japanese member of the IOC on Kanō's recommendation
· November 1933: Kanō attends another IOC meeting in Vienna, where he reports on the organization, venues, and costs for holding the Olympics in Tokyo
· May 1934: Kanō promotes the Tokyo bid by distributing photo albums of Japanese sports to IOC members at an IOC Session in Athens, where he also gets the general sense that Rome is the clear favorite as a candidate site; Soejima Michimasa is appointed an IOC member to replace Kishi Seiichi (1867–1933), who had passed away suddenly
· February 1935: Kanō sends Sugimura to attend the IOC Session in Oslo
· July 1936: Kanō attends and casts his vote at the IOC Session in Berlin
· March 1938: Kanō attends the IOC Session in Cairo

Kanō was already in his mid-seventies by the second half of the 1930s. Despite the physical toll all his travels must have taken, he thought nothing of the long voyages and continued to campaign for the Tokyo bid.

His hard work paid off. The IOC named Tokyo the site of the Games of the XII Olympiad (the 1940 Olympics) at an official IOC Session. Kanō's role in the victory is virtually impossible to overstate; his clear vision for the Tokyo Olympics and his keen eye for gauging the competition combined to land Tokyo an opportunity like none before.

During the IOC Session at the end of July 1936, where participants were voting to determine the host city for 1940, Kanō gave the following notice:

> I carry with me a grave resolve. It is natural that the Olympics should come to Japan. If they do not, it will be for an unjust reason. Since participation entails traveling across such a long distance from Japan to Europe, there will be no need to take part in the event if we fail, and Japan will be justified in staging an even larger international event.[2]

If it opted not to select Tokyo, Kanō declared, the IOC would be at fault—and Tokyo would be justified in holding its own, separate international event in lieu of the Olympics. Kanō went into the IOC Session with a firm conviction, supremely confident in his belief that Tokyo was to be the site of the next Olympics.

The logic behind the Tokyo bid

The logic underlying Kanō's drive for the Tokyo bid had a historical basis. "The Olympics, which had once been the domain of the Greeks, found new life in the modern age with the aim of spreading participation throughout the world," he wrote. "As such, the Games should not only belong to Europe and the United States, but must also take place in the Far East. Out of all the possible candidates, Japan is bursting with almost unrivaled enthusiasm."[3]

There was no such thing as air travel at the time, of course. To get from Europe to Japan, one would have to board a ship, sail through the Suez Canal and then traverse the Indian Ocean, take a waterway around North America, or ride the Trans-Siberian Railway across the Soviet Union—all routes that consumed nearly twenty days of travel time. Sending athletes to Japan must have seemed like a nearly unthinkable undertaking for the European world. Citing the sizable investments of time and money that an Olympic Games in Japan would entail for the participating nations, many IOC members voiced their opposition to the Tokyo bid.

Kanō (center) and Hirota Kōki (left) pose for a photo at the 1928 Amsterdam Olympics (courtesy of the Kodokan collection)

In response, Kanō deftly used the dissenting members'

arguments to his own advantage. Since Japanese athletes had consistently participated in the Olympics since 1912 in spite of the considerable challenges of long-distance travel, he argued, it would be fair to assume that European and American athletes would have the wherewithal to gather in Japan. Making a city in the Far East the host site of the Olympics would also help transform the Games from an exclusively European and American event into a global celebration. He turned his opponents' logic on its head to reinforce his own argument. For the creator of judo—an art that emphasizes using an opponent's force against him—the strategy could not have been more apt.

In addition to laying out a convincing rhetoric, Kanō also made sure to think pragmatically and take effective action. The key move involved persuading Rome to withdraw its bid. At the June 1933 IOC Session in Vienna, Kanō gave a report to the Tokyo Olympic Committee about the state of the bid competition. "Italy is an extremely strong contender, thanks in large part to its impressive existing Olympic stadium and geographical advantage," he explained. "Prime Minister Mussolini is fully behind the effort to secure the Olympics for Rome, but he, as a man of honor, may be willing to concede if we present him with our case and ask that he withdraw his nation's candidacy."[4] The mission for Japan was to convince Mussolini to withdraw Italy's bid. In February 1935, Sugimura Yōtarō and Soejima Michimasa met with Mussolini in Rome on their way to the IOC Session in Oslo.

3. Former Kanō students at the forefront of the Tokyo bid

Sugimura Yōtarō and Soejima Michimasa

Sugimura Yōtarō (1884–1939) and Soejima Michimasa (1871–1948), the IOC members who joined Kanō in pushing Tokyo's bid for the 1940 Olympics, were both former students of Kanō.

Sugimura graduated from the middle school affiliated with the Higher Normal School in 1901. For part of Sugimura's time at the middle school, Kanō had been principal. Their connection would later become closer, as Sugimura joined the Kodokan, enrolled in the Kanō Juku, and later even lived with Kanō—in essence, the link between the two was a mentor-mentee relationship. With that bond in place, Sugimura pursued his judo studies, eventually earning the rank of sixth dan in Kodokan judo. He was a remarkable swimmer, too. When the

Zōshikai (which Kanō founded by consolidating his own *juku* organizations) began teaching swimming, Sugimura took the initiative to master the Zōshikai swimming technique and, in 1900, became the first official "first-grade" rank holder in Zōshikai swimming. After later attaining a second-grade rank, Sugimura gave instructional swimming demonstrations at the middle school and Tokyo Higher Normal School. In both judo and swimming, he learned and thrived under Kanō's guidance. During his time serving as a diplomat in France, Sugimura helped popularize judo there. Thanks to his robust athletic build, he was no smaller than his French counterparts, standing 185 centimeters tall and weighing a full 100 kilograms.

Soejima Michimasa's relationship with Kanō, meanwhile, began at Gakushūin—but it was trepidatious at first. Soejima's grades were not outstanding, and Kanō, then the school's assistant principal, would often chastise him for his subpar academic performance. After graduating from Gakushūin, however, Soejima went on to study at the prestigious University of Cambridge, became president of the *Keijō Nippō* newspaper, and even sat in the House of Peers.

Soejima became an official IOC member in May 1934 after the death of Kishi Seiichi, who had been president of the Japan Amateur Athletic Association as well as a member of the IOC. At Gakushūin, Soejima had observed how formidable and demanding Kanō could be as an educator. As an IOC member, on the other hand, Soejima saw Kanō in a different light: he witnessed the respect his senior colleague had earned among foreign counterparts. According to Soejima, other IOC members saw Kanō not as just a fellow IOC member but as the "father of judo, a world-famous Japanese martial art, in their midst."[5]

Sugimura, too, went on to have a remarkable career. After graduating from the middle school affiliated with the Higher Normal School, he studied at the First Higher School, enrolled in the Faculty of Law at Tokyo Imperial University, earned his degree in 1908, and then secured a position at the foreign ministry. Determined to acquire more knowledge, Sugimura also obtained a doctorate from the University of Lyon (France) in 1910. He later went on to become the first secretary at the Japanese embassy in France in 1923, assumed the position of under secretary-general of the League of Nations in 1927, and served both in that role and as the League of Nations' director of political affairs until Japan withdrew from the organization in 1933. All told, Sugimura was one of the brightest Japanese stars on the contemporary international stage. He strove to utilize his standing as the League of Nations' under secretary-general to foster international cooperation, but Japan's decision to pull out of the United Nations in February 1933 nullified his efforts. As Sugimura struggled to recover from that disappointment, Kanō approached him with an opportunity that would allow him to continue pursuing his vision of international brotherhood: membership on the IOC. Sugimura took the proposal to heart and, at a June 1933 IOC gathering, became an official IOC member. Thus Kanō, Soejima, and Sugimura—the former teacher and two of his former students, united in their positive outlook on world affairs—would form the powerful engine behind the push to land Tokyo the Olympics.

Rome's decision to withdraw its Olympic bid

In January 1935, on Kanō's suggestion, Soejima and Sugimura (who was at the time the Japanese ambassador to Italy) met with Benito Mussolini in hopes of persuading the prime minister to withdraw Rome—then a leading candidate—from consideration for hosting the 1940 Olympics. In their plea, the Japanese duo focused on historical significance: the year 1940 marked the 2,600th anniversary of Japan's legendary creation, and Japan wanted to celebrate that important national milestone by hosting the Olympics. Soejima and Sugimura implored Mussolini to pull Rome out of the candidate pool for 1940—and only 1940—in light of Japan's unique situation. The two poured their hearts into the negotiations. Mussolini could tell that the 1940 Olympics held immense significance for Japan. Recognizing the merits of the Japanese cause, he told Soejima and Sugimura that he would be willing to compromise in the interests of the Japanese people and agreed to withdraw Rome's host-city candidacy. Kanō's influence on the entire process was clear; Sugimura had met Mussolini with Kanō's vision in mind, and he spoke on Kanō's behalf at the February 1935 IOC Session to lay out his former teacher's logical underpinnings for the Tokyo bid.

Rome's decision to pull itself out of consideration helped tip the momentum in Tokyo's favor. The Italian IOC member vehemently denounced what he saw to be political lobbying, but in the vote at the Berlin IOC Session in July 1936 Tokyo emerged victorious, fending off the challenge of Helsinki by a final tally of 36 votes to 27. The success was a combination of multiple factors—the language skills crucial to persuasive rhetoric on the global stage, a pair of motivated, optimistic Japanese proponents, and the overarching vision of their former teacher, Kanō Jigorō. In many ways, Tokyo's victory was a product of Kanō's educational pursuits.

IOC president Henri de Baillet-Latour made the following statement about Tokyo's win.

In all honesty, I had harbored certain doubts about Japan hosting the Olympics. When I visited Japan this past March, however, my misgivings were dispelled and, ever since, I have been a friend of Japan. I am incredibly grateful that the Japanese IOC delegation did such splendid work at the recent session, far exceeding expectations in making their case. Kanō and Soejima have devoted tremendous efforts toward securing Tokyo's bid to host the Games, all in the name of their country's citizens, a dedication that was stirring to behold. The votes were tallied by Lord Burghley of England, who placed every vote for Japan to his right and every vote for Finland to his left. On every occasion that a vote went to the right, one could see a smile appear on Lord Burghley's face, although it did appear that one of his fellow countrymen cast a ballot for Finland. Now that Japan has secured the Olympic Games, I encourage her citizens to channel their elation not toward simple merrymaking but rather toward fulfilling the true Olympic spirit. It brings me no greater pleasure to have the opportunity to visit Japan once again in 1940.[6]

De Baillet-Latour's March visit to Japan had been due to an invitation from Kanō, who wanted to give the IOC president a captivating experience of his

(L) Kanō departs for Berlin with an American IOC member; (R) Kanō leaves for Berlin (1936; courtesy of the Kodokan collection)

candidate city, the unique wonders of Japanese culture, and Tokyo's ongoing development. The very fact that Japan—a country that had spent several years in international isolation after leaving the League of Nations—could convince world leaders to hold the Olympics in Tokyo was, in and of itself, a remarkable feat.

Sugimura resigned from the IOC after the organization named Tokyo the host of the 1940 Games. Having served as Japan's ambassador to Italy since 1934, he became the ambassador to France in 1937. Unfortunately, he contracted stomach cancer and returned to Japan in 1938, where he died in office in 1939. His death came just one year after Kanō's.

4. The Olympics and the martial-arts spirit

Kanō's hopes for the Tokyo Olympics

Shortly after Tokyo secured the right to host the 1940 Olympics, Kanō addressed the IOC members in Berlin:

> The seeds I have planted for the Japanese Olympic Movement have finally borne fruit. . . . Now that Tokyo has secured its role as host of the Olympic Games, it must be an example to the world. Past Olympics have been exclusively in the West, a limitation that has prevented the realization of the true Olympic spirit. With Tokyo welcoming the twelfth Games, however, we have an opportunity to make the Olympics a truly global event and reveal to the world what Japan truly is—a doubly fortuitous outcome.[7]

Noting that his twenty-seven years on the IOC had finally seen the Olympic Movement attain complete fulfillment, Kanō painted the achievement in broad, sweeping strokes. The Tokyo Olympics, as he envisioned them, could be a model for the world to aspire to and put the Olympics on course to become

A group celebrates Tokyo's successful bid to host the Olympics (courtesy of the Kodokan collection)

a part of global culture. Instead of basking in the glories of a successful Olympic bid, Kanō was already assembling his vision for the ideal Tokyo Olympics. It was a magnanimous outlook, a characteristic feature of Kanō's mindset.

After Tokyo landed the bid to host the 1940 Olympics, Kanō gave an interview with an American broadcaster. The interviewer asked Kanō whether he thought Tokyo's preparations would follow a scope similar to what Germany had done for the previous Games. "Not if it means that every host country will ceaselessly try to outstrip the other nations of the world," Kanō replied. "Were that the case, I fear that the Olympic Spirit itself might be lost to the burdens of cost and the pitfalls of extravagant spending."[8] Having witnessed the Berlin Olympics, Kanō was concerned about the dangers of Olympic sprawl.

Fusing the spirit of the Olympics and the spirit of martial arts

What exactly did Kanō mean by making the Olympics into a part of global culture? He meant weaving the spirit of martial arts, with roots in Kodokan judo, into the Olympic Spirit.

On the domestic front, Kanō had his sights set on the development of national physical education. That was not his only aim, of course; internationally, his goal was to fuse the Olympic spirit with the spiritual heart of martial arts. The Olympic spirit is an extension of Hellenistic philosophy, seeking a harmonized development of mind and body, whereas the spirit of martial arts, in Kanō's mind, was aimed at training both mind and body so as to contribute to society. Far from contradicting the Olympic ideals, the martial-arts philosophy represented an extension of the Olympic philosophy. Kanō's take on martial arts, of course, found concise expression in the ideas of *seiryoku zen'yō* (maximum efficient use of energy) and *jita kyōei* (mutual prosperity for oneself and others); that is, utilizing the most effective methods for achieving goals in real life, thereby enriching society.

The precepts of *seiryoku zen'yō*, *jita kyōei*, and *seiryoku saizen katsuyō* (the best use of one's energies) firmly lodged themselves in Kanō's vocabulary as specific points of emphasis around the time of the Kodokan Culture Council's founding in April 1922. A reading of the Council's founding principles reveals the centrality of those core ideas: "Those with long experience of research in Kodokan judo have adopted the principle of *seiryoku saizen katsuyō*, the best practical use of one's energies, putting one's efforts to good use for the benefit of both oneself and society. By the establishment of the Kodokan Culture Council, this principle can be systematically promoted and make a further worthwhile contribution to the well-being of the public at large."

Kanō laid out the following goals for the Kodokan Culture Council (see part 1, chapter 2 for more):

· To seek the perfection of each individual, physically, intellectually, and morally, thereby developing their capacity to benefit society
· To esteem the national polity of Japan and the history of Japan, and to work to improve whatever is deemed necessary for the good of the nation
· To contribute to the harmonization of society by means of mutual help and mutual compromise between individuals as well as between organizations
· To seek the peaceful elimination of racial prejudice worldwide through the promotion of cultural pursuits

The idea that a single individual could contribute to the betterment of society, the nation, and the world as a whole through the simple act of physical training was something that magnified the value of judo—and that of sport itself. Also noteworthy was the fact that Kanō's thoughts and actions implied a rejection of the racial prejudice that was rampant in the highly imperialistic context of the time. In certain ways, Kanō essentially formed his own brand of Olympism through his unique position as a judoka-cum-IOC member amid the growing tide of the Olympic Movement. It all came down to a process by which the individual could achieve self-perfection *through*, not *despite*, devotion to others, thereby driving the development of society. That other-centered philosophy was evident in Kanō's pioneering efforts to bring Chinese students to Japan, for example. Through his personal experiences in both judo and international student education, Kanō developed a powerful belief in the concepts of *seiryoku zen'yō* and *jita kyōei*.

His hope was to add the spiritual threads of martial arts, typified by *seiryoku zen'yō* and *jita kyōei*, to the tapestry of Western athletic culture with a focus on both body and mind. The 1940

IOC members greet Kanō (1938, courtesy of the Kodokan collection)

Tokyo Olympics would be an ideal platform for that vision to flourish.

5. Kanō and the 1964 Tokyo Olympics

The death of Kanō Jigorō

Over time, Tokyo's delays in its Olympic preparations and Japan's intensifying war with China began to raise red flags at the IOC. Taking stock of the situation, IOC members were soon exchanging furtive whispers about urging Tokyo to relinquish its host-city status. The members convened in 1938 in Cairo, planning to discuss the Tokyo issue. With worries about the Tokyo Olympics mounting, Kanō—then seventy-seven—headed into the IOC Session to argue on behalf of Japan.

Kanō asserted that political climates and other such factors should have no effect on the Olympics. Not a single IOC member raised a dissenting opinion. Kanō had gone straight for the ethos of sport itself, and his argument resonated with the audience, gaining support for his cause. Grateful for the widespread support he received, Kanō sought out European and American IOC members to show his appreciation and gain additional backing for the Tokyo Olympics.

The ocean liner *Hikawamaru* left Vancouver, with Kanō aboard, bound for Yokohama. On the way, Kanō contracted pneumonia and passed away a short time later. He died on May 4, 1938, two days before the ship's arrival in Yokohama.

News of Kanō's death broke immediately in Japan and spread quickly to the United States. The *New York Herald Tribune* ran a detailed, seventy-line tribute to Kanō on its May 4 obituary page, complete with a picture.

Dr. Kano Dead; Japan's Agent For Olympics
World Committee Member, 77, in House of Peers, Passes on Ship at Sea Returning From Cairo

TOKIO, May 4 (Wednesday) A radio dispatch from the liner *Hikawamaru* in the Pacific today reported that Dr. Jigoro Kano, Japan's member of the International Olympic Committee, has died of pneumonia. He was seventy-seven years old. He was on his way home after attending the Olympic meeting in Cairo two months ago.

Kano, a member of the House of Peers, was honorary president of the Japan Amateur Athletic Association.

Got 1940 Games for Tokio

Dr. Kano, who was credited with obtaining the 1940 Olympic Games for Tokio, arrived in the United States three weeks ago after attending the conference of the International Olympic Committee in Cairo. He was confident that the 1940 Olympic games would be held in Tokio, despite Japan's undeclared war with China. "Even if there is no change in the China situation by 1940," he said, "I foresee no reason for not holding the Olympics in Tokio. The games are independent of politics or other influences."

Besides being a leader in athletics, Dr. Kano, a member of the Japanese House of Peers, was a noted educator. He was councillor and director of the Common Education Bureau of the Japanese Education Department, and Director of Higher Schools. In 1901 he organized a society primarily to educate Chinese.

A small, serious man, Dr. Kano was Japan's leading exponent of judo, a formalized method of jujutsu, with all bone-cracking and pain-causing holds barred. He weighed on [sic] 105 pounds, but on his recent visit to New York he floored a 200-pound reporter by "having an object or aim clearly before the mind and finding the means to fulfill the aim most efficiently." Judo, he explained, was what Americans described as "efficiency."

Dr. Kano was the founder of the Kodokan (Judo Training School), and organized the Kodokan Cultural Society in 1922. Two years ago women in New York were reported taking up Judo under the auspices of the New York Dojo, which followed the rules set down by Dr. Kano.

One woman, who said she was the first in the United States to study Judo, asserted that it helped in reducing [sic], provided mental training and exercise and whetted the appetite.[9]

Kanō's death came at a time when relations between Japan and the United States were deteriorating rapidly. Despite the worsening diplomatic ties between the two countries, an American newspaper devoted substantial space to an obituary mourning Kanō and detailing his achievements. That a Japanese figure could merit such a prominent place in a publication stateside in the late 1930s is a testament to Kanō's extraordinary personal diplomacy; one shaped by the growing presence of judo and his embrace of the Olympic Movement.

Condolences from fellow IOC officials were further evidence of Kanō's reputation as an exemplary educator as well.

IOC president de Baillet-Latour remembered Kanō as a true educator of youth, and called the Tokyo Olympics the fruit of Kanō's lifelong dedication to elevating Japanese athletics to their current lofty standards.

Carl Diem, the secretary-general of the Organizing Committee of the Berlin Olympics, lauded Kanō as a man of integrity and one of the foremost sports educators the world has ever seen; American IOC member and US Olympic Committee president Avery Brundage (1887–1975) also called Kanō a model educator. Francois Piétri (1882–1966), another IOC member and president of the French Olympic Committee, exhorted the Japanese people to be extremely grateful for Kanō's sincere, valiant efforts. Clarence Bruce, the third Baron Aberdare (an IOC member from the British Olympic Association) said that he would be thrilled to honor Kanō's dying wishes by doing everything possible to facilitate the Olympic Games in Japan, pledging his efforts to the Tokyo Olympics.

IOC Technical Adviser Werner Klingeberg echoed a similar commitment to seeing the Tokyo Games through, saying, "It is the duty of all who hold Kanō in respect to make the Tokyo Olympics a success."

In addition to galvanizing other IOC members, Kanō's death also made officials in the Japanese foreign service determined to usher the Tokyo Olympics to success. Diplomat Hirasawa Kazushige (1909–77), who had shared the first-class cabin on the *Hikawamaru* with Kanō, issued the following remembrance.

When I think about what Kanō Sensei must have been going through in his dying hour, just two days away from arriving in Yokohama, a flood of emotions rushes over me. Having been fortunate enough to spend the final eleven days of Sensei's life with him, having now spilled my emotions on the page with Sensei lying in repose in the neighboring house, I hold in the depths of my heart a fervent hope that the Tokyo Olympics will meet with success.[10]

Tokyo's victory in landing the 1940 Olympics was a testament to the trust and respect Kanō had earned from his peers on the IOC. The triumph was in vain, unfortunately. Just two months after Kanō's death, Tokyo forfeited the Games.

Making the 1964 Tokyo Olympics a reality
After World War II, Japan once again launched a bid to host the Olympics

in Tokyo. American Avery Brundage became IOC president in 1952. A close friend of Kanō, Brundage had been a supporter of the 1940 Tokyo Olympics to the end. In a speech to the IOC, he recalled how Kanō and Kishi Seiichi (the second president of the Japan Amateur Athletic Association) touched a chord in him, inspiring his support for a Japanese Olympics through their philosophies on athletics.[11] Brundage continued to push for the Tokyo bid in the postwar era. Hirasawa Kazushige, the diplomat who had been with Kanō when he passed away aboard the *Hikawamaru*, gave the final address in support of the Tokyo bid at the 1959 IOC Session in Munich—an impassioned speech in which he held a textbook in his hand, explaining that its pages described the Olympics to elementary-school students across Japan. In delivering the address, which apparently moved the voting IOC members powerfully, Hirasawa was surely shouldering Kanō's unwavering commitment to education. Hirasawa attributed Tokyo's successful bid not to the speech he had given but rather to the ground-work that Kanō had laid in the prewar years. In his writings, Hirasawa remembered long-serving IOC members talking to Tokyo representatives about their memories of Kanō, fondly reminiscing about the man who had, in so many people's eyes, made the Tokyo Olympics possible.[12]

The 1959 IOC Session in Munich officially made Tokyo the host of the Games of the XVIII Olympiad. Two years later, the members reached a resolution to introduce judo at the Tokyo Olympics. The International Judo Federation and the European Judo Federation worked tirelessly to make judo an Olympic event. French IOC delegate Francois Piétri, long an admirer of Kanō, put his weight behind the effort, as well. Through an emphasis on using judo to educate young minds and the personal network he had built over twenty-nine years as an IOC member, Kanō was instrumental in both making the Tokyo Olympiad of 1964 a reality and initiating judo into the family of Olympic sports.

Rather than just making judo an Olympic discipline, however, it had been Kanō's aim to embed the spirit of martial arts into the Olympic Movement. Kanō's vision of the martial arts spirit was on full display at the 1964 Olympics, personified by Anton Geesink (1934–2010) of the Netherlands in the judo open-weight division. At the moment his victory became official, Geesink waved off delighted countrymen as they attempted to rush to the mat; the scene epitomized the concept of courtesy, an element so central to the martial-arts philosophy. The image of a Dutch *jūdōka* embodying the time-honored spirit of Japanese martial arts is more than just a compelling cross-cultural phenomenon—it also highlighted the indelible stamp of Kanō Jigorō's legacy on the 1964 Tokyo Olympics.

The goal of expanding the Olympic Movement from a Western dominion to a global scale informed Kanō's work on the 1940 Tokyo Olympic bid. Rather than abiding by the traditional IOC doctrine, though, he outlined a vision of an Olympic ideal for the future from the viewpoint of both a judoka and an educator. That juncture—and Kanō's beliefs—will go down in the history of the Japanese Olympic Movement. With judo and taekwondo now among the list of Olympic sports, Kanō's hopes of bonding the spirit of martial arts to the spirit of the Olympics certainly seem to have come true.

The last note former IOC president Coubertin ever committed to paper touched on the connection between the Tokyo Olympics and the Olympic spirit. "The task of celebrating the XIIth Olympic Games [in Tokyo] . . . does not mean merely to . . . unite the whole of Asia with the modern Olympism in a most cordial manner," he wrote, "but also to combine Hellenism, the most precious civilization of ancient Europe, with the refined culture and art of Asia."[13] In his dying days, Coubertin stressed that the Olympic ideal had to evolve with the times. He may have sought a beginning for that process in Japanese culture.

What made it possible for Tokyo to win its bid for the 1940 Olympics in the early 1930s was, in significant part, a vision of making the Olympic Movement part of the world's shared cultural fabric. Shaping that perspective was Kanō's long-sought ideal, a grand design where the spirit of martial arts from the Far East and the spirit of Olympism in the Hellenic heritage came together.

Notes:

1 Kanō Jigorō, "Nihon Taiiku Kyōkai no sōritsu to Sutokkuhorumu Orinpikku Taikai yosen-kai kaisai ni kan suru shuisho" [Memorandum of intent on the establishment of the Japan Amateur Athletic Association and the qualifying trials for the Stockholm Olympics], 1911.

2 *Tokyo Asahi Shimbun*, July 31, 1936.

3 *Tokyo Asahi Shimbun*, July 25, 1936.

4 Tokyo City Hall, "Dai jūni-kai Orinpikku, Tōkyō Orinpikku, Tōkyō-shi hōkokusho" [Tokyo City report on the 12th Olympic Games in Tokyo], 1939, 10.

5 Soejima Michimasa, "Watashi to Kanō-sensei" [Kanō-sensei and me], *Jūdō* [Judo] 9, no. 6 (1938).

6 *Yomiuri Shimbun* (extra edition), August 1, 1936.

7 Ibid.

8   Kanō Jigorō, "Tōkyō Orimupikku ni kitare" [Come to the Tokyo Olympics], *Orimupikku* [Olympic] 14, no. 12 (1936).

9   *New York Herald Tribune*, May 4, 1938.

10   Hirasawa Kazushige, "Kanō-sensei ga kyūsei serarete" [On Master Kanō's sudden death], *Jūdō* [Judo] 9, no. 7 (1938).

11   Avery Brundage, translated by Miyakawa Tsuyoshi, *Kindai Orinpikku no isan* [Legacy of the modern Olympics] (Tokyo: Baseball Magazine Sha, 1974), 90, 272.

12   Hirasawa Kazushige. Fukushima Shintarō, eds., *Kokusai shakai no naka no Nihon: Hirasawa Kazushige ikōshū* [Japan in the international community: The posthumous writings of Hirasawa Kazushige] (Tokyo: Japan Broadcast Publishing, 1980), 158.

13   Pierre de Coubertin, *Olympism: Selected Writings*, ed. Norbert Muller (Lausanne, Switzerland: International Olympic Committee, 2000), 705; Coubertin's message was dated July 29, 1937, one month prior to his death.

A heritage unbroken

Kanō trains with Mifune Kyūzō (10th dan) (courtesy of the Kodokan collection)

*Chapter 1 was written in English by Andreas Niehaus and has not been altered from its original state.

Chapter 1

Judo's path to the Olympics

Today, judo is trained all over the world. No other Japanese martial art has gained that much international acceptance. Just to give you some numbers from Germany: the German Olympic Sport Federation lists for the year 2009 180,599 members for the German Judo Federation, followed by karate with 106,569 and jujutsu with 54,594 members. The two major Aikido Federations have approximately 15,000 members. Similar numbers can be found all over Europe. Among the sixty sport federations in Germany, judo places twenty-one in size of members.

There are a number of reasons that help to explain the success of judo in Europe. The main reasons are in my opinion:

A judo demonstration in London (1923, courtesy of the Kodokan collection)

1. Kano Jigoro, who actively promoted judo in Europe and America by lecturing, demonstrating and awarding dan-graduations to key figures in the European jujutsu world. Also, his IOC membership helped him to promote judo around the world.

2. Organizational structure: in contrast to martial arts like jujutsu or karate, judo was and is based on a unified system, whereas karate and jujutsu fall apart in different

styles, which makes it difficult to agree on a unified tournament system.

3. Historical advantage: jujutsu and judo were the first martial arts to enter Europe, thus having the advantage of time but also the advantage of defining the image of Japanese martial arts.

4. General exotic fascination with Japan that places martial arts and also judo in the realm of mysticism and Asian spirituality.

Judo instruction at the University of Berlin (1923, courtesy of the Kodokan collection)

5. Sportification: judo developed along the lines of Western sporting traditions. And especially the inclusion of judo into the Olympic program of 1964, meant not only a further step towards sportification, but also a further step to international recognition.

In this paper, I will analyse judo's way into the Olympic program and ask the question what this inclusion meant internationally as well as nationally, and what obstacles judo faced in the 50s and 60s. I will argue that these obstacles are rooted in the Western (European) perception that were connected to stereotypical images of the Far East and Japanese imperialism. My primary sources for this analysis will be the correspondence concerning the inclusion of judo in the 1964 Olympics that can be found in the IOC Archives in Lausanne.

1. The road to hosting the 1964 Tokyo Games

First of all, it is important to note that judo would have not been included that early into the Olympic program in 1964 without the Olympics being held in Tokyo. Therefore, it is necessary to briefly comment on the significance of the decision to hold the Olympics in Japan. John MacAloon has written the following on the meaning of a nation's participation in the Olympic Games: "To be a nation recognized by others and realistic to themselves, a people must march in the Olympic Games Opening Ceremonies procession."[1] However, the IOC denied Japan the right to "march" in the first post-war games of 1948. Japan's rehabilitation as a member of the world community only began when the Japanese Olympic Committee (JOC), that had been re-established in May 1948, was recognized in 1951 on the Vienna meeting of the IOC—the same year Japan signed the peace treaty and one year later regained her sovereignty. The reintegration of Japan into the world community was strongly supported by Douglas MacArthur, the Supreme Commander for the Allied Forces in Japan. In a letter addressed to J. J. Garland, the US IOC member, MacArthur writes: "It is my personal hope that conditions will make it possible for Japan to be a competitor with the other nations of the world in 1952. Performances in swimming during the Occupation indicate that, in this sport particularly, the Japanese may be expected to make outstanding records. Participation in the Games at Helsinki should contribute greatly to a deeply felt and desirable goal of the Japanese people to join again with other nations in peaceful and cultural pursuits."[2] On June 25, 1950, the Korean War had started, marking a course turn in the politics of the occupational authorities in Japan. Japan became an important factor in the fight against Communism. Although Article 9 of the Japanese constitution denied the right to have an army, a "Police Reserve Force" was established the same year and with the support of the US, former wartime leaders (including convicted war criminals) were able to occupy influential positions in the government, bureaucracy and industry once again. By the participation of Japanese athletes in the Olympics, MacArthur, whose attitude towards Japan had always been a paternalistic one, wanted to show that the "bad child" was allowed to "play with the others" again. And Japan "played" considerably well in the 1952 Olympics in Helsinki: 72 athletes participated, winning one gold (free-style wrestling), six silver, and two bronze medals. In the end, Japan placed 17th in the total medal ranking; one place before Britain and way ahead of Germany that ended up 28th.

Taking part in the Games is therefore not only a question of being recognized, that is to present the nation to the outside, but is also a question of cultural and national identity. The Olympics itself as a symbol of peace and international friendship helped to present to the world a peaceful and loving Japanese nation; actually reinventing the former symbols of war: the emperor and the military, now called self-defense forces. Attesting to the validity of these observations, the Olympic Games had played a vital role in Japan's international rehabilitation, as well as restoring Japanese national identity following the nation's defeat in World War II. An observation that is true not only for Japan, but also for Italy (1960) and West Germany (1972).

Aware of the symbolical meaning of hosting the Olympic Games, the Tokyo metropolitan assembly decided to apply for hosting the Games of 1960 already in 1952. However, the election in 1955 decided for Rome, but immediately Tokyo decided to apply for the Games of 1964.

When the Japanese decided to apply for the Games of 1964, state organs took the leading role on all levels of decision making. Important meetings of the commission to prepare the games were held at the residence of prime minister Kishi Nobusuke and the organizational efforts were bundled within the Ministry of Education. Under the guidance of the Ministry of Education, the Games were programmatically used to re-socialize Japan into the world community as well as to promote and strengthen the Japanese identity, which centered around the terms *hitozukuri* (forming people) and *konjōzukuri* (building spirit, building perseverance). Seki Harunami, in his book *Sengo Nihon no supōtsu seisaku* ("Sport politics in Postwar Japan"), shows that Japanese sport politics in Japan after WWII—under the guidance of the occupational forces—went through a short process of democratization only to find a goal that better suited their goals in the 50s: medals. After all, in the end it is not enough to just march in the Games, but in order to be recognized among the competing nations, it is the medals that finally count. In order to enhance the chances of medals, sport education and governmental sport sponsoring became centered around the building of athletes that were able to win in international competitions.[3]

The question of the hosting city of 1964 was discussed at the 55th IOC Session in 1958 that was held in Tokyo. Although the question of the hosting city was postponed to Munich, the members of the IOC were able to get a first-hand impression of the sport situation in Japan. Especially as they could witness the organizing qualities of the Japanese during the Third Asian Games —opened, as well as the IOC meeting, by the Japanese emperor—that took place at the same time (opened May 24th in Tokyo, so in fact directly after the IOC meeting). An account in the *Bulletin du Comité International Olympique* summarizes: "They [the members of the IOC] were pondering, while witnessing the Games, whether Japan is likely to be a worthy successor to Rome in the matter of organizing the next Olympic Games. One can almost guess that they left Tokyo most favorably impressed."[4]

The decision for the XVIII Games was thus to be made in Munich in 1959 and the JOC, especially its president Azuma Ryōtarō, tried to find allies for the Japanese bid and it was Avery Brundage, who became the most important supporter and actor behind the scene. During the Munich session, the Tokyo delegate (Hirasawa Kazushige and Yasui Seiichirō), presented their bid and answered questions on May 25th from 4:55 p.m. onwards. Tokyo was elected with 34 votes (Detroit 10, Vienna 9, and Brussels 5) during the next day's session.

Hosting the Games in Tokyo meant that the Organizing Committee had considerable influence on the selection of the sports to be conducted during the Games and the Japanese organizers were able to have judo included in the program for the first time. It has been argued that the inclusion of judo in the Olympic program was a generous gesture towards the host of the Games; however, this statement ignores the fact that not only Japanese politicians and sport administrators, but also sportsmen from Japan, Europe and the United States pressed for Olympic judo. The inclusion of judo into the Games was thus not a mere generous gesture, but the result of a variety of factors.

Judo (as well as were other martial arts) was prohibited by the Allied Forces in the first years after the war, as it was considered to have considerably contributed to the ideological propaganda of the wartime machinery. The inclusion of judo in the Olympic program thus came equal to internationally rehabilitate judo in particular, and the Japanese martial ways in general. Judo was shown as a modern Japanese sport that could contribute to a world in which different nations compete peacefully. A line in the *enka* (Japanese ballad) song called *Judo Ichidai* (A life for judo) by Hoshino Tetsurō (1963) expresses this idea perfectly. Here we read (or hear): "Judo ichidai / Kono yo no yami ni ore wa hikari o nageru no sa" (A life for judo / I throw a light into the darkness of the world).

But this was only one side of the coin: in the Japanese discourses of the post-war period—in movies, literature and songs—judo can be seen as a metaphor of Japan as well as a means to transmit post-war values. To use just one more *enka* song titled *Sugata Sanshirō* (text by Sekizawa Shinichi) —referring to Tomita Tsuneo's 1942 wartime novel, made into a movie by Kurosawa Akira one year later:

Keep in your heart the saying
"It is not important to win against others,
but to win against yourself."
Train hard without complaining.
The moon laughs, Sugata Sanshirō

More than the flowering grass
I love the spirit of the grass that has been trampled down
but is still alive
What I love is the love that is forbidden.
When I cry it rains,
Kodokan.

"Train hard," one of the major maxims of sport politics in the late 50s and 60s mirrors the spirit of the post-war years, in which the nation's efforts were bundled in the task of rebuilding the country (*kunizukuri*) and putting Japan on the road to economical growth and prosperity. Rebuilding the country asked stamina as well as personal sacrifice from everybody and this "patriotic" spirit is connected to Kodokan judo. In the metaphorical framework of these popular songs, judo and the Kodokan serve as the homeland (*furusato*) of an imagined community: Japan. It should not be forgotten that judo training had been part of the education for most Japanese men in their 30s and they had incorporated and memorized not only the moves, but also the atmosphere of the training halls and the training spirit. Judo thus became a space of shared nostalgia; a place where the past was connected not only to the present but to a (shining) future as well.

By including judo in the Olympic program, another of Japan's "wartime tools" was thus rehabilitated and the value of tradition that forcefully had to be denied in the early post-war years was shown not only to the world, but also to the Japanese people. 1964 in this sense marks an important year in which tradition was to become a reference of and source for a cultural and national self-identity again.

After having these notes on the role judo played concerning the re-acceptance of Japan internationally and the rebuilding of a Japanese identity, the focus will now turn towards the actual process of "en-shrining" judo into the Olympiad of sports.

Anton Geesink, winner in the open weight division at the Tokyo Olympics (courtesy of the Kodokan collection)

2. Finally, Olympic judo

Kanō Risei (1900-86)—son of the founder of Kodokan judo, Kanō Jigorō— head of the Kodokan and president of the International Judo Federation (IJF), had officially asked to include judo into the Olympic program in 1953.[5] The IJF had been recognized by the IOC only one year earlier (September 15, 1951) as representing an international body of the non-Olympic sport, judo. The question of an Olympic judo was thus put on the agenda of the Mexico meeting in 1953. However, during this session, it was decided to postpone the discussion whether judo should be including into the list of optional sports to 1954. Ironically enough, the question was then placed in the agenda under "Reducing the Games' Program." And the odds were against judo in 1954. The Executive Committee of the IOC decided at their meeting in Athens "that no new sport shall be introduced at the Melbourne Games of 1956." In a letter to Kanō Risei, Avery Brundage—in a more personal judgment—actually mentioned three reasons that spoke against a successful application at that time: 1. the general tendency to reduce the program, 2. the notion that judo is "too new a sport internationally" and 3. that judo has "too few participants" (eighteen affiliated nations in 1953).[6]

During the meeting of the IOC which followed that of the Executive Committee, the final decision was postponed after the French representative Armand Massard, 1920 Olympic gold medalist in fencing, argued that volleyball, roller-skating and judo could "well be entered on the list of optional sports." The question of including judo (as well as volleyball, archery, and roller-skating) into the program of the Olympic Games was thus discussed again on the 50th Session of the IOC 1955 in Paris. However, none of these four reached the necessary quorum of two thirds (in this case, 34 votes). Judo even ended last with only three votes (volleyball 26, archery 19, roller-skating 7). It was certainly too early for a Japanese sport to enter the Olympics. It should also not be forgotten that the JOC had only been recognized in 1951 at the Vienna meeting of the IOC, and that its members still had reservations towards the Japanese.

But when in 1960 the IJF asked again to include judo into the program of the Olympic Games (Kanō Risei to Avery Brundage May 14, 1960), Tokyo was already chosen to host the 1964 Summer Games, and Kanō Risei could rely on political support in Japan. Besides the strong support of by then-Tokyo governor Azuma Ryōtarō, the motion was supported by the "Judo Federation of Japanese Diet Members" that was formed in 1961. The president of the federation Shōriki Matsutarō describes the groups aims "to make the whole nation raise the Olympic Movement, to make complete arrangements for the enforcement of the judo event at the 18th Olympic Games to be held in Tokyo" (Shoriki Matsutarō to Otto Mayer, June 6, 1961).

When the candidature of the IJF to list judo as an optional sport was discussed during the 57th IOC Session in Rome (1960), it was at the same time connected to the question, whether judo should be included into the Tokyo Games: "This federation [IJF] asks to be recognized as an Olympic sport, and that JUDO [sic] be included in the programme of the Tokyo Games."[7] The Japanese representative Azuma Ryōtarō strongly supported the candidature of judo during this session and expressed his hope that judo might be included in the program of the Tokyo Games. The assembly, after hearing the members—Francois Piétri, Josef Gruss and Ferenc Mezö—decided to accept the candidature by 39 to 2 votes. Despite this decision, it was not yet certain that judo would be on the program.

The decision to accept the candidature left the IOC members as well as the Organizing Committee with the question of how to reduce the program of the Games. The plan to limit the sport events had been on the agenda of the IOC for a while and a commission was supposed to propose a change of Rule 30, which stipulated the number of sports for the Games. When the question of judo was discussed, Brundage made clear that "the mere fact of including judo in the Tokyo Games inevitably calls for an adjunction to the list of sports prescribed in Rule 30." During the Session in Rome, K. Andrianov and A. Romanov proposed a change to the first sentence of Rule 30, which allows only for eighteen sports, and the following change was decided: "The official program shall include minimum eighteen and maximum twenty-one of the following sports. . . " However, in the end Rule 30 reads as follows: "A minimum of fifteen and a maximum of eighteen of the events enumerated above must figure in the program."[8]

Already during the JOC Congress in December 1960, the Organizing Committee of the Tokyo Games, which had been organized in September 1959, decided to put judo on the list of sports to be practiced during the Tokyo Games. Following Rule 30, the Tokyo Committee first limited the events of the Tokyo Games to eighteen: "The Tokyo Committee suggests the elimination of the Modern Pentathlon (owing to lack of horses in Japan) and the rowing events.

On the other hand, it asks for including judo and finally proposes a maximum of eighteen sports to figure in the program of the 1964 Games."[9] However, on the next day (June 21), a heated debate around the number of sport events for 1964 arose. Brundage had already one day earlier mentioned that the number of sports did not matter, as long as they were in accordance with the Olympic Rules. After further discussion, the final vote decided on twenty events, eliminating handball and archery. But judo was only an optional sport. And the officials of the IJF already knew in 1963 that judo would not be part of the Games in 1968.

The success of the IJF candidature certainly owes substantially to the support of IOC chancellor Otto Mayer. In a letter to Kanō Risei, Mayer wrote: "You may be assured that I shall do all what is in my power to help you" (May 28, 1960). To make sure that the members of the IOC are "acquainted with this sport," Mayer advised his friend Eric Jonas, who at that moment was vice-president of the European Judo Federation, to contact the IOC members individually and also encouraged the publication of an article entitled "The phenomenal development of Judo" that appeared in the *Bulletin du Comité International Olympique*, No. 71, August, 1960.

But what were the arguments that were put forward in favor of Olympic judo? The letters in the IOC Archives stress the following points:

1. Judo is international and growing in numbers;
2. Judo is a pure sport;
3. Judo is an amateur sport;
4. Kanō Jigorō wished judo to be Olympic;[10]
5. The inclusion of judo would mean a "true" internationalization of the Olympic Movement

Especially the argument of judo being a "pure sport" as put forward by the International Judo Federation and Kanō Risei clashed with the way judo and martial arts were generally perceived in the West. To show the Western view on judo and line of argument put forward against Kodokan-style judo, I will base my arguments on the letters sent to the IOC by the International World Judo Federation (IWJF), an international judo organization that struggled for representing judo as a governing body in the Olympic movement as well. The IWJF combined different forms of jujutsu and European judo, like judo-*do*, developed by Julius Fleck in the late 40s in Austria, under its wings. The arguments against the recognition of the IJF put forward by the representatives of the IWJF reflect not only the sport political controversies of the time, but also an ideological frame in which the dominance of the Kodokan was seen as a threat to the cultural and religious identity of the West and connected to Japanese imperialism.

In February 1955, Jack Robinson, president of the IWJF and president of the Johannesburg-based Judokwai, asked for affiliation of the IWJF and for the inclusion of judo into the Games of 1956.[11] Jack Robinson, a self-awarded 10th dan, had immigrated to South Africa from Britain and started to teach his own form of judo. He had founded the South African National Amateur Judo Association (SANAJA) and worked as instructor for the police and the military. Already in this first letter to the IOC, Robinson connects the choice of the international body that will present judo sport to an ideological choice between the West or the Far East (Japan). Robinson argues that in judo "the Western World are superior to Japan" and that the Japanese are avoiding "combat" as their defeat "is a moral certainty," more over ". . . I must state there [sic] principles and rules could never be accepted by the Western world, who refuses to bow on there [sic] knees." Robinson is seemingly referring to the ritual of greeting, but metaphorically transfers this ritual on an ideological level: the West will not surrender to the East. The matter was handed over to Otto Mayer, who informed Robinson that the IJF was already registered with the IOC and that therefore his application could not be accepted. Additionally, Mayer advises Robinson to get into contact with the IJF and form one international body. But the International Judo Federation was not willed to merge with the IWJF, an organization that was too diffuse in its administration, as well as sporting aims. In his answer letter, Robinson turns towards a more or less open "racist" vocabulary—referring to the "white men" and expressing his hope, "that every country will be officially recognized, and not only the yellow race." Robinson's approach certainly has to be seen in the perspective of the relationship between South Africa and the IOC during the late 50s and 60s. The problem of Apartheid and racism in South Africa was a sensitive issue for the IOC and the pressure to exclude the South Africans from the Games became stronger and stronger from inside and outside the IOC. And Robinson's vocabulary certainly did not fit into the Olympic idea of nations peacefully engaging in sports.

A second issue that was discussed around the recognition of the IJF and inclusion of judo into the Olympic program is connected to the question of religious teachings in judo. The diffusion and exterritorialization of judo in fact also implied an exotification of judo, as it was in the West connected to spirituality and Zen Buddhism. That Kanō Jigorō did not connect judo with Zen Buddhism or Buddhism was of no relevance in this perception.

Knud Janson, who had taken over the presidency of the IJWF, writes in a letter to the IOC: ". . . Judo for the Japaneses [sic] and their followers is not alone a sport, but a 'bodily way' for working with Zen Buddhism (Buddhism of Samurai etc.) and codex of Bushido"; and he accuses the International Judo Federation of ". . . working on 'a cocktail' of Zen Buddhism, mysticism, Bushido . . . ."[12] The IWJF clearly interprets the dominance of Kodokan Judo as a threat to the Western world and claims to protect the Christian world and Christian values from Buddhist infiltration, and in fact from *religious imperialism*: "We in IWJF like judo as a fine sport, therefore we are trying to save it from the grip of mysticism and aggressive Buddhism [sic] missionary work."[13] In order to solve the question of an assumed religious background in judo, Mayer consulted with the Japanese representative in the IOC, Azuma Ryōtarō, who denied any religious dimension in judo.[14] The problem is further pushed in the early 1960s, when Janson visits Mayer in Lausanne and hands over a *memorandum* on the issue, in which he warns, that ". . . the united Buddhism these years is trying to make a great push inside the Christian Western culture" with its "main weapon," Zen Buddhism. The fact that the members of the IOC might not have heard about the synthesis of judo and Zen Buddhism is in his view, "because a Japanese—f.i. a high-graduated Judoka—does not speak much about Zen Buddhism, "he lives Zen instead of speaking it."[15]

When judo administrators in the IJF and EJU hoped to turn judo Olympic, a paragraph concerning amateurism was added into the statutes of the IJF in 1961. "Only judokas who are amateurs strictly in respect of the rules defined by the International Olympic Committee can take part in the Olympic Games." This was an important move, as during the presidency of Avery Brundage (1952–72), the attempt to keep the ideal of amateur sportsmen was one of the major issues within the IOC. Brundage, like Coubertin, saw the Olympic Movement as a religion: "A religion, whose ethical component Brundage summed up in the single word: amateurism."[16] The question of amateurism thus was also a welcome argument for the IWJF representatives. And not only Robinson, but also Stefan Aschenbrenner and Knud Janson, a Danish judo-pioneer as well as secretary and later president of the IWJF accused the IJF of being a professional and commercial organization: "Can IOC recognize a body (IJF) which as its presidium has a professionel [sic] Judo high school (Kodokan)?"[17] However, personal and sport political ties inside the IOC are strong. And Mayer turns toward Azuma, the former judomen and supporter of Kodokan judo, to ask for clarification. In his answer letter to Janson, we read: "There is no professional amongst the leaders of that Federation in Tokyo. There are of course some teachers, but who are not leaders of the Federation" (August 12, 1960). The Kodokan had in fact already in 1909 been transformed from a private enterprise to a foundation.[18] And Kanō Risei could thus state in a letter to Brundage: "The International Judo Federation is naturally an amateur organization, and we will at this time renew the spirit of amateurism" (May 8, 1961). Yet the existence of professional judo teachers could not be denied and in the already mentioned IJF letter to the IOC from June 5, 1961, we subsequently read: "It is absolutely clear that judo professors cannot take part in the Games."

3. Competition at the Tokyo Olympics and developments following 1964

The judo competitions of the 1964 Tokyo Olympics took place in the Nippon Budokan, a "sport" hall that was especially built for these Olympic events. The Japanese fighters were clearly dominating the competition by winning three gold medals in four competitions: the gold medal winners were in the category -68 kg Nakatani Takehide, Okano Isao in the -80 kg division and finally Inokuma Isao in the category +80 kg. Despite these victories, however, it was the victory of the Dutch Anton Geesink in the open category that came to be the place of memory internationally as well as nationally in Japan, and that finalized judo's internationalization; as now it became clear to the audience that judo was not just a Japanese sport that could only be mastered by the Japanese.

However, it could already be seen earlier that the dominance of Japanese judo fighters would be ending in the 60s. The first post-war world championships were held in Japan in 1956 and 1958. In both years Japanese fighters placed first and second. It seemed that the world came (back) to the birthplace of judo, only to be shown that the Japanese were still superior in their fighting skills. In contrast to the European weight classes, the first three world championships only knew the open weight category. This meant that the comparable small Japanese fighters had to face bodily stronger European and American fighters. Fighting in only one weight category went in hand with one of Kanō's main idea's that "a weaker person can overcome a stronger through technique and spirit." And the Japanese technique and spirit was seemingly better in the 1950s. But already in 1961, when the Championships were held outside Japan for the first time, Anton Geesink won the title of world champion. The decision to have different weight classes during the Olympics in Tokyo certainly helped Japan to win as many as three gold medals and one silver medal in the four weight categories. But 1961 was also foreshadowing Geesink's victory at the Olympics and the end of the dominance of the Kodokan in terms of administration, rules, and fighting skills. The position of the Kodokan inside the International Judo Federation weakened after 1964, when the British Charles Palmer (1930–2001) took over the IJF presidency in 1965, ending the hegemony of the Kodokan for the following fourteen years. The presidency of the IJF came back to Japan with Matsumae Shigeyoshi (1979–87), however, by then also Japanese judo was not a monolithic block anymore, but internal frictions between Matsumae, the student organization, the All Japan Judo Federation and the Kodokan had broke out concerning the "right" way of Olympic and competitive judo. It is also no surprise that Anton Geesink, the winner of the open category in 1964, developed a training system during the 1970s in contrast to the Kodokan system, that was generally adopted in Europe. It was also Anton Geesink who in 1986 suggested one of the most controversial developments in judo during the last 30 years: the introduction of the blue *jūdōgi*, which was realized in 1997. The blue judogi was to make it easier for spectators and referees to distinguish between the competitors.

4. Conclusion

Olympic judo in 1964 helped to internationally rehabilitate Japan and Japanese tradition: to present a positive image to the world. At the same time it helped Japan to reinvent a national identity that was not burdened by its wartime past, but could still rely on tradition as a force within modernity. However, the loss of Kaminaga Akio against Anton Geesink also resulted in a deep crisis in Japanese judo and was followed by a power turn away from the Japanese center inside the International Judo Federation.

But despite the fact that judo became an Olympic sport in 1964, in the international public discourse judo did actually not lose its "Japaneseness."

Notes:

1 MacAloon, "The Turn of Two Centuries," 42.
2 *Bulletin du Comité International Olympique*, No. 21-22 (June-August 1950), 14.
3 Seki, Sengo Nihon no supōtsu seisaku, 87-170, esp. 152-154.
4 *Bulletin du Comité International Olympique*, No. 53 (August 1958), 45.
5 Kanō Risei to Avery Brundage, March 18, 1953.
6 Avery Brundage to Kanō Risei, September 14, 1954.
7 Extracts of the minutes of the 57th Session of the International Olympic Committee in Rome, August 22nd to August 23rd 1960, in *Bulletin du Comité International Olympique*, No. 72, (November, 1960), 63.
8 Extracts of the minutes of the 57th Session of the International Olympic Committee, August 22nd to August 23rd 1960, *Bulletin du Comité International Olympique*, No. 72 (November 1960), 69. However a final decision was not yet reached as M. Bolanaki proposed some minor adjustments. Ibid. A final text that limited the sports to 18 was agreed upon only in 1962. Extract of the minutes 59th Session of the International Olympic Committee Moscow 1962, in *Bulletin du Comité International Olympique*, No. 80 (November 1962), 50. This change of rule goes in hand with the general tendency to reduce the Olympic program, but takes not into account the decision to include judo into the next program. And subsequently the IOC eliminated judo from the games in 1968.
9 Minutes of the 58th Session of the International Olympic Committee, Athens 1961. *Bulletin du Comité International Olympique*, No. 75 (August 1961), 77.
10 Kanō Risei in a letter to Brundage in 1953 speaks of a "long cherished wish" of his father and in his petition in 1960 he writes: "He [Kanō Jigorō] wished for long space of years the participation of Judo in the Olympic Games and made a supreme effort for the realization of the organization of the World Judo System." (Kanō Risei to Avery Brundage, May 14, 1960)
11 Letter from Jack Robinson to Avery Brundage, February 16, 1955.
12 Letter from Janson to Mayer, August 5, 1955.
13 Letter from Janson to Mayer, January 21, 1956 and Janson to Mayer, January 3, 1956. Stephan Aschenbrenner (general secretary IWJF) and Julius Fleck (Disziplinpräsident IWJF) also argue from the standpoint that judo is promoting religion. However in their letters the argument is based on the notion, that what is called education in judo is nothing more than religious education. Stephan Aschenbrenner to Comite International Olympique, August 2, 1956 and Fleck to Brundage, August 10, 1956.
14 Mayer to Janson, February 14, 1956.
15 Letter from Janson to IOC, August 20, 1962.
16 Guttmann, *The Games Must Go On*, 116.
17 Janson to Mayer, August 7, 1960. See also the letter by Janson to Mayer from August 20th 1962. The issue of education was also delicate inside the IJF. The Europeans were moving towards a clear definition of judo as a sport, whereas the Japanese stressed the educational value of judo.
18 Cf. Niehaus, *Leben und Werk Kanō Jigorōs (1860-1938)*, 219.

Chapter 2

The Japan Amateur Sports Association and "lifelong sports"

1. The dream of "lifelong sports"

Establishing the Greater Japanese Amateur Athletic Association

Dai Nihon Taiiku-Kyōkai (The Japan Amateur Athletic Association), founded under the leadership of Kanō Jigorō in 1911, eventually became the Dai Nihon Taiiku-Kai (The Japan Amateur Athletic Association) as part of a national policy initiative in 1942. The organization then took another new name, Nihon Taiiku Kyōkai (The Japan Amateur Athletic Association, JAAA) in 1948, following Japan's defeat in World War II.

The "Nihon Taiiku Kyōkai no sōritsu to Sutokkuhorumu Orinpikku Taikai yosen-kai kaisai ni kan suru shuisho" (Memorandum of intent on the establishment of the Japan Amateur Athletic Association and the qualifying trials for the Stockholm Olympics) articulated Kanō's vision for promoting physical education and sports, a pivotal building block of the Japan Amateur Athletic Association. In addition to underscoring the need for a formal athletic framework, the memorandum also made specific reference to the element of "lifelong sports."

The rise and fall of the nation hinges on the prosperity of the national spirit, the national spirit on the strength of the national physique, and the strength of the national physique, as is common knowledge throughout the world, on the degree to which the individuals and groups constituting the citizenry of the nation heed the need for physical education. In the countries of the West, every individual sees his personal health as his own livelihood, while every governmental body sees its constituents by building facilities for physical education as part of its obligation to its constituents. In both the private domain and the public realm, therefore, the West embraces the notion of physical education, demonstrating a thoroughly commendable commitment. While Japan has strived hard to absorb a vast amount of Western civilization since the Meiji Restoration, the nation has incorporated virtually nothing in the way of physical education. Of actual facilities for the purposes of athletics, there is little to speak; of educational practices, what little we do have goes no further than the gymnastics that form part of curricular physical education and the disorganized exercise in extra-curricular settings. It is no coincidence, then, that our youth are growing feebler by the year—and that said physical decline is far more evident in school graduates than it is among the unschooled. We must not ignore the possibility that our nation may be confronted with a grave situation should it continue down its current path. To rescue Japan from its current predicament, therefore, the most pressing tasks at hand are to establish an official organization to promote and develop physical education in accordance with steadfast policies and begin practicing a unified system of physical education for every youth in every corner of the nation, from the largest cities to the smallest rural communities.

Kanō saw the fate of the nation as a transitive link: the welfare of the nation depended on the spirit of the nation, which rested heavily on the physical fitness of the people as a whole, which hung on the extent to which individual citizens and relevant organizations were aware of the need for physical education (or sports, essentially). Operating on that assumption, Kanō looked at Japan and saw a weakening link—the declining physique of the Japanese youth population—threatening to thwart the entire equation. Furthermore, the institutional framework for promoting sports paled in comparison to those in the West. What Japan needed, in Kanō's eyes, was a centralized organization for the promotion of physical education. He thus created the Japan Amateur Athletic Association, which in part served to organize and facilitate Japan's participation in the Olympic Games, with that very need—to bridge the athletic gulf between Japan and the West—being its chief aim. Kanō's commitment to fostering the growth of sports in Japan extended past the school walls and into society at large, a far-reaching ideal that would help mold the Japan Amateur Athletic Association around the ideal of "lifelong sports."

Promoting sports in postwar Japan

Japan's downfall in World War II made it an international pariah. Along with facing the isolation of being a defeated combatant, the country soon found itself on the outside looking in on the sporting front as well, as the International Olympic Committee (IOC) and International Sports Federations (IF) revoked Japan's membership in their respective organizations. Japanese leaders in the field knew action was imperative. A group of Japan Amateur Sports Association (JASA) directors, including Tabata Masaji (1898–1984), Sawada Ichirō (1894–1984), and Takashima Fumio, assembled an International Intelligence Committee, held gatherings with physical education–related personnel from the occupying American forces, and pushed activities designed to foster domestic interest in international athletic competition, all the while taking steps to pave the way for Japan's readmission into the IOC and IF. The drive fell short of securing Japan a spot at the 1948 London Olympics, but subsequent efforts were enough to persuade Olympic organizers to allow Japanese athletes back onto the international stage for the 1952 Games in Helsinki. JASA resumed its previous role as Japan's National Olympic Committee, which functioned as more than just an official body for Olympic activities—the ramifications of the organization's activities also extended into ending Japan's diplomatic exile.

Japan has taken part in the Asian Games, which convenes every four years, since its inception in 1951. In 1958, Tokyo's Kasumigaoka National Stadium was the primary venue for the third Asian Games. For Tokyo, which was hoping to land an Olympic bid, hosting the bulk of the Asian Games was a prime opportunity to showcase its capabilities in organizing and running a full-scale sporting event to a multinational audience.

Another building block for the effort to promote sports was the Sports Badge test. The test began to take shape in May 1947, when a committee consisting of Mizumachi Shirō, Iwata Masamichi, Ōtani Buichi, Noguchi Genzaburō, and

Kanō Jigorō, IOC member

Kurimoto Yoshihiko, working under chairman Ogasawara Michio, devised a system under which people could earn "badges" by meeting the minimum standards for athletic ability at three levels—beginner, intermediate, and advanced. What gave the members pause, however, was the possibility that observers might see the initiative as an unwelcome revival of state power, a dynamic that had given birth to the "Physical Fitness Badge Test" during the war. Those concerns led Ogasawara to consult numerous times with the Civil Information and Education Section at General Headquarters, the Supreme Commander for the Allied Powers (GHQ), where he laid out the program's specifics and focused on assuaging whatever apprehension the American occupying forces might have had to secure approval. After roughly two years of research, investigative work, and liaison activities, the committee finalized the Sports Badge Test in June 1951, and the program began administering tests that September.[1]

2. The establishment of the Japan Junior Sports Clubs Association

The Preparatory Committee for Promoting the Olympic Youth Movement
Tokyo's successful bid for the 1964 Olympic Games prompted JASA, the heir to Kanō's hopes for "lifelong sports," to pursue a dual focus: helping Japanese athletes hone an elite-level competitive edge and promoting sports across the entire Japanese demographic, particularly among the youth segment. At the core of the organization's policy initiatives was the creation and development of the Japan Junior Sports Clubs Association.

Tokyo was officially named the host of the 1964 Olympic Games at the May 1959 IOC Session in Munich, West Germany. The Tokyo Olympic Athlete Training Headquarters was established in January of the following year, with Tabata Masaji and Ōshima Kenkichi (1908–85) appointed director and deputy director, respectively. A primary focus for this body was to create the "Five-Year Plan for Athlete Development," which charted out a road map for Japan to follow in the lead-up to the Tokyo Olympics. The first year of the five-year plan, 1960, included the drafting of a European Survey Report designed to help iron out a timeline for seeing the basic plan through. The delegation to Europe, with Ōshima at the fore, spent most of its time in West Germany, which was a "second home" of sorts for Ōshima. There, he encountered an idea largely foreign to the contemporary Japanese consciousness—the "Sports for All" concept—and the "West German Golden Plan," an initiative to bolster the country's sports facilities. Inspired by what he saw, Ōshima came back to Japan and wove similar components into the Five-Year Plan.[2]

To coincide with the Five-Year Plan, JASA proposed an "Advisory Board for Promoting the Olympic Youth Movement" in May 1960. On December 9, 1960, the advisory board voted to move forward and institute a "Preparatory Committee for Promoting the Olympic Youth Movement" in hopes of giving the movement a more concrete foundation. JASA then convened a special subcommittee for establishing the Olympic preparatory committee a few days later, on December 13, and the group selected and delegated a preparatory committee roster: Takeda Tsuneyoshi (1909–92; JASA's Executive Director) in the chair position, along with two deputy chairs, twelve standing committee members, twenty-five committee members, three advisors, thirteen executive secretaries, and six representative committee members. Judging from the size of the committee, which boasted a whopping sixty-two members, JASA was obviously serious about the project. The standing committee met for the first time on January 17, 1961, at Kishi Kinen Taiiku Kaikan (Kishi Memorial Hall), and issued a statement articulating its central purpose.

The Spirit and Purpose of the Preparatory Committee for Promoting the Olympic Youth Movement[3]
1. Never before have problems among juveniles posed a more dire concern. While measures to address the issues at hand already abound in a variety of forms, there are now mounting calls for the sporting community to play a role in ameliorating the crisis among the nation's youth.
2. Fortunately, Tokyo will host the 1964 Olympics. As we progress toward the culmination of the Games, we will organize a variety of Olympics-related youth programs and work with existing organizations in hopes of pointing the masses of youth, now so prone to wayward, aimless drifting, in a healthy direction.
3. Projects for fulfilling the aims of the movement may include the following.
    i. Establishing the Youth Sports Badge program (similar to the Physical Fitness Badge Test from years ago)
    ii. Popularizing the Youth Olympic Anthem (whose lyrics have already been selected by the JASA from a pool of submissions in accordance

with a proposal from advisory board members)
iii. Organizing Olympic tree-planting projects and other activities
iv. Holding Olympic Camps
v. Cultivating an international public spirit
vi. Publishing an Olympic pictorial newspaper

The statement of purpose marked a departure from the conventional approach to popularizing the Olympic Movement among the youth segment, which centered on event-oriented functions like "Olympic Day." What informed the preparatory committee's outlook was an emphasis on sowing the spirit of Olympism and giving the younger generation a stronger physical foundation through sports themselves, not events—the same concept that would later shape the creation of Japan's junior sports clubs.

The preparatory committee's first project was the "Olympic Youth Gathering," which convened at the Tokyo Metropolitan Gymnasium on March 7, 1961 and also featured the debut performance of the "Shōnen Orinpikku no Uta" (Youth Olympic Anthem).

The chair, deputy chairs, standing committee members, and advisors of the Preparatory Committee for Promoting the Olympic Youth Movement were as follows. The leadership was a veritable who's who from the contemporary Japanese physical education and athletic communities.

Preparatory Committee for Promoting the Olympic Youth Movement: Membership roster[4] [Names given in no particular order]
· Chair: Takeda Tsuneyoshi (executive director, JASA)
· Deputy Chair: Kurimoto Yoshihiko (director, JASA)
· Deputy Chair: Hisatomi Tatsuo (director, JASA)
· Standing Committee Member: Nozu Yuzuru (president, Japan Football Association)
· Standing Committee Member: Shiozawa Kan (director, JASA; director-general, Organizing Committee Secretariat)
· Standing Committee Member: Nishida Taisuke (physical education official, Ministry of Education)
· Standing Committee Member: Ozaki Gōki (director, Tokyo Metropolitan Physical Education Department)
· Standing Committee Member: Matsuzawa Ikkaku (deputy director-general,

Organizing Committee Secretariat)
· Standing Committee Member: Ōshima Kenkichi (deputy director, Tokyo Olympic Athlete Training Headquarters)
· Standing Committee Member: Nakahara Kanji (director, JASA)
· Standing Committee Member: Takasaki Yonekichi (member, Athlete Training Committee; executive director, All Japan High School Athletic Federation)
· Standing Committee Member: Furuhashi Hironoshin (member, Olympic Youth Committee)
· Standing Committee Member: Yoshikawa Yoshiji (executive director, Elementary School Physical Education Association)
· Standing Committee Member: Yamaoka Jirō (executive director, Nippon Junior High School Physical Culture Association)
· Standing Committee Member: Asakura Masayuki
· Advisor: Tsushima Juichi (president, JASA; chair, Organizing Committee)
· Advisor: Azuma Ryōtarō (member, IOC)
· Advisor: Takaishi Shingorō (member, IOC)
· The committee is also to include a representative from the Nippon Junior High School Physical Culture Association, two from the All-Japan High School Athletic Federation, and one each from the Primary School Principals Association, the Junior High School Principals Association, and the High School Principals Association.

Two of the key players on the Preparatory Committee for Promoting the Olympic Youth Movement were Ōshima Kenkichi and Nozu Yuzuru (1899–1983; then president of the Japan Football Association). Nozu, in addition to being proficient in the German language, also had close ties with West Germany; he brought West German Dettmar Cramer over to serve as the first foreign-born coach of Japan's national soccer squad, as well. Nozu noted in his memoirs (*Nozu Yuzuru no sekai: Sono subarashiki nakama-tachi* [The world of Nozu Yuzuru: Friends and colleagues beyond compare]) that the model for the "junior sports clubs" established by the Preparatory Committee for Promoting the Olympic Youth Movement was West Germany's "Sportjugend" (German sports youth):

Our efforts to establish junior sports clubs draw significantly on the Sportjugend movement, our predecessor, with which we have forged still-ongoing exchange programs for youth groups and instructors alike.[5]

The Preparatory Committee for Promoting the Olympic Youth Movement switched gears—and its name—slightly in the run-up to and during the Olympic Youth Gathering, sharpening its focus as the "Olympic Youth Gathering Executive Committee." On March 12, 1961, after the Gathering wrapped up, the organization held its second meeting as the Preparatory Committee. There, the members drafted a policy that entailed forming and pushing the development of "junior sports clubs." To establish a logistical structure for creating the clubs, the preparatory committee resolved to select members from its own roster to form a subcommittee, lay out a basic concept for the organization process, and discuss specifics. With the explicit purpose of establishing junior sports clubs, the new subcommittee convened for the first time on May 19 and set out a timeline that would have the preparatory tasks complete in time for the Japan Amateur Sports Association's fiftieth anniversary in 1962, roughly a year away. In the period between its first gathering in May 1961 and February 1962, the subcommittee met a total of nine times. The organizational framework had firmed up by the group's eighth meeting on December 18, 1961, laying the foundation for concrete initiatives. At its ninth meeting on February 9, 1962, the group then moved to form pilot junior sports clubs, mostly in Tokyo, and finalize a corresponding preparation plan with an end objective of officially establishing Japanese junior sports clubs to commemorate JASA's fiftieth-anniversary on Olympic Day (June 23), 1962. The JASA board of directors received a prospective plan for the Preparatory Committee for Promoting the Olympic Youth Movement and, at its fourteenth meeting in December 1961, officially resolved to establish junior sports clubs.

Instructors from the West German Sportjugend organization came to Japan for a research conference in October 1963. The connection would continue to grow from there, with an annual youth-exchange program between Sportjugend and Japan's junior sports clubs being launched in 1965. Nozu and Ōshima constituted the driving force behind the international-exchange activities linking West Germany and Japan.

The formation of the Japan Junior Sports Clubs Association
The Japan Junior Sports Clubs Association officially formed as part of JASA's fiftieth-anniversary celebration on June 23, 1962, coinciding with Olympic

Day. To mark the occasion, representatives from the individual junior sports clubs received official organization flags at the ceremony.

The target of Japan's junior sports clubs—the country's first youth-sports organizations at the community level—went beyond the specific audiences of schoolteachers, the sports world, coaches, and people with an interest in youth education. On a broader scale, the essential purpose was to make the goal of developing a healthy youth segment matter to the entire Japanese population. That founding ideal is manifest throughout "Nihon Supōtsu Shōnendan no kessei ni kyōryoku o yōsei suru" (A solicitation for cooperation in forming the Japan Junior Sports Clubs Association), a document distributed to readers in a variety of fields on April 26, 1962. Attributed to JASA president Tsushima Juichi, the piece later appeared in the 110th issue of JASA's newsletter, Taikyō jihō, dated June 20, 1962.

A Solicitation for Cooperation in Forming the Japan Junior Sports Clubs Association[6]

The precipitous pace of scientific progress since the midpoint of the twentieth century has prompted the mechanization and collectivization of the means of production, which have thereby given rise to urban expansion and fueled the spread of consumption culture. By extension, these transformations have had an enormous effect on the human mind, transformed the material world around us, and brought about massive changes in society.

Amid this new reality, the challenge of living sound, healthy lives and building robust social communities is no easy task.

The gravity of the situation weighs particularly on our impressionable young citizens, the generation of tomorrow. As the times continue to shift, I cannot bear to look idly at the effects that the changing circumstances may bring.

The only means of redemption for the youth of our nation is the further endowment of education. In enriching youth education, above all, we must first devote our energies toward physical education and sports, those pathways so vital to nurturing pride, ability, and a healthy constitution in our young fellow citizens.

It goes without saying, of course, that there are two settings in which young people engage in the pursuits of physical education and sports: the school and the community at large.

As school curricula are continuously overflowing with a massive influx of knowledge to impart to students, however, we must now venture outside the realm of education and turn to the broader community to fill the rising need for new athletic settings.

That brand of community-based physical education has been largely dormant in Japan, however.

Compared to the nations of the West, where physical education and sports have made dramatic strides at the community level in recent years, Japan lags far behind—and that gulf, I am all too aware, continues to grow.

Every last child has a love for sports. Every last child treasures the ability to develop, both mentally and physically, through athletic pursuits.

Today, however, formal education alone fails to provide boys and girls with sufficient opportunities and ample environments for engaging in sports.

The upcoming 1964 Olympic Games present us with a golden opportunity to propel youth sports forward.

Under the Sports Promotion Act, which recently came into effect, we also have a responsibility and an obligation to promote youth sports.

Now, therefore, is the time to embrace the cause of youth sports in the community, nurture their growth with conviction, and use that athletic foundation to provide our young counterparts with what they need to thrive in a new day and age. The importance of that responsibility is impossible to overstate.

Drawing on our experiences, we have concluded that the best practical means of bringing that aim to fruition lies in forming and cultivating junior sports clubs with the capacity to facilitate organized physical education and sports.

That goal, however, is a collective pursuit, and one that relies on the good conscience and good faith of all our fellow citizens.

We thus call on the entire nation—not only the central government, the members of the Diet, governors, mayors, and boards of education nationwide but also teachers, athletes, physical education instructors, and every individual to whom youth education matters—to share in the spirit of our cause and lend their support to the development of junior sports clubs.

April 26, 1962

Tsushima Juichi
Chair, Japan Amateur Sports Association

JASA's decision to go as far as publishing an official, public "solicitation" for support in the name of its chair sprung from the contemporary context. In the postwar years, Japan had experienced an extraordinary economic boom, one that catapulted the country forward at a speed the world had never before seen. With that massive growth came industrial mechanization and modernization, which opened the doors to the pervasive spread of consumption culture and other side effects. While the transformations ushered the Japanese populace into a lifestyle full of material wealth and abundance, the corresponding impact on the people's mental and physical state were, as Tsushima saw it, decidedly detrimental—particularly among the younger generation. Greater affluence led to less physical activity, thereby contributing to reduced strength; upswells in consumerism drained the traditional local community of its influence, which led to dwindling numbers of youth groups, a rise in juvenile delinquency, and an increasingly younger average delinquent age. Sports, then, represented a potential path to the development of a healthier youth segment and the rebuilding of the local community itself. In Japan, the domain of school education was largely where sports had established roots and grown. By broadening the scope of sports from school settings to the larger community, Tsushima asserted, junior sports clubs could tap the effectiveness of organized athletics in addressing the social needs of the time.

Against that backdrop, Tsushima's "solicitation" appealed to the nation at large to join the movement behind junior sports clubs. The effort centered on creating new opportunities for athletic engagement at the community level, which would help nourish a healthier youth generation through ongoing programs of systematic, well-organized sporting activities.

The concrete approach to establishing junior sports clubs had a far-reaching scope from the outset. Instead of basing the activities at schools, the clubs would operate on a broader community foundation, giving students opportunities to play sports outside of their time in school and at home; instead of specializing exclusively in more advanced competition sports, likewise, the clubs would incorporate sporting activities with developmental benefits. The clubs would also extend their reach into areas as diverse as learning activities, outdoor activities, recreational activities, social activities, and cultural activities.

The reasoning behind Japan's junior sports clubs

Along with Tsushima's "solicitation," the issue of *Taikyō jihō* dated June 20, 1962, also included a piece detailing the rules, regulations, and basic principles of the newly formed junior sports clubs. Titled "Naze supōtsu shōnendan o tsukuru hitsuyō ga aru ka" (Why Japan needs junior sports clubs), the article laid out the conceptual justification for the groups.

1. Why Japan Needs Junior Sports Clubs[7]

The expanding stores of human knowledge will never cease to amaze, but recent advances in science are truly astonishing.

Scientific progress has transformed our lives and brought us a host of benefits, both in professional settings and day-to-day life. At the same time, though, we also run the risk of forgetting important truths, losing sight of what really matters, in our attempts to keep pace with the frenzied escalation of material civilization.

Research on nuclear science provided the foundation for nuclear weaponry, but that very progress is fraught with the risk of cataclysmic destruction; one misguided judgment has the potential to eradicate human life as we know it.

Advances in transportation and communications have made everyday life more convenient by leaps and bounds, as well. At the same time, however, that very progress now forces us to contend with a profusion of unwelcome noise and an excess supply of media clamor in the absence of even the slightest human compassion.

Machines are making work more and more efficient, always churning out new products. While those innovations enhance productivity, the people who work with the machines have little choice but to sacrifice their human ingenuity and succumb to the exhaustion of monotonous piecework.

Scientific progress is a remarkable achievement with numerous benefits, to be sure. However, our wondrous modern civilization may, in fact, breed human suffering unless we bring our modes of life into harmony with the development of material civilization or refashion our practical existence before material civilization takes another leap forward. This is the vital issue at hand. Human happiness entails pursuing one's work or study with a sound mind, a healthy body, and a heart brimming with hope in a trusting, cooperative connection with one's fellow man. If material civilization develops too quickly, humans will find themselves being used, even exploited by machines, their inherent human nature lost, their good health endangered and, before they know it, their happiness replaced by misery.

Science is sure to keep evolving into the future, and the advances will certainly bring welcome progress. Whatever benefits may lie in store, though, we need to fortify our own positions in relation to material civilization by fortifying our spirituality, morality, and health, a process that will help us not merely live as mere *users* of machines but rather flourish in our new roles as the *protagonists* of scientific progress.

For no one is that more important than the children and adolescents among us. Our young, with their futures full of promise, need the ability to live rich, thriving lives without ever losing sight of themselves—but they must also have opportunities to develop that ability. Therein lies a fundamental purpose: to provide the younger generation with opportunities to develop their own vitality. It is that aspiration, and that aspiration alone, that calls us to establish junior sports clubs for the benefit of all.

Tsushima's "solicitation" and "Why Japan Needs Junior Sports Clubs" both echo the same basic tenet: that society needs to establish a basic spirit, a standard of health, that might help the human race keep pace with the ever-churning march of material civilization, fueled by advances in science and technology. Essentially, junior sports clubs represented an attempt to energize physical education and youth sports in order to ensure that Japan's young population grew in a healthy, wholesome way.

As the idea for Japan's junior sports clubs emerged from that practical need, JASA steered the clubs' formation along its own philosophical course. The organization not only demonstrated a concern for the contemporary social context but also evinced a sensitivity to the legacy of Japanese athletics—the past, present, and future of the country's physical-education and sporting communities. Tsushima's "solicitation" frames promoting sports on the community level to nourish Japanese youth as a serious obligation, calling the "importance of that responsibility . . . impossible to overstate." The upcoming Tokyo Olympics helped foment the organization's reflective sense of duty, which it proceeded to act on by advocating the creation of junior sports clubs. At the 62nd IOC Session (October 7–9, 1964), shortly before the Tokyo Olympics, then-IOC president Brundage touched on the true purpose of the Olympics in his opening address.

> ... the true objective [of the Olympics] is not the transitory glory of a few medals and broken records by a highly trained sports elite, but the development of a strong and healthy youth brought up on the highest principles of the amateur code.[8]

Reading Brundage's words, one can identify the same spirit that shaped Japan's junior sports clubs: using amateur athletics to nurture a robust youth population and, by extension, better citizens. The primary focus was on that ideal, not competition in and of itself. Likely due to its clear, incisive understanding of Olympism, in large part, JASA successfully grew that seed into the Olympic Youth Movement and ultimately Japan's junior sports clubs.

Even after the establishment of the junior sports clubs, JASA continued to take up a variety of new projects in hopes of furthering the development of a healthy youth segment. In June 1963, for example, the organization required junior sports club members nationwide to take part in sports tests. That January, a training center in Asaka-chō, Saitama Prefecture, hosted the First Central Instructor Seminar, one of several organized programs for training physical-education instructors. The First National Youth Sports Festival took place that July at the National Central Youth House (now the National Chuo Youth Friendship Center) in the city of Gotemba, Shizuoka Prefecture. JASA has since sponsored numerous other instructor workshops and exchange-oriented programs, many of which continue to this day.

3. Junior sports clubs and Kanō's philosophy

To celebrate the twentieth anniversary of the junior sports clubs' founding, JASA published *Nihon Supōtsu Shōnendan sōsetsu nijusshūnen kinen: Nijū-nen no ayumi* (A twenty-year commemorative history of the Japan Junior Sports Clubs Association). The foreword, by then-president of the Japan Amateur Sports Association, Kōno Kenzō, included the following statement:

> The Japan Junior Sports Clubs Association was created in 1962 to mark the fiftieth anniversary of JASA's founding. In doing so, the Association was aiming to fulfill the lifelong mission of its first president, Kanō Jigorō: the

Kanō (left) on his way from Cairo to Europe
(courtesy of the Kodokan collection)

healthy development of young people through sport.[9]

Kōno thus positioned the creation of Japan's junior sports clubs as part of Kanō Jigorō's "lifelong mission," which dovetailed with Avery Brundage's definition of the true Olympic spirit: "[N]ot the transitory glory of a few medals and broken records by a highly trained sports elite, but the development of a strong and healthy youth brought up on the highest principles of the amateur code." It also echoed the concepts of *seiryoku zen'yō* and *jita kyōei*, the two essential elements of Kanō's philosophy.

Kanō originally founded the Japan Amateur Athletic Association with the aim of fostering the "spread and advancement of physical education and sports for the people of Japan in light of the country's current circumstances and trends in the international community." Tracing the trajectory of that founding vision, one can see that junior sports clubs were the conceptual heirs to Kanō's dream of athletics on a society-wide level.

Japan's defeat in the Pacific War also marked a major turning point for the country's political, administrative, and educational frameworks. As it transitioned into a new age, Japan had to embark on the road to recovery as a defeated nation—a position it shared with Germany. That shared bond may have been part of why Japan's junior sports clubs took cues from West Germany's Sportjugend movement and developed through exchanges between the two sides.

Even more important, however, was the fact that Kanō's personal philosophy resonated so powerfully both before and after the pivotal historical juncture of World War II. His vision of peace and his stance on education had a universal appeal, a foundation so enduring that it could withstand the tides of time. In that sense, calling the creation of Japan's junior sports clubs a "return to the Kanō philosophy" fails to do the process complete justice; framing it as "return" makes it sound as if the heritage was broken and then reclaimed, which would gloss over the larger picture. Kanō's philosophy maintained a constant presence, with legions of the like-minded passing his spirit on and into Japan's junior sports clubs—a lasting testament to his vision.

Notes:

1   Japan Amateur Sports Association, *Nihon supōtsu hyakunen* [A century of sports in Japan] (Nagoya: Nagoya Times, 1979), 141–146.

2   Nakajima Naoya and Ban Yoshitaka, *Supōtsu no hito: Ōshima Kenkichi* [Man of sports: Ōshima Kenkichi] (Suita, Osaka: Kansai University Press, 1993), 184–199.

3   "Orinpikku Seishōnen Undō Suishin Junbi Iinkai no seikaku oyobi shushi" [The spirit and purpose of the Preparatory Committee for Promoting the Olympic Youth Movement], Taikyō jihō [JASA newsletter] 97 (1961).

4   "Orinpikku Seishōnen Undō Suishin Junbi Iinkai meibo" [Preparatory Committee for Promoting the Olympic Youth Movement: Membership roster], Taikyō jihō [JASA newsletter] 97 (1961).

5   Nozu Yuzuru, *Nozu Yuzuru no sekai: Sono subarashiki nakama-tachi* [The world of Nozu Yuzuru: Friends and colleagues beyond compare] (Osaka: Kokusai Kikaku, 1979), 119.

6   "Nihon Supōtsu Shōnendan no kessei ni kyōryoku o yōsei suru" [A solicitation for cooperation in forming the Japan Junior Sports Clubs Association], Taikyō jihō [JASA newsletter] 110 (1962).

7   "Supōtsu Shōnendan to wa!!" [What are junior sports clubs?] Taikyō jihō [JASA newsletter] 110 (1962).

8   Japan Amateur Sports Association and Japan Junior Sports Clubs Association, Nihon Supōtsu Shōnendan sōsetsu sanjū-nen-shi [A thirty-year history of the Japan Junior Sports Clubs Association] (Tokyo: Japan Amateur Sports Association, 1993), 16.

9   Japan Amateur Sports Association and Japan Junior Sports Clubs Association, *Nihon Supōtsu Shōnendan sōsetsu nijusshū-nen kinen: Nijū-nen no ayumi* [Twenty years of the Japan Junior Sports Clubs Association] (Tokyo: Japan Amateur Sports Association, 1983), 2.

A return to Kanō's philosophy

1. Promoting kata research

Kata: Defining the forms

Internationalization brought numerous changes to judo. The appearance of colored judo attire, a departure from the traditional garb, is just one example of how the sport, as many observers saw it, was beginning to shift away from its roots. At the same time, attempts to return judo to the Kanō philosophy began to gain traction. A renewed focus on kata and the advent of the "Judo Renaissance" attest to that movement.

There are two basic modes of judo training: *randori*, which involves practicing and competing in a freestyle format, and kata, a systematic curriculum of forms. Before Kanō established Kodokan judo, kata was the only—or at least the primary—training method for most *jujutsuka*. Kata eventually spawned *randori*, as well. When two practitioners would face off in an arranged pattern of kata, for example, or an opponent's failure to land the intended *waza*, or technique, required a practitioner to respond with his own *waza*, a back-and-forth of maneuvers would naturally ensue. The *randori* method evolved out of such exchanges.[1]

As judo spread across borders, *randori* displaced kata as the dominant training format. In recent years, however, kata have made a comeback and gained a growing international following—one strong enough to spur the creation of the World Kata Judo Championships in 2009. Part of the basis for the reemergence of kata lies in the roots-reclamation movement: dissatisfied with the contemporary state of judo, some are shifting their focus toward understanding the *waza* and spirt of judo as Kanō envisioned them. Whether the sport will make a return to the Kanō philosophy is a question that falls to the Kodokan and the rest of the Japanese judo community.

Kanō noted several specifics pertaining to the nature and development of judo kata.[2]

1. Consider the relationship between kata and *randori* to be similar to the relationship between grammar and composition.
2. The main basis for the creation of kata was the increasing numbers of students at the Kodokan, which made it impossible to provide the individualized instruction that the institution had originally offered. The study of Kodokan judo thus required a systematic, rational system of patterns that would facilitate group instruction.
3. At the request of the Dai Nippon Butoku Kai, I [i.e., Kanō] first created *nage no kata* [throwing forms], then *katame no kata* [grappling forms], and, some time later, *kime no kata* [combat forms], after which I gave the forms further consideration and compiled them into the official syllabus of Kodokan kata.
4. I created *jū no kata* [forms of gentleness] not at the request of Dai Nippon Butoku Kai but rather as an original set of unique Kodokan forms.
5. Kata exist not only for the purposes of physical education and martial arts but also aesthetic development through the forms of *koshiki no kata* [ancient forms] and *itsutsu no kata* [the five forms], among others.
6. The syllabus of Kodokan kata shall continue to grow into the future.

As Kanō's explanation implies, *randori* and kata are complementary essentials in judo training: practitioners have to learn both, given how each affects the other. *Randori* eliminates dangerous *waza*, thereby creating a feasible freestyle format where judoka can attack and defend full-bore, but it leaves practitioners no recourse if an opponent should apply a prohibited *kansetsu* (joint) *waza* or *atemi* (body-striking) *waza*. On the other hand, kata abides by set sequences and methods—and, as a result, any attack that breaks from the predefined mold requires a response that goes beyond their scope. Kata and *randori* go hand in hand; without training in both, a judoka lacks the ability to adapt to all conceivable situations.

The Kodokan judo kata
Kodokan judo has nine kata categories: *nage no kata*, *katame no kata*, *kime no*

kata, *jū no kata*, *itsutsu no kata*, *Kōdōkan goshin jutsu* (Kodokan self-defense forms), *koshiki no kata*, *gō no kata* (force forms), and *seiryoku zen'yō kokumin taiiku* (maximum-efficiency national physical education).

Kanō emphasized the importance of practicing kata with a complete understanding of their different purposes, which ranged from competition and physical education to aesthetic sensitivity.[3] In modern-day kata competition, athletes perform in seven kata groups—all but the *gō no kata* and *seiryoku zen'yō kokumin taiiku* categories.

1. *Nage no kata* (throwing forms)
There are three types of judo techniques: *nage* (throwing) *waza*, *katame* (grappling) *waza*, and *atemi* (body-striking) *waza*. The *nage no kata* group comprises three representative techniques from the five categories of *te* (hand) *waza*, *koshi* (hip) *waza*, *ashi* (foot and leg) *waza*, *masutemi* (forward sacrifice) *waza*, and *yokosutemi* (side sacrifice) *waza* for a total of fifteen maneuvers. The *nage no kata* was created to help judo practitioners understand the basic techniques of *nage waza*, such as how to set up, execute, and receive each *waza*.

2. *Katame no kata* (grappling forms)
The *katame no kata* comprises five representative techniques from the *osaekomi waza* (pins), *shime waza* (strangling), and *kansetsu waza* (joint locks). By learning the *katame no kata*, judo practitioners can acquire the essential principles of pinning and grappling, controlling their bodies, and maintaining the proper attitude, among other concepts.

3. *Kime no kata* (combat forms)
Kanō created the *kime no kata* to give judo students a simple, effective way to defend against a variety of attacks via applications of *nage waza*, *katame waza*, and *atemi waza*. Several years after establishing the Kodokan, Kanō devised thirteen (originally ten) *shinken-shōbu no kata* (combat-forms) to accompany the *randori kata*.

4. *Jū no kata* (forms of gentleness)
Combining the *riai* (the principle of using correct, sufficient motion to perform each technique properly with maximum efficiency) and methods of attack and defense in forms of smooth motion and aesthetic lines, the *jū no kata* consists

of fifteen techniques that serve to foster vitality and nurture enrichment both internal and external. The *jū no kata* can be performed anytime, anywhere, and in any type of clothing by both men and women regardless of age.

5. *Itsutsu no kata* (the five forms)

The *itsutsu no kata* comprises five forms, but the group is incomplete, and the individual forms have no names. The first two show clear similarities to kata from Kitō-ryū jujutsu. The forms are said to evoke the appearance and principles of natural forces.

6. *Kōdōkan goshin jutsu* (the Kodokan self-defense forms)

Created in January 1956, the *Kōdōkan goshin jutsu* is a collection of judo *waza* for the purposes of defending against external dangers. The group, which includes twenty-one forms (twelve in the "unarmed" category and nine in the "armed" category), centers on the practical mastery of responding to attacks upon contact.

7. *Koshiki no kata* (ancient forms)

The *koshiki no kata* group is mostly *nage waza* intended for armored grappling in ancient times. The group consists of fourteen *omote* (front) and seven *ura* (back) forms.

Kanō essentially appropriated the Kitō-ryū kata, which he had studied before founding Kodokan judo, into his own curriculum's *koshiki no kata* as-is for their technical merits, theoretical quality, and spiritual virtue. The principles behind the stately elegance of the *omote kata* and quick-acting resolution of the *ura kata* reflect that heritage.

The fourteen *omote* (front) *kata*
· *Tai* (Ready posture)
· *Yume no uchi* (Dreaming)
· *Ryokuhi* (Strength dodging)
· *Mizu-guruma* (Water wheel)
· *Mizu-nagare* (Water flow)
· *Hiki-otoshi* (Draw drop)
· *Ko-daore* (Log fall)

· *Uchikudaki* (Smashing)
· *Tani-otoshi* (Valley drop)
· *Kuruma-daore* (Wheel throw)
· *Shikoro-dori*
  (Grabbing the neckplates)
· *Shikoro-gaeshi*
  (Twisting the neckplates)
· *Yūdachi* (Shower)
· *Taki-otoshi* (Waterfall drop)

The seven *ura* (back) *kata*
· *Mikudaki* (Body smashing)
· *Kuruma-gaeshi* (Wheel throw)
· *Mizu-iri* (Water plunge)
· *Ryūsetsu* (Willow snow)
· *Saka-otoshi* (Headlong fall)
· *Yuki-ore* (Snow break)
· *Iwanami* (Wave on the rocks)

Kanō performs kata (1929, courtesy of the Kodokan collection)

The Kodokan Waza Research Division: Background, development, and activities

The Kodokan Waza Research Division was founded on July 1, 1954. "Considering the current status of judo that has been spreading on a global basis," the statement of purpose read, "the Kodokan, which is the origin of judo, has the responsibility of studying, standardizing, establishing, and explaining both *waza* and kata. Moreover, these activities are extremely important in the aspects of diffusion and development. This is why we are forming this research division."[4] The Kodokan Waza Research Division originally consisted of the Nage Waza Research Group, the Katame Waza Research Group, and the Kata Research Group, which pursued their respective studies accordingly. The Nage Waza Research Group and Katame Waza Research Group focused on the names of the growing number of new *randori waza* whose *riai* were difficult to assign to an existing *waza* category, while the Kata Research Group standardized techniques to establish model kata for learners to emulate.

The three groups eventually integrated in 1977, forming a unified organization that would tackle one research area at a time.

After first assigning new names to *nage waza*, the consolidated research wing proceeded to choose new names for *katame waza* and then standardize the remaining uncategorized kata. In 1992, the organization finished standardizing the entire kata curriculum with the *itsutsu no kata*.

2. International kata championships

The creation of the Kata Commission and the IJF Kata World Cup

Official kata competition has spread steadily on the intercontinental stage, especially since the turn of the twenty-first century. After the Pan-American area got a relatively early start in holding kata tournaments, the European Judo Union followed suit in 2005 with the first Kata European Judo Championships (London). Next came Southeast Asia, which incorporated kata competition (*nage no kata* and *jū no kata* only) into the Southeast Asian Games in 2007. In Japan, the diffusion of kata competition began in 1997, when the Kodokan and the All-Japan Judo Federation held the first All Japan Judo Kata Championships.

After ten Japanese national championships in Japan, the growing momentum for organizing international kata tournaments spurred the creation of the Kodokan Judo Kata International Tournament, which convened for the first time at the Kodokan's Grand Dojo in 2007.

In 2007, new International Judo Federation (IJF) President Marius L. Vizer proposed a new project: the development of an official framework for kata competition. The IJF then began preparations for a world-championship tournament to be held in 2009.

In January 2008, the Kata Commission met for the first time in Paris, with Development Project Committee Chair and IJF Director Jean-Luc Rougé (president of the French Judo Federation) playing the leading role. Kata Commission Chair Franco Capelletti (Italy) headed up the meeting, which was attended by representatives for Europe (Sugiyama Shōji, Italy), Pan-America (Takeuchi Kuniko, United States), Asia (Komata Kōji, Japan), and Oceania (Ivor Endicott-Davies, Australia). Africa did not take part in the gathering.

At the meeting, the attendees set to discussing the specifics of the following year's inaugural world championships. The talks resulted in several rules and regulations: each continental delegation would select official judges for certification by the IJF; the competition would involve performances of five Kodokan kata groups (*nage no kata*, *katame no kata*, *kime no kata*, *jū no kata*, and *Kōdōkan goshin jutsu)*; scoring would adhere to the European Judo Union criteria; and each participating country would be able to enter a set number of competitors and judges in the competition.

The first IJF Kata World Cup took place in November 2008 at the dojo adjoining the French Judo Federation's headquarters, drawing athletes from twenty-three countries. Europe accounted for most of the turnout, which also included two countries from Asia (Japan and Iran), three from the Pan-American zone (the United States, Canada, and Colombia), one from Africa (South Africa), and one from Oceania (Australia).

Looking at the breakdown by category, eighteen pairs from fourteen countries competed in the *nage no kata* category, sixteen pairs from fourteen countries in *katame no kata*, thirteen pairs from eleven countries in *kime no kata*, seventeen pairs from thirteen countries in *jū no kata*, and thirteen pairs from eleven countries in *Kōdōkan goshin jutsu*.

The *nage no kata* and *katame no kata* competitions took place on day one, followed by the remaining three categories on the second day. All five categories had separate preliminaries and finals. Five judges watched the athletes' performances from the front (*shōmen*) side, sitting at one-meter intervals.

Japanese athletes dominated the competition, taking first in every category except *nage no kata*, which the Romanian team won. All in all, the tournament was a resounding success: despite organizers initially envisioning the competition as a platform for certifying judges, the Kata World Cup—in both name and quality—proved to be far more than just a test event for future world championships.

The first World Kata Judo Championships

After the success of the 2008 World Cup, the IJF sponsored the first World Kata Judo Championships in Malta in October 2009. The event, like its predecessor, featured judoka from twenty-three participating countries, the same competition categories (*nage no kata, katame no kata, jū no kata, kime no kata*, and *Kōdōkan goshin jutsu*), and a new addition: the Judo Show World Cup.

The competition allowed for up to two pairs of competitors from each country. In total, the *nage no kata* category fielded nineteen pairs, *katame no kata* eighteen pairs, *jū no kata* sixteen pairs, *kime no kata* fifteen pairs, and *Kōdōkan goshin jutsu* fourteen pairs. The Japanese contingent had one pair in each category. Besides competing in the official tournament, seven pairs took part in the Judo Show—a relatively small side event that was closer to entertainment than an actual competition. The demonstration showcased the sport in a variety of different formats, but the nominal "scoring" system was ambiguous at best. Lukewarm to the whole idea, Japan decided not to enter any athletes or judges in the Judo Show.

On the judging side, the event enlisted twenty-six (twenty from Europe, two from Asia, one from the Pan-American zone, and three from Oceania) of the thirty-two judges that the IJF had authorized via the previous year's World Cup. The participating judges assembled for a full-day judging seminar on the day before the tournament, where they reviewed World Cup footage to help establish a consensus on *waza* scoring criteria, did judging simulations, and underwent individualized judging assessments, with Commission members on hand in advisory roles.

The scoring rubrics for Japanese competitions and international competitions differ in certain respects. At Japanese tournaments, the maximum score for any given *waza* is 10 points. Judges award participants 9 or 10 points for "Excellent" performance, and lower scores correspond to lower-quality execution: 7 or 8 points for "Good," 5 or 6 for "Correct," 3 or 4 for "Nearly correct," and 1 or 2 for "Poor." Besides the number of *waza* a competitor performs, "overall flow and rhythm," "courtesy," and other criteria also factor into each assessment, giving every kata a different perfect score. Once the scores from all five individual judges are in, the highest and lowest marks are discarded; the judoka's final score is the total of the remaining three judges' scores.

European tournaments, meanwhile, employ a "points-off" scoring system. Assessing each performance against the maneuvers in Kodokan kata videos, which serve as the primary models for perfect execution, judges deduct points for mistakes in a judoka's performance according to the severity of the error. Competitions define the specific movements that constitute mistakes in three categories: large mistakes (a five-point penalty; maximum of one per performance), medium mistakes (a three-point penalty; maximum of one per performance), and small mistakes (a one-point penalty; maximum of two per performance). In addition to assessing mistakes (number and severity only), the judges also give each competitor a score for "fluidity," "course," and "rhythm," similar to the "overall flow and rhythm," "courtesy," and other elements in the Japanese system. The process of tabulating a judoka's final score is identical to the Japanese pattern, as well, with the highest and lowest scores from the five judges eliminated from the total.

In *randori* competition, rules customarily prevent a judge from working any match that involves a judoka from his or her own country. In kata competition, however, there are no stipulations against a judge and a performer sharing the same nationality.

The first World Kata Judo Championships spread across two days, with *nage no kata*, *katame no kata*, and *jū no kata* on the first day and *kime no kata*, *Kōdōkan goshin jutsu*, and a Judo Show on the second. Each performance was assessed by five judges and one commission member sitting on the *shōmen* side so that they could assess the kata from the same vantage point.

One of the major differences between the Kata World Cup in 2008 and the World Kata Judo Championships in 2009 had to do with the order in which qualifying judoka performed in the finals. While the 2008 competition had the qualifier with the lowest preliminary score perform first in the finals, the 2009 championships selected the order via a lottery.

Japanese judoka packed the podium, placing first in all the events. The only other countries with athletes placing in the top three were Spain (with three pairs coming in second and one pair in third), Italy (two pairs in second and three pairs in third), and Romania (one pair in third). Among the higher-finishing foreign judoka, several had taken part in Kodokan Summer Courses. In terms of overall judo quality, the competition was a marked improvement on the performances at the World Cup.

Kata performances were once little more than decorative garnishes to accompany tournament competition—and, for many years, that secondary status never warranted a panel of judges.

Now that the judo community has official kata competitions on a global scale, however, kata performance finds itself in the category of judged "routine" sports. That evolution has had its share of consequences, of course. People fear that kata performances will become more rote, by-the-book replications, with performers so anxious about making "mistakes" that their execution falls flat or strays from the *riai*. In some cases, meanwhile, performers overexaggerate to the point of bordering on theatrics. Observers are concerned about a possible rise in kata performers pandering to the judges, using artifice in hopes of gaining higher scores. To many, the true essence of kata may be fading.

The fact that kata judges currently are allowed to evaluate performances by judoka from their home countries raises obvious questions about impartiality, as well.

While competitive kata may thus have several concerns to iron out, the framework has also had a positive impact. Athletes from countries that have never fared well in *randori* competition now have more chances to garner medals on the international stage, a development that helps level the playing field and extend judo's global reach. At the Southeast Asian Games, for example, a Laotian judoka took home a gold medal.

Clarifying competition rules, standardizing scoring criteria, and deciding how to handle additions of new kata are just several of the challenges that the IJF will need to address—and Japan will likely need to play an even larger role in seeing the efforts through. The future of kata competition will depend largely on how well the leaders of the judo community can preserve the spirit central to Kanō's vision, from an emphasis on smooth, flowing execution to the importance of courtesy and core judo principles. In that sense, the process of learning kata will need to go beyond simply mastering the movements—an understanding of Kanō's vision and the history of judo itself will also be vital.

3. The "Judo Renaissance"

The stirrings of the "Judo Renaissance" movement (2001–November 2004)

Judo has gone global. Waves of internalization have helped the sport take hold in countries around the world. With an increasingly diverse mix of countries earning medals in competition, too, judo is on its way to reaching an even larger audience. At the same time, however, far-reaching expansion can also lead to dilution. There is real concern that judo might be drifting away from its roots, and some groups are making efforts to address the situation. One example is the Judo Renaissance movement, which originated in at the turn of the twenty-first century. It aimed to solidify judo's basis in the founding vision of Kanō Jigorō and move away from an overemphasis on competition in favor of a focus on human education.

The Judo Renaissance grew out of a suggestion by Nakamura Ryōzō (then a professor at the University of Tsukuba and IJF education and coaching director) and an official proposal by Kanō Yukimitsu (then president of the Kodokan and president of the All Japan Judo Federation). In 2001, the Kodokan and the All Japan Judo Federation teamed up to create a joint Judo Renaissance Committee.

The project began with a lineup of four committees:

1. Committee I (Chair: Yamashita Yasuhiro): Personal-development and campaign activities

Objectives: Committee I will help the members of the judo community establish a renewed awareness of *seiryoku zen'yō* and *jita kyōei*, which constitute the essence of judo, and understand their identity as the embodiment of the judo ideal. From that frame of mind, judo practitioners will be able to become models of responsible conduct and appearance in daily life for other athletes to aspire to and, by extension, develop as individuals capable of making positive contributions to society.

2. Committee II (Chair: Satō Nobuyuki): Educational and promotional activities

Objectives: Committee II will encourage children in youth judo programs to devote themselves to their studies, in addition to engaging in judo training, and be considerate of others, thereby cultivating personal qualities befitting the leaders of tomorrow.

The Committee also strives to encourage effective instruction by discouraging biased, win-at-all-costs coaching and advocating approaches that guide athletes toward performing to the best of their abilities in competition. At the same time, the Committee will require instructors to value effort and assess athletes based not only on their results but also on their progress in practice.

3. Committee III (Chair: Uemura Haruki): Volunteer activities

Objectives: Committee III will establish rules requiring all judo events, including competitions and seminars, to introduce and implement the IJF "Fair Play Award" given the need for models of upstanding behavior amid the failing morals and lack of respect for public facilities pervading society. The effort will help make judo venues—where clean, orderly, and respectful use will be the norm—into exemplary venues for other sporting-competition sites to emulate.

4. Committee IV (Chair: Nakamura Ryōzō): Exchange activities for people with disabilities

Objectives: The Committee will make judo venues as barrier-free as possible and facilitate access via wheelchairs and other adaptive devices to help establish the sport as a spectator-friendly, accessible martial art. The Committee will also actively support the Paralympics and strive to increase practitioner numbers across the board.

Judo Renaissance activities (phase one) (November 2004–March 2006)

When the Judo Renaissance movement began, the term "Judo Renaissance" grabbed more attention than the actual motivations of the initiative. The novelty of the name led many to see the "renaissance" as a superficial movement, a simple program that would amount to little more than organizing cleanup activities or practicing proper etiquette. Gradually, however, the message got through to the target audience. People—both in Japan and overseas—began to embrace the idea of passing Kanō's judo vision on to coming generations.

The four existing committees eventually merged into a single entity in November 2004. Working with the All Japan Judo Federation's various expert panels and other groups, bodies, and organizations, the unified Judo Renaissance Committee began formulating plans for more concrete projects.

The efforts had an expansive, all-inclusive scope. Setting its sights on the judo community five and ten years down the road, the Committee sought to establish judo in the public consciousness as a sport with both educational merit and a competitive appeal—ingredients that could help judo win a broader interest base. The whole initiative centered on the interface with the public, so the Committee avoided taking a one-sided approach to implementing its ideas. Incorporating input from a variety of sources, the members concentrated on setting every project in motion on a foundation of mutual understanding.

Judo Renaissance activities (phase two) (April 2006–present)

In 2006 and 2007, the Judo Renaissance Committee turned its attention to executing concrete projects. Bolstering its connections with expert panels and other organizations, the group began delegating promotional work and activities to the appropriate parties. The logistical framework firmed up, too, as the Committee organized the various activities under its umbrella into eight project-specific subcommittees. Expanding the scale of the Judo Renaissance effort was another priority, which the Committee did by networking with prefectural institutions around Japan. In 2007, the second year of the phase-two initiatives, the Judo Renaissance Committee started organizing at the prefectural level, and a variety of independent initiatives ensued.

The Judo Renaissance movement, which launched in 2001 to help return judo to its roots in Kanō's vision, to use the sport as a vehicle for "human education," and to sustain the judo tradition in its proper form, reached its tenth year of existence in 2010. At that juncture, movement leaders transitioned into discussions about how they would turn their past decade of far-reaching activities and the coming decade of future initiatives into a complete, twenty-year culmination of their efforts.

Judo Renaissance activities on the prefectural level, meanwhile, were fostering a growing number of independent activities on organized foundations—but not every prefecture took the same approach. To help bridge the gaps that were beginning to appear, the Judo Renaissance Committee brought prefectural Judo Renaissance personnel together for a "Judo Renaissance Forum" and began working to give independent projects across the country a stronger push.

At the end of the forum, the participants adopted The Judo Renaissance Declaration 2010.

The Judo Renaissance Declaration 2010
1. We shall encourage instructors to straighten up and take responsibility for upholding the ideal of "completion of self and contribution to the well-being of society at large."
2. We shall focus on teaching *waza* in a principled, rational way and value *ippon*-style judo.
3. We shall strive to popularize and develop judo with a focus on safety so that men and women of all ages can fully enjoy the sport.
4. We shall be and train learners to be judoka with a sense of courtesy, proper etiquette, and dignity.

The Judo Renaissance was a natural product of the need to pass judo—and Kanō's teaching's—on to future generations as accurately as possible.

Kanō Risei, the third director of the Kodokan, argued that the judo community should not simply *aspire* to the ideal of *jita kyōei* but rather *embody* the realization of *jita kyōei*. Ideally, there would never have been a need to organize a Judo Renaissance movement. Looking to the future, however, the judo community will have to create more opportunities for exploring ways of developing the sport: how to pass the correct judo techniques on, convey the fruits of judo training, nurture international exchange through judo, and translate the sport into the betterment of society.

4. The return to Kanō Jigorō

Revising the judo judging conventions (International Judo Federation)

The evolution of the IJF's judging conventions offers revealing insight into the organization's stance on the sport. For several years after its founding in 1952, the IJF used the Kodokan's judging rules. When the organization established its own judging conventions for the first time in 1967, the stipulations still bore a strong resemblance to the Kodokan conventions. The first significant departure came in the IJF's 1974 revisions, which added *yūkō* and *kōka* scores to accompany the conventional *waza-ari* score. A *yūkō* equated to a "near-*waza-ari*," while a judge would award a *kōka* for a maneuver giving a judoka a technical advantage (the positive equivalent of a *shidō* penalty). In the Kodokan rubric, however, the *kōka* concept applies exclusively within the execution of an attack—the organization does not treat *kōka* as an independent *waza* score.

In 2009, the IJF decided to do away with the *kōka* score and institute a ban on directly grabbing an opponent's pants. The alterations to the judging conventions essentially represented a course correction: the IJF wanted to put the emphasis back on the *ippon* style, and the changes appear to have had the desired impact. At the World Judo Championships in September 2010, the year the IJF's new judging conventions went into effect, victories by *ippon* increased considerably. The effort to make *ippon* a focus harmonized with the theme behind the whole competition: a return to judo's roots. The medal design even featured an engraved portrait of Kanō Jigorō.

Organized competition has obviously had an enormous influence on judo, spurring the development of a point system that determines athletes' eligibility for the Olympics and other tournaments. The recent shift toward back to an earnest, *ippon*-focused style—competitive judo at it most elegant—represents a reclamation of the sport's original roots. Judo continues to globalize and develop, but current trends show that the judo community is trying to steer the sport's progress to its source: Kanō, whose defining imprints need to be evident in judo as it evolves.

5. The efforts of the Associazione Italiana Sport Educazione (Italy Association for Sport Education)

Looking around the judo world outside Japan, one can see ample evidence of the movement toward Kanō's philosophy. The Associazione Italiana Sport Educazione (Italy Association for Sport Education), for example, has embraced the ideas Kanō held as an educator and made the concepts of *seiryoku zen'yō* and *jita kyōei* into centerpieces of its various activities. The Associazione Italiana Sport Educazione, a group with roughly 3,500 members, operates with the official approval of the Italian Ministry of Health and Ministry of Education, University and Research. Originally founded by leaders in the judo community, the organization centers its mission on teaching authentic judo in line with Kanō's *Jūdō kyōhon* (The fundamentals of judo; 1931)—the *ippon* style—and cultivating Kanō's ideal of *jita kyōei* (the concept of devoting oneself to others to enable both self-realization and social prosperity). The group's activities stretch across a broad athletic scope, including sports, yoga, dance, aikido, and kendo, and include a variety of programs:

1. Judo workshops for young people
In its judo workshops and summer camps for young people, the association emphasizes the *ippon* philosophy over the point system and holds competitions with special rules that approximate Kanō's original judo practices.

2. Judo instruction for people with disabilities
To embody the *jita kyōei* concept, the association organizes judo workshops for people with disabilities.

3. Initiatives to develop female leaders in the sports world
The association also holds various judo training sessions and seminars to help bring more female leaders into the sports community.

4. Farming programs
Collaborating with partner universities, the association organizes programs that give students opportunities to appreciate the importance of natural resources and the environment through firsthand farming experiences.

The association clearly places Kanō's *jita kyōei* tenet in the foreground, aiming to nurture that ideal in program participants. Ever since Kanō gave judo demonstrations and lectures in Italy in 1928, the sport has enjoyed an enthusiastic reception in the country—a fertile environment for developing educational programs in Kanō's name.

In 2010, the year that would have marked Kanō Jigorō's 150th birthday, the Associazione Italiana Sport Educazione sponsored twelve seminars in Rome, Milan, Palermo, and other Italian cities to give audiences a clearer understanding of what Kanō built his philosophy around and how his ideas translate into real-world, everyday settings. The group also held an international symposium in October, Kanō's birth month. In attendance at the event was Japanese judoka Tanimoto Ayumi, who gave guests a glimpse of *randori* practice. That same month, the association also published a book on Kanō's impact as an educator.

Ivana Gaio Barioli, president of the Associazione Italiana Sport Educazione, contributed the following message to commemorate the unveiling of the Kanō statue at the University of Tsukuba on December 10, 2010:

We have long immersed ourselves in the sport of judo. Over time, however, we gradually realized that our focus on the Olympics was no more than one small step forward within the scope of moral training central to Kanō-sensei's vision.

The practice of judo, like "samskara," the Sanskrit word for the "formations" of the Buddhist tradition, leads the individual to fuller completion as a human being. In our educational efforts in dojo and school settings, we focus on helping students follow that path toward self-realization and gain the abilities to benefit human progress.

While scientific advances continue to press forward in today's modern age, that constant evolution is outpacing human development—we have not yet progressed to a level where we can make effective use of all the science in our midst.

For that reason, we encour-

International Symposium for Sport: Commemorating the 150th Anniversary of Kanō Jigorō's Birth

age schools around the world, especially those in civilized nations, to adopt developmental curricula with a grounding in holistic human development and a sense of responsibility—an ideal that has faded in the face of intellectualism.

We know that Kanō-sensei's judo can provide us with education to benefit human progress and offer the young people of the world such a valuable philosophy to learn from.

To create a true human race of men and women in the place of uncompassionate individualism, to ensure that our youth can carry society further forward, we need to place an emphasis on understanding the aesthetic dimensions of human life.

November 2010
Milan, Italy

Ivana Gaio Barioli
President, Italy Association for Sport Education

The movement to make a return to Kanō's central philosophy is gaining momentum across divides the world over, spanning the International Judo Federation, the rest of the judo community, and even foreign educational organizations behind specialized programs for judo, workshops for other martial arts, and school curricula. The IJF's official definition of judo reads, "Judo was created in 1882 by Professor Jigoro Kano. As an educational method derived from the martial arts, judo became an official Olympic sport in 1964." By making that statement part of its canon, the IJF firmly grounds the sport in Kanō's heritage: everyone in the judo community thus knows that Kanō continues to occupy a central position in the sport and offers a touchstone to rely on. Given the importance of that foundation, the Kodokan and All Japan Judo Federation need to keep up their efforts to spread Kanō's philosophy—both in Japan and abroad—in ways that resonate with contemporary audiences.

Notes:
1   Kanō-sensei Denki Hensan-kai, ed., *Kanō Jigorō* (Tokyo: Kodokan, 1964), 374.
2   Daigo Toshirō "Kōdōkan jūdō no 'kata' ni tsuite (7)" [The Kodokan judo *kata* (7)], *Jūdō* [Judo] 80, no. 4 (2009).

3   Daigo Toshirō "Kōdōkan jūdō no 'kata' ni tsuite (1)" [The Kodokan judo *kata* (1)], *Jūdō* [Judo] 79, no. 10 (2008).
4   Daigo, "Kōdōkan jūdō no 'kata' ni tsuite (1)" [The Kodokan judo *kata* (1)].

*Chapter 4 was written in English by Andreas Niehaus and has not been altered from its original state.

Chapter 4

Expectations toward budo on the European front

Introduction

Japanese budo today is trained throughout the world and we can certainly speak of an international budo-boom. However with its diffusion, budo also adapted to a certain degree to the sporting traditions and body cultures of the countries budo was "exported" to, and by that losing some of its distinctive cultural markers; a process that has also been described as exterritorialization.[1] The described development is, however, only partially influenced by the traditions of different cultures, but it can be argued that the perception of Japanese culture is mirrored in the perception of budo and that budo is adapted to this idea of Japan. These findings leave the question whether there still is a common denominator to all budo, international as well as Japanese? I will argue that there is something common to all budo, which can be found in the value budo can have for society.

1. Characteristics of budō

Budo obviously subsumes a broad variety of martial ways that differ in terms of body techniques, as well as philosophical or theoretical framework. The stated diversity of budo makes the attempt to identify common budo values rather difficult. Yet there are, in my opinion, certain aspects that form a uniting denominator for all budo. And the declaration of the *Budo Charter*, which has been signed by the major Japanese Martial Arts Federations (including the All Japan Judo Federation) has to be seen as an attempt to create a binding framework.[2] Speaking about budo also means speaking about sport, as both are often seen as antagonistic in nature. Talking to *budōka* in Europe, sentences like "Aikido is not sport, it is budo," and "Karate is not sport, it is budo" can be heard. Even in judo, which is considered certainly by the definition of the International Judo Federation to be a sport, this sentence is regularly applied. Clearly, budo and sport are considered to be different. Competition certainly can not serve to differentiate between budo and sport, as most of the modern budo include competition in their systems. So is there a difference in competition itself? Is an *ippon* system budo and a system that allows for a point system sport? Are budo and sport indeed different in nature?

All budo systems involve a certain degree of physical activity. In this regard budo does not diverge from sport, and the immediate benefits of budo and sport for the human body are consequently identical: they strengthen an individual's physical fitness, which in turn has a positive effect on a person's health. The necessity of executing complicated body movements and synchronizing those movements with those of a partner or an opponent further supports physical coordination. Beyond these physical benefits budo is, in the same way as wrestling and boxing are, a martial activity through which skills for self-defense can be acquired (the usefulness is highly depending on which budo is practiced and how it is learned). These skills, in return, result in growing self-confidence concerning one's ability and potential. This aspect of budo was already stressed by Kanō Jigorō in his lecture in 1889 in front of the Educational Society of Japan, a lecture that is certainly crucial in understanding Kanō's approach to judo and budo. But also in his lectures given in an international context, Kano stressed these benefits of judo.[3]

The practice of budo is secondly also a social activity that asks for nonverbal (bodily) and verbal interaction between individuals as well as (inter-)group communication. Budo thus extends beyond the frame of the actual training reality of a dojo or fixed practice times; it manifests itself in joint social activities which involve participation in a range of activities, where social skills can be developed. This is an important aspect of budo in Europe. After budo (jujutsu and judo) was introduced to Europe in the beginning of the twentieth century, it first was connected to fight halls as well as circuses and thus commercialized. Only in a second step did judo then find its way into the non-profit clubs of towns, villages, neighbourhoods, companies, schools, and universities. These clubs are until today not commercial and socializing is a very important factor in attracting new members. A beer after the training, weekends spent together . . . Even holiday trips are a regular pastime in these clubs. Not to speak of the numerous budo workshops all over Europe, where besides intensive training, social interaction is of utmost relevance. Here, another value of budo, which is often ignored as it is considered to be trivial in nature, comes into focus: budo is recreation. Especially in modern societies in which sedentary activities are the reality of everyday work life, physical performance has a therapeutic effect. Time, space, and realization of budo practice are recreational in essence. They are separated from the work sphere and have a positive effect on wellness, satisfaction, and ultimately in an individual's quality of life.

All of the abovementioned beneficial aspects of budo are shared by sports in different degrees. It is unquestionable that modern budo has developed along the lines of modern (competitive) sport and that it has incorporated and continues to incorporate sporting characteristics to different degrees. Where Olympic judo has gone through a complete process of sportification, other budo, such as sumo or kyudo, show lesser degrees of sportification. And even inside one form of budo, the stress might differ significantly. Judo is a perfect example for that: not only do we find what is termed Olympic judo, but also a judo that stresses character-building and social relevance, of which the Kodokan is a representative. Lately, as a counter movement to competitive judo, the exercise of kata has become more popular in Europe and a growing interest in educational values of judo can be observed.

Budo specialists argue that budo surpasses sport because it is supposed to develop character and consequently goes beyond being a purely competitive physical activity. Nevertheless, this notion reveals a misunderstanding of the characteristics of European athletic or sporting traditions. The idea of a correlation between character and physical activity can already be found in the Greek athletic tradition, and in modern times the founder of the Olympic Movement, Pierre de Coubertin, developed his thoughts on Olympism and sport along that Greek tradition. Thus, the main difference between budo and sport in modern times is not found in the existence or absence of character building values but rather lies in its

Sugimura Yōtarō, Japanese ambassador to France, judges a judo match (courtesy of the Kodokan collection)

primary objectives; in sport, breaking a record or winning a competition is central, and the idea of building character is considered marginal in the mainstream whereas in mainstream budo culture, the perfection of a bodily technique in order to build character is central and part of the practitioner's self-conception. Rather than being a temporary physical activity, budo is considered to be "a way of life."

2. Perceptions of budo in Europe

Naturally, the reasons for beginning a martial way are as diverse as budo systems themselves are. Yet when starting with budo training, the practitioner will come into contact with educational core concepts and theories that I see as a common denominator to all budo. In modern budo, it is believed that the enhancement of personality and character leads to a certain kind of "wisdom," that can—in contrast to Western ideas of attaining wisdom—only be developed and attained by exercising both body and mind together. In most budo, the concept of the unification of body and mind encloses spiritual elements, thus giving budo a degree of seriousness and severity that is lacking in modern sport.[4] Self-development and self-perfection in budo is in itself not a self-centered activity, but is seen as a social activity that aims at the betterment and improvement of society. Wisdom, consequently, does not remain an abstract concept, but must be verifiable through a person's deeds. "Deeds" in this context does not refer to tying records but to the social relevance of human actions. This picture is also given in the public media, in books and TV series. Just to name one example that shows how budo and moral development are connected in the public discourse: one of the most popular European child detective series is called "TKKG", an acronym of the children's names. In this series four children (aged around fourteen) solve crimes, and the leader of the group is a judo fighter, named Tarzan (later Tim). In the novels his character has very clear, rather conservative moral values to help the weak, protect women and only use force when being attacked.[5] Budo in Europe is in the public, as has been shown above, very often ascribed a spiritual or even supra-human sphere. A person practicing a Japanese martial art is seen as calm and controlled; attributes the *budōka* acquired through training. Above that, in the perception, the *budōka* possesses, despite his or her average or small physical stature, superb fighting skills. Especially the notion of a smaller person defeating a stronger person by technique and will and/or wit rather than by brutal force is a recurrent motive that is closely connected to the European idea of the small Japanese.⁶ Already, when the first jujutsu fighters came to Europe and then Germany, it was exactly this image that determined the reception of the discipline.⁷ Comparable to Riki Dōzan who fought against fierce-looking Americans, rather small-looking European or Japanese fighters applied Japanese martial arts to beat huge European-style wrestlers. In Germany, Ōno Akitarō taught jujutsu as early as 1906 to the military in Berlin. Even earlier, the *Illustrierte Athletik-Zeitung*, in 1903, announced that the jiujitsu fighter Tani Yukio would come to London to fight at a circus:

> The famous Japanese wrestler Tani has come to London, where he will fight in the "Camberwell-Theatre." The famous Scottish athlete Apollo has taken Tani under his protection, so to speak. He is so convinced of the power of this man that he will give any person that can throw the Japanese 2500 Frcs. Everbody who can endure a fight longer than 10 minutes will receive 500 Frcs. Tani is 22 years old, 1.56m tall and weighs 90kg. The style of wrestling Tani is performing is not the so called Greco-roman style, but a special form of free wrestling, in which he uses his hands as well as his feet. He is so skilled that even the strongest men have to surrender. Especially as the small Japanese, who seemingly knows very well the human anatomy, places his hands and feet, where he can cause great pain.⁸

He and other fighters like Katsukuma Higashi showed their skills in circuses, variety theaters and music halls and it was in these places that the common cliché of the tiny and weak Japanese found extensive use, for the purposes of advertisement and profit. The advertising pamphlets and posters usually promised fights between a "diminutive Japanese" and huge, seemingly-invincible European boxing or wrestling champions. One example I will give is taken from the *Illustrierte Sportzeitung* from 1909, in which we find an article entitled *Tani Yukio, the Japanese world champion* which, when referring to Tani only uses diminutive expressions like "cute Japanese," "chappie" or "plain little Japanese":

> It is now five years ago that one day in the London office of the magazine *Sporting Life*, stood a plain, little Japanese who claimed to be 18 years old and to have been arrived by ship from Japan. He asked the editor to publish that he, Yukio Tani, would be willing to pay 100 pounds to the person that

would be able to defeat him in his native martial art of jujutsu. The chap—Tani weighed just 100 pounds at that time—performed on a stage in a suburb of London and challenged, as mentioned, everybody to fight him for the price money. Attracted by the plain, light stature of Tani, many opponents applied, including men of more than 200 pounds, square-built characters, among them skilled boxers, catch-as-catch-can wrestlers, etc.; in short, everybody that belongs to professional athleticism in London. But then, what a surprise! The chappie finished all his opponents easily in two, three, four minutes. He defeated men close to whom he looked like a dwarf and nobody could hold their grounds. In just eight days, as everybody in London is a sportsman, London was talking about him and in just four weeks the cute Japanese who appeared suddenly like a meteor became a celebrity.[9]

This view on budo is deeply rooted in the above European discourse on Japan and also connected to the idea of the samurai. The samurai and their fighting skills had fascinated Europeans right from the first contact in the sixteenth century. The Japanese victory over Russia in 1905 and also WWII (although a catastrophe for Japan and the world) enhanced the image of strong and fierce Japanese fighters, which was, strangely enough, turned into a "positive" stereotype born from fear and admiration.

The practice of budo ideally extends into the practice of daily life and aims to improve society in general. In this sense, modern budo is, as pre-modern Japanese martial ways were, a form of moral education. It was Kanō Jigorō who coined the term *jita kyōei* (mutual welfare and benefit), and Sō Dōshin uses the phrase *jita kyōraku* to refer to the value budo is supposed to have for society. It is most interesting that the educational aspects of budo are most strongly advocated in judo, which in budo circles is often characterized as not being budo but "pure" sport. The example of judo shows that budo and sport do not have to be antagonistic and that they are complementary in nature. Budo actually can facilitate the means to refocus athletes' objectives away from the often criticized materialism and record hunting in sport (which has led to multi-layered problems such as doping) toward the direction of developing character and promoting the betterment of society through physical activity. I regard the described inherent educational values as most important regarding the question how budo can be beneficial for society in the twenty-first century, and educators as well as politicians in many countries have already acknowledged its educational values by integrating judo, karate, or aikidō into their school curricula. Through the practice of budo, children not only improve their health, but they also learn to value and trust a teacher, to respect and support partners in practice, to become part of a group and mutually develop.

3. International budo and Japanese budo

Today, Japanese budo is truly international, and Kanō Jigorō has certainly contributed to this development. As result of a historical process Japanese budo has lost the hegemony to define budo to different degrees. When jujutsu and judo came to Europe in the early twentieth century not much was known about Japanese martial arts and what was taught often merely resembled the Japanese original.[10] When Japanese teachers came over, with the possibility to go to Japan to study martial arts, a translation of primary Japanese sources for deeper understanding of budo was attained. The following step, namely a sort of exterritorialization, was inevitable. Similar developments can be observed in other budo systems as well; although these happened much later as karate, kyudo, *iaidō* or kendo were introduced much later to Europe. The development can be described by a process of learning, which is known in budo as *shuhari* (obey, break, leave).

European budo diverges from Japanese traditions as it adapted local (sporting) traditions.[11] Yet most of the budo schools overseas preserve the Japanese words for techniques as well as gear, wear Japanese clothes, and follow the Japanese customs of greeting, etc. Above that, training in Japan is still seen as an important factor in mastering a martial way. It is like coming back to the homeland of budo.

Budo offers an opportunity for international exchange on the physical as well as intellectual level, and can help to eliminate stereotypical ideas about societies. Budo in this sense can be seen as an important "soft power." As a teacher of Japanese studies in Europe, I have noticed that there are two main reasons for students to begin their studies in Japanese language and culture: manga and budo. The Japanese Government recognized the relevance of manga and anime for the international image of Japan in March 2008 when it named the manga character Doraemon "Anime Ambassador." In my opinion, however, it has been overlooked that also budo can beneficially be used to internationally promote a better understanding (also) of modern Japan beyond traditional stereotypical notions and to improve intercultural dialogue and understanding.

Conclusion

Despite the fact that budo is trained around the world and has lost some of its cultural markers, budo still has not lost and will also in the future not lose its "Japaneseness"; a "Japaneseness" which is constructed outside of Japan as well as in Japan. Budo should, however, not be understood as a container for Japanese traditions that have been transmitted to our century from a glorified past without change. Budo as we know it today is the (temporary) result of a historical process in which combat systems were increasingly seen as educational tools. Also the judo of Kano Jigorō developed over the years, including new elements and eliminating others. Budo still transmits its specific cultural assets but has adapted to modern times and because of its adaptability and flexibility, it continues to be beneficial to society on different levels that range from health and ethics to mutual welfare and international understanding. In order to have a value for society in the twenty-first century, budo thus must continue to develop and adapt to the needs of our time. Or to speak with the *Hōjōki*: "The current of the flowing river does not cease, and yet the water is not the same water as before."

Notes:

1   See Frühstück; Manzenreiter, 'Neverland lost,' 69-93.
2   See Bennett, 'Introduction', 1-7.
3   For example Kanō's speech given at the University of Southern California (1932) or his lecture to the prestigious and influential Parnassus Society in Athens (1934).
4   Deeply rooted in the European view on budo is the idea that it is based on religion, especially on Zen Buddhism. In her article *Fascination with the Exotic: On the Development of Jujitsu and Judo in Germany*, Gertrud Pfister asserts the following: "On the way from Asia to Germany, jujitsu apparently lost much of its religious meaning and the last vestiges of this vanished in circus acts and music hall performances, where audiences wanted to see a show with artistic skills without any religious ballast. Furthermore, the rationalization of jujitsu as a means of self-defence and its later 'sportification' not only required, but also furthered its 'secularization'." (ibid., 20) Also this approach is based on the European view of Japan as being a haven of a 'pure' form of spirituality and religiosity, which has been lost in the West during the process of industrialization.
5   Also characteristic is the fact that although the main character is practicing judo, the techniques applied in the series are not always judo techniques, but also aikido or jujutsu techniques; thus hinting at the fact that in the public opinion budo is generally not clearly differentiated in different styles, but rather seen as one.

6   For the European construction of Japan see esp. Schaffers, Uta: *Konstruktionen der Fremde*.

7   The first German jujutsu school was founded in 1906 by Erich Rahn in Berlin. However, it was difficult for Rahn to rent a suitable location. In the end, he was forced to a dance hall adjoining a bar for his lessons. The reason he found it so difficult to rent somewhere suitable is connected to jujutsu's poor reputation at the time. On the one hand, jujutsu was a "mysterious Eastern martial art form," but on the other hand it was perceived as an activity pursued by the lower classes, connected to circuses and variety theaters. Also, Rahn had performed in circuses, appearing in prize fights with wrestlers and boxers, as well as members of the audience (these kinds of fights between a professional and a member of the audience can still be witnessed in fair booths around Europe today). Jujutsu's banishment to the back rooms of pubs also damaged its reputation. In Berlin jujutsu and boxing were even prohibited for several years before the outbreak of the First World War. For Rahn and his view on jujutsu see especially: Rahn, '50 Jahre Jiu-Jitsu und Judo'; Rahn, 'Die unsichtbare Waffe (Jiu-Jitsu)' and Rahn, 'Neue Kniffe'.

8   *Illustrierte Athletik-Zeitung*, 1903, 116.

9   *Illustrierte Sportzeitung*, 1909, 296.

10   Rather than referring to Japanese sources, European sportsmen became the source for knowledge. One of the main informants in the early years is the German doctor Erwin Bälz, who is often considered to have rediscovered and re-animated jujutsu. It has also been suggested that it was him, who literally inspired Kanō Jigorō to study jujutsu. Another example would be Irving Hancock with his book *The Complete Kanō Jiu-Jitsu*, which was published in 1906. Bälz's as well as Hancock's explanations on jujutsu and judo became accepted as common knowledge on jujutsu and judo in the following years.

11   As well as in Japan, judo had been prohibited by the allied forces for three years and Rhode as well as his companions wisely refrained from using ideological messages, but concentrated on the sporting elements and on the form (this is a development we can observe in other fields as well; e.g., literature). The orientation towards sport and competition was followed by a concentration on and development of European training methods and training theories. The fact that Anton Geesink, who defeated Kaminaga in 1964, was one of the first to develop a new training concept is no surprise in light of this historical context. And it is exactly this historical victory that Hofmann, one of the most influential judo teachers in Germany after the war, uses in 1969 in the magazine as an argument to underline the necessity of detaching the German judo system from Japanese tradition (Hofmann in *Judo*, No. 9, 1969, 6-8).

Kanō Jigorō the man

Caption: Kanō and his family (around 1902, courtesy of the Kodokan collection)

Kanō and his students

1. Kanō and students at the Kanō Juku

Everyday life at the Kanō Juku

Kanō Jigorō opened the Kanō Juku, his own private academy, to coincide with the foundation of the Kodokan. Students at the Kanō Juku shared their living arrangements with Kanō, even eating with him, and underwent a diverse mix of training. While the frequency with which students came and went makes the academy's exact enrollment hard to define with any accuracy, observers estimate that enrollment topped out at fifty in 1898 and had likely surpassed a total of 300 by the time the Kanō Juku ceased operations in 1898. Students basically fell into three categories: the sons of members of Kanō's extended family, the sons of Kanō's acquaintances, and the sons of people who specifically sought out Kanō's instruction.

Kano's growing renown as an educator put his tutelage in high demand; requests came pouring in from people hoping to make him a mentor for their sons. Those who did secure a place at the Kanō Juku entered an institution that Kanō envisioned as a locus of both learning and human development,[1] a place for the cultivation of character. Considering how carefully he hoped to mold his students as people, not just learners, Kanō went about day-to-day life with his pupils to set an example for them to follow.

By 1886, however, Kanō's duties as a public servant had grown so busy that he no longer had much time to spend with his students. To make sure that the students would have guidelines to model their behavior around even in his absence, he wrote up a "Juku Rulebook" that laid the behavioral standards to which students were to adhere.

A good number of the students at the Kanō Juku came from privileged backgrounds, which is why Kanō opted for a strict, hard-and-fast regimen of school rules: he wanted to accustom his pupils to a set rhythm and way of life, one that would discourage them from behaving selfishly and prevent them from feeling overly complacent in the lap of luxury. For Kanō, that meant doing away with any arrangements that might enable students to fall into those patterns. The students were thus responsible for every last facet of their day-to-day lives at the Kanō Juku.

The daily routine followed a rigid structure. Waking up before the sun rose, students quickly split up to clean the facilities (both inside and outside), gardens, and gates before reporting to the dojo for a morning assembly at 5 a.m. They then studied by themselves until 6 a.m., when they met for breakfast, and next went back to their studies before heading to school. When the school day was over and the students arrived back home at the Kanō Juku, they went right back to work tending to their accommodations, with pupils cleaning the baths, lamps, and other facilities on a rotating basis. Lamp duty was quite the chore, apparently; the process involved trimming the wick and cleaning the soot off each lamp (of which there were more than ten). Winter work was especially grueling, as the lack of any fireplaces or other form of heating forced everyone to toil at his task in the cold. The rules also stipulated that every student had to wear a *hakama* (formal divided skirt) at all times and sit *seiza*-style (kneeling on the floor with their buttocks resting on their heels) during study hours.

Early every Sunday morning, Kanō lectured the academy's students on proper conduct. The sessions were the primary interface between Kanō and his pupils, and Kanō strove to make the time constructive in forging bonds.

Kanō's weekly lectures touched on a variety of instructions, including:[2]

· Dedicate your every effort to a purpose in life.
· Aspire to greatness in the future instead of fretting about worries in the present.
· Apply yourself with conviction, knowing that your individual strengths can benefit the country.
· Become cornerstones for the nation to better Japan's position in the international community.

It must have been extremely hard for the younger pupils at the Kanō Juku to

maintain their proper *seiza* postures for the duration of their headmaster's lectures, which often stretched on for more than an hour. In spite of what was surely considerable discomfort, however, they apparently received Kanō's message—an exhortation to think on big, international horizons, not just the "now now," and thrive as drivers of society at large—clearly.

Kano in his late fifties (courtesy of the Kodokan collection)

Kanō scheduled Sunday-night "chats" where students could interact with him and their peers. In addition to serving as a forum for tossing around ideas on the various issues that came up at the establishment, the gatherings also included students' readings of their own poetry and presentations of research reports. The Juveniles' Quarters also hosted "readings" of useful texts on Saturday evenings. Through these various get-togethers, Kanō and his students built a rapport via mutual interaction.

The Kanō Juku's alumni roster is full of notable names: educators like Andō Masatsugu (who went on to serve as the president of Taihoku Imperial University), Kawaguchi Yoshihisa (president, Nihon University), Tomabechi Hidetoshi (principal, Otaru Higher Commercial School) dot the list, as do other prominent figures such as Sugimura Yōtarō (diplomat and Under-Secretary General of the League of Nations), Ōkura Naosuke (president, Ōkura Fire and Marine Insurance Company), Kanō Tokusaburō (vice-president, Bank of Chosen), and Nangō Saburō (president, Japan Cotton Trading Co., Ltd.).

Kanō and students at the Higher Normal School's affiliated middle school

Kanō's coupled his role as principal of the Higher Normal School with his position as principal of the institution's affiliated middle school, another institution with an affluent student makeup. Concerned that the students' coddled upbringings might foster apathy and indolence, he created a framework for spurring friendly competition among pupils by making judo part of the required curriculum and creating the Kōyūkai (School Council) to head up student activities. In 1897, he officially named the Kōyūkai the "Tōinkai" and set up clubs for judo, kendo, baseball, soccer, and other sports under the organization's oversight.

He also had students run monthly races, with upperclassmen in charge of coaching.

The Tokyo Higher Normal School's affiliated middle school (ca. 1940)

Besides making institutional arrangements to facilitate sound student development at the affiliated middle school, Kanō also looked after the students on a more personal level. Reforms to the nation's educational system eventually made it possible for fourth-year middle school students to apply for admission to higher schools. A handful of fourth-year students from the Higher Normal School's affiliated middle school took advantage of the change and applied to enter higher schools in the first year of the new system, but they all came up empty-handed. The students returned to the middle school frustrated and crestfallen, their pride in tatters. When Kanō heard the news, he sought out the students to impart some words of wisdom:

It's a good thing, what happened. This institution is a five-year school. No matter what school you go to, you can't skip a year of the curriculum and expect to have all the education you need. If I were you, I'd be happy that I was coming back to the middle school to get those finishing touches.[3]

For Kanō, missing out on admission was no failure by any means—it simply meant that the students could complete the full course of their education at the middle school. The story shines a light on Kanō's reassuring humanity, illuminating a sense of affection for his students and highlighting his trademark optimism.

An official diploma from the Tokyo Higher Normal School (ca. 1904; courtesy of the Nakamura Tōtarō collection)

3. Kanō and the international students at Kōbun Gakuin

Connecting with Chinese students

Ekiraku Shoin and Kōbun Gakuin, both of which Kanō founded out of his own pocket, together accepted a total of over 8,000 students from China. The first group of thirteen government-funded Chinese students came over in 1896, shortly after the Russo-Japanese War. Seven of the students completed three years of study and received diplomas at a graduation ceremony, which featured an address that helped illustrate the relationship between the international cohort and their headmaster:

> The Ministry of Education entrusted our education to our venerable Professor Kanō, whose earnest, dedicated teachings, needless to say, have provided us a font of learning and wisdom across numerous disciplines over the past three years. The wisdom you have been so kind to impart unto us on occasion over the last three years, Sensei, has permeated our minds, thoroughly transforming us. How could we ever contain our excitement, our joy, at learning from such a fine teacher?
>
> . . . Honoring your instructions, we shall go forth and sate our brains with the learning of the world and cultivate a spirit of independence, which we shall then apply in navigating the great difficulties facing our country. Should we succeed in achieving the necessary political reforms, fashioning China into a second "New World," and elevating the nation to stand shoulder to shoulder with the community of civilized nations, it will be to none other than the foundations of virtue and wisdom that you have instilled in us that we owe our success.
>
> April 16, 1900[4]

As the speech suggests, Kanō approached international students the same way he did his Japanese students: with a commitment to providing guidance in whatever way necessary, a dedication that earned the students' respect.

Like the Higher Normal School, Kōbun Gakuin put a substantial emphasis on physical education and sports. After Japanese classes, gymnastics occupied the second-largest chunk of the international students' course load—a full five hours per week. The institution had clubs for tennis, archery, and distance running, while the Ushigome athletic grounds began playing host to annual Kōbun

Gakuin athletic meets in 1906. For the international students, the competitions were thrilling, unlike anything they had ever seen.

Records also include an account of a visit to Kōbun Gakuin by world-renowned pole vaulter Fujii Minoru, a student at the Imperial University. The international students apparently gaped in awe as Fujii did a live demonstration of the event, their eyes glued on his figure catapulting into the air.[5]

Meanwhile, Kanō also worked to enrich the curriculum. The academic focus on Japanese language accompanied an aim to acquaint in-

Lu Xun during his time at Kōbun Gakuin

ternational students with Japanese culture. To give students firsthand experience with the cultural dynamic, Kanō often took groups on tours of famous sights around the Tokyo area.

He also designated the Kōbun Gakuin judo dojo as the Ushigome branch dojo of the Kodokan, which made it easier for international students to join the Kodokan while enrolled at Kōbun Gakuin; Chinese writer Lu Xun (born Zhou Shuren) was one of the Kōbun Gakuin students to do so. Through judo and a variety of other sports, Kanō forged bonds with the international students at his institution.

Those connections remained strong, as well. International students would often write letters to Kanō after graduation to extend gratitude for their time at Kōbun Gakuin, introduce new prospective students, and report on their activities back home.

For example, Tang Bao E went on to serve at the Hunan Provincial Normal School after graduating and returning to China. Due to his young age and inexperience, however, Tang struggled to make progress in his post. He thus decided to seek out the help of his former teacher. Tang wrote to the Shandong *xunfu* (the governor of Shandong), asking him to request a letter of recommendation from Kanō.[6] Many other graduates solicited Kanō for recommendations, and he was always eager to comply.

Several high-performing Chinese graduates stayed on at Kōbun Gakuin to work as interpreters. One was Fan Yuanlian, who, besides earning admission to the Higher Normal School after securing his diploma, interpreted at Kōbun Gakuin from 1902 to 1904 at Kanō's request. At Jissen Women's University, too, Fan interpreted Principal Shimoda Utako's morals (*shūshin*) lectures—without a prepared text to work from, no less—as a supervisor for international students. Upon returning home, Fan set to work on establishing a broader base for normal education in China. He, too, sent Kanō a letter expressing his gratitude:

> Kanō Sensei, I will always admire the impassioned education you provided me and the way you so thoughtfully molded your teachings around a far-reaching perspective. In the years to come, I hope that you accept even more international students, offer them full facilities, and cultivate young men with the power to benefit the Orient, an objective of profound, well-considered import. While I may yet lack intelligence and knowledge, I feel an enormous sense of responsibility to confront and overcome whatever difficulty I encounter. Drawing always on your valuable teachings, Sensei, I look forward to traversing the road ahead.[7]

Fan Yuanlian became a leader in the realm of Chinese education. In addition to occupying the post of Minister of Education on three separate occasions, he also served as president of Beijing Normal University and helped lay the formative groundwork for the Taiwanese educational system. Fan was just one of the many Chinese students who shared lasting bonds with Kanō, even after they left Kōbun Gakuin.

Carrying on the legacy at the Tokyo Higher Normal School
Following the closure of Kōbun Gakuin, Kanō continued to welcome twenty to thirty international students a year to pursue studies at the Tokyo Higher Normal School—the institution essentially inherited the acceptance policy that had been in place at its now-defunct counterpart. International students accounted for a sizable percentage of the Tokyo Higher Normal School's student body for a considerable stretch, hovering around 15 percent all the way through the 1930s. The international contingent was by no means isolated, either: they took active part in various School Council doings, competed in athletic meets and boat races, played on the school's soccer team, and had a presence on the rosters of the other athletic clubs, as well. Upon receiving their diplomas, many of the Chinese students embarked on careers along high-profile paths in academics—including scholarly positions at the prestigious Peking University and

Beijing Normal University, for example—as well as politics and a wide range of other fields.

Japanese teachers also went over to China at the request of the Chinese government. Uchibori Korebumi, a faculty member at the Tokyo Higher Normal School, assumed the position of principal at the new Shandong Normal University on an official request and proceeded to establish close ties with Kōbun Gakuin and the Tokyo Higher Normal School. Shandong Normal University started out with just sixty or seventy students, but the steady stream of students returning from Kōbun Gakuin—impressive in both number and ability—prompted an expansion of the school's enrollment to 300 students. Uchibori attributed much of the growth to Kanō's stature. "Professor Kanō's repute as a prolific educator was enormous to begin with," Uchibori said. Subsequent developments added to his prominence. "The heroic deeds of Lieutenant Commander Hirose Takeo, Lieutenant Yuasa Takejirō, and Captain Honda Chikatami during missions to blockade Port Arthur had captured attention in China," Uchibori explained. "When the Chinese learned that each of the three war heroes had studied under Kanō, his renown as an educator only grew."[8]

Another Japanese teacher who headed to Shandong Normal University at Kanō's behest was natural history scholar Nakamura Kakunosuke, who made his way to China in 1905. Nakamura was more than just an academic, however—he was a standout athlete and dedicated sports advocate, too. Not only did he help lay the foundation for the soccer club at the Tokyo Higher Normal School, but he also earned the first *shodan* rank in swimming in the Higher Normal School program that Kanō instituted in 1902.[9] As part of the soccer club, meanwhile, Nakamura even penned the first technical soccer book ever to come out of Japan: *Assōshiēshon futtobōru* [Association football]. Nakamura's official responsibility at Shandong Normal University was to teach natural history, but he almost assuredly gave students a taste of soccer, too. Though an illness cut his life short in 1906, Nakamura was one of the many first-rate professionals who made positive contributions to China on official assignment from Kanō—an arrangement through which Kanō's relationship with China developed on an educational level. When Kanō attended the Fifth Far Eastern Championship Games in Shanghai at the end of May 1921 as an International Olympic Committee member, as many as fifty Chinese Kōbun Gakuin and Tokyo Higher Normal School graduates were on hand to welcome him. For many of Kanō's Chinese students, evidently, the time that they spent with their teacher in Japan formed important experiences—ones that they continued to treasure long after making their homecomings.

4. Kanō and students at the Tokyo Higher Normal School

"Bring it on, damn it."

Kanō may have been an administrator at the Higher Normal School, but that did not stop him from connecting with students—in fact, he made his relationships with the student body a vital component of his work as principal. Believing that focusing exclusively on school administration would render his role as an educator pointless, Kanō worked to create as many opportunities for direct contact with students as he could.

First of all, Kanō gathered students in the lecture hall (or classrooms) on a weekly basis for "principal's exempla" (instructive tales) that mainly covered his basic precepts on life. Gotō Keita (1882–1959), then a student and later the founder of the Tokyu Corporation, remembered the impact of Kanō's lectures:

Principal Kanō gave us weekly lectures on morals at the Higher Normal School. The talks were unusual; from start to finish, he focused on nothing but his personal maxim of "Bring it on, damn it." It all centered on the indomitable spirit that you could derive from the practice of judo. Win or lose, you had to refuse to let up—Kanō wanted us to demand more and keep pushing to be better, always embracing that "bring-it-on" tenacity, regardless of the outcome.

At first, I thought it was a bit of a strange thing to be teaching. After hearing that same refrain for a whole year, however, I gradually came to understand what he was on to; it all started to make sense, though I still lacked the life experience I needed to appreciate it fully. It was only when I left the confines of the school and started making my own way in the world that I really grasped the idea. I learned so much at the Higher Normal School, from English, geography, and history to pedagogy, but I have forgotten the bulk of that knowledge over the years. What has stuck with me most, however, is "Bring it on, damn it." Professor Kanō kept saying that as long as we remembered those words, we could handle whatever life might throw our way. He was right.[10]

Kanō also called small groups of soon-to-be graduates into the principal's office and had the students ask him questions to make sure that his teachings had gotten through. According to graduates, their principal offered words of wisdom on a variety of themes:[11]

"Feel free to drink alcohol as long as your finances, morals, and health permit."
"Never let your students see you going off to the bathroom."
"Approach everything with a bring-it-on attitude."
"No graduate of this school shall ever lose his embrace of a broad, far-reaching educational spirit."

Kanō Jigorō at age 68 (courtesy of the Kodokan collection)

"The teaching profession is not the only path forward. Be it in business, in politics, or anywhere in between, do what you feel called to do as long as you have confidence in yourself and know that you can fill a social need."

Rational sensibility

Rather than just pass on his teachings in formal, pedagogical settings, Kanō involved himself in actual student life on a regular basis. Athletics, naturally, were part of that communion. Students at the Tokyo Higher Normal School took part in distance-running competitions, and Principal Kanō often ran the course with them—he joined 600 students for the 1908 fall footrace, for example, a 6-*ri* (roughly 23.4-km) run from the Tokyo Higher Normal School to Ōmiya. Students responded with gratitude, inspired by their principal's commitment to erasing boundaries of age and status.[12]

According to 1906 enrollee Ueno Atsushi, Kanō joined a group of students playing a game of *bō-oshi* ("pole-pushing") at the School Council's welcoming party for new students. After a while, he started to challenge students to matches—and roundly defeat whoever toed the line. Ueno had a tough time believing what he was seeing: a principal throwing down the gauntlet and leveraging his impressive strength to overpower his young pupils. In his younger years, evidently, Kanō rarely passed up a chance to exercise with his students.

Given how eager Kanō was to build camaraderie, one might assume that he took every opportunity to accommodate his students' wishes. That was not always the case, however. If a request from the students made rational sense, he was happy to oblige; if it was unreasonable, he dismissed it.

At a certain point, the school's boat fell into disrepair. The students came to a consensus that they needed a replacement built. Ueno, then a leader of the School Council, thus brought a formal request to Kanō (the organization's chair). Kanō refused, saying that he would not authorize any new construction. The boat's considerable distance from the water would make the process unnecessarily time-consuming, he contended, and the substantial costs would be economically disadvantageous. Ueno stood his ground. For three hours, he implored Kanō to understand the request represented the collective will of the student body—the very thing that the School Council was supposed to embody. As the chair of the organization, Ueno claimed, Kanō had a responsibility to honor the request. Kanō asked Ueno about the expenses, and Ueno responded that the organization planned to cover the costs with donations from students, personnel, and graduates. Kanō wanted a specific estimate of how much the group planned to collect, which Ueno gave him. At that point, after Ueno had laid everything out in clear terms, Kanō relented and signed off on the project— but also adamantly refused to make any out-of-pocket contribution whatsoever to the fundraising effort. When the project finally reached its end, with the new boat built and the launching ceremony complete, Kanō handed Ueno a celebratory gift of 15 yen (equivalent to 60,000 yen, or roughly 600 dollars, in today's money). "You worked hard, Ueno," Kanō told him. "I can tell you've got a lot of fire, which I must say I admire, but you just have to know how to use it—you can't let that passion get the best of you."[13] For Ueno, Kanō's gentle rebuke proved pivotal: he began to recognize the potential pitfalls of his fiery streak, an awareness that he said helped him avoid future mistakes. Kanō had his students' futures, not just their formal education, in mind.

5. Kanō's love for education

"It was good, I'd say, for the most part"

Education was something that Kanō had an irrepressible, deep-seated love for.

"Education is a pure delight. Once one knows how satisfying it can be, nothing else comes close," he explained. "Physical pleasure inevitably loses its allure over time; the longer one basks in it, the less satisfying it becomes. But the only thing that remains gratifying no matter how much one indulges in its joys, the one undertaking that becomes even more deeply satisfying nature the more one pursues it, is education."[14]

Kanō's calligraphic rendering of *tsutomureba kanarazu tassu* ("Striving surely results in achieving"; courtesy of the Kodokan collection)

To relish those inherent joys, Kanō urged his fellow educators, one needed to develop a deep, thorough understanding of what education was all about.

As he frequently reminded his teaching faculty at the Higher Normal School's affiliated middle school, the wonders pervading education were actually easier for educators to grasp when they reaped fewer material rewards from their profession.

Teachers who enjoy better treatment than they actually deserve end up perceiving themselves as bearers of massive debts, thoughts of what they "owe" to others weighing heavily on their minds. On the other hand, teachers who receive less than they might deserve see themselves as lenders; never under the onus of any perceived obligation, they are free to relish the pure joys of education in contentment.[15]

Echoing that common refrain at virtually every faculty meeting, Kanō strove to ensure that the teachers at the affiliated middle school were content with their vocation and shape their perspectives in his vision of education, the calling he so wholeheartedly loved.

One of Kanō's pet phrases was "It was good, I'd say, for the most part," which he would usually append with a fine-pointed critique or cautionary remark. Somewhere in that standard preamble, though, students sensed tolerance and care, a nuanced warmth that could mitigate even the harshest standoffs and win over adversaries.

Morohashi Tetsuji (1883–1982) recalled his own firsthand experience of Kanō's educational style:

There was a pattern to how Professor Kanō went about educating people. First, he would chastise the person. When the person countered his

293

opinion, he would listen, gently taking in what the person had to say. Finally, he would patiently guide the person through the lesson to be learned, taking painstaking care to make sure that the person understood. It was through that methodical process that his nature as an educator—magnanimous and driven—came gradually into view. When I was a student at the Higher Normal School, the library was a small operation with hardly any budget to speak of. There were stacks of books, but there were no reading rooms—students had to relocate to the corridor next to the lecture hall and set up chairs to read in. While we went on studying in cramped, uncomfortable conditions, our principal built an enormous dojo—bigger than what any other school had. Convinced that something obviously unfair and unjust was going on, I decided to voice my frustrations to Principal Kanō. I can still remember how he responded. "I understand what you're saying," he began, "but there's nothing stopping you from reading books in a corridor. You can't practice judo without a dojo," he said, grinning. It may have sounded like sour grapes to me at first, but there was a warmth in how he came across; his words had an unmistakable depth, a pull that hinted at what he was trying to do—guide his students forward with the sincerest, kindest care. As that indescribable aura filled the air, I took his words to heart and simply backed away.[16]

That giving, generous side was evident in how Kanō handled students facing financial difficulties, as well. When a student in a pinch turned in his tuition envelope, Kanō would often hand it right back without opening it. He even let needy students live at the school. Kanō's big-hearted generosity extended to his teaching faculty, as well.

Always look on the bright side
Kanō also earned a reputation for being an optimist through and through. Murakami Kunio, a judoka at the Tokyo Higher Normal School, learned from Kanō that judo meant never taking a pessimistic outlook:

At its essence, judo teaches you to apply your best possible effort in whatever situation you find yourself. If you confront a larger opponent, you accept the difference in size and act accordingly; if your opponent is stronger than you, you adapt to the imbalance accordingly. The idea is to do the very best you can in light of the circumstances at hand. You never look at things in a negative light or abandon hope. Upon grasping that fundamental teaching of judo, a judo practitioner will likely never take a pessimistic view of anything. No matter what the circumstances are, regardless of how trying the situation may be, a judoka does the best he can in the context of the that specific situation. Kanō Sensei, with thorough, scrupulous care, taught me that pessimism has no place in a judoka's mind.[17]

In an article for the *Osaka Mainichi Shimbun*, journalist Hasegawa Nyokezan wrote that Kanō was a judoka in life—not just in the dojo.

I once got into a bit of a heated discussion about the Olympic spirit with someone at a meeting. Kanō stepped in and told us that our arguments, though different in form, were one in spirit. I had never learned the practice of judo from him, but it was at that moment that I learned the judo of life from him. From what his friends and acquaintances tell me, he was a judoka in how he lived. No doubt that "way of gentleness," the precept on which he based his very way of life, played a vital role in his Olympic negotiations, as well.[18]

As the 1938 IOC Session in Cairo drew near, contemporary events were putting plans for the 1940 Tokyo Olympics in a precarious position. IOC members were talking behind the scenes about the possibility of moving the Games to another location in light of concerning shifts in Japan's political landscape, particularly its increasingly brittle relations with China. Just before leaving for Egypt, Kanō told a group of reporters at the port of Shimonoseki that all the talk about the United Kingdom opposing the Tokyo bid was "gossip." He wanted to hear what the delegates actually had to say before he started planning his approach. "I'm not going to start fretting now," he said. "Needless anxiety is just a good way to go bald." In the end, he said, he would just "play judo's ace in the hole: adapt to the circumstances."[19] At the meeting in Cairo, Kanō emphasized the need to make the Olympics independent of politics—and his message resonated. He had done exactly what he told the reporters he would do. Throughout his life, Kanō lived by judo's principle of adapting flexibly to an opponent's use of force and then responding in the most efficient way possible to secure victory. He practiced what he preached as both a representative of Japan and an educator, passing his vision on in a way that made an indelible impression on his students.

Notes:

1 Kanō-sensei Denki Hensan-kai, ed., *Kanō Jigorō* [Kanō Jigorō] (Tokyo: Kodokan, 1964), 121–122.
2 Ibid., 131.
3 Ibid., 227.
4 Ibid., 169.
5 Yokoyama Kendō, *Kanō-sensei-den* [The life of Professor Kanō] (Tokyo: Kodokan, 1941), 191.
6 Ibid., 185.
7 Yokoyama Kendo, *Kanō-sensei-den*, 192.
8 Kanō-sensei Denki Hensan-kai, ed., *Kanō Jigorō*, 184.
9 "Kōyūkai kakubu hōkoku: Yūei-bu" [School Council club reports: The swimming club], *Kōyūkai-shi* [School Council journal] 5 (1904).
10 Kanō-sensei Denki Hensan-kai, ed., *Kanō Jigorō*, 220.
11 Ibid., 218–219.
12 "Kōyūkai kakubu hōkoku: Hobu [School Council club reports: The track and field club], *Kōyūkai-shi* [School Council Journal] 17 (1908).
13 Ueno Atsushi, "Waga Kanō-sensei" [Our Professor Kanō], *Kōyūkai-shi* [School Council Journal] 67 (1920).
14 "Kanō-sensei o toburau" [Mourning the loss of Professor Kanō], *Kōyūkai-shi* [School Council Journal] 67 (1920).
15 Saitō Hishō, "Omoideru koto-domo" [Remembrances], *Kōyūkai-shi* [School Council Journal] 67 (1920).
16 Kanō-sensei Denki Hensan-kai, ed., *Kanō Jigorō*, 661–662.
17 Murakami Kunio, "Onshi" [Forever my teacher], *Kōyūkai-shi* [School Council Journal] 67 (1920).
18 Hasegawa Nyozekan, "Kanō-sensei" [Professor Kanō], *Jūdō* [Judo] 9, no. 6 (1938).
19 Yokoyama Kendō, *Kanō-sensei-den*, 246–247.

Chapter 2

Kanō and his fellow IOC members

1. Kanō's place on the IOC

"It's that Nippon jujitsu—watch out!"

He founded judo. He created the Kodokan, Kōbunkan, Kōbun Gakuin, and Kanō Juku. He served as the principal of the Tokyo Higher Normal School and a member of the House of Peers. That legacy, forming in the prewar climate between the middle of the Meiji period and the early stages of the Shōwa period, undoubtedly made Kanō Jigorō a paragon in Japan's public consciousness—especially in the eyes of judoka and Higher Normal School graduates. Aside from his roles as an originator and educator, Kanō was also Asia's first member of the International Olympic Committee (IOC). How did he reflect in the eyes of his fellow IOC members? An issue of *Jūdō* (Judo) offered a short anecdote about Kanō and other IOC members at the 1938 IOC Session in Cairo, providing a glimpse at perceptions of Kanō within the organization.

> While some IOC members were more advanced in years, Kanō was still the sixth-oldest of the group. His peers from around the world held him in high regard, affectionately calling him "Good Ol' Kanō," and many trusted that their dear Kanō would see the Tokyo Olympics through to successful fruition. . . . At banquets and other gatherings, people sidled up to him time and time again and wrapped their big arms around his little shoulders. Kanō would make the deftest adjustment, escape the hold, and put up his guard, at which his friendly foe would say, "It's that Nippon jujutsu—watch out!" and run comically off, playing up the moment in jocular fun. I can still picture all that good-natured ribbing like it happened yesterday.[1]

Always mediating between his fellow IOC members, Kanō strove to serve Japan's best interests at every juncture—and he did so with a unique charm and a winning smile. He thus drew people in naturally; no matter who called out his name or how often they came to him, he would give them the same cordial treatment.[2]

Kanō was selected to become an IOC member in May 1909, at the age of forty-eight. As the above accounts suggest, he had evidently formed a friendly rapport with his colleagues—and earned their respect—by 1938. That distinct brand of camaraderie had taken shape through roughly three decades of interpersonal exchange.

The next anecdote captures a scene that took place in 1934, when Kanō was on his way from that year's IOC Athens Session to Olympia with IOC members to attend a ceremony celebrating the 40th anniversary of the Olympic revival.

The mayor of Tripoli [Greece] held an official city luncheon for the IOC members. . . . Bottles of champagne were uncorked, glasses were poured, and even the face of Kanō Jigorō, the Japanese IOC representative and famed founder of jujutsu, flushed red. These types of banquets almost always sink into a malaise as soon as the toasts begin, but the speeches at the IOC fete were actually quite interesting. The mayor began by addressing the gathering in Greek (which only the Greeks in attendance could understand), after which President Latour returned the favor in French (which few could understand). What then ensued was captivating. The Japanese representative stood up and delivered a speech in his own language, which, again, no one understood. Though impossible to discern, the address fascinated the assembly because the pronunciation and tone of the tongue was so unfamiliar [Kanō also noted that he deliberately affected his manner of speaking]. Seeing the assembly's reaction to the Japanese address, members of all stripes began to take the floor one after the other and address the group in German, Italian, English, French, Spanish, Dutch, Hungarian, Swedish, Czechoslovak, Serbian, and more, replying and offering thanks in their native languages in what proved to be an entertaining, boisterous conclusion to the festivities.[3]

With a feel for the room and a dash of wit, Kanō helped steer the IOC luncheon to a rousing finish. He changed the entire complexion of the gathering in the time it took to give a short speech, transcending the boundaries of language and winning over his fellow members with a cheerful charm. Kanō's stature as a master of judo and eminent school principal may have inspired a solemn reverence in Japan, but his IOC colleagues saw him in a decidedly different light: he was their lovable man of the world, a little old man with a big sense of humor.

How Kanō became an IOC member

Kanō's first encounter with the Olympic Movement came when he made his first encounter with Pierre de Coubertin (1863–1937), the founder of the modern Olympics.

In 1908, Coubertin was in London attending the fourth Olympic Games. On October 24, just as the competition was drawing to a close, Coubertin penned a letter to French Ambassador to Japan Auguste Gérard, seeking his assistance in identifying an ideal candidate to represent Japan on the IOC. It was this letter that would eventually forge a link between Coubertin and Kanō.

I was intending to reply to your letter dated October 24 [1908] earlier. I wanted to inquire as to what exactly you had in mind for the "right man" to represent Japan on the International Olympic Committee. (Letter from Gérard to Coubertin, dated January 19, 1909; IOC Archives)

Gérard was more than just a French diplomat—he also had a thorough grasp of Olympism. During his tenure as the French ambassador to Belgium, he had helped organize the 1905 Olympic Congress in Brussels.

Coubertin's letter arrived from London roughly four and half years after the Brussels Congress. To honor Coubertin's request for help locating a fitting leader to be Japan's IOC delegate, Gérard first sought the advice of his close acquaintance Motono Ichirō, then Japan's ambassador to Russia. Motono suggested Kanō, whom Gérard then met with on January 16, 1909. The very next day, Gérard wrote Coubertin about the conversation and informed him that Kanō had immediately accepted the invita-

Pierre de Coubertin (oil portrait; courtesy of the French Olympic Committee)

tion. The IOC unanimously approved Kanō's nomination at the Berlin Session at the end of May, making Kanō the first IOC member from Asia.

The IOC was fraught with turmoil at the time. The Greek delegation, first of all, was trying to drum up support for making Athens the permanent site of the modern Olympic Games. Surging waves of nationalism were manifesting themselves at Olympic venues. Political unrest had begun to spawn clashes between members, who wrangled over political, diplomatic, and ethnic issues. With disorder reigning, Coubertin was clamoring to rebuild the IOC as quickly as he could. Most of all, he was looking for members who were sympathetic to the concept of Olympism from an educational perspective and willing to back IOC initiatives in the interest of international cooperation. Gérard knew what Coubertin needed. With that profile of the ideal member in clear view, Gérard found his way to Kanō Jigorō: someone who had championed educational reforms around a core of physical education, eager to fuse Western learning and the Japanese spirit. Coubertin thus found the "right man" to represent Japan on the IOC, thanks in large part to Gérard's shrewd insight into the needs of the IOC.

2. Kanō and Coubertin

Prior to the Stockholm Olympics (1912)

After joining the IOC ranks in 1909, Kanō had his first face-to-face meeting with Coubertin three years later in Stockholm, the site of the fifth Olympic Games. In the interim, Kanō had written Coubertin on two occasions (September 14, 1909, and May 24, 1911; IOC Archives). Kanō's two letters shed light on how his relationship with Coubertin took shape.

On June 15, 1909, approximately two weeks after the conclusion of the IOC Berlin Session on June 2, Coubertin sent Kanō a letter that offered his congratulations on becoming an IOC member and asked about whether Kanō would be attending the IOC Budapest Session (1910) and Stockholm Olympics (1912). In his reply, dated September 14, Kanō told Coubertin that he was thrilled to be part of the IOC but still unsure about his attendance at the upcoming session and Olympic Games. It was a noncommittal response, but one can understand why Kanō would have been undecided: not only did he lack sufficient, accurate information on the modern Olympics at that stage, but voyages to Europe in the early 1900s were also extremely cost- and time-intensive undertakings.

The correspondence also suggests that Kanō had received copies of *Revue Olympique* (The Olympic review) and Coubertin's just-published *Une Campagne de vingt-et-un ans* (The twenty-one-year campaign). *Revue Olympique* was an IOC periodical, consisting mostly of writings by Coubertin; essentially, it was Coubertin's mouthpiece in print. Through the medium of *Revue Olympique*, Coubertin worked to provide IOC members with an understanding of Olympism and information on IOC operations.

Une Campagne de vingt-et-un ans, meanwhile, comprised a progress report on the movement that Coubertin had launched in 1887 to propel educational reforms via athletics. Tracing the development of the Olympic Games and detailing the particulars of various meetings, the book surveyed a broad scope through the lens of an Olympic revivalist on the front lines of progress. *Revue Olympique* and *Une Campagne de vingt-et-un ans*, both of which were in Kanō's possession, represented vital foundations for understanding the Olympic Movement.

Kanō's second letter to Coubertin was dated May 24, 1911. Beginning with an apology for failing to respond promptly to Coubertin's earlier letter due to an illness, the letter also included Kanō's confidence vote for the selection of new IOC members. Considering the nature of the content, the letter appears to have been a reply to Coubertin's mailing to IOC members on January 28, 1911.

From the Stockholm Olympics (1912) to World War I

The 1912 Stockholm Olympics were where Japan made its Olympic debut and where Kanō first met Coubertin in person. What follows here is an account of Kanō's dealings with Coubertin around the time of the Stockholm Games, a chronicle that draws primarily on the abridged translations of Kanō's English journals in Katō Nihei's *Kanō Jigorō* (Tokyo: Shoyo Shoin, 1964). On June 8, 1912, Kanō boarded a train in Shimbashi and set off for the port town of Tsuruga. He then boarded a ship and made his way to Vladivostok, where he set off for Saint Petersburg aboard the Trans-Siberian Railway. From there, he embarked on the last leg of his journey: a steamship voyage to Stockholm by way of Helsinki. He finally arrived at his destination at 2 p.m. on June 26—a full sixteen days after leaving Japan. At some point during his travels at sea, Kanō met Turkish IOC Member Selim Sırrı Tarcan, whom he quickly befriended. There was no rest for the weary, however; Kanō hit the ground running in Stockholm. As soon as he arrived, he met with Swedish IOC member (and chair of the Olympic organizing committee) Captain Viktor Balck at the Olympic Stadium and then proceeded to watch football (soccer) and tennis matches on June 29 and 30.

The first verifiable meeting between Kanō and Coubertin occurred on the afternoon of July 2, when Kanō paid Coubertin a visit at the Grand Hotel in Saltsjöbaden. Despite talking with Coubertin for two hours, Kanō made no mention of any details of the conversation in his English journals. The two likely discussed the root concepts of the Olympics at the Grand Hotel, possibly touching on the educational value of boxing, wrestling, and judo, though any guesses as to what they talked about are merely speculation.

After their chat, Kanō and Coubertin saw each other several times at various meetings (including an official IOC Session) and competitions during the Stockholm Games.

> July 8 (Monday) Went to a meeting of committee members at the parliament building. Had lunch and then visited the stadium, where Coubertin introduced me to Lafrete. . . Told Coubertin that I would send him a letter when I departed for Paris.[4]

While the identity of the "Lafrete" connection is uncertain, the above entry shows that Coubertin played a role in helping Kanō forge a network of personal connections. Kanō was also eager to continue developing the relationship, apparently; no more than a week after their previous conversation on July 2, Kanō also informed Coubertin that he would be visiting Paris after the Stockholm Olympics, insinuating that he wanted to meet with Coubertin again during his stay.

> August 3 (Saturday) Arrived in Saltsjöbaden at 3 and set off for the Grand Hotel. Baron Coubertin was out for a walk along the lakeshore. Had a look at the swimming area before returning to the hotel. Saw Baron de Blonay, who kindly went off to locate Coubertin for me. Spoke with Coubertin upon his return and promised to visit him in Paris at the end of August. Coubertin said that he would be going to Alsace to see his mother-in-law and son before heading to Paris.[5]

Kanō left Stockholm for a European survey tour on August 4, which means that the events in the above entry took place on eve of his departure. Kanō was clearly trying to squeeze in one last face-to-face with Coubertin, especially considering that he evidently made another trip to the Grand Hotel after missing Coubertin the first time. In all likelihood, Kanō wanted to reiterate his hopes for another meeting with the IOC President in Paris. Godefroy de Blonay, who went off to find Coubertin for Kanō, was Coubertin's closest confidant on the IOC.

On his subsequent trip through Europe, Kanō went from Stockholm on to Copenhagen, Berlin, Vienna, Geneva, and other locations before reaching Paris on December 1 (or sometime in late November). Upon arriving in Paris, Kanō wasted no time in writing Coubertin (in French) to request an appointment. Coubertin received the letter on December 1 and, without delay, reached out to Kanō to schedule a meeting for the evening of December 4. The two rendez-voused at the Japanese embassy shortly after five p.m. on the fourth, went off to watch some boxing and fencing, and then parted ways; Kanō arrived back home "around 7:30 in the evening." Given that Kanō and Coubertin both shared an interest in combat sports, the fact that they took in boxing and fencing was almost surely no mere coincidence.

Kanō's interest was evident in his 1889 "Jūdō ippan narabi ni sono kyōiku-jō no kachi" (Judo and its educational value). In the text, he wrote about the need for *atemi* [body-striking] *waza* in judo; he apparently saw the delivery of blows to the body, a part of numerous combat sports, as vital parts of the judo reper-toire, as well. He also showed an interest in *bōjutsu* (staff techniques), *kenjutsu* (swordplay), wrestling, boxing, and combat sports of all kinds—both Japanese and Western—in his later years, aiming to incorporate their most redeeming features into judo. Combat sports also captivated Coubertin. Not only did he box and fence himself, but he also specifically identified the educational value pervading the practices and make them key components of his stance on sports education.

For Kanō, who was aiming to expand the depths of judo, connecting with Coubertin opened up valuable opportunities to explore the nuances of Western combat sports. The meeting had similar benefits for Coubertin, who got the chance to explain the educational merits of boxing and fencing to someone who would have undoubtedly been interested in those dimensions—Kanō, the mind behind the art of judo. On that early-winter evening in Paris, Kanō and Coubertin spent roughly two hours in each other's company. One can easily imagine their conversation flowing through themes that they both loved: the educational value of sports like boxing, fencing, and, most likely, judo.

Ten days later, on December 14, Kanō called on Coubertin again. Coubertin was out, however, so Kanō left a calling card and returned home.

Connecting with Coubertin was clearly a priority for Kanō in Paris. Kanō made arrangements to meet with Coubertin as soon as he arrived in Paris and clearly intended to bid Coubertin farewell just prior to his departure. In the scope of Kanō's personal network of associations, Coubertin appeared to have been taking on a larger presence. On August 18, 1913, around five months removed from the Stockholm Olympics and his European study tour, Kanō sent his fourth letter to Coubertin. The letter included Kanō's confidence vote for the selection of new IOC members, conveyed his apologies for not being able to attend the 1913 IOC Session or Olympic Congress in Lausanne, Switzerland, and expressed his hopes to be at the 1914 IOC Session and Olympic Congress, scheduled to convene in Paris.

The confidence vote had to do with the election results, which were already in. After placing his vote, Kanō expressed his regrets for his absence at the IOC functions. He noted that he was happy that the gathering was a success, suggesting that Kanō had seen the report on the Congress in the July 1913 issue of Revue Olympique before writing the letter. Although he also told Coubertin that he was looking forward to the upcoming IOC Session and Olympic Congress, writing that he had a keen interest in what would transpire, 1914 would see Kanō miss his second consecutive year of IOC gatherings.

After World War I

The outbreak of World War I resulted in the cancellation of the 1916 Berlin Olympics, but the subsequent 1920 Antwerp Games got the modern Olympics back on their standard quadrennial track and brought Kanō and Coubertin together once again. That reunion in Belgium, however, would be their last face-to-face meeting. Kanō did not make an appearance at the Paris Olympics in 1924, and Coubertin resigned as IOC President the following year to concentrate on educational reforms.

The IOC Archives are home to three letters from Kanō to Coubertin that date to after the conclusion of World War I: August 1, 1921; November 17, 1921; and February 3, 1924. The first of the three (August 1, 1921) detailed the results of the Fifth Far Eastern Championship Games (the "Far Eastern

Games"), event by event. Featuring athletes from countries around Asia, with large delegations from Japan, China, and the Philippines, the Far Eastern Games convened for the first time in Manila in 1913. The fifth edition of the competition took place in Shanghai, running from May 30 to June 4, 1921. According to his letter, Kanō had, "in accordance with the action taken at the Antwerp meeting last summer," attended the Fifth Far Eastern Games "in the capacity of special representative of the International Olympic Committee." Kanō thus wrote the letter as an IOC envoy of sorts, reporting to President Coubertin.

Three months later, on November 17, Kanō sent another letter to Coubertin about the fifth Far Eastern Games from Kobe. Unlike the previous letter, the November 17 mailing was handwritten on Kobe Oriental Hotel stationery—and the tone was more personal.

> . . . I wish to add one thing which I do not like to write in an official report but only with you to understand that such was the case. In short, I was not treated in China with due importance which a special representative of the International Olympic Committee should be.[6]

At the time, the major powers of the world were gradually turning China into a semicolonial state. Japan, for example, had thrust the "Twenty-One Demands" on China in 1915. Four years later, student protests erupted into the "May Fourth Movement"—a massive anti-Japanese demonstration—and Sun Yat-sen founded the Nationalist Part of China. The pushback against colonization would continue to grow as a new revolutionary government, which would later go on to form the basis of China's Nationalist government, set up operations in Guangzhou in 1921. China was in a political maelstrom, and Kanō was aware of the implications. In his letter to Coubertin, Kanō noted that the chilly reception he received in China was partially a product of the "political relations between China and Japan" and may have also stemmed from the "lack of understanding" that China (and the Philippines, both of which had yet to participate in the Olympics) had of the IOC.

The third letter from Kanō to Coubertin was dated February 3, 1924. In the aftermath of the Great Kantō Earthquake (September 1, 1923), Coubertin had sent Kanō a letter asking if he was safe. Kanō immediately replied via telegram, but he followed up with the February 3 letter to describe the disaster in more detail and inform Coubertin that the rest of his family was safe. After discussing the earthquake, the letter continued with two notes on Olympic-related matters, a request, and a report on the Far Eastern Games:[7]

i. Due to the effects of the earthquake, Japan was "obliged to curtail the number of competitors" in its delegation to the Paris Olympics (1924)

ii. For the same reason, the House of Peers would need to meet under an extraordinary schedule, making it impossible for Kanō to be away from Japan (and attend the Paris Olympics)

iii. Kanō wanted Coubertin to admit Kishi Seiichi as one of the members of the International Olympic Committee for Japan; otherwise, Kanō wrote, "I wish you would admit Dr. Kishi, I resigning."

iv. Kanō was present at the previous year's Sixth Far Eastern Games (Osaka) and "conveyed the greetings of the I.O.C. as one of its members."

At its Paris Session in 1924, the IOC officially approved Kishi as Japan's second IOC member. President Coubertin had evidently honored Kanō's request in full.

The February 3 letter is the last of Kanō's letters to Coubertin in the IOC Archives. There may well have been more going on behind the scenes, however. If historical evidence corroborating the following episode were ever to turn up, it would prove that the relationship between Kanō and Coubertin had a second act.

He (Coubertin) was then lodging at a hotel on Saltsjöbaden, a picturesque island off the shores of Stockholm, and it was in a room there that I first made his acquaintance. . . . We grew closer and friendlier over the course of frequent meetings coinciding subsequent Olympic Games. After he resigned his post as Committee President, however, we never again had the opportunity to meet in person; our only communication was through the exchange of an occasional letter.[8]

3. Kanō and other IOC members

Godefroy de Blonay

When Kanō began his career as an IOC member, Swiss IOC representative Godefroy de Blonay (1869–1937) was in charge of the organization's accounting. The IOC Archives are home to two letters that Kanō sent to Blonay to notify him of an annual-fee payment (dated October 10, 1909, and November 4, 1910).

Blonay was also the one who went out looking for Coubertin when Kanō was hoping to meet with the IOC President on August 3, 1912, shortly after the conclusion of the Stockholm Olympics. Kanō departed on his European tour the following day and, exactly a month later (September 3), wrote Blonay a letter (in French) from Geneva (IOC Archives). In the letter, Kanō told Blonay that he had hoped to visit him at his home in Grandson (Neuchatel), Switzerland, while in the area. As Blonay was out at the time, the letter continued, Kanō left him a telephone message in his absence.

When World War I erupted in 1914, Coubertin named Blonay the acting president of the IOC—partly because he was one of Coubertin's closest allies on the organization, and partly because Blonay represented a permanent neutral state, Switzerland, and was thus impervious to any conflicts of political interest. On October 15, 1918, Blonay sent the IOC members a letter (presumably in the capacity of acting president) regarding a confidence vote concerning new IOC members, the creation of the Olympic Institute (in Lausanne), and the annual IOC dues. Kanō responded roughly six months later (May 1, 1919), again in French. The reply included Kanō's confidence vote for the appointment of new IOC members, thanked Blonay for taking on the role of acting president, and extended his congratulations on the founding of the Olympic Institute.

As far as the historical records show, the next—and last—interaction between Kanō and Blonay was an exchange of correspondence (a telegram and a letter) during the bidding process for the Games of the XII Olympiad in 1940 (well after Blonay's service as acting president had come to a close). In the telegram, dated February 13, 1935, Kanō asked Blonay to cast his vote for Tokyo at the approaching IOC Session in Oslo (February 28–March 1), where the members were scheduled to decide on a site for the 1940 Games. Blonay responded in a letter dated February 20, 1935. While extenuating circumstances would prevent him from attending the meeting in Norway, Blonay wrote, he was "fully prepared to do everything in [his] power in support of Japan's plan," which required "both the approval of the IOC and the attention of all the IOC members." Coubertin, who had always longed to see Olympism grow in a truly international mold, was supportive of Tokyo's bid—and Blonay's message to Kanō suggests that Coubertin's vision had made its mark on his close colleague and former temporary successor. In the end, however, then-IOC President Baillet-Latour decided to postpone the host-city vote until the following year's

Berlin Session.

Jiri Guth-Jarkovsky (1861–1943)

Jiri Guth, one of the founding IOC members in 1894, served longer than any other member. Although political and ethnic strife across Europe in the late-nineteenth and early-twentieth centuries sometimes put Guth in unenviable, precarious circumstances on the IOC, Coubertin came to his defense at every juncture. That support helped Guth sustain his career as an IOC member all the way to 1943, nearly half a century after he first took his post. For Kanō, a contemporary in terms of age, Guth was the IOC member with whom he had the longest relationship.

Unfortunately, the only historical documentation of the connection between Kanō and Guth is from Kanō's European tour after the 1920 Antwerp Olympics. According to the available records,[9] Kanō arrived in Prague, Czechoslovakia, on September 24 and immediately headed to Guth's residence. He had preceded his visit with a letter to Guth a few days before his arrival in Prague, but the letter's intended recipient never saw it; Guth was away, and his wife left the envelope sealed—when Kanō showed up, then, it obviously came as quite the surprise to Mrs. Guth. Her husband did return the following day, however, and accompanied Kanō to a meeting with President Tomáš Masaryk (1850–1937). Kanō had been looking forward to the opportunity to talk with Masaryk, the father of Czechoslovak independence, and Guth helped bring that hope to fruition.

Sigfrid Edström (1870–1964) and Henri de Baillet-Latour (1876–1942)

Sigfrid Edström, a Swede, was the fourth president of the IOC (serving from 1946 to 1952). Just after becoming an IOC member in 1921, Edström took a place on the newly established Executive Board and became one of the IOC's key internal players. He also traveled to Japan in October 1929, the year after the Amsterdam Games, and spent two days in Tokyo and one in Kyoto with Kanō, who offered to entertain Edström during his stay. The connection between Kanō and Edström would again emerge about three years later. When Kanō announced Tokyo's host-city bid at the official Los Angeles Session on July 30, 1932, Edström chimed in with a "compelling speech in support of the motion."[10]

Henri de Baillet-Latour succeeded Coubertin as IOC President in 1925.

He first became an IOC member in 1903, so he and Kanō had known one another for quite some time. The defining feature of their relationship was a delicate, sometimes uneasy balance. After Kanō paid Latour a visit for a private conversation about Tokyo's Olympic-bid plans ahead of the IOC Session in Los Angeles on July 27, 1932, the bid became the centerpiece of their

Kanō welcomes IOC President Latour to Tokyo (1936; courtesy of the Kodokan collection)

relationship. Just before the 1935 IOC Session in Oslo, where the selection of the 1940 host site was on the agenda, Kanō sent Latour a letter carefully spelling out the significance of a Tokyo Games and urging Latour to back Tokyo's bid (Letter from Kanō to Latour, dated January 10, 1935; IOC Archives).

The vote to determine the site of the 1940 Olympics would be postponed until the 1936 IOC Session in Berlin, however. Prior to the meeting in Berlin, President Latour headed to Japan for a firsthand look at the state of Japanese sports in March 1936. He was in the country for some three weeks—and Kanō spent nine of those days entertaining Latour, a man sixteen years his junior. For almost half of Latour's stay, then, Kanō was essentially his attendant. Upon returning home from his Japan tour, Latour wrote Coubertin about how the Olympic spirit was swirling in Japan, which he deemed a fitting site for the Games of the XII Olympiad (Letter from Latour to Coubertin, dated May 22, 1936; IOC Archives). Kanō, who had known Latour for a quarter of a century, surely must have had a hand in stirring that enthusiasm by demonstrating how far Japanese sports had come since the country debuted on the Olympic stage. Two years later, however, came an abrupt change of tone and course. While Latour's role as president of the IOC bound him to the mission of bringing the Olympics to fruition, he sent a stern warning to Kanō on the heels of the IOC Session in Cairo about the fate of the 1940 Tokyo Games. If the war had not come to an end by 1940, Latour wrote, there would be consequences for the Japanese Olympic Committee.[11]

4. What the connections reveal

Coubertin's vision of Olympism and Kanō's philosophy of judo

What gave Kanō such a singular presence on the IOC was his commitment to explaining the theoretical dimensions of judo, which he took numerous opportunities to do at various Olympic Games, IOC Sessions, and more, often demonstrating techniques himself. At gatherings around the world, he presented the martial art—a practice of his own creation—in 1920 (London), 1921 (United States), 1928 (Italy, the United Kingdom, and Berlin), 1932 (Los Angeles), 1933 (Vienna, Berlin, London, France, and Singapore), and 1934 (Athens, Vienna, and London).

Kanō was over sixty years of age when those demonstrations began. He had a diminutive frame, paling in comparison to many of his larger colleagues. When he showed audiences how he could throw brawny men seemingly twice his size with ease, it was an adage personified—mind over muscle, the weak trumping the strong. Watching logic-defying displays unfold before their very eyes, the IOC members saw the tenets of judo in action. Kanō gave the IOC members a revealing glimpse, one that made a significant impression on those in attendance. British IOC member Clarence Napier Bruce, Lord Aberdare (1885–1957), for example, noted the experience in his memoirs: "When we sat for a lecture and demonstration of judo by Kanō, who was around seventy-five

Kanō Jigorō departs Vancouver
(courtesy of the Kodokan collection)

or seventy-six years of age at the time, he would make quick work of much younger opponents, throwing them to the ground in less than a minute. I will never forget the sight of it all, Kanō's courage and proficiency astounding the entire audience." In the words of German IOC member Ritter von Halt, "Listening to Kanō speak about judo and watching him demonstrate the art in Vienna in 1933, I marveled at what an extraordinary person he was."[12]

Under the intriguing pull of the lectures and demonstrations ran a deeper significance: Kanō leapt at the opportunity to show his fellow IOC members that the philosophy of judo, which he had defined as the most effective application of one's mental and physical abilities (1915), merited broader applications in the social sphere. In Berlin, after the 1928 Amsterdam Olympics, Kanō spoke about "applying the principles of judo in various aspects of society." At a meeting in Vienna following the 1934 IOC Session in Athens, Austrian IOC member Theodor Schmidt assured Kanō that Austria would "make efforts to promote the spirit of judo," which had "deeply resonated" with him. Coubertinian Olympism (here, Coubertin's educational philosophy) aspired toward a world where the education value innate in sports would apply in real, everyday life. In that sense, Kanō's vision for judo—a process of enrooting the tenets of *seiryoku zen'yō* and *jita kyōei* in the social landscape—harmonized with the spirit of Olympism that his IOC colleagues were striving to spread. Kanō's judo was Japanese Olympism.

International understanding through sports

It was 1922 when Kanō first verbalized his concept of *jita kyōei*, which advocated seeking benefits both for oneself and for others, serving both one's own country and other nations, and striving for mutual prosperity. The origins of that vision, however, stretch back to when Kanō began accepting international students as principal of the Higher Normal School in 1896. The seeds of the concept took root in that context. Kanō's relationships with IOC members then cultivated that conceptual soil, the feedback he received from his audiences sparking a growing confidence in his ideas. When the seeds eventually sprouted, they budded the *jita kyōei* philosophy.

The objectives of these quadrennial gatherings are to promote physical education by uniting the athletes of the world in competition, firstly, and to help establish the proper policies on physical education. However, it is also the hope of the committee's leading members that the gatherings foster exchange among members and among youth, which thereby forges common emotional bonds, facilitates mutual understanding, and consequently nurtures harmony between nations, another objective of no small import. The committee member representing the United Kingdom is a true, fervent advocate of that purpose. . . . At the very least, the members, assembling from nations across the globe, have shared a warm, emotional bond. As I myself saw during my subsequent travels, every fellow member to whom I paid

Kanō Jigorō in his later years (courtesy of the Kodokan collection)

a personal visit has given me a warm-hearted welcome and shown me a special type of affectionate, kindhearted goodwill. I have always found myself overcome with a feeling of closeness, a pleasurable sensation, for some reason that defies simple explanation.[13]

Whenever I attended a meeting of the International Olympic Committee, the constant refrain was that the Olympics are to unite the youth of the world with no distinction of nationality. All the members of all the participating countries, I recall, were of one mind in calling for the Games to be a means of joining hands in harmony and facilitating international cooperation. Therein lies the value of competitive sport.[14]

The above passage captures a line of thought that Kanō often used when discussing the value of athletics in the Olympic context: that sports held the potential to be a medium of international understanding. He also openly credited his fellow IOC members for shaping that understanding, as their commitment to the pursuit of international cooperation through sport had made a significant impact on him.

Kanō won over his colleagues on the IOC with an inimitable charm and unique presence, forging relationships that would continue to grow through written correspondence and personal visits. Over that process, he found kindred spirits with similar stances on the educational value of sports (Coubertin's vision of Olympism and Kanō's conceptualization of judo), a commonality that brought him together into trusting relationships with fellow members. Those connections, for Kanō, sustained his development as a leader and a person. After Kanō's death, the condolences from IOC members (and officials) often spoke to that dynamic:[15]

"... Mr. Kanō was a *samurai* of the finest order and a model educator whose contributions to sport will long be remembered."

—Avery Brundage, later the fifth IOC President

"He was a man of integrity, one of the foremost sports educators the world has ever seen. His death is a regrettable tragedy not only for Japan but also for the worlds of sport and education."
— Carl Diem (1882–1962), Secretary General of the Organizing Committee of the Berlin Olympics

"[Kanō] was a true educator of youth. . . . The Tokyo Olympics are the fruit of Kanō's lifelong dedication to elevating Japanese athletics to the lofty standards they now occupy."
—Henri de Baillet-Latour, IOC President

Notes:

1 Nagai Matsuzō, "Kairo sōkai no Kanō-san" [Mr. Kanō at the Cairo Session], *Jūdō* [Judo] 9, no. 6 (1938).
2 "Ko-Kanō Jigorō-sensei tsuitō zadankai" [A roundtable remembering the late Dr. Kanō Jigorō] *Orimupikku* [Olympic] 16, no. 6 (1938).
3 Kanō Jigorō, "Shihan no otayori roku-gatsu tsuitachi-hatsu, Atene yori" [Master Kanō's June 1 letter from Athens] *Jūdō* [Judo] 5, no. 8 (1934).
4 Katō Nihei, *Kanō Jigorō: Sekai taiiku-shi-jō ni kagayaku* [Kanō Jigorō: A luminary in the world history of physical education] (Tokyo: Shoyo Shoin, 1970), 165.
5 Ibid., 170.
6 Kanō Jigorō to Pierre de Coubertin, November 17, 1921.
7 Kanō Jigorō to Pierre de Coubertin, February 3, 1924.
8 Kanō Jigorō, "Kūberutan-dan o omou" [Remembering Baron de Coubertin], *Orimupikku* [Olympic] 15, no. 10 (1937).
9 Kanō Jigorō, "Kokusai Orinpikku Taikai o oete (dai-ni)" [Reflecting on the Games of the II Olympiad (part II)] *Yūkō no katsudō* [The principle of effective activity] 7, no. 3 (1921).
10 Kanō Jigorō, "Tobei no ninmu o oete" [Reflecting on my work in the United States] *Sakkō* [Promotion] 11, no. 9 (1932).
11 Nakamura Tetsuo, "IOC Kaichō Baie-Rastūru kara mita Tōkyō Orinpikku" [How IOC President Baillet-Latour saw the Tokyo Olympics], in *Maboroshi no Tōkyō Orinpikku to sono jidai* [The phantom Tokyo Olympics and the context of the times], ed. Sakaue Yasuhiro and Takaoka Hiroyuki (Tokyo: Seikyūsha, 2009), 51–52.
12 "Kanō-sensei no chōsei o itamu" [Mourning the death of Dr. Kanō], *Orimupikku* [Olympic] 16, no. 6 (1938).
13 Kanō Jigorō, "Ōbei junshikan: Taiiku no hōshin" [Thoughts from my tour of Europe and the United States: Policies on physical education], *Kyōiku jiron* [The educational review] 1013 (1913).

14 Kanō Jigorō, "Kyōgi undō no mokuteki oyobi sono jikkō no hōhō ni tsuite" [On the purpose and implementation of competitive athletics], *Chūtō kyōiku* [Secondary education] 52 (1925).

15 "Sekai no nageki" [The world grieves] *Jūdō* [Judo] 9, no. 9 (1938)

The University of Tsukuba and the legacy of Kanō Jigorō

Kanō Jigorō served as the principal of the Higher Normal School and Tokyo Higher Normal School for a total of twenty-three years, spanning three separate terms between 1893 and 1920. While Kanō's renown has obvious roots in his role as the founder of judo, now a sport with a global reach, he also had a lasting impact on the Higher Normal School and, by extension, its successor, the University of Tsukuba. Centering his outlook on the philosophical constructs of *seiryoku zen'yō* (maximum efficient use of energy) and *jita kyōei* (mutual prosperity for oneself and others), Kanō worked to enhance the Higher Normal School, drive educational reforms to better the state of middle schools and higher schools for women, underline the need for extended periods of study amid calls for the closure of higher normal schools, and put the pieces in place for the Higher Normal School's promotion to university status. Institutional improvements were just one facet of Kanō's many contributions. He was also a pioneering force in fostering international study; more than a century ago, he admitted roughly 8,000 Chinese students to his institutions and provided the enrollees with an education that would help them flourish in the future. From his educational leadership to his dedication to international exchange, Kanō left an enduring legacy on innumerable fronts.

In 2010, the University of Tsukuba celebrated the 150th anniversary of Kanō's birth with a slate of different events and programs. By revisiting Kanō's philosophy and achievements, both as a forward-looking educator and visionary force in the international community, the initiative aimed to foster a deeper discussion of the University's identity, its ideals in shaping human resources for the future, its educational practices, and Japan's roles on the global stage.

Given our lasting ties to the legacy of Kanō Jigorō, we at the University of Tsukuba need to understand and appreciate that heritage. A basic timeline of his impact on education, research, international exchange, physical education, and sports illuminates just how vital Kanō was in laying the school's foundation.

1893: Kanō becomes principal of the Higher Normal School at age thirty-two

1894: Higher Normal School holds an athletic meet, with all students and faculty members taking part

Period of study extended from three years to four years

1896: Athletic Association established to encourage student involvement in sports

Kanō begins accepting students from China to study at his private academy

1898: "Healthy-leg race" (marathon), mandatory for all students, established

1901: Athletic Association dissolved and replaced by the School Council, designed to encourage student participation in extracurricular activities

1902: Higher Normal School renamed Tokyo Higher Normal School

1907: Bylaws for the acceptance of special international students established, and enrollment slots for students from China expanded

1908: Judo and kendo required for all students, and mandatory distance-running competitions (spring and fall) established

1915: Four-year faculty of physical education established at the Tokyo Higher Normal School

1918: Movement to promote the Tokyo Higher Normal School to university status gains momentum

1919: "Sen'yōka" ("enhancement song") written in support of the university-promotion movement

1920: International students represent 15 percent of the Tokyo Higher Normal School's total enrollment

1922: Kanō publishes an article explaining his philosophies of *seiryoku zen'yō* (maximum efficient use of energy) and *jita kyōei* (mutual prosperity for oneself and others)

1929: Tokyo University of Literature and Science opened

A student doing gymnastics (1940)

316

1936: IOC names Tokyo the host of the 1940 Olympic Games
1938: Kanō dies at the age of seventy-seven
1949: Tokyo University of Education opened
1973: University of Tsukuba opened
2010: 150th anniversary of Kanō's birth

1. Elevating the university to a center of world-class research

One can gauge Kanō's impact from a historical distance, but a closer reading of how his initiatives unfolded in real time provides an even more revealing glimpse. What were things like at the Tokyo Higher Normal School—and its successor, the Tokyo University of Literature and Science, which opened in 1929?

In *Nijūisseiki taiiku e no teigen* (Proposals for physical education and sport in the twenty-first century) (Tokyo: Fumaidō Shuppan, 2005), former Tokyo Higher Normal School student (and my former teacher) Kinpara Isamu (1914–) discussed the faculty of physical education at the Tokyo Higher Normal School and the education and research that took place at the Tokyo University of Literature and Science. The conceptualization of physical education pervading the specialized studies in the faculty of physical education, Kinpara wrote, "fell in line with a sports-oriented approach that focused on human development, an orientation that bore strong evidence of Professor Kanō Jigorō's influence." Sports thus occupied a sizable portion of the physical-education curriculum, at least relative to academic lectures; unlike the physical education of today, which has evolved to a point where instructors can give exhaustive, theoretical lectures on a variety of themes in the world of physical education, there was simply not enough existing research in Kanō's day and age to enable deep, scholarly dives into the discipline. However, Kinpara also explained that the general education and pedagogical instruction he received at the Tokyo Higher Normal School were first-rate. His teachers, many of whom were prominent figures in their fields, provided him with sophisticated instruction. After graduation, Kinpara went on to study at the Tokyo University of Literature and Science. There, he found a wealth of cutting-edge research facilities, ample educational establishments, and sound frameworks for facilitating academic work. The environment had all the markings of a top-quality graduate institute, even when it came to research on the still-developing fields of physical education and sports. Kanō's impact, especially in his consistent emphasis on human development, had begun to foster a tradition of pursuing advanced research, offering thorough education, and cultivating high-caliber human resources.

Kanō was always intent on raising the academic bar at the Tokyo Higher Normal School. By assembling a faculty of superb educators, he constantly worked to enhance the institution's capabilities in education and research. "The professors at the Higher Normal School must have an educational background of the finest quality," he wrote. "This institution requires instructors who have studied at universities abroad, learned at universities in Japan, or otherwise undergone a similar regimen of education and acquired the necessary abilities." He also laid the foundation for the Tokyo Higher Normal School's ascension to the university ranks, the process by which it became the Tokyo University of Literature and Science. By molding the institution around a commitment to profound scholarship, he built an environment that would produce steady streams of instructors with specialized expertise and a long list of renowned educators and researchers. That component of Kanō's legacy lives on at the University of Tsukuba, which continues to secure its foothold as a world-class research university.

2. *Seiryoku zen'yō, jita kyōei,* and internationalism

In the world of traditional Japanese physical arts, from jujutsu to *kenjutsu* (swordplay), technical skills are often secondary to a more philosophical emphasis: the development of one's mind and the cultivation of one's character. That focus on self-perfection tends to direct practitioners' attention inward and, as a result, away from the world outside their individual selves—namely, the community, the country, and the world. Kanō was well aware of that dynamic. While he constructed judo on a basis in traditional jujutsu, he appears to have eschewed the inward-looking tendencies so prevalent among Japan's traditional approach to training. His role as an international-minded "citizen of the world" speaks to that stance: he engaged with the world outside, and he encouraged his fellow Japanese citizens to do the same. He wanted them to broaden their perspectives, to recognize the community around them, to turn their gaze to the globe as a whole. In his departure from the internal focus common to Japanese physical arts, Kanō emphasized the idea of using one's energies as effectively as possible to foster mutual prosperity the world over.

Kanō was also the first educator in modern Japan to admit international students. He schooled his first group of students from abroad at Kōbun Gakuin, his private academy, and then continued to accept international students at the Higher Normal School from 1899 onward. While the idea of cross-border education might seem commonplace today, Kanō was doing it more than a century ago—it must have been an enormous undertaking at the time, one teeming with logistical challenges and hurdles that we would hardly be able to fathom now. Kanō, though, was resolute in his belief that only through friendly neighborly relations can people and countries thrive. At Kōbun Gakuin and Tokyo Higher

(Top) Participants gather in Italy for a symposium commemorating the 150th anniversary of Kanō's birth;
(Bottom) Tanimoto Ayumi teaches a judo workshop (Italy, 2010; courtesy of the Associazione Italiana Sport Educazione)

Normal School, Kanō supervised the education of some 8,000 Chinese students. Many would go on to pursue careers in the educational sphere, with some landing positions at prestigious universities (Peking University and Beijing Normal University, among others) and others cementing their reputations as leading scholars. The Kōbun Gakuin and Tokyo Higher Normal School graduate rolls contain an impressive collection of names, including famed author Lu Xun, literary giant Tian Han, and Yang Changji—an educator who taught Mao Zedong. In that same spirit, the University of Tsukuba has made openness a core value ever since its founding. Embodying a willingness to engage both inwardly and outwardly, the University has earned a place on the Japanese government's Global 30 funding project (an initiative to promote the internationalization of academic environments at Japanese universities)—and put itself in position to inherit Kanō's legacy of internationalism for years to come.

3. The traditional dimensions of physical education and sports

As an educator, Kanō saw educational merit in judo:

> After a few years of training in jujutsu, however, I found that my health had improved. As a result, I had become calmer and possessed much greater self-control. I also concluded that the same spirit necessary to prevail in a life or death struggle against an enemy . . . could be similarly applied in an attempt to overcome difficulties that we often have to face in our daily lives. The training to acquire competent fighting skills that enable one to defeat an enemy in battle is, in a sense, also very valuable as intellectual training . . . I concluded . . . that after modification, many of these same jujutsu techniques . . . could be of a practical nature for modern-day life and could be of value in the exercising of one's intellect, body, and moral character" (Kanō Jigorō, interview by Ochiai Torahei, "Jūdō-ka to shite no Kanō Jigorō (san)" [Kanō Jigorō, the judoka (III)], *Sakkō* [Promotion] 6, no. 3 (1927); English translation based on Brian Watson, *Judo Memoirs of Jigoro Kano* [Bloomington, IN: Trafford Publishing, 2008], 15)

Kanō would thus go on to found Kodokan judo and promote the art as a means of human education, of course, but his embrace of physical activity stretched far beyond judo. At the Tokyo Higher Normal School, he made distance running and swimming mandatory for the entire student body and worked to encourage extra-curricular athletics as chairman of the Tokyo Higher Normal School's School Council. With the wide-ranging exposure to sports that they received at the Tokyo Higher Normal School, graduates—and not just those who had studied in the faculty of physical education—had a background that made them natural ambassadors for sports. Sports spread across Japan, and the teachers coming out of the Tokyo Higher Normal School played a pivotal part in that process.

The history of physical education and sport at the University of Tsukuba traces back to the National Institute of Gymnastics, which opened its doors in 1878. That beginning spawned a tradition that survived and developed at the Tokyo Higher Normal School, Tokyo University of Education, and now the University of Tsukuba—an institution that stands at the forefront of Japanese physical education and sport. Over those more than 130 years, public perceptions of physical education and sport have evolved. The corresponding environments have changed, as well. Not only have people connected with the joys of competition, from contests of strength to tests of skill, but they now recognize physical education and

The Tsukuba Marathon

sport as parts of a bigger picture: living healthier lives, communicating with others, engaging with the environment, fostering relationships on an interregional and even international scale, and energizing communities and economies. From low awareness, physical education and sports have lodged themselves in the public consciousness as sources of meaningful value on a far-reaching scope.

Sports play a substantial role at the University of Tsukuba, as well, which has held Sports Day events in the spring and fall since its founding. Team sports are thriving, too. That flourishing sport environment has roots that reach back in a natural succession to Kanō Jigorō: the educator who had all of his students learn judo, encouraged participation in a variety of different sports, and created the Athletic Association and School Council to facilitate athletic activities on a school-wide basis. From the standpoint of today's educational field, where sports are becoming an increasingly important part of liberal-arts programs, Kanō's foresight and commitment to action take on a compelling layer of significance.

4. Producing human resources capable of thriving on the global stage

Kanō was also a politician in the House of Peers—and a capable one at that. Though he probably could have been prime minister, considering all the resources and abilities he had at his disposal, Kanō decided to make education his focus. Kanō was of the belief that there was virtually nothing more important for contemporary Japan than education, and he wanted to entrust that education to the best possible people. To produce those types of exceptional educators, Kanō believed, normal schools and normal education would need

Calligraphy of *issei kaiku*

to implement the finest education available. That set the stage for his educational reforms, which he drove ahead with tenacity and zeal. "The work of an educator is only of value if the educator himself believes in the fulfilling worth of education and applies his vocation toward the benefit of the nation."

Nothing under the sun is greater than education. By educating one person and sending him into the society of his generation, we make a contribution extending a hundred generations to come.

Seiryoku zen'yō, jita kyōei, and *issei kaiku* (the teachings of one can influence a great many, and one's life work will last for generations) are concise, elegant distillations of Kanō's philosophy, but the man behind them was more than just a font of lofty ideals. Remembering his time at the Tokyo Higher Normal School, former student Gotō Keita (and later the founder of Tokyu Corporation) sat for morality-themed lectures that emphasized Kanō's more dogged, never-say-die attitude.

"The talks were unusual," he wrote. "From start to finish, he focused on nothing but his personal maxim of 'Bring it on, damn it.'" Gotō continued, saying, "Sensei explained how to make effective use of force—but he never imposed anything unreasonable on anyone. In judo, forcing the situation and wasting energy are two things to avoid at all costs. But the fighting spirit of Principal Kanō's 'bring-it-on' maxim was something different. He once said that the magic of life lies in the conjunction of those two seemingly contradictory ideas: the determination to keep tackling whatever might come one's way and the avoidance of forcible imposition." Kanō was advocating an extremely rational, sensible way of life, but at the same time, he was urging his students to back up that level-headed outlook with an indomitable spirit. The University of Tsukuba is not a normal school, nor is it a teacher-training university—but it is, all the same, an educational institution. As such, it needs to be an environment where the faculty can both educate their students from a foundation in leading-edge research and keep learning together with their students at every level of study. People often say that great scholars are great educators. That would be an oversimplification, however. A more accurate interpretation would be that great scholars have the potential to be great educators. Whether or not quality researchers can realize that potential would depend on how fully they recognize the vital importance of *kaiku*—Kanō's notion that the education one passes along continues to grow and evolve, broadening both in the scope and the duration of its impact.

If the entire community at the University of Tsukuba roots its educational activities and research pursuits in a commitment to bettering the world, that spirit so central to Kanō Jigorō's basic philosophy, the legacy that he bestowed on the University will not just live on—it will develop and foster new traditions. I can almost hear him talking to us, urging us onward as he did so many of his students. "I left so much unfinished, but I know that I made at least some measure of contribution to the world in my twenty-three years here," Kanō might say. "The University of Tsukuba still has unfinished tasks to take care of, as well. While you have charted a successful course over the last thirty-eight years, you still have a long way to go. Never lose sight of the future, and never stop making forward progress."

Ae Michiyoshi
Dean
School of Health and Physical Education
University of Tsukuba

Bibliography (in order of year of publication)

Kyōiku jiron [The educational review]. Tokyo: Kaihatsu-sha, 1885–1934.

Kokushi [Patriot]. Tokyo: Kodokan, 1898–1903.

Kyōiku [Education]. Tokyo: Meikeikai, 1900–59.

Kōyūkai-shi [The journal of the School Council]. Tokyo: Higher Normal School Kōyūkai, 1902–29.

Honkō sōritsu yonjūnen kinen Kōyūkai hatten-shi [Commemorating the fortieth anniversary of the school's founding: A history of the School Council]. Tokyo: Tokyo Higher Normal School Kōyūkai, 1911.

Jūdō [Judo]. Tokyo: Kodokan, 1915–19, 1922–23, 1930–2011.

Kanō, Jigorō. *Kōdōkan no enkaku, shimei oyobi sono jigyō* [The history, mission, and initiatives of the Kodokan]. Tokyo: Kodokan, 1917.

Yūkō no katsudō [The principle of effective activity]. Tokyo: Kodokan, 1919–22.

Sakkō [Promotion]. Tokyo: Kodokan Culture Council, 1924–38.

Kanō, Jigorō. *Jūdō kyōhon: Jō, ge* [The fundamentals of judo, vols. 1 and 2]. Tokyo: Sanseidō, 1931.

Tokyo University of Literature and Science and Tokyo Higher Normal School. *Sōritsu rokujū-nen* [Commemorating our sixty-year history]. Tokyo: Tokyo University of Literature and Science, 1931.

Yokoyama, Kendō. *Kanō-sensei-den* [The life of Professor Kanō]. Tokyo: Kodokan, 1941.

Kanō-sensei Denki Hensan-kai, ed. *Kanō Jigorō* [Kanō Jigorō]. Tokyo: Kodokan, 1964.

Katō, Nihei. *Kanō Jigorō: Sekai taiiku-shi-jō ni kagayaku* [Kanō Jigorō: A luminary in the world history of physical education]. Tokyo: Shōyō Shoin, 1970.

Oimatsu, Shin'ichi. *Jūdō hyaku-nen* [100 years of judo]. Tokyo: Jiji Press, 1970.

Watanabe, Ichirō, ed. *Shiryō meiji budō-shi* [The documented history of martial arts in the Meiji period]. Tokyo: Shinjinbutsu Ōraisha: 1971.

Ōtaki, Tadao. *Kanō Jigorō: Watashi no shōgai to jūdō* [Kanō Jigorō: My life and judo]. Tokyo: Shinjinbutsu Ōraisha, 1972.

Noritomi, Masako. *Joshi jūdō kyōhon* [The fundamentals of women's judo]. Tokyo: Junsensō, 1972.

Hasegawa, Junzō, ed. *Kanō Jigorō no kyōiku to shisō* [The education and thought of Kanō Jigorō]. Tokyo: Meiji Shoin, 1981.

Japan Amateur Sports Association. *Nihon Taiiku Kyōkai nanajūgo-nen-shi* [The 75-year history of the Japan Amateur Sports Association]. Tokyo: Japan Amateur Sports Association, 1986.

Committee for the Publication of the History of the Tokyo Higher Normal School Judo Club. *Tōkyō Kōtō Shihan Gakkō jūdō-bu-shi* [The history of the Tokyo Higher Normal School judo club]. Tokyo: Gyōsei: 1987.

Kodokan, comp. and ed. *Kanō Jigorō taikei* [An introductory overview to Kanō Jigorō], 15 volumes. Tokyo: Hon no Tomo-sha, 1987–88.

Saitō, Akio, Doi Masaoki, and Honda Kōei, eds. *Kyōiku no naka no minzoku: Nihon to Chūgoku* [Peoples in the context of education: Japan and China]. Tokyo: Akashi Shoten, 1988.

Murayama, Masaaki. *Kanō Jigorō-shihan no omoide* [Memories of Master Kanō Jigorō]. Tokyo: Shinsei Shobō, 1994.

Funaki, Toshio. *Kindai Nihon chūtō kyōin yōseironsō-shiron* [Tracing the history of the controversy surrounding secondary teacher training in modern Japan]. Tokyo: Gakubunsha, 1998.

Murata, Naoki. *Kanō Jigorō shihan ni manabu* [Learning from Master Kanō Jigorō]. Tokyo: Nippon Budokan/Baseball Magazine Sha, 2001.

Editorial Committee for the History of the University of Tsukuba Swim Team. *Meisui hyaku-nen-shi*. Tsukuba: University of Tsukuba Swim Team, 2002.

Tōdō, Yoshiaki. *Jūdō no rekishi to bunka* [The history and culture of judo]. Tokyo: Fumaidō Shuppan, 2007.

Nagaki, Kōsuke. *Kanō jūdō shisō no keishō to hen'yō* [Kanō's judo philosophy: Legacy and transformation]. Tokyo: Kazamashobō, 2008.

Shōgenji, Kisaburō. *Jūdō to Nihon-teki hassō* [Judo and the Japanese mindset]. Tokyo: Bungeisha, 2008.

Chronological Table

Year	Education/Sports	Kanō Juku/Judo	Society/International community
1860	· Kanō born December 10 in Mikage, Ubara-gun, Settsu Province		*Kanrin Maru* (warship) sets sail for the United States Sakuradamon Incident
1861			Spencer's *Education* published
1863			Coubertin born in Paris
1866			Satsuma-Chōshū Alliance formed
1867			Imperial rule restored
1869	· Kanō's mother, Sadako, dies of an illness		Boshin War ends
1870	· Kanō travels to Tokyo with his father · Kanō studies Chinese classics		
1871	· Kanō studies calligraphy at Seitatsu Shojuku		Domain system abolished
1872	· Kanō studies English literature		Fukuzawa Yukichi's *Gakumon no susume* [An encouragement of learning] published
1873	· Kanō enrolls at Ikuei Gijuku; studies English and German		Conscription Ordinance issued; land-tax reforms implemented
1874	· Kanō enrolls at the Tokyo School of Foreign Languages; studies English and general subjects		
1875	· Kanō graduates from the Tokyo School of Foreign Languages and enrolls at Tokyo Kaisei School		Japan signs Treaty of St. Petersburg with Russia
1876			Japan–Korea Treaty of 1876 signed (Korean ports opened)
1877	· Tokyo Kaisei School renamed Tokyo University; Kanō transfers into the Faculty of Letters as a first-year student	· Kanō studies jujutsu under Fukuda Hachinosuke, a Tenjin Shin'yō-ryū master	Satsuma Rebellion (Seinan War)
1878	· National Institute of Gymnastics established		
1879		· Kanō demonstrates jujutsu for US President Ulysses Grant during a visit to Japan	Japan annexes the Ryukyu Islands to establish Okinawa Prefecture
1881	· Kanō graduates from the Department of Political Science and Economics of the Faculty of Letters at Tokyo University; enrolls in a special course on moral science and aesthetics (and graduates the following year)	· Kanō studies jujutsu under Iikubo Tsunetoshi, a practitioner of the Kitō-ryū	

1882	· Kanō becomes an instructor at Gakushūin (teaching political science and finance) · Kanō establishes the Kōbun-kan, an English school, in Minami-jinbō-chō	· Kanō establishes the Kanō Juku and Kodokan at Eishō-ji temple, Inari-chō	Bank of Japan founded
1884			First ball held at the Roku-meikan
1885	· Kanō becomes administrator and professor at Gakushūin · Team of Kodokan judoka easily defeats teams from other schools at the Metropolitan Police Martial-Arts Competition · National Institute of Gymnastics becomes an affiliate of the Higher Normal School		Cabinet system established (Itō cabinet)
1886	· Kanō becomes professor and assistant principal at Gakushūin · National Institute of Gymnastics closed; gymnastics special course offered		
1887		· Kodokan establishes *jū no kata* and *katame no kata*	
1889	· Kanō travels on an official mission to Europe, visiting Paris and Berlin by way of Shanghai	· Kanō addresses Minister of Education Enomoto Takeaki and other guests at a meeting of the Educational Society of Japan on "judo and its educational value"	Constitution of the Empire of Japan promulgated
1890	· Kanō visits Berlin, Vienna, Copenhagen, Stockholm, Amsterdam, and London		Imperial Rescript on Education issued Inaugural Imperial Diet convened
1891	· January: Kanō returns to Japan via Cairo · August: Kanō marries Takezoe Sumako · August: Kanō appointed principal of the Fifth Higher Middle School in Kumamoto and counselor to the Ministry of Education (serving through January 1893)		
1893	· June: Kanō appointed principal of the First Middle School (serving through September) · September: Kanō appointed principal of the Higher Normal School (serving through 1897)	· Ashiya Sueko joins the Kodokan · New Kodokan building completed in Shimotomisaka, Koishikawa	

1894	· Higher Normal School holds a track-and-field meet, with all students and faculty taking part · Mission of the Higher Normal School expanded from "training teachers" to "training teachers and principals" · Period of study at the Higher Normal School extended from three years to four years	· Judo clubs created at the Higher Normal School and affiliated middle school · Katsu Kaishū and other guests attend the dedication ceremony for the Kodokan dojo	Sino-Japanese War begins (eventually ending April 1895) Revival of the Olympic Games becomes official (in Paris)
1895	· Military organization at the Higher Normal School boarding house abolished	· Lafcadio Hearn writes "Jiujitsu," introducing judo to Western audiences	Treaty of Shimonoseki signed Triple Intervention
1896	· Higher Normal School Athletic Association established to encourage student participation in sports · Kanō begins accepting Chinese students at his private academy	· Research into dumbbell gymnastics takes place at Kanō Juku · Kanō Juku students participate in swimming practice in Matsuwa, Miura District (Sagami Province)	Games of the I Olympiad (Athens)
1897	· July: Kanō dismissed as principal of the Higher Normal School · November: Kanō reappointed principal of the Higher Normal School (serving through 1898)		
1898	· Kanō appointed director of the Ministry of Education's Common Education Bureau (serving through November) · June: Kanō dismissed as principal of the Higher Normal School · "Healthy-leg race" (marathon), mandatory for all students, held · Kanō's private *juku* academies integrated to form the Zōshikai	· Judo matches between teams from Gakushūin and the Higher · Normal School's affiliated middle school held · First issue of *Kokushi* published	
1899	· Ekiraku Shoin, a school for international students, established · Gymnastics special course offered	· Professor from Yale University (US) tours the Kodokan	Middle School Order, Vocational School Order, and Girls' High School Order promulgated Treaty revisions implemented
1900		· "Kodokan judo *randori* match and officiating regulations" created · Kodokan *yudanshakai* and Kodokan Research Group established	Games of the II Olympiad (Paris) Nitobe Inazō's *Bushido: The Soul of Japan* published
1901	· Kanō begins his third term as principal of the Higher Normal School (serving through 1920) · Kanō dissolves the Athletic Association and establishes the Kōyūkai (School Council)	· Kodokan membership reaches 6,000 · British Consul and British naval officers visit the Kodokan	Nobel Prize established

1902	· Ekiraku Shoin expanded to form Kōbun Gakuin (in Ushigome) · March: Higher Normal School renamed Tokyo Higher Normal School · Tokyo Higher Normal School offers moral gymnastics special course · July: Swimming club established under the School Council; swimming practice at Hōjō (Bōsō Peninsula) · July–October: Kanō visits China on the invitation of the Qing government and discusses education with Zhang Zhidong	· May: Kanō's student Yamashita Yoshiaki travels to the United States and introduces judo	Anglo-Japanese Alliance signed
1903	· Faculties, departments, and weekly class hours at Tokyo Higher Normal School revised	· Kanō establishes the Kodokan Ushigome branch dojo for international students · Kodokan midsummer practice begins	
1904			Russo-Japanese War begins (ending the following year) Games of the III Olympiad (Saint Louis)
1905	· Two-week swimming practice held in Tateyama, with all preparatory course students of Tokyo Higher Normal School taking part		Treaty of Portsmouth signed
1906	· Tokyo Higher Normal School offers special course in arts and gymnastics and establishes gymnastics, judo, and kendo majors		Intercalated Olympic Games (Athens)
1907	· Bylaws for the acceptance of special international students established · Number of Chinese students increases significantly · Confucius Festival at the Yushima Seidō's Taiseiden Hall revived	· Shimotomisaka grand dojo completed	
1908	· Secondary Education Research Society established, with Kanō serving as chair · All students take part in summer/fall footrace competitions	· Judo and kendo made required electives for all Tokyo Higher Normal School students	Games of the IV Olympiad (London)

1909	· Kanō appointed Asia's first IOC member · Kōbun Gakuin closed · International students take part in the Tokyo Higher Normal School track-and-field and aquatic athletic meets	· Kodokan incorporated	Itō Hirobumi assassinated Great Depression
1910	· Tokyo Higher Normal School international-student soccer team plays match against Toshima Normal School · Seinen shūyō-kun [Teachings for the cultivation of the young] published		Japan annexes the Korean Peninsula
1911	· Japan Amateur Athletic Association established, with Kanō serving as the organization's first president (through 1921) · Tokyo Higher Normal School celebrates 40th anniversary	· Swordsmanship and jujutsu become electives via amendments to the Middle School Ministerial Administrative Ordinance	Japanese tariff autonomy restored Xinhai Revolution
1912	· Kanō leads Japanese delegation to the Games of the V Olympiad (Stockholm), where Kanakuri Shisō (Tokyo Higher Normal School) and Mishima Yahiko (Tokyo Imperial University) compete		Republic of China established
1913	· Japan Amateur Athletic Association holds first National Athletics Championships, which become annual events · Tokyo Higher Normal School international-student soccer team plays a match against a team of Korean students in Japan		
1914	· Japan Amateur Athletic Association holds first National Swimming Championships, which become annual events	· First Technical College Judo Championships held · Kodokan Jūdōkai established; first issue of Jūdō published	World War I begins
1915	· Tokyo Higher Normal School Regulations revised, creating two faculties (arts and sciences) and establishing a special four-year faculty of physical education · Tokyo Higher Normal School international-student soccer team plays match against Saitama Normal School	· Judo instruction permitted at girls' schools and women's normal schools · Kodokan midwinter practice begins	Japan sends China its "Twenty-One Demands"
1916			Games of the VI Olympiad canceled due to World War I
1917	· Kanō attends the First Far Eastern Championship Games (Shibaura, Tokyo)		Russian Revolution begins

1918	· Kanō argues for a normal-university system at the Special Council for Education, initiating the movement to promote the Tokyo Higher Normal School to university status	· Budokwai established in London	World War I ends with Germany's surrender
1919	· Kanō Juku closes · "Sen'yōka" written as part of the university-promotion movement	· *Jūdō* renamed *Yūkō no katsudō* [The principle of effective activity] · First National Middle School Judo Championships held · Kanō explains judo to American educator John Dewey	May Fourth Movement begins
1920	· Kanō steps down as principal of the Tokyo Higher Normal School · Tokyo Higher Normal School enrollment reaches 724 (as opposed to 86 when Kanō took over as principal) · Kanō attends the Games of the VII Olympiad (Antwerp) · Kanō lectures on judo in London and Los Angeles	· Kanō instructs students at the London Budokwai	League of Nations forms
1921	· Kanō demonstrates judo for the Prince of Wales at the Imperial Palace · Kanō attends the Fifth Far Eastern Championship Games (Shanghai) as an IOC member · Kanō resigns as president of the Japan Amateur Athletic Association, becoming honorary president	· Kodokan membership surpasses 22,000, with 6,400 dan holders	Kishi Seiichi appointed president of the Japan Amateur Athletic Association
1922	· Kanō becomes a member of the House of Peers · Proposal to promote Tokyo Higher Normal School to university status passes the Special Council for Education (university opening delayed until 1929 due to the Great Kanto Earthquake)	· Kodokan Culture Council established · Kanō verbalizes concepts of *seiryoku zen'yō* and *jita kyōei*; prime minister Takahashi Korekiyo, home affairs minister Tokonami Takejirō, education minister Nakahashi Tokugorō, and Tokyo governor Usami Katuso attend	Fifth Far Eastern Olympics (Shanghai)
1923	· Tokyo Higher Normal School celebrates 50th anniversary	· Kanō demonstrates judo in Sakhalin	Great Kanto Earthquake
1924	· Kanō named Tokyo Higher Normal School professor emeritus · Kanō unable to attend Games of the VIII Olympiad (Paris) for health reasons		
1925	· Kanō attends the Meiji Shrine Games		Public Security Preservation Law and Universal Manhood Suffrage Act promulgated

1926	· Kanō appointed president of Founding Committee for English Association · Kanō visits Taiwan	· Kodokan Women's Division established; women's judo training sessions held	
1927	· Ministry of Education Institute for Research in Physical Education established; judo demonstration held at the institute · Kanō addresses graduates at the Tokyo Higher Normal School · Kanō meets with Korean graduates · Kanō gives lectures on *seiryoku zen'yō* and *jita kyōei* nationwide	· Kanō tours Okinawa, watching *bōjutsu* (staff techniques) and karate; also gives lectures · Former Kanō Juku student Sugimura Yōtarō appointed Under-Secretary General of the League of Nations	
1928	· Tokyo Higher Normal School's affiliated middle school institutes bylaws on judo and kendo courses · Kanō delivers lecture to students in the Tokyo Higher Normal School's faculty of physical education · Kanō attends the Games of the IX Olympiad (Amsterdam) · Kanō visits Berlin, Paris, Rome, London, Amsterdam, and League of Nations Headquarters (Geneva)	· Kanō studies Katori Shintō-ryū swordplay and *bōjutsu* · Kanō has the Kodokan provide instruction in *bōjutsu* · Kanō attends the dedication ceremony for the construction of the Keijō Kodokan branch	Zhang Zuolin assassinated in the Huanggutun Incident
1929	· Kanō attends the Teachers' Conference on Secondary Science Education · Tokyo University of Literature and Science established, with Kanō attending the celebratory reception · Kanō attends the Romajikai (Society for the Romanization of the Japanese Alphabet) · Kanō demonstrates judo at the Ministry of Education Institute for Research in Physical Education	· Judo matches held at the Imperial Palace with the Emperor in attendance; Kanō and Yamashita demonstrate *koshiki* maneuvers · Kanō explains judo to Professor Hudson (from Oxford University) · Kanō lectures on judo at the Etajima Imperial Japanese Naval Academy	
1930	· Kanō delivers a lecture to students in the judo course at the Tokyo Higher Normal School · Kanō discusses European affairs with Sugimura Yōtarō · Kanō gives a celebratory address at the opening ceremony of the Far Eastern Championship Games (Tokyo), representing the IOC	· Kodokan membership reaches 48,000, with 23,000 dan holders · Sugimura Yōtarō appointed director of political affairs for the League of Nations · Kanō attends the inaugural ceremony for the Sakhalin branch of the Kodokan Culture Council	London Naval Disarmament Conference

1931	· Kanō delivers a lecture to students in the faculty of physical education at the Tokyo Higher Normal School · Tokyo Higher Normal School celebrates 60th anniversary	· *Jūdō kyōhon* [The fundamentals of judo] published	Tokyo Municipal Diet resolves to submit bid to host the Olympic Games Manchurian Incident
1932	· Kanō attends the inaugural reception for Minister of Education Hatoyama at the Tokyo Higher Normal School's affiliated middle school · Kanō attends the Games of the X Olympiad (Los Angeles) · Kanō reads and explains Tokyo's official bid (by Nagata Hidejirō, mayor of Tokyo) at the 1932 IOC Session · Kanō visits Hawaii and other locations in the United States		
1933	· June: Kanō attends the 1933 IOC Session (Vienna) · Kanō receives honors from the French government for his contributions to physical education · Kanō attends the Deutsches Turnfest (German Gymnastic Festival)	· Kanō teaches judo at a training session organized by the Bavarian government · Kanō lectures on and demonstrates judo in London · Kanō addresses attendees at a judo competition in Singapore	Japan withdraws from the League of Nations Sugimura Yōtarō appointed IOC member
1934	· Kanō attends the 1934 IOC Session (and 40th anniversary of the Olympics) in Athens, also visiting the United Kingdom, France, and other European countries · Meets with Carl Diem	· Dedication ceremony for the new Kodokan building in Suidōbashi held · Kodokan celebrates 50th anniversary · Proposal for the World Judo Federation drafted	Soejima Michimasa appointed IOC member
1935	· Kanō delivers lecture to students in the Tokyo Higher Normal School's faculty of physical education · Kanō meets with Wang Zhengting (Republic of China) on Soejima's invitation	· First model *randori* presentation held	Soejima and Sugimura meet with Mussolini Second London Naval Disarmament Conference
1936	· Kanō attends the Games of the XI Olympiad (Berlin) · IOC names Tokyo host of the 1940 Olympics · Kanō visits the United States, United Kingdom, Poland, and Romania · Bronze statue of Kanō Jigorō unveiled at Tokyo University of Literature and Science	· Showcases women's judo in Sasebo, Nagasaki	February 26 Incident IOC President Latour visits Japan Sugimura resigns from the IOC
1937	· Kanō attends the Nagoya Pan-Pacific Peace Exposition and Buddhism Exposition (Nagoya)	· *Kamidana* (Shinto altar) installed at the Kodokan	Second Sino-Japanese War begins Anti-Comintern Pact signed

1938	· Tokyo approved as host of the 1940 Summer Olympics and Sapporo as host of the Winter Olympics at the 1938 IOC Session in Cairo · After visiting Greece and the United States, Kanō dies of pneumonia at the age of 77 during his return voyage from Vancouver to Japan (May 4)		National Mobilization Law enacted
1952			Tokyo Metropolitan Assembly resolves to submit an Olympic bid
1956		· First World Judo Championships held in Tokyo	Games of the XVI Olympiad (Melbourne)
1958	· Bronze statue of Kanō Jigorō erected in the Senshun'en Gardens at Tokyo University of Education (a bronze statue built in 1938 had been seized for metal collection during World War II)		
1959			Tokyo named host of the 1964 Olympics at the 1959 IOC Session in Munich
1960		· Judo approved as an Olympic sport at the 1960 IOC Session in Rome · Kodokan celebrates the 100th anniversary of Kanō's birth and unveils a commemorative bronze statue of its founder	Games of the XVII Olympiad (Rome)
1964	· Games of the XVIII Olympiad (Tokyo)		

Afterword

Kanō Jigorō served as the principal of the Tokyo Higher Normal School, which later evolved into the University of Tsukuba, for twenty-three years. To coincide with the 150th anniversary of Kanō's birth, the University of Tsukuba thus decided to organize an official commemorative celebration spanning a wide range of different initiatives and activities.

Memorial symposia convened in December 2009 and June 2010, providing participants with revealing looks at Kanō's wide-ranging achievements. In an effort to enrich its faculty-education offerings, meanwhile, the University began offering a comprehensive course on Kanō. In December 2010, the Tsukuba Campus added a visual testament to Kanō's legacy with the installation of a bronze statue by Order of Culture recipient Asakura Fumio. Another part of the project to honor Kanō's legacy was the publication of a new book on his educational legacy—the book you now hold—which the contributing authors began writing in the summer of 2009.

The editors decided to title the work *Kigai to kōdō no kyōikusha: Jigorō Kanō* [The Legacy of Kanō Jigorō: Judo and Education], which reflects key elements of Kanō's identity. Sensei was no armchair theorist. He put his beliefs into practice and constantly worked to refine his ideas, engaging with global audiences and reincorporating his experiences into a richer philosophy that he then strove to disseminate. At the heart of his career as an educator were a passionate determination and a commitment to action.

Kanō founded judo and helped it evolve into a sport with a global reach, but judo was just one facet of his career. He also poured his energies into educating international students, reforming educational systems, promoting the concept of lifelong sports, and developing the Olympic Movement.

A closer look at Kanō's myriad achievements reveals a common thread: his tireless focus on the future. When he adapted jujutsu traditions into judo, for example, he envisioned his creation as a means of building a better society. That outlook found expression in his concepts of *seiryoku zen'yō* (maximum efficient use of energy) and *jita kyōei* (mutual prosperity for oneself and others), which apply just as much today as they did nearly a century ago. As young people of today's generation struggle to communicate, grappling with the isolation of modern-day society, Kanō's tenets might carry more weight than ever before.

Kanō's decision to educate international students was another product of his future-oriented vision and commitment to serving others. Believing that an individual's own prosperity and the well-being of the nation are only possible through a devotion to others, he began admitting students from other countries—and thereby established a fundamental policy that continues to shape international education. His legacy is manifest in the enduring concept of lifelong sports, as well. Distance running and swimming, the two athletic pursuits that Kanō advocated as ideal for the entire age spectrum, are now the most beloved sports in Japan. In Japan's close ties to the Olympic Movement, you can trace yet another direct line to Kanō. By ushering the country into the Olympic community, Kanō put Japan on a path that it has embraced and followed in playing an active role in the Movement and holding three Olympic Games on its home soil.

The International Olympic Committee and United Nations Educational, Scientific and Cultural Organization frequently call for the nations of the world to mandate physical education as part of their school curricula. Kanō was advocating the same idea in Japan more than 100 years ago. When you look at the state of modern-day Japanese athletics, where students begin a required regimen of physical education in elementary school, extra-curricular athletics thrive, and sports continue to develop, you can see evidence of Kanō's visionary perspective—one that was more than a century ahead of its time.

Two of the most notable biographies of Kanō Jigorō are *Kanō-sensei-den* (The life of Professor Kanō) (Tokyo: Kodokan, 1941), written by Yokoyama Kendō, and the voluminous *Kanō Jigorō* (Tokyo: Kodokan, 1964), edited by Morohashi Tetsuji. The afterword of the latter work lays out an ambitious goal for future research. "This book may provide the leading minds of the future with a substantial foundation for further works on the life of Kanō Jigorō, explorations that bring the glorious radiance of his legacy into a clearer, more illuminating light. Should this volume succeed in inspiring a work of that stature, the results will undoubtedly offer profound benefits for all across the ages to come." While the book you now hold may fall well short of those lofty aims, we hope it gives readers an understanding of what Kanō stood for, how he lived out his philosophies, and how we, as a society, might be able to draw on his ideas in forging a better future.

In closing, allow us to extend our sincerest gratitude to everyone who helped make this book a reality. Special thanks go to Tanikawa Akihide, the previous editor-in-chief at the University of Tsukuba Press, all the personnel at the University of Tsukuba Press, and Maruzen Publishing Co., Ltd. for all their kind, dedicated support.

April 2011
Ae Michiyoshi and Sanada Hisashi
Committee for the Commemoration of the 150th Anniversary
of the Birth of Jigoro Kano

Contributing authors

· Tōdō Yoshiaki (professor emeritus, University of Tsukuba): Part I, Chapters 1–2
· Yamaguchi Kaori (professor, Faculty of Health and Sport Sciences, University of Tsukuba): Part I, Chapter 3
· Ōtani Susumu (professor, Faculty of Human Sciences, University of Tsukuba): Part II, Chapter 1
· Sanada Hisashi (professor, Faculty of Health and Sport Sciences, University of Tsukuba): Part II, Chapters 2, 4; Part III, Chapter 3; Part IV, Chapter 3; Part V, Chapter 1
· Ōkuma Hiroaki (professor emeritus, University of Tsukuba): Part II, Chapter 2
· Itō Junrō (professor, Faculty of Humanities and Social Sciences, University of Tsukuba): Part II, Chapter 3
· Murata Naoki (curator and professor, Kodokan Judo Museum): Part III, Chapter 1
· Nagaki Kōsuke (professor, Faculty of Sports and Health Studies, Hosei University): Part III, Chapter 2
· Andreas Niehaus (professor, Faculty of Arts and Philosophy, Ghent University): Part IV, Chapters 1, 4
· Gotō Mitsumasa (professor, School of Political Science and Economics, Meiji University): Part IV, Chapter 2
· Okada Hirotaka (associate professor, Faculty of Health and Sport Sciences, University of Tsukuba): Part IV, Chapter 3
· Wada Kōichi (professor, Faculty of Global and Intercultural Studies, Ferris University): Part V, Chapter 2
· Ae Michiyoshi (professor emeritus, University of Tsukuba; professor, Faculty of Sport Culture, Nippon Sport Science University): The University of Tsukuba and the legacy of Kanō Jigorō

About the translator

Tom Kain is a US-born translator who lives in Saitama. After obtaining his bachelor's degree in history from St. John's University (MN), he spent one year teaching English and studying Japanese in Okinawa and then continued his studies in the Graduate School of Global Studies at Sophia University (Tokyo). Kain now teaches English composition at Bunkyo Gakuin University (Tokyo) and translates Japanese to English in a freelance capacity. This is his first published book translation.

Index (Names)

（英文版）気概と行動の教育者　嘉納治五郎
The Legacy of Kano Jigoro: Judo and Education

2020 年 3 月 27 日　第 1 刷発行

編　者　　生誕一五〇周年記念出版委員会
訳　者　　トム・ケイン
発行所　　一般財団法人 出版文化産業振興財団
　　　　　〒 101-0051 東京都千代田区神田神保町 2-2-30
　　　　　電話　03-5211-7283
ホームページ　https://www.jpic.or.jp/

印刷・製本所　　大日本印刷株式会社